*Trade Unions and
Industrial Relations*

TRADE

NEW YORK

UNIONS *and*
Industrial Relations:
An International Comparison
by EVERETT M. KASSALOW

University of Wisconsin

R A N D O M   H O U S E

PREFACE

This volume is an outgrowth of a pair of lectures I delivered some years ago at the Foreign Service Institute on the subject of trade union development abroad. In preparing one of these, the lecture on Western European unionism, I realized only partially that my effort to provide a summary view of European unionism for an American audience compelled me, in many instances, to take American unionism as a point of departure. Almost unwittingly, I decided that one can understand other countries and cultures better if one has a clearer insight into what is unique about his own.

When I came to the preparation of the present volume I followed this line of approach even more deliberately. Although it is intended as a general analysis of trade unionism abroad, it is also a comparative effort because it reaches back to U.S. union development for examples both by way of contrast and affirmation.

The comparative method can provide new insights for social scientists, and I admit my prejudice on its behalf. The usefulness and intelligibility of what might be termed the "continuously comparative" method, which the book employs, is in contrast to the few earlier volumes on the same subject. My own experience in teaching and lecturing to different groups has convinced me of the superiority of the genuinely comparative approach as opposed to the separate, country-by-country accounts one often finds in so-called comparative volumes. Moreover, the existence of many useful individual chapters in collections, journal articles, and monographs on the labor movements of practically every country of Europe (and numerous less-developed countries) renders any new series of chapters on particular countries superfluous. (The separate chapter on France and the extended section on the Swedish labor movement in Chapter IV have been included as ideal types of illustrations within the general comparative framework of the book.)

There is always a danger, however, that use of the comparative approach can become superficial and fail to set contemporary developments sufficiently into an historical background. The present volume seeks to avoid this, and (within the limits of space) it is both historical and analytical in explaining the current state and prospects of unionism and industrial relations. The first three to four chapters set forth a general, historical *pattern* of Western European trade union development. The review of this pattern is not intended as a normative device, but rather as an effort to distill trade union experience in that area and to make it intelligible for the reader. Comparisons with the United States are drawn again and again. A special chapter on France is included both because that country's labor development (as well as unionism in other European Latin nations) has diverged from the general pattern and because it seemed that the inclusion of a sharply divergent form of trade unionism would help illuminate the general pattern of Western unionism.

At some points the book deals with labor parties, workers' cooperatives, and similar groups. These are discussed because most labor movements abroad have been part of a total workers' complex that included labor socialist parties and cooperatives as well as unions. But the concentration is upon unions and related industrial relations systems. These systems (and their problems) are considered primarily from the viewpoint of trade unions—the central focus of the book. My effort, moreover, has been to portray these unions as functioning institutions in their own societies rather than to set forth detailed aspects of highly unique union or industrial relations practices.

The reader will not find a separate bibliography because the footnotes cite most major secondary works and important contemporary primary materials that should open the door to further study. Since I am writing primarily for American readers, I have confined myself largely to English sources, except in the material on France, where, of necessity, some reference is made to French sources. In order not to overburden the text itself, I have also used the footnotes to amplify, with additional examples and exceptions, many of the comparative generalizations made in the main body of the study.

In various places in the text, I have quoted at some length from original sources. As a teacher in this field, I have found that a substantial quotation from a British trade union journal, a speech by an Italian trade union leader, or a manifesto from the Indian National Trade Union Congress is apt to convey something much more effectively than any individual effort to summarize what is often exotic to American experience.

Although the choice of subjects inevitably involves some arbitrary decisions in a volume of this sort, those selected generally convey a comparative sense of trade-union character and development. A major share of the volume is devoted to Western trade unions and industrial relations systems. Unions have the longest history in these countries, and the largest "public" for comparative analysis is also to be found in the Western area. The final two chapters however, deal with union and industrial relations development in the new, less-developed countries. Admittedly, an author's ability to generalize about the less-developed countries is limited by the relative newness of unionism in these areas. Limits are also imposed by the enormous diversity in these countries' cultural, economic, political, and geographical structures. As development proceeds in the years to come, we shall doubtless find the need to construct new groupings or general types in describing unionism and industrial relations systems in the new countries.

The impact of international trade union organizations and of European integration has not been included for lack of space as well as a lack of major relevance to the book's main focus. The impact of European economic integration on industrial relations systems is likely to increase in the future, but its influence has only been marginal until now.

Unionism in communist countries has not been included for two principal reasons. First, the underlying premises of communist societies and unions remain substantially different from those of comparable institutions in the West, whose comparative analysis forms the core of the volume. Second, like most Western students I remain at a disadvantage because of my lack of firsthand communication with, and knowledge of, communist country institutions and practices. These still remain largely hidden from the eyes of all but superspecialists in those areas. Communist unionism and tactics as a force outside the communist world is dealt with to some extent in the chapter on France and briefly in the chapters on the less-developed countries.

My thanks are due to countless foreign friends in the union movement who have spent long hours discussing many of the ideas and concepts developed in the volume. The corps of foreign labor attachés serving in the various embassies in Washington—and particularly those from Great Britain, Germany, Sweden, and Switzerland—have been most helpful. Deep thanks are also due to friends who have worked with me in the continuing Seminar on Comparative Labor Movements (most recently sponsored by the University of Wisconsin) which it has been my pleasure to direct for the past six years in Washington, D.C. This seminar has included trade-union specialists from different branches of the AFL-CIO, several academicians, and career officials from the State and Labor Departments who have special competence in the international labor field. I should also like to mention grants from the University of Wisconsin which made possible several visits to Europe and Asia in recent years, and provided me with an opportunity to look into some recent foreign labor developments.

I must express my appreciation to two old friends, Paul Fisher of the

Social Security Administration, and Arnold Steinbach, recently retired from the U.S. Department of Labor. Both of them made helpful criticism on parts of an early version of the manuscript. Mr. John Chandler of the U.S. Department of Labor read and criticized a draft of Chapter XI, which deals with wage problems and trends. At Random House Miss Muriel Smith and Professor Albert Blum made helpful suggestions and numerous editorial improvements during the course of the book's preparation. Needless to say, none of those mentioned is responsible for the views set forth in the volume—indeed some of them might very well have differing opinions about my statement of the subject.

Finally, my deepest thanks go to my wife and children, who have patiently borne with me as this book was being written on long weekends, evenings, and holidays during the past few years. They have also been most understanding of those absences when I was abroad and much of the book was germinating.

Everett M. Kassalow
Madison, Wisconsin

CONTENTS

XV Industrial Relations in the New Countries: Economic Setting and Problems 308

Abbreviations Used in Text for Unions, Federations, and Political Parties

AEU	Amalgamated Engineering Union (Great Britain)
AFL	American Federation of Labor
AFL-CIO	American Federation of Labor and Congress of Industrial Organizations
ALP	Australian Labour Party
CCSLB	General Federation of Liberal Unions of Belgium
CFDT	French Democratic Confederation of Labor
CFTC	Confédération Française des Travailleurs Chrétiens
CGC	Confédération Générale des Cadres
CGIL	Confederazione Generale Italiana Lavoro
GGL	General Confederation of Labor (Italy)
CGT	Confédération Générale du Travail (France)
CIO	Congress of Industrial Organizations (U.S.A.)
CISL	Confederazione Italiana Sindicati Lavoratori
CNV	Protestant Christian National Trade Union Centre
CSC	Confederation of Christian Trade Unions (Belgium)
DAG	German Salaried Employees' Union
DBB	German Association of Civil Servants
DGB	German Trade Union Federation
ETU	Electrical Trades Union (Great Britain)
FDTU	Federation of Danish Trade Unions
FGTB	Belgian General Federation of Labor
FO	Force Ouvrière
FTF	Federation of Civil Servants and Salaried Employees (Denmark)
GAP	White Collar Workers' Union in Private Industry and Commerce (Austria)
GMWU	General and Municipal Workers Union (Great Britain)
HK	Danish Retail Clerks and Office Workers Union

ICFTU	International Confederation of Free Trade Unions
IFCTU	International Federation of Christian Trade Unions (see WCL)
IGM	German Metalworkers Union
ILO	International Labour Organisation, International Labour Office
IMF	International Metalworkers Federation
INTUC	Indian National Trade Union Congress
IWW	Industrial Workers of the World (U.S.A.)
KFL	Kenya Federation of Labor
LO	Swedish Federation of Labor (also used for Danish and Norwegian labor federations, but see FDTU above)
NALGO	National Association of Local Government Officers (Great Britain)
NEDC	National Economic Development Council (Great Britain)
NKV	Netherlands Roman-Catholic Trade Union Centre
NLRB	National Labor Relations Board
NUT	National Union of Teachers (Great Britain)
NVV	Netherlands Federation of Trade Unions
ÖGB	Austrian Trade Union Federation
OECD	Organisation for Economic Cooperation and Development (formerly OEEC)
PRI	Partido Revolucionario Institucional (Mexico)
SACO	Swedish Confederation of Professional Associations
SAF	Swedish Employers Confederation
SDAP	Social Democratic Workers Party (Sweden)
SFNCTU	Swiss Federation of National-Christian Trade Unions
SFPTU	Swiss Federation of Protestant Trade Unions
SFTU	Swiss Federation of Trade Unions
SIF	Swedish Union of Clerical and Technical Employees in Industry
SNTUC	Singapore National Trade Union Congress
TCO	Central Organization of Salaried Employees (Sweden)
TFL	Tanganyika Federation of Labour
TGWU	Transport and General Workers Union (Great Britain)
TUC	Trades Union Congress (Britain)
UAW	United Automobile Workers (United States)
UGTA	Union Générale des Travailleurs Algériens

UIL	Italian Union of Labor
USDAW	Union of Shop, Distributive, and Allied Workers (Great Britain)
WCL	World Confederation of Labor (formerly FCTU)
WFTU	World Federation of Trade Unions

Trade Unions and
Industrial Relations

PART ONE

Unions and Industrial Relations in the Western Nations

I

Western Labor Movements, Origins and General Characteristics

The Comparative Study of Labor Movements

RADE UNIONISM had become a world-wide phenomenon by the middle of the twentieth century. Unions were functioning in the Western, market-oriented, democratic countries, in the communist countries, and in the newly developing societies. In these different types of societies trade unions have some features in common, but they also have some important, fundamentally different characteristics. In this respect they are, of course, like the three groups of societies themselves.[1]

The comparative study of labor movements must inevitably lay greater emphasis upon how unions and industrial relations systems *differ* in various countries. It is this emphasis which enables the student to understand what is unique about foreign systems and to gain valuable insights concerning his own labor institutions.

This volume focuses first upon a comparative view of Western trade unions and industrial relations systems because they are more closely related than any others to those in the United States. Moreover, it is in the West that trade unionism and industrial relations systems have had their longest history and have become most securely institutionalized.

During the last hundred years or so, Western unions have developed rather steadily from a position virtually outside their respective societies to the point where they are today fundamental, representative forces in them. This evolution has produced transformations of some of the earlier programs, functions, and forms of the Western union movements. Despite these great changes, however, one can still find in these movements some of their origins.

Within the Western system of trade unions it is useful to distinguish certain subgroups. The Scandinavian countries, the Low Countries, Switzerland, Germany, and Austria form one such group. Even this subgroup can be separated, to some extent, in terms of historical development, with the Scandinavian countries standing somewhat by themselves.

British unionism shares many features with this first subgroup, especially with the Scandinavian countries. France and to some extent Italy constitute another subgroup. The United States is still another subgroup.

Nevertheless, it is the thesis of this volume that after allowances are made for variation, one can consider the development of Western union industrial relations as a whole for comparative analytical purpose.[2]

Many may believe that diversity is so great among these Western societies that they cannot be considered as a group. However, to group them otherwise among the world's nations seems less useful for comparative study. Moreover, to government officials, employers, and trade union leaders in the newly developing countries, the Western labor movements and labor systems clearly exhibit certain basically similar, major characteristics and qualities compared with the patterns of labor development in their new countries. This is not to argue that unions and industrial relations in the West are totally different from those elsewhere in the world but, rather, that they are distinguishable as a group and that this distinction is especially valuable for study purposes. This identity will also be demonstrated by the consideration of union and industrial relations in the less-developed nations, to which the volume turns in Part II.

Beginnings of Modern Western Labor Movements

Practically all of the present-day major Western labor movements trace their critical, continuing origins to the last half of the nineteenth century. There are, of course, fragmentary beginnings of unionism in many countries fifty years or more before this. The American labor movement looks back at the foundation of the American Federation of Labor in the 1880s as the point of departure for modern unionism in the United States; the labor movements of Western Europe also consider that their modern unionism started sometime in the last half of the nineteenth century. The philosophy, structure, and practices that were characteristic of the AFL and its constituent unions during that period, still have a critical influence in the American labor movement today. These characteristics include job consciousness and job control, business unionism, and an overwhelming emphasis on economic struggle and collective bargaining as opposed to broad political reform of the society and the economy.[3]

By the same token, the ideas, practices, and influences that helped shape the modern European labor movements in the nineteenth century continue to play an important role today. In their evolution these movements, though often interrupted by war, revolution, and dictatorship, have shown a remarkable resiliency and continuity. There has been change, of course, but this change can be understood only if the origins are also understood. For this reason it is useful to look backward to the beginnings of European labor movements.

Although some of the same social forces conditioned the American and European labor movements and date from roughly the same period, crucial differences between the societies in which they developed have produced significant differences in the philosophy and practices of these movements. Although many of these differences have become blurred in subsequent decades, the labor movements continue to reflect them in philosophy and practice.

Differences in the Background of U.S. and European Labor Development

Most striking of these differences, perhaps, is that modern European labor movements, unlike American unions, began their lives with a dedication to transform their own societies totally. In a sense, the labor movements were often colored by a revolutionary tradition and were very much under the influence of Marxism and other socialist or anarchist doctrines of the latter half of the nineteenth century.

In reviewing the labor movement, it has always been somewhat curious that the deep sense of class conflict and antagonism toward the capitalist order (including the desire to overturn it), should have been so much greater in Europe than in America. After all, it was in the United States that capitalism was more fully triumphant and less tempered by paternalism or other social restraints. Superficially, one might have expected this purer capitalism to have triggered a sharper sense of class conflict in its workers.

However, Louis Hartz, in a brilliant restudy of American political ideas, has suggested that the revolutionary tradition of Europe in the nineteenth century (and thereafter), and the deeper, socialist class ideology of the European working class, does not stem primarily from the influence of capitalism. Hartz believes that, contrary to Marx's conception, and indeed to much popular conception, the militant class character of socialism was not so much the product of "objective economic forces." Rather, he finds that it was "largely an ideological phenomenon"—a revolt against the old European class order that owes its character more to the carry-over of a feudal tradition than to the emergence of capitalism. Hartz argues: "It is not accidental that America which has uniquely lacked a feudal tradition lacked also a socialist tradition. The hidden origin of socialist thought everywhere in the West is to be found in the feudal ethos."[4]

Again contrasting the United States and Europe, Hartz adds (of the United States): "One of the central characteristics of a nonfeudal society is that it lacks a genuine revolutionary tradition which in Europe has been linked with the Puritan and French revolutions: that it is 'born equal,' as Tocqueville said."[5]

By comparison with European society of the same period, American capitalism was a more dynamic force, laid the basis for a more open class structure, and provided a foundation for a less class-conscious labor movement.

It is not surprising that modern European labor movements, created in a tradition where class privileges were deeply rooted and still entrenched, almost immediately and everywhere set themselves the task of radically transforming this society. Robert Heilbroner notes:

While capitalism in America managed without any effort to embrace the aspirations of its "lower orders," in Europe, already by the time of the revolution of 1848, these lower orders had turned their backs on capitalism as a vehicle for their hopes and beliefs.[6]

It would perhaps be more accurate to say that the labor movements had turned their backs upon the existing social, class orders as a vehicle for their hopes and beliefs.

As we shall see, this rejection of the social order was so deep that it lives on today in the jargon and the slogans of European labor movements, even if it does not always exist in their practices and programs. Indeed, so sharp was this antagonism that beginning in the latter part of the nineteenth century and continuing into the twentieth century it became popular for otherwise mature and "responsible" labor movements to couch their slogans and appeals in military terms—as though a great armed conflict was to be the ultimate expression of the workers' movement. Writing in 1915, Robert Michels could say:

The close resemblance between a fighting democratic party and a military organization is reflected in socialist terminology, which is largely borrowed, and especially in Germany, from military science. There is hardly one expression of military tactics and strategy, hardly even a phrase of barracks slang which does not recur again and again in the leading articles of the socialist press. . . . [these slogans recurred despite the fact that] In the daily practice of the socialist struggle preference is almost invariably given to the temporizing tactics of Fabius Cunctator.[7]

On the other hand, military rhetoric or conceptualization has been quite alien to the mainstream of American labor development.[8] In Western Europe today, such militancy has become largely outmoded as well, except perhaps for occasional rumbles in the communist labor centers in France and Italy. On the other hand, many of the old slogans, rituals, and battle songs continue to be heard at European labor meetings.

What did it mean to be a worker in a feudal-capitalist class structure? Generally, it meant that well into the latter part of the nineteenth century, and often into the twentieth century, one enjoyed no voting rights. Politically speaking, one was shut out of the suffrage, which was limited to the upper classes, feudal or bourgeois. High on the program of almost all of the Continental labor movements was the demand for universal male suffrage. And this became deeply involved with labor tactics and strategy.

At the first modern trade union congress in Austria in 1893 a proposal was made to authorize a general strike to achieve universal male suffrage. During the decade just before World War I, discussions in Germany about using the trade union apparatus to precipitate a general strike to break down restrictions on suffrage in Prussia were heated and intense. Some of the most important activity of the early Belgian union movement centered on efforts to win suffrage. The Norwegian labor movement, which one almost automatically associates with the socialist Labor Party in that country, was closely allied to the Liberal Party in the 1880s and broke with it largely because of the Liberal Party's equivocation on the suffrage issue. In Sweden unions helped to bring about universal male suffrage in that country in 1907 and 1909 by the use of the demonstration general strike.

These examples are cited to illustrated the atmosphere in which most European labor movements were born. They also indicate how much later than in the United States the matter of male suffrage became an issue. To realize the difference in timing, one need merely recall that the male suffrage issue was settled in the United States (aside from the Negro question) long before the Civil War.

Timing alone, however, is not the only difference between the way in which the resolution of the suffrage and related issues colored the typical European vis-à-vis the U.S. labor movement. Generally suffrage, and other rights were not won by European workers until they took *collective action* to gain them. Said Maurice Duverger, "For the European working classes . . . freedom was a collective conquest . . . no serious social reform took place until the proletariat discovered the weapon of its common liberation: common action."[9] The tradition of common action continues to be a strong one.

Such collective struggle for social freedom has never characterized the American labor movement on any large scale. The absence of important collective social triumphs in the past naturally reduced any collective spirit or class sense among American workers. It is not surprising, consequently, that one finds great differences in solidarity and ideology between the labor movements here and in Western Europe.[10]

Lack of suffrage was not the only problem in Western Europe. Illiteracy was often a severe problem among the lower classes. Such isolation from the learning and cultural process of a society easily leads any class to feel that only by overturning the society can it advance. For example, much of the early violence of Belgian labor has been attributed to "acts of anger" and "acts of violence" heightened by the frustrations of ignorance and illiteracy. In Italy, the recurring patterns of resignation and violent outbreaks among local labor bodies is attributed by Maurice F. Neufeld, in part, to illiteracy and abject poverty.[11]

If, in modern times, there is a single factor that keeps any class or group alienated from its own society, illiteracy fits the role. One must again recall that the battle for free public schools for white children had been won in the United States long before the Civil War. Even in Great Britain state education was introduced only in 1870 and made free only in 1891.[12]

Elsewhere on the Continent the development of free public education also lagged behind the United States. Moreover, long after free public elementary education was introduced in Western Europe the education system continued to operate as a class-creating vehicle. Working class children were generally prevented from attaining higher educational opportunities by the European system of separating academic secondary education from regular (more vocationally oriented) secondary schools. Moreover, working class children were virtually excluded from university life. Guenther Roth writes of the German situation:

. . . only pupils attending a secondary [academic] school could go to a university, and scarcely any working class children entered secondary school. The early starting age, ten years of age, and the tuition fees were effective deterrents, besides the other social handicaps and biases involved. This perpetuated the class cleavage between the working class and the upper and middle classes. . . .[13]

To a significant extent the European educational system has continued to the present time to function as a major instrument of class division, although it is now undergoing major modification in nearly every country.

Legal and Social Indignities of European Workers

The working class sense of being isolated and oppressed had a long history in Europe. Its origin was more feudal than capitalistic. But the burgeoning capitalism of the nineteenth century added to the burdens and sense of deprivation of the working classes, many of whom were being pulled into the new commercial and industrial process for the first time. Largely as a by-product of the emerging capitalism, so-called conspiracy and combination laws were enacted in almost every Western European country to prevent workers from combining to defend their interests. The earliest of the laws was the French statute of 1791 that stated:

Citizens of the same trade occupation, and workers or journeymen in any art or craft, may not, when assembled together, appoint a president, a secretary, or syndic, keep registers, make decisions or draw up any regulations concerning what they claim are their common interests. . . . Administration and municipal bodies are forbidden to receive any address or petition from any trade or occupation.[14]

In most countries employers had even resorted to direct control over the freedom of movement of their workers. Belgium was a notable example with its so-called worker's passbook (*livret*), which recorded whether he had discharged his obligations "properly" or "satisfactorily" to his previous employer. In the courts, severe legal inferiority was also visited upon the Belgian worker. As late as the first decade of the present century when AFL President Samuel Gompers visited Western Europe, he was struck by the fact that:

The European working-man's identification book is a badge of his still existing serfhood. While in America any one may freely roam the country over, in most countries in Europe the laborer must be prepared to produce his "legitimation" book on demand of the police or on applying for employment. . . . In Italy the laborer's book, besides giving his character as a workman, as seen by his successive employers, states whether he has ever been in prison for any cause whatever for more than ten days. The "labor agitator," subject to police hounding, is thus liable to be effectually squelched.[15]

According to the Belgian Civil Code (which was changed only after great agitation in 1883) the employer was believed on his own word so far as the payment of salary was concerned. In the case of a court suit, the worker had to prove his claims, while the employer's word was accepted.[16]

Until 1875 British workers who struck in breach of contract could be prosecuted for criminal charges under the Master and Servant Act and imprisoned. The very name of the legislation conveys the inferior legal position of workers, which was modified by the 1875 Employers and Workmen Act. This act limited charges for breach of contract to payment of civil damages.[17]

These examples of class barriers are drawn from basic legal and institutional practices prevailing in nineteenth century Europe. Still another example of the sense of class injustice felt by workers is taken from day-to-day social custom in Austria in the mid-nineteenth century. One of the important demands of the working class in the 1848 revolution was that "they be addressed by the formal *sie* rather than the familiar *du*."[18]

By way of contrast, consider the rather strict, ritualistic observance of formal social equality in America. Inequalities in wealth have always been tolerated, but pretensions to social or class superiority are exceptional. One student of American character writes,

Pulling one's rank has therefore been the unforgivable sin against American democracy, and the American people have accordingly reserved their heartiest dislike for the officer class in the military . . . it is permissible for an American to have servants (which is a matter of function) but he must not put them in livery (which is a matter of rank); permissible to attend public schools, but not to speak with a cultivated accent.[19]

The sense of class separation and social deference continues in many ways today, even among the typical socialist workers in Europe. When they visit European plants American trade unionists are often struck by the sense of deference on the part of European workers toward plant management—even in countries where a socialist party may control the national government.

In America the business classes, for the most part, have tended to be as casual about class symbols and class consciousness as have the workers. Hartz notes, "It takes the contemptuous challenge of an aristocratic feudalism to elicit such a consciousness. A triumphant middle class . . . can take itself for granted." In turn, this means that little counterclass consciousness is evoked among American workers. Hartz adds, "Marx himself used to say that the bourgeoisie was the great teacher of the proletariat."[20] In Europe, on the other hand, the bourgeoisie fashioned a liberalism that was honed by its sense of class revolt against feudalism. The European working class drew upon this same sense of class revolt when it formulated its own socialist ideology. That ideology has sustained and reinforced the sense of European class division. In the United States the working class has never been much more group class conscious than the American middle class.

The absence of a feudal system, coupled with a great western land frontier until the end of the nineteenth century, was another factor making for "freer" labor development in the United States.[21] Labor tended to be more scarce, although this was offset in part by the great tide of immigration from Europe. The flow of immigration, on the other hand, tended to *reduce* the possibility of class consciousness because the divisive ethnic factors often came to count for more than shared economic deprivation. Time and again employers were able to play one ethnic group against another and frustrate efforts to form a common front of employees.

Feudal Guilds and Unions in Europe

As a final point about the impact of an older, feudal tradition upon the working class movements of Europe, it is significant that several of these movements trace their lineage directly to the old journeymen's guilds. The tanners and leather workers of Vienna, for example, shifted from guild to union in 1870, reverted to a guild form in the 1880s, and finally became a union in 1896. In Switzerland the liquidation of the guilds provoked sharp competition in certain trades, and employers and unions joined together to form a general union to control competition. Gradually, the employers dropped out, and modern unions emerged. In Germany, too, there was a kind of gradual evolution from guild to union forms. Here the conspiracy doctrine was used against employee groups and played havoc with the old journeymen societies, but the skilled journeymen, especially after 1841, helped create the new unions.

Even where one cannot always trace direct connections, guild influence on the formation of the early trade unions can be significant. In Denmark 80 percent "of the 65 local trade unions established in Copenhagen from 1870 to 1880 were in trades in which a guild monopoly had existed."[22]

The guild connection or influence on European unionism is a general, but not a universal phenomenon. The great historians of British trade unionism have denied its role as a predecessor of modern trade unionism, particularly in Great Britain.[23]

The debate about guild influence on the development of European unionism is not worth pursuing. What does seem to be significant is that in every Western European country the tradition of collective grouping and collective action in social and economic life was thoroughly implanted as part of the old feudal and guild influences. In this sense, trade unionism was a more "natural" development, and more "naturally" accepted by workers and, ultimately, by employers, than was to be the case in the United States. Here the ethic of individualism held sway almost from the beginning of American history.

While virtually all of the labor movements of Western Europe went through a period of intense struggle for existence, the problem of just staying alive collectively has always been more difficult for unionism in the United States than in Europe.

This traditional advantage that Western Europe has in facilitating unionism continues to operate on today's labor problems. Clearly one of the reasons why Western European white-collar and government workers have taken to unionism in far greater numbers than have U.S. white-collar workers is their easier acceptance of the necessity for collective action and grouping.

Our concern here is not primarily with American labor development. However, before we turn to an analysis of the class character of European labor, we must add that the absence of feudal restraints in the United States also helps to account for the more dynamic character of capitalism here as compared with nineteenth century Europe. This situation laid the basis for higher living standards for workers and also created more promotional and business opportunities—both having the effect of draining off potential class consciousness.

Total Reaction of European Labor Movements

At the very moment when groups of Americans were painfully building union organizations that could defend and advance the economic rights and needs of their members almost exclusively in the business world, European labor movements went marching toward the ideal of an entirely new society.

American unions were almost inevitably exclusionist in nature—their overwhelming concentration was on winning and defending benefits for members only, without great concern for the social order as such. This concentration reflected in part their general lack of class consciousness and the lack of clearly defined and stable social classes in American society.

On the other hand, European unions were part of a wider social movement aimed at changing the whole society on behalf of *all* workers —not just union members. For the typical European worker, the distinction between the goals of his union, his socialist party, or his cooperative was not very sharp. Within this labor constellation the union may have had at times a somewhat more parochial view than the party; but, overwhelmingly, the drive of the combined movement was to replace the social order.

The European labor movements of the late nineteenth century naturally sought to embrace the entire life of the worker and his family. Organizationally they spread into most of the institutions that typically catered to the worker, and they offered him the vision of a new social order.

There is general familiarity with the strongly Marxian-oriented economic programs of European labor in the late nineteenth and early twentieth centuries. Plans for socialization of the means of production, the liquidation of capitalism, and the substitution of a society producing for social rather than private gain highlighted all these movements.[24]

British Unionism More Missionary than Marxist

Although it, too, came to advocate a "substitute" society, the British labor movement was a notable exception so far as any direct, major Marxian influence on its programs and slogans was concerned. The character of British socialism was shaped by a nonconformist religious tradition.

The British Marxist economic historian, E. J. Hobsbawm, has observed that British workers "learned how to run a trade union" by "modelling themselves on chapel and circuit" derived from Methodism. It was also from the Methodists that they picked up the "devices of mass agitation and propaganda." According to Hobsbawm, "The Primitive Methodists were to English mining or farm labor unions in the mid-nineteenth century what the Communist Party is to the French workers today, the cadre of leadership."[25]

The socialist ardor of British labor was not necessarily less, however, because of the absence of a strong Marxist tradition. Selig Perlman quotes a description of a 1926 meeting to honor one of the earliest union and socialist heroes, Keir Hardie:

Every year in Glasgow, the Socialist faithful gather together to preach and to pray in memory of Saint Keir Hardie. I went to this year's prayer meeting. The church was St. Andrew's, the largest public hall in Glasgow. Father and mother and the kids were there . . . up to five thousand. . . . Chairman Rankine swung into straight gospel preaching right soon—the gospel of socialism. . . . He used personal religious experience to vivify the thing. One night, when sleeping in the open he said that he found himself on a sudden in the presence and novelty of dawn. It was like something that Socialism was doing to the world today. His words put me in mind of the revelation of Saint John: "The new light and the new day," he ended, on a ringing note of ecstasy, "are not far away." Then Maxton preached. He told them promptly the misery was their own fault. They had been backsliders, lazy and shiftless, lacking energy, lacking faith in the religion that could serve them—Socialism. He beat and flayed them for their Socialist sins, for their supineness in action, their trade union laxity, their social heresy, their little faith. And they cheered him for these scourgings louder than for his curse of the capitalist. They were Presbyterians and had the conviction of sin in their hearts. . . . There was even more religion in George Lounsbury's half-episcopal and half-evangelical sermon than there was in James Maxton's. . . . "Our movement is the greatest religious movement the world has ever known. Tell people the truth, I say: that capitalism is on its last legs, and ask men to join with us in this, the only fight that matters, for the redemption of mankind. . . ." Then the choir rose and sang 'O Beautiful My Country.' "[26]

How confusing this kind of socialism could be to an orthodox European Marxist is well summed up in Leon Trotsky's reactions to a London labor meeting in 1902: "One Sunday I went with Lenin and Krupskaya to a London church where a social-democratic meeting alternated with hymn singing. A compositor who had returned from Australia stood up and talked about social revolution. Thereupon everyone got up and sang 'Almighty God, make it that there will be no more kings nor rich people.' I could not believe my eyes or ears."[27]

This strong influence of religion on the traditions, practices, and formation of the labor movement was unique in Great Britain when compared with the other nations of Western Europe.[28] Paul Malles argues that "in Britain the decline of established religion had not left the same emotional void which was filled by the messianic message of Marxism on the continent. The traditions, thought habits, and emotions of religious nonconformism remained strong among the British working class. British labor may have become estranged from the established church, but not free from the 'Chapel.'" [29] This contrasted, for example, with the growth of antichurch feeling among working class leaders in Continental, Catholic countries.

The leading historian of British socialism, G. D. H. Cole, has also stressed the influence of nonconformism on the origins of another key British labor institution, the cooperative movement. Cole states that Rochdale, birthplace of the modern cooperative movement, was outstanding in the number of "religious controversies and foundations" and was a veritable center of nonconformism. Cole also comments that the way in which the chapels genuinely ministered to the poor and the oppressed working class during the early decades of the industrial revolution was a great factor in "impelling the leaders of the workers into more sober courses of economic and political thoughts"—notably into unions and cooperatives. In particular, Cole notes that the cooperative movement led British workers away from revolutionary unionism into the so-called New Model trade unionism of the 1850s.[30]

From the 1850s on, the British labor movement moved in a more moderate (though ultimately socialistic) path than most of the Continental movements.

This religious nonconformist basis of the socialist ideology of the British labor movement has persisted into today's leadership. Harold Wilson, leader of the Labour Party at this writing (1968), is a striking example of this influence. Interviewed a few years ago on the forces affecting his own intellectual evolution, he commented: "In my own boyhood it was the chapel and the Scout movement, that kind of pattern. . . . I was impregnated with non-conformity. It was the soil out of which the Labour Party grew. . . . [Asked in this interview about 'How much has Marx influenced you,' Wilson replied, 'Not at all.' As to 'Who has influenced you,' he replied] . . . Well, as I have said, my parents and the Scout movement. The Fourth Scout Law, 'A Scout is a friend to all and a brother to every Scout. . . .'" Wilson also described the influence of two socialist schoolmasters whose personal examples of "unselfish and unstinting" devotion greatly affected him.[31]

The less doctrinaire character of British socialism and the British trade union movement is also due, of course, to the different political evolution of the country. Democracy, on the Continent, was very much a product of the violent French Revolution of 1789, which had its wave-like effect nearly everywhere in nineteenth century Europe. In Britain, however there had been the gradual evolution of democratic and civil rights over many centuries. The various forces of give-and-take between middle and working classes and the competition between middle class and tory class for working class support had all produced an atmosphere where class conflict was in a lower key than on the Continent.[32]

The struggle to extend the suffrage in nineteenth century Britain included middle-class reform in 1832 and after. Moreover, many important middle-class leaders fought to extend voting rights to the working class as well. By contrast, as a recent study notes, in Imperial Germany the middle classes and the landed aristocracy were content to accept full suffrage rights for themselves with only limited rights for the working classes. This development, the study adds, "left the German working class on its own. Class conscious organization appeared to some politically interested workers . . . as the only alternative; in contrast the English working class could for decades support the liberal bourgeoisie in the expectation of gradual democratization."[33]

In Britain there was also the phenomenon of Fabianism, a major middle-class reform movement effecting wide social reform on behalf of the labor movement and the Labour Party. Fabianism was another symptom of the broader accommodation between classes in that country. As Henry Pelling writes, "The Fabian Society performed the essential service of adopting Marxist theory to a form compatible with British constitutional practice." In so doing, the Fabians drew heavily upon indigenous British "radical ideas, on Mill and the Benthamites, on the Positivists and on the historical economists. All this work of synthesis was a vital contribution to the British Labour movement."[34] So moderate was the commitment of British labor to socialism that its formal endorsement was accepted only when the Labour Party platform was fundamentally revised in 1918.

Although the non-Marxist character of British labor must be stressed in the comparative analysis of union development, it should be added that the longer history of capital-labor relations in that country has left some of the most lasting vestiges of class difference and style of life anywhere in Western Europe. Industrialism came first to this country, and it was accompanied by the worst social conditions, including slum communities, child labor, and the like. The historian Val Lorwin has observed, "Where industrialization came late in the nineteenth century, the old evils did not have to plague man and child. Housing and sanitation, playgrounds and parks in workers' neighborhoods in Copenhagen, Stockholm, Amsterdam and Oslo were very different from the wretched conditions prevailing in early Manchester."[35]

The long misery of the British industrial revolution left its mark in the form of a persistent, deep sense of class cleavage. Despite the absence of substantial Marxist or other revolutionary influence, there seems to be less group consensus and integration of the human forces in British enterprise today than in most other countries of Western Europe.

European Labor Movements—a Separate Subculture

The quality of the European labor movements in the first decades of the twentieth century may be better grasped by examining some of their socially organized structures. The influence on the day-to-day lives of labor members was particularly significant in this regard. We refer here to the impact of labor cooperatives, clubs, schools, recreation societies, and the like. Kurt L. Shell has described this workers' network in Austria as follows:

The Movement . . . produced a home, literally as well as metaphorically, for a considerable part of the Austrian working class. It comprised clubs and associations whose scope and interests ranged from stamp collecting to militant atheism. Each one of these organizations insisted on drawing a clear class line between itself and the rest of society. Singing, hiking, playing chess, all these were carried on in associations proudly affixing the term "worker" to their title and maintaining affiliation with the Social Democratic Party. Through the Children's Friends (Kinderfreunde) and the Free School (Freie Schule) an attempt was made to ensure that the public school system should not alienate the growing working class child from his proletarian background or indoctrinate him with anti-socialist ideology. Through a determined drive against the use of alcohol, the workingman was to be rescued from this particular "opiate of the people." Through the organization of cultural activities—book clubs, theatres, libraries, and concerts—he was to develop a sense for the higher things of life; all this on the assumption that sober, well read and cultured, these rational workingmen would become conscious of the political position of their class, and join the struggle for a socialist society.[36]

The total substitute society, which seemed to be the aim of the European labor movements, is so remote from American labor philosophy that it is hard to grasp. The fact, for example, that most European labor movements took it upon themselves to try to control and curb the use of alcoholic drinks among workers is perhaps the most striking of these activities. Although alcoholism has probably been no more and no less a problem among American workers, the idea that the union could become the main center in the campaign against drinking is far-fetched in the United States, and it is a good index of the different character of the movements here and in Europe.[37]

A special word should be said about the role of workers' education associations. In the earlier days, when many of the now-accepted union activities were illegal, it was frequently the workers' education movement that provided the rallying center for workers' movements.

Training in such centers varied from literary instruction to the basics of socialism and trade unionism. In the earlier stages, at least, workers' education typically played a much larger role in Western European movements than in the United States.

On the ideological level, workers' education programs were important as a cementing, indoctrinating force in making socialist doctrine understandable to countless members in the labor movement.

One highly respected expert on American labor, Clark Kerr, has strongly argued that it would not be in the interest of democratic evolution in the United States for unions to "extend their sphere of activity until it covers more and more of the life of their members, not only as workers but also as consumers and citizens." He insists that each of the key U.S. institutions—the state, the corporation, the union, and others—"should be narrowly oriented toward its primary function, whether that function is production of goods or representation of economic interest, or the salvation of souls." Kerr asserts that "The institution which encompasses the totality of the life of the individual can subject him to its power and control in a way no limited-function institution can."[38]

The kind of European labor movement we have been describing here contrasts sharply with Kerr's conception of what is proper or best for U.S. labor as a functioning part of American democracy.[39] Certainly one must generally concede that the total impact of the European labor movements—parties, unions, cooperatives, clubs—generally helped to democratize their own societies in the twentieth century. Moreover, in the Scandinavian countries, where the movements are most integrated with a full sweep of unions, parties, and cooperatives, the devotion to democratic ideals and to an understanding of democratic restraint is also highly developed.

This is not to argue the case for total labor movements everywhere! As has already been suggested, these are usually a product of special social and economic forces. But European labor movement experience should suggest some caution about projecting purely American concepts of the nature of pluralism and a modern democratic order. The "total" European movements often made a major contribution to democratic development.

There are at least two additional aspects of this kind of total workers' movement that we have been describing above, that call for comment. (And we have, of course, taken Shell's description of Austria only as an example; the labor movements in Scandinavia, Germany, Switzerland, and some other countries could be similarly described.) It was a product, as Landauer says, of the fact that in most European countries society had built a "wall" in front of workers. If workers were to enjoy club life and a "share in the higher expressions of civilization," they had to create their own institutions.[40]

Again, the creation of labor institutions also reflected the kind of revolutionary reaction on the part of the European working class that has often typified classes in revolt against a social order. The development of this fabric of unions, parties, clubs, and societies represented a denial of the prevailing order, as well as a substitute for it.[41]

On a different plane, it is clear that these pre-1918 European labor movements possessed what one recent writer describes as their own "coherent world view which simultaneously linked it to, and separated it from, the dominant ideology" of the bourgeois class. This world view, armed largely with the dialectical philosophy of Marxism, was unified under the banner of Social Democracy.[42]

Adam Ulam has effectively argued the neat fit between Marxism and workers' reactions to the realities of the newly industrializing society in central Western Europe during the latter half of the nineteenth century. He writes:

The surplus labor theory may be "wrong" from the point of view of a non-Marxist economist, yet it implies the supreme value of human labor and individuality in the midst of societies where the worker views himself as an adjunct of the machine. The economic historian may patiently prove that under capitalism the fate of the worker has not grown worse, but this Marxist error still communicates to the worker in an *industrializing* society his loss of the stability and security he enjoyed in his previous status of peasant or craftsman.[43]

As Ulam adds, "In an industrializing society the appeal of Marxism rests on the fact that its *intermediate* aim, the overthrow of capitalism, coincides with the proletariat's instinctive reaction against industrialism." For these reasons, for workers "at the crucial point of transition from a pre-industrial society to a partly industrialized state, Marxism becomes in a sense the national ideology of that society and the most alluring solution to its problems."[44] Most of Western European labor gradually came to reject Marxist ideology as the twentieth century wore on, but there can be little doubt of its hold in the formative decades.

Again, this broad structure and world view or ideology, which was shared by the European working class movements, added immeasurably to their solidarity in the early years of union struggle. We have already remarked that a collective tradition made unionism's path easier in Europe than in the United States. As they embraced or expounded a full ideology, these European movements also were cementing themselves together in a way not open to the American labor movement.

More Limited Scope of the American Labor Movement

In the modern era, the American labor movement has developed as almost a purely trade union affair. Political activity, cooperatives, and other European-type labor endeavors played little or no role as the American labor movement evolved in the first decades of the twentieth century. U.S. labor could not call upon a common working class ideology to help it expand in the more or less continuous path pursued by most of European labor. Although American unionism was relatively more advanced than most European movements in the 1870s and 1880s when industrialization was proceeding rapidly in the United States, the spread of unionism in the first three decades of twentieth-century America lagged behind most of Western Europe.

Not until the 1930s did a mass union movement come into existence in the United States on a permanent basis. Before that time U.S. unionism of a continuing character was confined for the most part to skilled workers in a relatively small number of industries.

Most of the modern European union movements also had their beginnings among skilled craftsmen such as printers, machinists, carpenters, and the like. As the mass-production industries developed, however, a common feeling of class solidarity and a common ideology made it easier in Europe than in the United States to spread unionism to the newer parts of the economy.

This extension of unionism to semiskilled and unskilled workers tended to deepen and solidify the relationships between the union and the political arms of the European labor movements. Although skilled craft workers might depend on their pure bargaining or union power for economic gain, the semi- or unskilled worker, depended on more effective political action as an absolute essential for social and economic progress.

The example of British labor is particularly interesting. Beginning in the 1850s or so, Britsh labor leaders, unlike most of their Continental counterparts, tended to pursue a fairly conservative brand of unionism, which was concentrated among skilled workers. This unionism confined itself to fairly limited objectives, which included, among other things, wages and hours on the job and different forms of mutual aid for members only. During these decades there was no serious independent, union-backed labor party action.

In some important respects, British unionism of the 1850–1890 period resembled the continuous mainstream of American unionism as it developed in the 1880s and thereafter. Indeed, during the decade of the nineties, the American Federation of Labor officers took note in their convention reports that the AFL, like the British Trades Union Congress, based its efforts in the political field primarily upon lobbying activities through a parliamentary committee. As for proposals to support a labor political party, the AFL noted, "In view of our own experience, as well as the experience of our British fellow-unionists, it would be wise to steer our ship of labor safe from that channel whose waters are strewn with shattered hopes and unions destroyed." The AFL took the position that, far from supporting any party program, the unions should be "broad enough and liberal enough to admit all shades of opinion upon the economic and political and social questions." The AFL over the years remained convinced of the correctness of this position of being "partisan to principles and not to be partisan to political parties."[45]

About 1890, with the rise of the "new unionism" in Britain, which took in growing thousands of semi- and unskilled workers in many basic industries, the British union movement underwent profound changes. One of these came of its decision to reach out and help form a new labor party with a generally socialistic orientation. This movement to extend labor's political engagement met with opposition from leaders of some of the older, craft unions, who were hostile to overdependence on legislation or commitment to a single political party. It took several years of struggle to bring the British Trades Union Congress into official support of the proposed labor party.[46]

In contrast to his earlier approval of British labor's limited political approach, Samuel Gompers, long-time president of the AFL, did not agree with British labor's new venture into the political party field. From his observations he concluded that, despite various joint arrangements and relationships, "the executive committee of the labor party dominates the entire movement of England. . . . all the time I was in England I never heard of a phrase like this: 'The British trade union movement and the labor party . . .' It was always the labor party and the Trades Union Congress. The labor party of England dominates the labor movement of England."[47]

The process of spreading unionism to the semiskilled and unskilled workers was long delayed in the United States. It occurred only in the wake of the great social upheaval of the 1930s when unionism was finally extended to the mass-production industries. Partially as a consequence of this long delay, the leaders of the American unions of skilled workers created for themselves a special union ideology that "gloried" in its practicality and its pragmatism. The unions had no ideological approach to the economy and society as a whole. As we have already noted, the lack of a strict class conscious structure in America produced a relatively ideology-free union movement—in the traditional sense in which the word ideology is used.[48]

But strangely enough the so-called job consciousness or business unionism of the American labor movement, as contrasted with the general socialistic orientation of the European movements, came to be woven into a special form of American ideology.[49] That ideology can be summed up as a "more, more now" concept sought basically through collective bargaining and politically through lobbying before legislatures.

In the absence of a clear-cut general philosophy or ideology, it is not surprising, of course, that American labor's commitment to full-scale political action has always been less than its European counterparts. American labor political action, especially since the 1880s, has been undertaken on behalf of specific pieces of legislation and/or particular candidates, as opposed to fundamental, permanent union involvement with a particular political party.

It should be noted, however, that beginning with the unionization of millions of semiskilled and unskilled workers in the mass production industries in the 1930s and 1940s, the character of American union participation in national politics has changed significantly. Organized labor's interest in social and economic issues has enlarged considerably, and the set of resolutions adopted by the biennial AFL-CIO Convention in 1965 or 1967 adds up to one of the most broadly based political programs in the nation. This undoubtedly reflects the *necessary* shift of a labor movement, which was largely sectional in its representativity prior to the 1930s, to a more broadly based movement that could scarcely hope to meet its social and economic needs without making a wider impact upon public policy.

The nature of American society and politics continues to preclude any serious consideration of a union-supported labor political party. But the amount of resources and manpower that American unions now devote to national political action are quite different from what existed before World War II. Mention should be made of the deep involvement of the construction unions in local politics prior to World War II, though in an admittedly narrow range of issues. The railway unions tended to be in the vanguard in terms of interest in national political issues and candidates prior to World War II. That interest no doubt reflected the very national character of the problems of their industry. But even in this case, the interests of the railway unions in this period can hardly be compared to the scope of union labor's political program today.

However, in spite of the increased emphasis upon political action, it is obvious that U.S. unionism remains much less political than the movements of Western Europe. Its main thrust is still industrial in character.

The spread of labor activity over cooperatives, parties, and unions provides European labor with a wider field of action. It has made it easier to extend and maintain union organization as compared with the United States, even under adverse economic conditions. Given the existing class structure and traditions, many European workers are born into a complex of socialist parties, youth groups, unions, and clubs; joining this complex is almost an automatic thing to do.[50] American workers are not born into such a complex. Their determination to join a union may not be as automatic, and some may even have to be convinced of the immediate advantages of joining.

On the other hand, because unions are almost the sole economic-industrial instrument of organized American workers, their thrust on the bargaining front has typically been more effective than that of the European unions. American unions have concentrated on collective bargaining, the collective agreement, and control over wages and working conditions; their power at the job level exceeds that of their European counterparts. The militance and wide range of items covered in collective bargaining in the United States are often envied by some European union officials.

The lack of enduring class feeling and organization in the United States should not be equated with a lack of violence in American history. Such violence, for example, has generally been more common in union-management relationships in the United States than in Western Europe.[51]

N O T E S

1. A longer discussion of the author's reasons for believing comparative labor study is best approached by this division among three types of societies can be found in E. M. Kassalow, *The Comparative Labor Field: Research and Teaching.* This paper was presented to the First World Congress of the International Industrial Relations Association (Geneva: September 1967) and was published, in part, in *International Institute for Labour Studies Bulletin,* July 1968. For a different approach to the same subject see the article by Kenneth F. Walker in *ibid.,* November 1967. A more general survey of the field is Frederic Meyers, "The Study of Foreign Labor and Industrial Relations," in S. Barkin, W. Dymond, E. M. Kassalow and others, *International Labor* (New York: Harper & Row, 1967).

2. Western here really refers to market-oriented, democratic, industrialized societies. In addition to the United States and Western Europe, these include Canada, New Zealand, and Australia. Our reference to the latter countries will be peripheral only. See Kassalow, *The Comparative Labor Field.*

3. Philip Taft has argued that these same characteristics can be found throughout all periods of U.S. labor history. See "On the Origins of Business Unionism," *Industrial and Labor Relations Review* (October 1963). Taft's point is well taken, but it remains true that as a set of *continuing, dominant characteristics* and *practices* of American unions, "business unionism" dates from the 1880s or 1890s. For a recent study of the emergence of the philosophy of business unionism in the United States, see H. M. Gitelman, "Adoph Strasser and the Origins of Pure and Simple Unionism," *Labor History* (Winter 1965), 71–83.

4. Louis Hartz, *The Liberal Tradition in America,* Harvest Book 53 (New York: Harcourt, Brace & World, 1955), p. 6.

5. *Ibid.,* p. 5.

6. Robert Heilbroner, *The Making of Economic Society* (Englewood Cliffs, New Jersey: Prentice-Hall, 1962), p. 182.

7. Robert Michels, *Political Parties* (Glencoe, Illinois: The Free Press, 1949), p. 43.

8. For the sake of brevity and clarity of comparison, I am here ignoring the nondurable strands of American labor development such as the International Workers of the World, the Socialist Labor Party, etc. It is true that many new revolutionary slogans and songs bobbed up in the mainstream of a major part of the American labor movement during the union upsurge of the 1930s. This probably reflected, in part, the relatively weak acceptance by workers then of the ongoing American social structure. A few of the militant songs and slogans of the thirties live on in U.S. labor today, but they often seem anachronistic even to the labor educators who are "charged" with the task of preserving continuity with the past.

9. Maurice Duverger, *Political Parties*, 2d ed. (London: Methuen, 1959), p. 170.

10. The Negro civil rights movement of the 1950s and 1960s may, in this respect, usher in new forms of continuing, *collective* political action and organization with something of a class character. In the context of this movement a largely disenfranchised section of the population has made a collective "conquest" of new and important social and political rights. Will the collective character of these victories lead the Negro masses to maintain collective organization for future social and political gains? Conceivably this could mark a significant departure in American life. On the other hand, it can be argued that the diverse class character of the Negro civil rights movement makes it possible that it will not hang together this way but will diffuse and eventually fuse with other elements of the population—as, for example, immigrant groups did earlier in American life.

11. B. S. Chlepner, *Cent Ans d'Histoire Sociale en Belgique* (Brussels: Université Libre de Bruxeles, Institut de Sociologie Solvay, 1958), p. 29; Maurice F. Neufeld, *Italy: School for Awakening Countries, The Italian Labor Movement*, N. Y. State School of Industrial and Labor Relations (Ithaca, N.Y.: Cornell University, 1961), p. 211.

12. Henry Pelling, *A History of British Trade Unionism* (Baltimore: Penguin, 1963), p. 90.

13. Guenther Roth, *The Social Democrats in Imperial Germany, A Study in Working Class Isolation and National Integration*, (Totawa, New Jersey: The Bedminster Press, 1963), pp. 213–214.

14. Quoted in *Freedom of Association*, (Geneva: International Labour Office, 1959), p. 9. The doctrine of conspiracy was also employed against American unions in the first half of the nineteenth century.

15. Samuel Gompers, *Labor in Europe and America* (New York and London: Harper and Brothers, 1910), p. 217.

16. Chlepner, *op. cit.*, pp. 22–24.

17. Pelling, *op. cit.*, pp. 74–76.

18. Charles A. Gulick, *Austria from Hapsburg to Hitler*, Vol. I (Berkeley: University of California Press, 1948), p. 18.

19. Daniel Porter, "The Quest for National Character," in John Higham, ed., *The Reconstruction of American History*, Harper Torch Books, the Academy Library (New York: Harper & Row, 1962), Chap. 11.

20. Hartz, *op. cit.*, pp. 51–52.

21. Even if one concedes that the earlier frontier school of American history may have underestimated some of the difficulties confronting would-be worker migrants from East to West in the United States, the frontier did drain away some of the discontent and enhance general social mobility in the United States.

22. Walter Galenson, *The Danish System of Labor Relations* (Cambridge: Harvard University Press, 1952), p. 17.

23. Sidney and Beatrice Webb, *The History of Trade Unionism* (London, New

York, Toronto: Longmans Green, 1950), pp. 1–43. In his classical work *On the History and Development of Gilds and the Origin of Trade Unions* (London: Turner & Co., 1870), even Lujo Bremzano did not argue that European guilds had directly evolved into unions. He did stress the appearance of early unions in many of the same trades where guilds had previously operated to regulate economic and social conditions. See Chap. V especially.

24. The literature on European socialist doctrine is, of course, voluminous. Two major works are G. D. H. Cole, *History of Socialist Thought*, 5 vols. (London: Macmillan 1953–1960), and Carl Landauer, *European Socialism*, 2 vols. (Berkeley: University of California Press, 1959). An excellent short account of the development of European socialism up to the 1930s is Oscar Jaszi's article "Socialism" in the *Encyclopedia of Social Sciences* (New York: Macmillan, 1934). The influence of *Marxism*, among varieties of socialism, varied between countries. It was relatively much more influential in Germany and Austria, for example, than in Sweden or Denmark.

25. E. J. Hobsbawm, *Labouring Men* (London: Weidenfeld and Nicolson, 1964), pp. 373–374. Another author, E. P. Thompson, does not deny the positive contribution of Methodism to English trade union spirit and organization but lays emphasis upon the same religious doctrine as a great disciplining force of the rebellious, resistant working class in the early, grinding years of the industrial revolution. See his "The Transforming Power of the Cross" in *The Making of the English Working Class* (New York: Random House, 1966), Chap. 11. Robert F. Wearmouth has written a series of volumes on Methodism and the British working class movement. See, for example, his *Methodism and the Struggle of the Working Classes 1850–1900* (Leicester: Edgard Backus, 1954) and *Methodism and the Working Class Movements of England 1800–1850* (London: The Epworth Press, 1937).

26. Selig Perlman, *A Theory of the Labor Movement* (New York: Augustus M. Kelley, 1949; first printing 1928), pp. 139–140.

27. Quoted in *Encounter*, XXI (July 1963), p. 81.

28. In a later period, of course, the Catholic Church directly entered the picture on the Continent and helped to sponsor a series of Catholic union movements in several countries.

29. Paul Malles, *Draft Paper on Certain European Trade Union Movements and Their Relation with Social Democratic Parties*, (Florence, Italy: International Confederation of Free Trade Unions, United Nations Economic and Social Commission East-West Seminar, May 24–30, 1959), p. 8.

30. G. D. H. Cole, *A Century of Cooperation* (London: George Allen & Unwin, 1944), pp. 54–65.

31. "Who is Harold Wilson? A conversation with Labour's leader," *The Observer*, June 9, 1963.

32. Hans Kohn has argued that a similar gradual evolution, and the early emergence of religious tolerance in Switzerland, also helps to account for the deeper, more stable roots of democracy in that country as well as in Great Britain. See *Nationalism and Liberty* (London: George Allen & Unwin, 1956), pp. 13–17.

33. Roth, *op. cit.*, pp. 38–39. Although Germany, with its unfinished revolution of 1848, was to some extent a special case, the degree of middle-class support for working-class rights on the Continent nowhere matched the British pattern.

34. Henry Pelling, *The Origins of the Labour Party* (London: Macmillan, 1954), p. 231.

35. *Labor and Working Conditions in Modern Europe*, Val R. Lorwin, ed. (New York: Macmillan, 1967), p. 12.

36. Kurt L. Shell, *The Transformation of Austrian Socialism* (Albany: State University of New York, 1962), p. 11.

37. Some of the European labor movements are still at the center of the anti-

alcoholic movements in their respective countries. It is ironic that the reform-minded Knights of Labor, ultimately unsuccessful in harnessing social reform and trade unionism in the United States, did unenthusiastically accept temperance policy pronouncements under the influence of its chief officer, Terrence Powderly, and over the objection of the Brewers' union. See Norman Ware, *The Labor Movement in the United States, 1860–1895* (New York: Appleton, 1929), pp. 223–225. Samuel Gompers, and most of the AFL, later also came to oppose the growing prohibition movement in the early decades of the twentieth century. See Nuala McGann Drescher, "Organized Labor and the Eighteenth Amendment," *Labor History*, Fall 1967, pp. 280–289.

38. Clark Kerr, *Unions and Union Leaders of Their Own Choosing*, (Santa Barbara, California: The Fund for the Republic, 1957), pp. 19, 21.

39. In his pamphlet Dr. Kerr did not deal with European labor, and in the comments I have made here this should be clearly understood.

40. Landauer, *op. cit.*, Vol. I., p. 315.

41. The ascetic aversion to the social institutions and customs of a society against which they were "revolting" similarly characterized the rising capitalistic class in sixteenth century England. Writing of this, Max Weber compared the reaction of the ascetic middle class against the more luxury-minded feudal and monarchic way of life in the sixteenth century, with the "class morality of the proletariat and the anti-authoritarian trade union" and its rejection of the middle-class capitalist way of life in his day (1904–1905). Max Weber, *The Protestant Ethic and the Spirit of Capitalism* (New York: Scribner, 1958), p. 167.

42. George Lichtheim, *Marxism: An Historical and Critical Study* (New York: Praeger, 1961), p. 258.

43. Adam B. Ulam, *The Unfinished Revolution, An Essay on the Sources of Influence of Marxism on Communism* (New York: Random House, Vintage Book V-516, 1964), p. 9.

44. *Ibid.*, pp. 10 and 64. Ulam's insights on Marxism as the "natural" language of protest in a society in the early or intermediate stages of industrialization are extremely valuable. He has, perhaps, tended to avoid some of its other appeals, which may account for its persistent hold in "developed" countries like France.

Marxism as a protest language of workers in the early stages of industrialization is likely to flourish best in a society in which there is a clear-cut background of class development and structure. Where, on the contrary, the economy is being developed almost exclusively by state direction and state enterprise, as in some of the new countries of Asia and Africa, social conflict can and does arise, but it does not as readily take a Marxist form or tone.

45. From the Proceedings and Reports of the AFL Conventions in 1890, 1894, and 1923, as quoted in *American Federation of Labor, History Encyclopedia Reference Book*, Vol. I, 1919, pp. 317–318, and Vol. II, 1924, p. 213 (Washington, D.C.: American Federation of Labor).

46. Pelling, *A History of British Trade Unionism*, "New Unionism and New Politics, 1880–1900," Chap. 6.

47. Gomper's speech as endorsed in the 1919 Officers' Report. American Federation of Labor Book, *op. cit.*, Vol. II, p. 215. Curiously enough, in considering all the labor party-labor union complexes of Western Europe, students have in the past often been struck by the dominant role of the Trades Union Congress in its relationship with the Labour Party in Britain.

48. I refer here to those characteristics of ideology that can best be summed up in the sense that the unions and the working class lacked any general world view of their own as to the nature of society and the direction in which it was moving or should move.

49. See the interesting article by Michael Rogin, "Voluntarism, the Political Functions of an Antipolitical Doctrine," *Industrial and Labor Relations Review* (July 1962).

50. These traditions are changing, however, particularly as technological and labor-force changes produce a "new worker" in Europe.

51. Several historians believe that his essentially correct observation about the lack of permanent class attitudes in the United States has led Hartz, *op. cit.*, and other historians to exaggerate the degree of consensus and the lack of conflict in American history. See Richard Hofstader, *The Progressive Historians* (New York: Knopf, 1968) pp. 456–466.

II

Unions and Parties, A Relationship
of Interdependence

I N VIEW of the social and political conditions prevailing during the early years of the modern Western European labor movements, it is not surprising that the thrust of these movements was as much political as industrial. In most countries the working class groups were confronted with deep social and political inequities, as well as with industrial burdens and needs.

To the typical European trade unionist, therefore, a concerted, organized, independent labor political party was as natural and necessary as the trade union itself. To the great majority of American workers, however, during a comparable period of their trade union growth, such a permanent working-class based labor-socialist party might have seemed unnatural.[1]

We have already described the political, social, and industrial labor movement in Western Europe. Although this combination has undergone considerable evolution since the last half of the nineteenth century, it still remains a vital force. It is fair to say that the description made by the German socialist leader, Wilhelm Liebknecht, in 1893, still has validity for most European workers: "The working class movement with purely trade union organization cannot reach its goal. A working class movement with purely political organization cannot reach its goal. The two forms of organization are indispensable to each other. . . ."[2] In 1925 the official history of the Belgium trade union movement described the interrelationships thus: "If the Trade Union Commission is considered the economic expression of the Trade Unions in the sphere of class war, the Trade Unions no less consider the Belgian Labour Party to be the representative and defender of the working classes in the political sphere."[3]

Of course relationships between the typical union and party arms of the various labor movements have changed significantly since Liebknecht formulated this thesis; indeed, at the time he spoke they had already evolved from what they had been earlier. However, his is a fair statement of the way in which typical, organized European workers viewed their labor movements throughout most of this period and down to the present—with arms of union and party joining to form one social force.

In the twentieth century, the different arms of union and party came to be understood and indeed consciously employed as alternate routes to social and economic goals of the working classes. Emphasis would be placed first upon one, then upon the other route, depending upon circumstances and possibilities.

Students of the trade union movement have even developed a theory to explain the shifting emphasis on the various arms of the labor movement. Sidney and Beatrice Webb spoke "of the perpetual 'see-saw' within the Labor Movement, decade after decade, between an infatuation for industrial or 'direct' action and an equal infatuation for political or Parliamentary and Municipal action. . . ." They explained the shifts rather simply as a product of the frustations of working people when they do not "find themselves obtaining the results in their daily lives which they expected, and which they were, as they understood, promised. . . ."[4]

Other theories have suggested that in times of economic growth and expansion there is a satisfactory "bargaining margin" in the economy, and the unions can be expected to place a relatively heavy emphasis upon collective bargaining. In this connection, it seems significant that modern unionism in most Western European countries took firm root in the last decade of the nineteenth century and the opening decades of the twentieth century, a period when capitalism was beginning to flower and a good bargaining margin was available.

However, Adolf Sturmthal has suggested that no union movement can turn itself too steadily to economic-bargaining tasks until it has also come to terms with the social and political institutions of its own society.[5] This coming to terms, which in American society had occurred in the nineteenth century, did not fully occur in several countries of Western Europe until the end of World War I. (In Belgium and Germany, for instance, male suffrage was not fully realized until then.)

Again, even after unions gain a general bargaining margin through economic (or industrial) evolution, the onset of recessions and depressions is likely to shift emphasis back to political action.

The above explanations merely underline the fact that one course of action does not exclude the other but that both routes—political and economic—are always being employed to some degree. Therefore, it is impossible to understand the workings of European union movements without an insight into their relationships with their brother political parties.

Early Patterns of Unions and Parties

Prior to the launching of the various social democratic parties in the closing decades of the nineteenth century, there was a brief tendency in a few countries for unions to seek cooperation with the so-called liberal parties. This was notably true in Norway and Great Britain. Even in these countries, however, the alliances were broken in a relatively short period of time, and permanent relations developed between the emerging unions and socialist parties.

Although individual unions and some municipal and regional union bodies were established on a fairly wide scale on the Continent, in the 1870s and 1880s, it was generally the national labor or socialist party that was formed before the *national* labor federation emerged. Often, however, the *individual* unions were part of the founding of the national party.

Sweden: Case History in Interdependence

A good case in point is Sweden. Here individual unions, city federations, and the few national unions (such as the typographers and the postal workers) helped in establishing the Social Democratic Party in 1889.

The Swedish national labor federation (the LO), was not established until 1898. During this formative period from 1889—1898, the socialist party organization was the only national labor body.

. . . Party district executives served as central organization for union activities. It was to them that the local unions, and to some extent even the weaker national union, turned for counsel and support. Under these circumstances it is scarcely surprising that the Party organizations insisted upon having a say in decisions on union matters. On the district level these relations were direct and intimate, and Party officials played an important part in making decisions primarily of trade-union character.[6]

During those early years, Swedish socialists, like socialist leaders elsewhere on the Continent, looked upon the unions as "schools for socialism" to be used primarily to educate members in party programs and discipline.

In the 1890s, Sweden's rapid economic growth brought about the emergence of various national unions and each strove to centralize authority in its national headquarters. Particularly critical was control over strike policy and strike funds. The Social Democratic Party tended to judge strikes and to give or refuse aid on grounds other than purely trade union ones. In 1897 a mining strike in Malmberget was supported because "Malmberget is an important Party outpost." But a wage dispute in a Goteborg paint factory was not supported "because it was neither a question of lockout nor the right to organize, but only a wage issue." Donald J. Blake adds, "During the years immediately following the formation of the Social Democratic Party, it was common to regard the strike as an excellent form of agitation, win, lose or draw. This view was soon abandoned as experience demonstrated that poorly planned strikes were seldom successful and frequently costly."[7]

It is therefore not surprising that those unions that were most advanced in national development chafed at party "intrusion" in trade union affairs which they regarded as their own province. This kind of dualism in the control of purely trade union affairs would not be long tolerated.

The growth of the Swedish economy and the sheer increase in the number of workers in industry opened new trade union possibilities. With increasing concentration and specialization in employment, it became feasible, and indeed desirable, to think of more national unions to cover particular industries or crafts. Moreover, the growth of central employer organizations in Sweden and in other countries compelled serious consideration of a national trade union federation.[8]

Trade union membership in Sweden, which was estimated at 14,000 or 15,000 in 1890, had reached 65,000 by 1900. The necessity to move toward a central union body distinguished from the Social Democratic Party was heightened by the growth of union membership. Also, the unions wanted to obtain fuller control over strike policies and funds. Although the party did strive to extend organization and to serve as coordinator for the unions, especially in economically strategic industries, the dictates of more complete union strategy called for more independent union organization.

Under pressure from the emerging national unions, a resolution was finally passed at the 1897 party convention authorizing the unions to develop a more effective organization, while at the same time "safeguarding the cooperation with the Party." To guarantee such cooperation, first proposals for the constitution of the Swedish Federation of Labor (the LO, established in 1898), provided for compulsory affiliation of all local unions with the Social Democratic Party. Party headquarters initiated a campaign in favor of compulsory affiliation with the Social Democratic Party just prior to the founding convention of LO, and the requirement of party affiliation was finally accepted at the convention. (The provision specified that local unions affiliated with the LO had to affiliate with the SDAP in 3 years.)

The second convention, or congress, of the Swedish Federation of Labor, LO, formally dissolved the compulsory affiliation requirement. Instead, the constitution was amended in 1900 to provide that one of the aims of the LO was to *work for the affiliation* of every trade union with the *local* party organization and through it with the national party.

The clause urging the LO to work for union affiliation with the party was continued in the constitution for the next nine years, but opposition to it mounted. The two largest LO unions campaigned against the clause and argued that any relationship which implied that union members would be compelled to join the party undermined the unions' independence and hindered recruitment of union members. Under this pressure, the LO congress in 1909 finally repealed the party affiliation declaration. Since then there have been no provisions in the LO rules for *compulsory* cooperation between it and the Social Democratic Party.[9]

As the LO was evolving, it also came into conflict with the basic Social Democratic Party structural forms. For the party the local commune or municipality and the larger district or region were the key building organizational blocks. At the first congresses of the LO, the commune organizations were accepted and represented as trade union bodies, just as the various national unions were.

By 1903 the LO secretariat was arguing that only national unions should be represented in the congresses, and by 1906 the LO congress voted to exclude the commune unions.[10]

This process of differentiation and separation should not be misunderstood. It did not represent any serious ideological or policy split between the party and the unions. When viewed retrospectively, it can be seen as part of the pluralizing process that typically spawns a larger number of powerful, independent institutions in a more fully developed modern industrial society. The sheer growth in the number of industrial workers made it possible to think about separate union organizations in Sweden and elsewhere during this period.

In Sweden the *enduring* relationships between party and union were well summed up in the 1909 resolution offered by the LO chairman. (This was the very year when the LO constitution was amended to eliminate the compulsory clause for union affiliation with the Social Democratic Party.) Speaking of this decision to change the LO constitution, the chairman noted:

This decision does not involve any change whatsoever in the ideological unity and solidarity of the labour movement, which from the beginning has bound together the Swedish trade union movement and social democracy. Congress considers that the social democratic party is the natural and obvious vehicle for the political aspirations of the Swedish working class.[11]

While party-union relationships had their points of tension during these formative decades, the relationship then and later continued to be one of mutual dependence. Prior to the establishment of the LO, the party organization provided critical services for the unions, especially those weaker unions that were in a great majority. Blake notes that after the formation of the LO itself, the weaker national unions, in turn, looked to it for strong central support and direction. The stronger national unions, which had led the movement for the establishment of a labor federation separate from the party, were skeptical about a strong centralized LO and preferred to emphasize their own autonomy. This is a pattern which one can observe in some other countries, as for example Norway.

In the period before 1909, before male suffrage had been more fully won, the party came to have a certain dependence upon the unions. As Blake notes, "As long as labour was grossly under-represented in the Riksdag, extra parliamentary weapons had to be held in readiness." As suffrage was extended and the Social Democratic Party gained legislative influence, the party was important "to the union movement as the guardian of its interests in the national legislature. Thus a new form of mutual dependence began to evolve . . . an interpretation of Swedish developments as a process by which the unions wrested their independence from Party domination is over-simple and fundamentally inaccurate. . . . Briefly stated the union party relationship was one of inter-dependence."[12]

This characterization of the relationship as one of interdependence is a sound one. By and large it best sums up the union-socialist party relationships for most of the period since the various, modern Western European labor movements have developed. This, of course, does not gainsay the fact that there are issues and periods of tension between parties and unions. At times one arm or the other may gain or drift into a state of dominance. But clashes or differences are overcome, since both party and union have come to be essential in the minds of their constituents.

Some International Parallels

Although the relationship and evolution of the Swedish labor movement that we have described here was not duplicated precisely, it can be taken as a broad example of the way in which the process proceeded in most of the other Western European countries. Even though individual unions and worker education groups were established at an early date, in practically all cases the first *national* labor organization to emerge usually was the socialist or labor party. (England is an exception which has already been referred to.)

Even on the international front it is significant that in the first years of the Second or Socialist International (founded in 1889) unions were members along with parties. It was not until 1903 that a separate international trade union secretariat was established, and for most of its early years, it was not much more than a weak body, a "mail box" to use one writer's description. The Socialist International was looked upon as *the center* of the international labor movement. The union secretariat was converted into the International Federation of Trade Unions, with a formal constitution, in 1913.

The international labor movement, and one might more properly describe it as a European-wide movement in the pre-1914 period, went through an evolution that bore an "organic" resemblance to what was happening within each nation. At first the all-embracing labor organization was the socialist political party; later it was the Socialist International to which many labor unions, as well as political parties, were also affiliated. In the late 1880s and 1890s a series of international trade-union secretariats, or international union bodies, were founded. These international bodies, such as the Hatters secretariat, the Miners secretariat, and others, grouped the national unions operating in the same industry or craft in different countries. As previously noted, an overall international union organization combining country-wide trade union federations, as such, was established only in 1903.[13]

To summarize, then, the pattern of evolution in a given country generally began with *local* unions, often affiliated to a socialist party, then proceeded to the establishment of some key *national* unions (printers, tobacco workers, metalworkers, and the like) and advanced to the creation of a national or country-wide trade union federation to which the national unions were affiliated.

Other Examples of Unions' and Parties' Relationships

In Norway, the Labor Party was established in 1887 and remained the national center for union and party bodies until the Norwegian Federation of Labor was established, as the trade union center, in 1899. The decade of the nineties witnessed the rise of national unions in various crafts, such as metals, bakers, and so on. The development of these national unions was a "natural" forerunner of the move for a national trade union federation separate from Norway's Labor Party.

In Denmark, during the 1880s, the Social Democratic Party functioned as a "coordinating body for the socialist trade union" in a manner similar to that described for Sweden. A national trade union federation did not emerge until 1898.[14]

The Belgian Workers Party was formed in 1885, and among its affiliates were many unions, workers' mutual societies, and local party groups. The growth in the union movement led the Belgian Workers Party to set up a Trade Union Standing Committee in 1898. As the name implies, however, the union body was subordinate to the party. Throughout most of the pre-1914 period the trade union movement in Belgium remained in the shadow of the party, and for a number of years the party granted the union movement a subsidy to cover the expenses of the Trade Union Study Committee. Unions not affiliated with the party, however, could join the Standing Committee, so long as they "believed in the principle of the class struggle."[15]

The situation in Austria followed the general pattern. A full-fledged national trade union federation did not clearly and fully emerge there until 1928. The Austrian Socialist Party, on the other hand, was firmly established in 1889. The Vienna unions, which were part of the Austrian Socialist Party complex, established an overall Provisional Commission for themselves shortly thereafter. In 1893 the first congress of Austrian unions was held, and the Provisional Commission was converted into a National Trade Union Commission. It was not until 1928, however, that this commission was reorganized into the Federation of Free Trade Unions of Austria.[16]

In Switzerland, control over strike funds lay at the heart of the process whereby the Swiss Federation of Trade Unions gradually structured itself into a strong independent force in the nation's social and economic life. (This recalls a similar contest for control over strike action and funds in the Swedish movement.) The federation arose in this way:

Because Swiss trade unions had been few in number, they did not set up a national labor federation in the 1870s; instead they joined with other workers' political and friendly societies and, in 1873, established the Swiss Labor League. This body was hurt by the impact of a severe economic crisis and by 1880 had fallen apart. In October of that year, a small number of unions met and established the Swiss Federation of Trade Unions. For the next five or six years, however, this body was extremely small both in numbers and in strength.[17]

In the mid-1880s there was an improvement in economic conditions. This gave rise to an upsurge of labor militance, which led to several critical strikes. Many workers found themselves "victimized" (laid off because of union activity) by employers, and a cry rose for the establishment of strike reserve funds.

The Grutli Association, a workers' organization founded in 1838 for educational purposes, but which had evolved into a broad political labor center, took the lead. In 1886 it passed a resolution calling for a general "strike and victimization fund" and proceeded to contact kindred bodies in Switzerland to find resources for the fund.[18]

The unions, who were uneasy at the prospect of nonunion management of the proposed fund, offered some resistance. Moreover, for the Swiss Federation of Trade Unions, the Grutli-managed strike fund was a significant competitor in the federation's efforts to affiliate different unions.[19]

The unions' position was rendered particularly difficult because it was stipulated that the managers of the fund were not only to authorize strike pay support but also to investigate "where grave dissension arises between workers and employers; to attempt to obtain settlement with the employers or arbitration of the dispute . . . and if the case calls for it, to approve a strike. . . . [and] to promote as far as possible the organization of the workers into trade unions."[20] Thus the Reserve Fund, in which the Swiss Federation of Trade Unions had only a modest role, had negotiating power and organizing power, as well as control over strikes. As the official history of the pre-World War II Swiss socialist union movement notes, the Grutli Association "claimed undue powers in judging of purely economic questions and in unionizing movements, activities for which, being a political organization, it was in no way qualified."[21]

The unions, moreover, were dissatisfied with the loose, purely voluntary contribution system employed in raising the Reserve Fund and called for compulsory contributions. The Grutli Association, a loose political-education body, was unenthusiastic about this proposal. Finally, however, the fund was (1891) put on a compulsory basis, and made an integral part of the Federation of Trade Unions. A decisive step had been taken in the development of the Swiss trade union movement.

Union Right and Party Left: Germany the Classic Case

The evolving relationship between the German Social Democratic Party movement and the German trade union movement is almost a classic example of the stages and problems in pre-World War I party-union ties in Western Europe. Moreover, many of the generalizations that can be made about this party-union relationship in Germany apply to the entire party-union process throughout Western Europe.

During the 1870s and 1880s the labor movement in Germany was largely conceived of in political terms. Many basic voting and citizenship rights still remained to be won. The famous Gotha program of the Social Democratic Party, adopted in 1875, called upon workers to affiliate with the party, saying that only the party could win the proper political and economic conditions for the proletariat. German socialist leaders of the time belittled trade unions, so much so that Friedrich Engels for whom attainment of political power was certainly central, nevertheless could criticize the Gotha program, writing, "There is not a word about the organisation of the working class as a class by means of the trade unions. . . . [despite] the importance which this form of organisation has also attained in Germany." He argued that it was "necessary in our opinion to mention it in the programme and if possible to leave open a place for it in the party organisation."[22]

The bitter conflicts so characteristic of the German socialist-party movement in the 1870s and 1880s had repercussions in the unions. The official history of pre-World War II German unions states that as each party faction forced "the vigorous new life of the trade unions into channels dictated by the interests of the political party," the unions were weakened.[23] Not only were they weakened as unions, but the very nature of the conflict tended to make their identification with the party (or parties) all too total.

Until the last decade of the nineteenth century, the unions generally played only a minor role in the vigorous German working-class movement. The prestige and growth of the Social Democratic Party left the workers with "the belief in the all-conquering might of the Party. . . . All was to be risked on that card alone: The trade unions too were to subserve political purposes."[24]

Industrial growth, the rise of national unions, and growing and concerted opposition from employers began to produce (the now familiar) strains among the local unions. Increasingly they realized that it was impossible for them to risk all on the political card. Finally, in 1890, under the influence of a number of Social Democratic Party leaders, but not the party officially, a separate National Executive Commission was established for the union movement as such. By 1892 the concept of national trade union federation was further strengthened when representation in this commission was limited to national unions (craft or industrial, as the case might be); local union organizations were excluded. Recognition of a national center in this form meant, again in the words of the unions' official history, "an end to the endeavors of the local organisation to convert the trade unions into auxiliaries of the Party, subordinated to its influence and fighting its battles. . . . [It] was a declaration by the trade unions of their determination to go their own way independent of . . . any . . . party, in accordance with their own rules." Moreover, the establishment of a National Executive Committee welded the unions "together into a Movement."[25]

The unions continued in close relationship with the party, however, and the move toward independence still remained very much in its infancy. Carl Legien, chief leader of the pre-World War I German union movement and chairman of the new union Executive Committee, continued to minimize union effectiveness in the workers' movement. In 1893 he stated that unions were nothing "but a palliative within present-day bourgeois society." He continued to characterize them as "recruiting schools for the party."[26]

For the moment Legien may have been correct in his estimate of the relative weight of party and union movements. In 1893 when union membership was 223,530, the Social Democratic Party vote was eight times greater. (Party *membership* figures, as opposed to party *votes*, are not available for some of the earlier years.)

The relationships between party and unions were to change radically in the next two decades. By the time of the 1903 elections the ratio was down to three to one, and by 1912 the party vote was 4,250,000 and union membership 2,530,000—in other words, a ratio of less than two to one. *Membership* figures available for 1912 indicate that union membership was two and one-half times party membership.

Cast in a role of more or less permanent opposition to the existing government, socialist party leaders and theoreticians could and often did continue to voice the old revolutionary programs and slogans. Opposition, in this pre-World War I period, bespoke a kind of revolutionary irresponsibility in most socialist parties.

In contrast, union leaders were typically caught up in the day-to-day business of administering labor-management agreements, mutual benefit funds, social security funds, and the like. Again, as union membership expanded rapidly, union treasuries did, too, and magnificent buildings often were built—whereas party membership and party dues were typically much smaller.[27]

With variations, of course, the general pattern of relationships that emerged in Western European labor movements in these pre-World War I years was one in which the party and its leaders stood on the left and the unions and their leaders stood on the right.

Though socialist parties may have remained to the left of the unions, they frequently depended on labor organizations for financial assistance. Such dependence continues in most of Western Europe today, although in a few countries the old formal ties of affiliation have been broken and contributions to the party are on a purely individual subscription basis.

As might be expected, a certain amount of tension developed between the different wings (union and party) of some of the workers' movements. Generally speaking, the bureaucratic union leaders restrained the more revolutionary party wings. This situation was well expressed by Robert Michels, who, on the eve of World War I, wrote:

Two qualities in which most of the trade-union leaders unquestionably excel are objective gravity and individual good sense (often united with a lack of interest in and understanding of wider problems), derived from the exceptionally keen sense they have of direct personal responsibility, and in part perhaps from the dry and predominantly technical and administrative quality of their occupations. The trade-union leaders have been deliberately contrasted with the verbal revolutionists who guide the political labour movement . . . and, not without exaggeration, there has been ascribed to the former a sound political sense which is supposed to be lacking in the latter—and insight into the extraordinary complexity of social and economic life and a keen understanding of the politically practicable. The nucleus of truth which such observations contain is that the trade-union leaders (leaving out of consideration for the present those of syndicalist tendency) differ in many respects from the leaders of political socialism.[28]

There has been some tendency to exaggerate the dichotomy of the union and party movements. But for the great mass of workers both bodies had their legitimate status and roles and were looked upon as one "movement."

Since history is most often written by people who are theory- or ideology-oriented, the unions seem to come off badly in comparison with the parties. Given the nature of democratic processes, the predominantly nonproletarian character of European society, and the opportunities for gradual rather than revolutionary advance, the kind of caution with respect to reform that the unions advocated in the first three decades of the twentieth century seems, in retrospect, to have been largely appropriate for the times.

The Cautious Route of the Unions

A British writer recently stressed the value of the cautious approach. He noted that in Britain the unions exercised a dominant role in the combined labor movement from the outset; the Labour Party itself, as well as its program, were therefore always more gradualistic in character. The result was a greater degree of social reform and, on balance, greater democratization of the society.

By holding down the pace of proposed change to what their instincts told them would be acceptable to a steadily widening range of working-class opinion, the trade unions in fact speeded up the pace of effective change. The longest way round proved the shortest way home. A comparison of the achievements of the [British] Labour Party with those of continental socialist parties provides ample proof of this, and the continental parties themselves recognised this when, after the Second World War, tacitly admitting that their short-cut techniques had taken them much less far, they acknowledged the *de facto* leadership within the Socialist International of the Labour Party, whose original application for membership had been accepted in 1908 only after much hesitation.[29]

This problem of pace and style between labor union and labor party has been a persistent one in modern European history.

Curiously enough, one of the clearest distinctions between the unions' step-by-step approach to social and economic change as contrasted with the more sweeping conceptions of socialist parties was made by a recent leader of the Communist-dominated General Italian Federation of Labor (CGIL). In his farewell address (on his retirement) to the federation's 1965 convention, Fernando Santi, a left-wing socialist, declared:

. . . one of the trade union's basic characteristics is that of being a mass organisation. It is made up of human beings, of human beings exactly like us, with differing political opinions or without any particular political views, with a mind open to changes and suggestions, having hopes and fears.

They are human beings who, at times, do not march in step but who nevertheless want to go ahead, who daily become aware of their conditions and of the necessity to change them. This is why I believe that there is an invisible law that governs—whether we want it or not—the activity of the trade union: the law of graduality. The trade union cannot make appointments with history. Political parties can do so and even they only within certain limits. Each day the union must give an account of itself, of its activity. I would say it must conquer something each day. That is why we must avoid sterile impatience, as we must avoid culpable renunciations. I believe in the secure gain of each day; I believe in the necessity of incorporating the workers' gains in the customs, regulations and laws in order that they be safeguarded and become the civil patrimony of the entire national society.[30]

In quoting William S. Pickles and Fernando Santi, we have jumped far ahead in time—and we have done so in order to give an overview of the situation as it may appear today. But it is useful and instructive to look back at the interplay between party and union in the formative years, when the union's right-wing role was quite conspicuous. Germany, to repeat, is the classic example.

We have already noted that even Carl Legien, long-time top leader of the German labor movement, was inclined to minimize the relative importance of the unions in the early nineties, describing them as mere "recruiting schools for socialism." Almost at the same time, however, Legien was beginning his argument for formal trade union neutrality on political questions, on the grounds that many workers were not yet "ripe" for socialist ideas.

German Unions Move Toward Independence of Party

By the early 1900s union and party leaders were in occasional and serious conflict over certain tactics and programs. Some of the German Social Democratic Party leadership, for example, placed great reliance on the mass, general political strike as a means of "activating the political consciousness of the backward positions of the population." Gradually the mass general strike became a favorite tactic, even a program, of much of the left socialist leadership of Western Europe. In Germany, the idea of using such a strike to break down the remaining barriers to universal male citizenship and voting rights in Prussia became particularly popular.[31]

The German unions, with their collective agreements, buildings, treasuries, and the like, were less than enthusiastic about the use of their resources and power for such political objectives. The rising power of employer organizations also tended to make the German union leaders fearful of any political "adventures." Union power and wealth had been accumulated slowly and painfully, and they regarded with suspicion proposals for mass general strikes, since in the words of the official union history, "They had too much to lose and too much to risk."[32] At their triennial Cologne Congress in May 1905 the unions decided to tackle the mass strike issue before the Social Democratic Party Congress could act definitively upon it. One of the key union leaders declared

"To develop our organizations further, we need peace in the labor movement. We must see to it that the discussion of the mass strike disappears." The congress itself adopted a resolution which declared the general strike "indiscussable" and told the unionists "not to let themselves be distracted by the reception and propagation of such ideas from the small day-to-day tasks of building up the organization of labor."[33]

Party theorists were offended, for the most part, by this action of the Free Trade Union Federation.[34] At its congress in Jena, in September 1905, the Social Democratic Party went into heated debate on the political mass strike. Finally, the congress voted party leader August Bebel's resolution accepting the mass strike primarily as a defensive tool, to be used against an attack on either universal suffrage or the right of association.

For the moment it appeared as though the "radicals" on the party left had triumphed. Actually it was at best only a compromise since the mass strike had not been accepted as a central tactic or as part of the program to bring about the new socialist order.

These debates were going on against the background of the Russian Revolution of 1905, with its spectacular political strikes, which had stirred socialists everywhere. Socialists were stirred, too, when in Austria the Socialist Party congress and the unions adopted the principle of the mass strike to obtain universal suffrage in 1906. In Germany, a series of suffrage crises in different states seemed on the verge of provoking the mass strike that union leaders feared so much.

The top leadership of Germany's Social Democratic Party was in turn fearful; it felt that resort to mass political strikes would alienate the trade unions from the party. At a secret conference held early in 1906, the party executives agreed to "try to prevent as much as possible" any mass strike. If such a strike did break out, its leadership would be a party affair, and the costs of the strike would have to be borne by the party alone.

The debate continued at the party's congress at Mannheim in September 1906. Despite the radical spirit that seemed to prevail among most delegates, the congress accepted the party principle that declared, "In actions which affect equally the interest of trade unions and party, the central leadership of both organizations should seek a mutual understanding in order to achieve a unified procedure." The resolution dealing with the mass strike accepted the union's 1905 Cologne resolution, which had opposed it, and tried to reconcile this with the party's resolution at Jena, which had favored it. Clearly the party's ability to engage in revolutionary action was now firmly compromised by the fact that it had to act in concert with the trade union movement.[35]

The Mannheim Party Congress resolution was a milestone, and not merely because it resolved the general strike issue. The very phrasing of the resolution denoted, as the official German union history states, "the recognition of the claim of the unions to tactical independence and separate leadership. . . . Thus was the way cleared for cooperation on the basis of mutual understanding."[36] Prior to this resolution, the primacy of political goals and needs was implicit and explicit in virtually all socialist theory.

It should be added that the kind of clear-cut collision and resolution between party and union that occurred in Germany was an exception rather than the rule. Generally, on the Continent, the union and party forces reached a position of equality of status and interdependence more gradually and more peacefully.

German Unions Oppose Party in May Day Demonstrations

For the same reasons they opposed the general political strike, the German trade unions came to be less than enthusiastic about the traditional May 1 demonstrations or strikes. Even before 1900, individual employers had acted in reprisal against strikers by permanently locking them out or discharging them. By 1900 the unions were arguing that workers should be given the option of joining or not joining the May 1 demonstrations (as against being required to join them). An official trade union history notes that union progress "had been built up by slow degrees under collective wages agreements . . . social legislation [etc.] . . . [a] system developed on the principle of cautious progress." They had much to lose, and they could not see risking severe employer reprisals for the demonstrative value of the May 1 strike.

The 1906 Mannheim Party Congress, in addition to dealing with the issue of the general strike, also took some action on the May Day strike problem. It ruled that in the future the costs of supporting the victims of any May Day strike would be borne jointly by the party and the unions (clearly a more disproportionate burden for the party).[37]

The May Day strike itself continued to enjoy popularity among the workers, but the union leaders remained concerned about the problem of reprisals. In April 1907, arguing that many unions were already engaged in industrial strikes and that important wage discussions were nearing a climax, the union executives persuaded the party executives to issue a release advising against a May Day strike if a lockout threat existed. Finally, in 1909, under a plan adopted by the party congress at Leipzig at the urging of the unions, it was agreed that general trade unions funds were not to be touched for May Day demonstrations and that special regional funds were to be created to support them. Much of the motivation was thereby weakened for participating in this traditional day of "defiance."[38]

Robert Michels, Carl Schorske, and others have graphically described the braking action of unions on their brother parties, especially in the pre-World War I period. Indeed, Michels virtually made a sociological law out of the unions' right-wing, oligarchic-like force in the party-union relationship. He argues that the unions, with their day-to-day needs, inevitably became a conservative force undercutting any serious socialist, revolutionary appeals and programs.

There is, however, another important aspect of union influence. As we have previously suggested, in many respects the sometimes cautious, less doctrinaire tactics of the unions were better adapted to the real social needs and opportunities of the day.

Socialist Parties and Unions in the Great Depression

German history provides a striking example of the unions' greater realism. In the late 1920s the Weimar Republic was confronted with a crisis in the economy, accompanied by rising unemployment. Like virtually all other Western European (and American) governments, the German republic met this threat with classic deflationary policies. Efforts to balance the budget and reduce expenditures became the order of the day.

The crisis deepened, however, and grew into the depression of 1929. The chief economic adviser of the German unions, W. S. Woytinsky, developed a counterdeflationary program that involved outlays for public works and a program of monetary expansion to create additional purchasing power in the economic system. This was a Keynesian proposal, formulated even before John Maynard Keynes published his famous *General Theory of Employment, Interest, and Money.*

Woytinsky continued his agitation into 1930 and 1931, and by that time he had convinced the trade union leadership of the wisdom of an antideflationary spending program to reverse the trend of the depression. But Woytinsky and the unions came into sharp conflict with the Social Democratic Party and its theoreticians. The leader among these men was Rudolf Hilferding, whose traditional, doctrinaire Marxian economics could brook no middle-ground policy, such as Woytinsky was proposing, between pure capitalism and pure socialism. Hilferding continued to support traditional deflationary measures designed to defend the German mark.

The unions pressed for a spending program to restore the economy, but the party remained opposed and effectively blocked action. Finally, party and union leaders met in a dramatic confrontation. Woytinsky debated Hilferding, arguing that easier credit, public works, and the like could help restore the economy.

Hilferding clung to " 'Marx's theory of labor value' and the conviction that depressions 'result from the anarchy of the capitalist system. Either they must come to an end or they must lead to the collapse of this system. . . . [no] program can mitigate a depression.' " By definition such a program as Woytinsky was proposing would not be Marxist, since it was conceived of in terms of reforming the capitalist economy—something not admissible in Hilferding's "system."

The party leadership, unable to face a break with Marxism, sided with Hilferding, and the German tragedy moved to its terrible climax.[39]

Curiously enough, most American writers on the subject of German trade union-socialist party relationships, especially when they write about the period from 1900 to 1933, almost invariably side with the party, which tends to be more "radical." Commenting on these relationships, Richard N. Hunt in his recent *German Social Democracy* is critical of the trade unions for refusing to go along with the socialist-led government in its efforts to reduce unemployment benefits in 1929. One would imagine that by now it would be appreciated that the union's antideflationary position was basically correct, as opposed to the party's "neoclassicism"![40]

This traditional, one can call it neoclassical, approach to the Great Depression of 1929 was typical of the path pursued by almost all of the European socialist parties. Imprisoned by traditionalist ideology, the typical European socialist parties could not come to grips effectively with the problems of economic policy in the 1930s. Their failure to do so paralleled a similar ineffectiveness among the various conservative and liberal party leaders elsewhere on the Continent, prolonged the depression, and ultimately helped the spread of fascism as another type of response to the breakdown. The totality of this process has been described by one student as *The Tragedy of European Labor*.[41]

In England the British Labour Party also foundered and finally split because its top leaders could propose nothing but a general deflationary program, including cuts in unemployment benefits, to counter the depression. Significantly enough, the trade unions to some extent tended toward a more pragmatic approach. In order to reverse the economic tide, at least one leading trade union leader worked his way through the morass of traditional governmental fiscal and monetary institutions and policies to advocate a policy of inflation and public spending. In 1930, sitting with

Keynes and ten other members of the Macmillan Committee on Finance and Industry, Ernest Bevin, General Secretary of the Transport and General Workers Union, broke with economic orthodoxy; he argued for positive fiscal action to restore the economy. Despite the efforts of Bevin, Keynes, and a few others, Labour Party Prime Minister Ramsay MacDonald was never persuaded to pursue strong counterdeflationary fiscal action to turn back the depression.[42]

Sweden was the shining exception to the inability of socialist labor movements to come to grips with the depression. Taking office in 1932, the crisis point of the economic downturn, the Swedish Social Democratic Party embarked upon a vigorous program of public investment, financed by borrowing. In a sense the groundwork for the successful Swedish Social Democratic attack upon traditional economic policy and the depression had been prepared years before. Both the socialist party and trade union leaders had broken with old dogmas, and the country had produced a brilliant generation of economists (including socialists like Gunnar Myrdal and Erik Lindahl), who helped provide a theoretical framework for the successful program that had just about eliminated unemployment by 1938. But, as noted, Sweden was largely an exception (although it did influence developments elsewhere in Scandinavia to a degree); only after World War II did it begin to serve seriously as a model in democratic planning.[43]

NOTES

1. For interesting statements of why the American labor movement has avoided independent labor-socialist action, see Walter Galenson, *Why the American Labor Movement Is Not Socialist*, Reprint No. 168, Institute of Industrial Relations (Berkeley: University of California, 1961), and John H. M. Lasler, "Socialism and the American Labor Movement: Some New Reflections," *Labor History* (Spring 1967).

2. James Joll, *The Second International, 1889–1914* (New York: Praeger, 1956), p. 66.

3. C. Mertens, *The Trade Union Movement in Belguim,* (Amsterdam: International Trade Union Library, No. 1, International Federation of Trade Unions, 1925), pp. 15–16.

4. Sidney and Beatrice Webb, *The History of Trade Unionism* (London, New York, Toronto: Longmans Green, 1950), p. 706.

5. Adolf Sturmthal, "Unions and Economic Development," *Economic Development and Cultural Change* (January 1960), p. 201.

6. Donald J. Blake, *Swedish Trade Unions and the Social Democratic Party: The Formative Years.* Reprint No. 166, Institute of Industrial Relations (Berkeley, University of California, 1961), p. 26. I have drawn heavily from this excellent study in my description of the evolution of the Swedish unions and the Social Democratic Party in the decades from 1880 to 1910.

7. Blake, *op. cit.,* p. 25.

8. The European term for what we call a "federation," (for example, the AFL-CIO), is normally "confederation." The word "federation," when employed in Europe, normally signifies a national union covering a particular craft or industry. We shall use American terminology wherever possible, and the term federation will be reserved for the national, central labor body such as the Swedish LO, the British TUC, the American AFL-CIO, etc.

9. T. L. Johnston, *Collective Bargaining in Sweden* (Cambridge: Harvard University Press, 1962), p. 26. The LO statutes adopted in 1909, and still in force, do declare "the Social Democratic Party is the natural bearer of the political aspirations of the trade union movement." *Trade Unions in Sweden,* (Stockholm: LO, 1961), p. 44.

10. *Ibid.*

11. Quoted in *ibid.,* p. 27.

12. Blake, *op. cit.,* pp. 42–43.

13. Walter Schevenels, *Forty-Five Years, International Federation of Trade Unions, 1901–1945* (Brussels: 1956), Chaps. II and III.

14. Walter Galenson, *The Danish System of Labor Relations* (Cambridge: Harvard University Press, 1952, pp. 24–26.

15. B. S. Chlepner, *Cent Ans d'Histoire Sociale en Belgique* (Brussels: Université Libre de Bruxelles, Institut de Sociologie Solvay, 1958), pp. 115–116.

16. Charles A. Gulick, *Austria From Hapsburg to Hitler,* Vol. I (Berkeley: University of California Press, 1948), pp. 20–21.

17. Edward Weckerle, *The Trade Unions in Switzerland* (Berne: Swiss Federation of Trade Unions, September 1947), pp. 14–15.

18. *Ibid.,* pp. 16–17.

19. N. Meister, *Fifty Years of Trade Unionism in Switzerland,* (Amsterdam: International Federation of Trade Unions, 1933), p. 43.

20. Weckerle, *op. cit.,* p. 17.

21. Meister, *op. cit.,* p. 43.

22. Friedrich Engels, letter to August Bebel, March 18–28, 1875, in Karl Marx, *Selected Works in Two Volumes* (Moscow: Cooperative Publishing Society of Foreign Workers in the U.S.S.R., 1936), Vol. II, pp. 590–591.

23. Richard Seidel, *The Trade Union Movement of Germany,* No. 7–8 (Amsterdam: International Federation of Trade Unions, 1928), p. 18.

24. *Ibid.,* p. 31.

25. *Ibid.,* pp. 31–32. The process whereby the local, geographically centered union bodies embracing all trades were subordinated to the national, more industrially oriented union bodies went on in nearly every European country around the turn of the century. In his visit to Western Europe at about this time, Samuel Gompers complained about the activities of those "local labor unions" in Switzerland that took in any businessman or professional who wished to join, as well as local unions of the various national unions. Gompers quotes the Swiss *Revue Syndicaliste* as criticizing the local unions for being " 'the arena of the champions of local politics.' " The local unions precipitated strikes, boycotts, and the like, without reference to the national unions. The *Revue* also noted, " 'Certain politicians of the locality profit so much from the 'local labor union' as a source of power that the wage workers get disgusted with the movement and quit.' " Samuel Gompers, *Labor in Europe and America,* (New York and London: Harper & Row, 1910), p. 121.

26. Quoted in Carl E. Schorske, *German Social Democracy, 1905–1917* (Cambridge: Harvard University Press, 1955), p. 12. In the succeeding sketch of the German union-party relationships I have leaned heavily on this outstanding work.

27. One is reminded of French labor's witticism concerning pre-World War I German trade unionism: that it suffered from "la maladie de la pierre"—literally, "a

sickness of the stone."—Georges Lefranc, *Le Syndicalisme dans le Monde* (Paris: Presses Universitaires, 1961), p. 20.

28. Robert Michels, *Political Parties* (Glencoe, Illinois: The Free Press, 1949), p. 301.

29. William S. Pickles, "Trade Unions in the Political Climate," in B. C. Roberts (ed.), *Industrial Relations: Contemporary Problems and Perspectives* (London: Methuen, 1962), pp. 34–35.

30. *CGIL News Bulletin,* April/May, 1965, pp. 23–24. Santi's words seem to echo Rinaldo Rigola, leader of the pre-World War I Italian General Confederation of Labor, who, challenging left-wing socialist forces in 1914, declared: "But the labor movement is not able to be intransigent because it is only a way of achieving successive reforms. . . . whoever believes that the emancipation of the proletariat must come only through catastrophe cannot be a labor organizer. . . . If our action has been tepid and reformist, I promise you the same course of action in the future." Quoted in Maurice F. Neufeld, *Italy: School for Awakening Countries, The Italian Labor Movement* (Ithaca, N. Y.: N. Y. State School of Industrial and Labor Relations, 1961), p. 362.

31. Again I am indebted to Schorske, *op. cit.,* for much of this description of the pre-World War I party-union situation in Germany.

32. Seidel, *op. cit.,* p. 55.

33. Schorske, *op. cit.,* pp. 39–40.

34. Edward Bernstein, distinguished reformist socialist leader, was one notable exception. He correctly noted that the party theory tended to remain basically "pessimistic," or what we might in more modern terms call apocalyptical. The unions with visible evidence of day-to-day progress could not and did not share this pessimism, and with it the necessity for a mass, final confrontation with capitalism as such. Curiously enough, however, the unions never formally identified themselves with Bernstein's struggle within the Social Democratic Party during this period even though his "evolutionary theory" of socialism largely accorded with their practices and policies. As Peter Gay suggests, all of "these matters, to them, were intellectual pastimes of no value for practical affairs." *The Dilemma of Democratic Socialism, Edward Bernstein's Challenge to Marx* (New York: Collier Books, 1962), p. 138.

35. Schorske, *op. cit.,* pp. 46–51. Schorske notes that conditions were favorable for restricting the use of the general strike for the party leaders were becoming more conservative and were willing allies of the union group. By the time of the International Socialist Congress at Stuttgart in 1907, the combination of party executive and trade unionists, joined by the so-called revisionists or evolutionists in the party, together voted against acceptance of the mass strike as a tactic against militarism and war.

36. Seidel, *op. cit.,* p. 56.

37. Seidel, *op. cit.,* pp. 54–56.

38. Schorske, *op. cit.,* pp. 91–97. Ironically enough, the problem of May Day celebrations and demonstrations continued to beset the German union movement. Acting independently, and indeed against the wishes of socialist party leaders, the German unions sought to cooperate with the Nazi regime in its early phases and even marched in celebration of May Day in 1933. The very next day the Nazis liquidated the union movement and took over its property. Sensitivity on the issue continues in German union ranks, and in May 1965 the president of the German Federation of Trade Unions felt it necessary to issue a statement on "Are May Day Celebrations Still Necessary?" He argued that although the struggle of labor today does not have the same setting as at the time of its birth, "that which was born in the revolt against injustice and oppression must be ever and anew reemphasized as

the innate purpose of the 1st of May, as a public confession of faith in the solidarity of human ideals, reemphasized in the consciousness of our strength and achievement, joyfully and confidently as the greatness of the ideal demands." *DGB Newsletter*, May 1965, p. 2.

39. See W. S. Woytinsky, *Stormy Passage* (New York: Vanguard, 1961), pp. 462–472; also Fritz Baade, "Fighting Depression Germany," in *So Much Alive, Contributions in Honor of W. S. Woytinsky* (New York: Vanguard, 1962). Gaining acceptance of an antideflationary program in a Germany that only a few years before had experienced a catastrophic inflation was especially difficult. Woytinsky also recognized that it would be difficult for Germany to act alone in Western Europe, in view of its dependence on foreign markets. As part of his campaign for vigorous spending measures to combat the depression, he sought to enlist support in other countries by an extensive correspondence campaign.

40. Richard N. Hunt, *German Social Democracy* (New Haven: Yale University Press, 1964), p. 187. Hunt does describe effectively the heavy bureaucratic tendency of the German trade union movement in the 1920s and the way in which it hung over the Social Democratic Party. For an interesting critique of American writing on the German socialist movement, parties, and unions in the 1900–1933 period, see Klaus Epstein, "Three American Studies of German Socialism," *World Politics* (July 1959), pp. 629–651.

41. Adolf Sturmthal, *The Tragedy of European Labor* (London: 1944), *passim*.

42. Allan Bullock, *The Life and Times of Ernest Bevin* (London: Heineman, 1960), Vol. I, pp. 425–439.

43. Sturmthal, *op. cit.*, pp. 140–146.

III

Reversal of Traditional Roles of Contemporary European Unions and Labor Parties

WE HAVE OBSERVED that, up to the 1930s and even up to World War II, European unions stood on the right of the labor movement while, in a more purely socialist stance, the party stood on its left. However, one can see signs of change during the twenties, which was a transition period. But only in the post-World War II period did a more lasting shift occur.

Union economic effectiveness, in terms of significant gains and the achievement of any substantial power in various industries, dates from the first decade of the twentieth century in most European countries. Socialist parties, by contrast, came to power, alone or in coalition, only after World War I. For example, during the twenties the British Labour Party was called upon for the first time to form a government. Also during the twenties, the German Social Democrats were in and out of government coalitions under the Weimar Republic. Swedish Social Democrats came to power in 1932 and, at this writing, still have not relinquished control of the government. Since World War II socialist parties everywhere in Western European countries have ruled alone or in coalition on numerous occasions.

The needs and dictates of staying in power or coming to power, as well as the significant social changes that had occurred nearly everywhere in Western Europe between World War I and the end of World War II, made an enormous impact on the party and the party-union coalition. The development of great social security systems in several countries well before World War I, the success of far-flung cooperative housing programs, the acceptance of positive government fiscal action to maintain full employment (after World War II), and the extension of unionism to the great majority of industrial (and often government) workers—all had quietly transformed the societies in which the labor movements were operating—a transformation to which the labor movements had, of course, made a great contribution.

Aware of these changes and confronted with the need to make the kinds of concessions that go with responsibility for national government (and even when they were not governing, the various socialist parties had to conduct themselves as possible future governments), the parties often found themselves shifting to the right, moving past the trade unions, who tended to remain less mobile.

The problems of ruling a country could not be met by adherence to old dogmas. In most instances in which a socialist government has come to power in Western Europe, it usually has done so as a minority, dependent upon some support from other parties and, to some extent, from non-worker interests. The kind of total and completely uncritical support that socialist parties had given to union action in the past was no longer easy to continue.

Union-Party Tensions: The Socialist Party in Power

An almost classic example of the tension that can develop between the twin poles of party and union under these circumstances appears in the brilliant biography by Alan Bullock of the great British union leader, Ernest Bevin. The first Labour government in Great Britain took office at the end of 1923, during an economic upswing, and Bevin, on behalf of the dock and tramway workers, was eager to restore wage cuts that had been suffered in past years. He moved swiftly, and after a successful strike the dock and tramway workers won an impressive economic victory.

Bullock notes, however, that Bevin's great satisfaction with these strikes

was not shared by the Labour Government. MacDonald, in particular, out of sympathy with down-to-earth trade-union demands and increasingly inclined to take a high line about national responsibilities, was greatly angered by the strikes and never forgave Bevin for the embarrassment he caused the Government. This did not worry Bevin. But there were others in the Labour Party besides MacDonald who felt that Bevin had behaved irresponsibly and shown less than the loyalty the unions owed to the first Labour Government ever to take office. This impression was strengthened by the aggressive manner in which Bevin asserted his independence and expressed his contempt for politicians as a race.

A controversy broke out in the socialist press in which the economist, J. A. Hobson, accused the unions of following a "separatist" policy, and Bevin had to deal with the question of whether it was incumbent upon the unions to wait for the government to set up some new machinery to settle the workers' wage claims or whether the unions' strike action was correct. He commented:

We are all too aware of the Government's difficulties and desire as much as anyone to assist in the success of Britain's first Labour Government. A policy of industrial truce would, in our view, even if it were possible, not be to the best interests of the Government. There is work to do on the industrial field as well as in the political arena. While it is true that the two are to some extent part of the same effort, we must not lose sight of the fact that governments may come and governments may go, but the workers' fight for betterment of conditions must go on all the time.

Bullock adds his own comment:

Nor did the rank-and-file members of the Union disagree with Bevin. They had waited a long time to recover the wage cuts they had suffered and to see some practical benefit from the Union they supported. They saw no reason why, the first time they gained the advantage in a dispute, they should not press it home simply because a Labour Government was in office. If that fact made the employers more reluctant to fight it out, so much the better: what did they pay the political levy and support the Labour Party for, if not to secure such advantages? No one could say the employers were reluctant to take advantage of the Tories being in office to force wages down and use the power of the State to defeat the miners. It was too high a price to pay for office if the only way the Labour Government could retain the Parliamentary support of the Liberal Party was to take sides against the unions in the legitimate defence of their members' industrial interests.

There is a postscript, however, to this interesting interlude. Unlike the 1923 Labour government, when Labour came to power in 1945, it had gained a clear majority in the Parliament, and Bevin was willing to face the issue of the national responsibility of the labor movement as opposed to the immediate sectional interests of the trade unions. As a member of the government, he recommended to the unions a policy of "wage restraint which placed a heavy strain on the loyalty and forbearance of the trade unions."[1]

Whether in a majority or a minority position, the Labour government is almost driven to act as a restraining force on the unions. Examples abound. In April 1963, anticipating the general election of 1964, Party Leader Harold Wilson intervened with railway union leaders to prevent a scheduled protest strike; he did so on the grounds that such a strike would damage Labour severely in public eyes and jeopardize its position in the elections. In commenting on this action *The New York Times* noted, "Fresh in every Labour politician's memory is the six-week London bus strike of 1958. The strike has been considered a major reason for Labour's overwhelming defeat by the Conservatives a year later."[2]

On election eve in the fall of 1964, when a strike of 300 automobile inspectors threatened to idle tens of thousands of additional automobile workers, Harold Wilson charged that the stoppage was deliberately provoked by Conservative opponents in order to embarrass the Labour Party in the imminent election.[3]

After taking power in 1965, Wilson induced the trade unions to exercise a system of voluntary wage restraint. Later, in 1966, his government enacted a compulsory type of wage freeze. Serious friction between the Labour Government and the unions has persisted since 1966. In part the British "case" can be explained by the unusual historic dependence of the party on the unions, with the consequence that the latter approaches the party more as a client than as a social "partner," as is the case in most of continental Europe.

This reversal of roles, in which the union has come to behave or talk less "responsibly" than the party, has some parallels almost everywhere in European socialist movements. Since World War II the West German Social Democratic Party, in its efforts to convince German voters that it can be the best guarantor of continued growth and prosperity in the nation, has undertaken a complete revision of its old Marxist-oriented program. Among other things, it sets forth as its new economic goals: "the stability of the currency . . . the achievement of a free-competitive economy . . . the free market economy." It adds that it will "not intervene in the decision making of the entrepreneurs, nor shall we attack private property. Rather, shall we endeavor to work together in mutual trust with all sections of the economy and its organizations." The Party also supports welfare reform and collective agreements and opposes concentration of wealth.[4]

This program as a whole is a giant step away from the older tradition. Indeed it is a long way even from more moderate socialist notions of at least limited socialization of industry and more intensive economic planning.

This sharp swing from the left to the center may appeal to the middle classes, the farmers, and other groups. However, it has provoked considerable unhappiness among a number of trade union leaders. The leadership of the giant German Metalworkers Union (IGM), in particular, has been critical of these moves, as it clings to older socialist doctrines. The program of the union parent body, the German Federation of Trade Unions (DGB), lays much more stress on "planning" and clearly regards "competition" in a different light from that of the party program. The tone of the DGB program has a different ring from that of the party. Like the party, it makes no serious commitment to traditional socialism and extensive public ownership, but it continues to feel that some "transfer into public ownership [must be] . . . included in the catalogue of measures required for public control of economic power. . . . public ownership is also of decisive importance for economic planning." While the party program stresses such things as "stability of currency" and "the achievement of a free-competitive economy," the DGB still talks of a "determination to transform the social and economic order in accordance with the concept of social justice."[5]

One student of the German labor movement has noted that the DGB stands today virtually alone in German society in its strong, unequivocal support of national economic planning. The Social Democratic Party, which was born, as he writes, in the tradition of planning, currently presents itself "before the general public as a defender of economic liberty and the spirit of free competition."[6]

Key DGB leaders, including its president and the presidents of its important unions, continue to be active in the socialist party, but at least some of them are clearly to the left of the party's economic program.

Even in Sweden, where for a long time party and union have generally cooperated closely in supporting a reform economic program of the planning type—which support runs counter to traditional socialist-Marxist demands—there is some occasional irritation or friction. To stay in power, for example, the party, which does not quite have a majority in the parliament, has in the past supported various farm programs (to keep agrarian party votes) that are not always pleasing to the trade union movement with its more consumer-oriented interests.

Irritation with party efforts to "modernize" socialist platforms has not been confined to Western Europe. Ken Baxter, Secretary of the New Zealand Federation of Labour, bitterly criticized the action of the New Zealand Labour Party for having changed its objective from "the socialisation of the means of production, distribution and exchange," to the objective "to promote and protect the freedom of the people and their political, social, economic and cultural welfare." He pointedly charged that "no 'new look' can overcome the fact that there is a class struggle." The new objective was so vague, he argued, that Tories or workers could subscribe to it. He insisted that the Labour Federation continue to adhere to the belief that "there is an irreconcilable conflict of interest between the two classes."[7] He was referring, of course, to workers and capitalists.

Radicalism and Conservatism: Shifting Party and Union Roles

"Left" and "right," "radical" and "conservative"—these are no longer correct terms to describe this shifting phenomenon whereby parties and unions seem to be reversing the roles they occupied forty or fifty years ago when Michels and others were analyzing their relationships. The seeming leftism of trade union leaders may in many cases stem primarily, not from genuine radicalism, but from an inability to shift their allegiance from older programs that have nostalgic appeal. This "persistent leftism" may actually spring from a kind of conservatism.

Caught up in the delicate task of formulating economic policies and programs that can no longer be simple socialist or capitalist prescriptions, party leaders are constantly compelled to reexamine their old ideologies and commitments. Similar forces operate on the socialist parties in the foreign policy field, where their governments must frequently make alliances with democratic capitalist powers against so-called Marxist-oriented dictatorships.

Party leaders have also been compelled to take note of the changing class character of their own societies as they try to frame election appeals. Hugh Gaitskell, the late leader of the British Labour Party, showed clear recognition of this when he tried to explain the election failures of the British Labour Party between 1951 and 1959. He reported to the Party Congress:

What has caused this adverse trend? It is, I believe, a significant change in the economic and social background of politics. First, there is the changing character of the labour force. There are fewer miners, more engineers; fewer farmworkers, more shop assistants; fewer manual workers, more clerical workers; fewer railwaymen, more research workers. Everywhere the balance is shifting away from heavy physical work and towards machine maintenance, distribution and staff jobs. Go to any large works in the country, as I happened to have done a good deal in the last couple of years, and you will find exactly the same story. It is an inevitable result of technological advance. But it means that the typical worker of the future is more likely to be a skilled man in a white overall, watching dials in a bright new modern factory, than a badly paid cotton operative working in a dark and obsolete 19th century mill."[8]

Gaitskell came to the conclusion that one of the factors that was weakening the appeal of the Labour Party for new young voters, as well as for white-collar and middle-class groups, was Clause 4 in the party's 1918 constitution, which made a generalized commitment to nationalization of the means of production. At the Labour Party Conference in Blackpool in November 1959, Gaitskell suggested that Clause 4 be revised. Extending nationalization, save in the case of one or two industries, had not been a serious issue for years in the Labour Party. But Gaitskell's proposal started a storm, not only among traditional leftist leaders but also among a number of so-called right-wing trade union leaders who had always been counted as "safe" in any right-left struggle within the party or the union movement. As one reads the union journals or party debates of this period, it seems fairly clear that the opposition of many leading trade union leaders to revising Clause 4 arose less from any burning radicalism than from a desire to cling to past doctrines and from resentment against a coterie of party intellectuals who were trying to take upon themselves the responsibility for rewriting the old program.[9] Gaitskell was defeated in his move to rewrite Clause 4.

The Trend of Party-Union Relationships to Party Leadership

As already indicated, party-union tensions are, of course, nothing new in the labor movement complexes of Western Europe. Doubtless these tensions will continue, but it would seem that the changing nature of work and of classes in society, as well as the increasing priority being given to state economic planning, may lead to permanent dominance by party forces. Walter Galenson, examining this problem in Denmark some years ago, concluded:

It is virtually impossible for one who has not participated in the decision making process to determine conclusively whether in the last analysis it is the party or the trade unions that have the final say on disputed issues that cannot be compromised. To an outsider there are reasons for believing the preponderance lies with the party. . . . Perhaps the most important factor in party predominance is that it is the party and not the trade unions that is confronted with the more basic problems; the wage decisions of the trade unions are only part of the economic issues with which the party must deal, but the converse is not true: many party decisions are outside the range of trade union competence. It seems almost inevitable that the accession of a labor party to political power means ever increasing supremacy over its allied trade unions.[10]

The very nature of the trade union leader's intense, highly pragmatic, more practical, and less conceptual type of activity prepares him much less adequately for the kind of broad sociopolitical decisions that party leaders are constantly called upon to make. In a certain sense trade union leaders have tended to take pride in practical as opposed to theoretical approaches. The notion of "planning" trade union administration and programs has been relatively rare both abroad and in the United States. The very nature of most problems in industrial relations compels unions and union leaders to place a premium upon day-to-day ingenuity, rather than upon long-term considerations.[11]

This same problem—the relative disadvantages of trade union leaders as compared with labor political party leaders in the national political sphere—was neatly anticipated decades ago by Sidney and Beatrice Webb. Commenting on the tendency for the British Labour Party to choose somewhat fewer trade unionists to sit in Parliament, they noted:

As the Parliamentary Labour Party, claiming today to represent, not the Trade Unionists only, but the whole community of "workers by hand or by brain" expands from sixty to four or six times that number—as it must before it can be confronted with the task of forming a government—it will necessarily come to include an ever increasing proportion of members drawn from other than trade union ranks; whilst even its trade union members cannot fail to acquire more of that habit of mutual intercourse and that art of combined action which, coupled with the Parliamentary skill and capacity for public administration of those who rise to leadership, is the necessary basis of successful party achievement.[12]

The Webbs' forecast has proven to be quite correct so far as the selection of union leaders for parliamentary seats is concerned. The proportion of union-member-held seats of the Labour Party's parliamentary group has shown a distinct decline, especially since the end of World War II, when the party came to assume a permanent mass shape in the Parliament. By 1959, in the 258-strong Parliamentary Labour Party (as the group of Labour's members in Parliament is termed), there were 92 trade union members, 5 less than in the 191 Labour group in the 1923 Parliament.[13]

One writer on British politics, Jean Blondel, has noted the increasing tendency toward a predominance of middle-class types in both major British parties, Conservative and Labour. He comments:

Whether one likes it or not, politics is a middle class job, and the training appropriate for middle class jobs is also a training for politics. The dice are loaded [against manual workers] by the present structure of society as well as by the natural conditions which govern the job of politics in any society. The administrative skill and the training acquired at school or on the job automatically help potential politicians.[14]

Structural Aspects of Party-Union Relationships: The British Case

There is no single formula to define the actual legal or working relationships and linkages between European union movements and their brother socialist parties. Perhaps the most significant starting point in an analysis of these relationships is the fact that in no instance is a socialist union movement financially dependent upon its political party counterpart.[15] Indeed the reverse would seem to be true; in other words, in most countries nowadays the labor parties depend upon the unions for major financial contributions. As previously indicated, on the Continent in the early days the parties often were the center of financial strength.

Maurice Duverger has drawn a distinction between direct and indirect parties. In the former, membership is direct by individual membership subscription. In indirect parties, affiliation is primarily by bloc, especially by trade unions on behalf of their members.[16]

Duverger goes on to argue that in *direct* parties radicalism and close adherence to socialist doctrine and theory prevail. By contrast, *indirect* parties, where union affiliation and financial support is decisive, tend to be more "practical" and realistic in their day-to-day programs, and less doctrinal in character.

The outstanding examples of *indirect* relationships are in Great Britain and Scandinavia (especially Sweden), where the bulk of union members are affiliated indirectly through their unions with the labor-socialist parties.

In Great Britain individual national unions affiliate with the British Labour Party on behalf of their membership.[17] With relatively few exceptions union members are consequently members of the British Labour Party only via the affiliation of their unions. This system assures the large unions, which are the party's principal financial support, a preponderant vote at the party's annual congress. (Union contributions total as much as 90 percent of the party's financial support during a national election campaign.) Voting together, a handful of large unions can have virtual bloc control of the congress. Criticism of so-called bloc voting at party congresses has been exaggerated, however. On key issues coming before the congress in the past decade, division among the large unions has been as common as unity.[18]

Even in cases where bloc union voting can put through a political policy resolution at the party congress, the Parliamentary Labour Party and its leadership may refuse to follow the resolution. Such, for example, was the case in 1960 when a handful of large unions succeeded in swinging the party congress vote in favor of a resolution supporting unilateral nuclear disarmament for Britain. Hugh Gaitskell refused to follow this resolution in subsequent years, and eventually the party congress reversed itself.

Broadly speaking, it seems increasingly apparent that the Parliamentary Labour Party will take a fairly independent line vis-à-vis its union "brother," particularly when questions of a general political character are involved. On more purely industrial matters such as legislation affecting industrial relations or working conditions, party leaders will continue to be more highly responsive to union needs and wishes.

Australia: Structural and Policy Rigidities in a Labor Complex

The Australian labor-union-party complex is an example of some of the difficulties that can beset a labor party today; here the alliance has been traditionally "over"-dominated by the union side. In Australian life, as in other Western democracies, issues such as education, foreign policy, and international trade and development are taking on major importance.

Yet, as James Jupp writes, these are issues that "are largely outside the range of the unions' interest." Nevertheless the unions dominate the party machinery, and unlike the situation in the British Labour Party, "the A.L.P. [Australian Labour Party] does not allow autonomy to its parliamentarians." The result is a lack of flexibility and innovation on the labor parliamentary side. Jupp adds that the Australian Labour Party "machine at present gives this element [the trade unions] a more dominant position than in any major party anywhere. Unless the party broadens itself . . . it will remain futile on the national scale," having lost seven successive elections anyway.[19]

The past virtues of the Australian labor movement tend to become vices today, as far as political progress is concerned. Jupp points out that by British standards Australian trade unions have been very radical and have gained high standards for their members. But this has been principally an industrial or collective bargaining radicalism with great indifference to theory or ideology. "The A.L.P. has never developed a middle-class wing, nor encouraged intellectuals other than lawyers, who are valued for their skill rather than their education."[20]

Yet, as we have suggested, the intricacies of modern Western politics today place a premium on middle-class "skills." Moreover, the changing character of the labor force makes it imperative for a modern labor party to appeal beyond the manual working class to "middle-class" groups if it is to achieve power today.

Change comes hard, but the defeat in the spring of 1965 of the ALP in the Australian state of New South Wales, where it had held power since 1941, appears to have shaken the party badly. Most of the blame for the defeat was attributed to the exploitation by the opposition party leader, Sir Robert Menzies, of the fact that the parliamentary Labour Party is virtually dictated to by a conference of thirty-six delegates (largely under trade union domination)—a conference in which the parliamentary leaders have no vote. One leading Labour Party leader, recognizing the need to rid the organization of the overly dominant trade union influence, announced that a program was being undertaken to increase the role and authority of "Parliamentary leaders . . . in the formulation of policies" and to improve the party's "public standing."[21]

In passing it should be noted that a split between right-wing and left-wing forces that occurred in the Australian Labour Party some years ago and that led to the creation of a second labor party has also been a major factor in its electoral defeats.

Structural and Financial Party-Union Relationships

The pattern of union affiliation with socialist parties in Sweden and Norway is at the local union level, and it is here that union financial support is significant; but in neither case does bloc union support approach the percentage it constitutes of total financial support for the British Labour Party. Representation at party congresses in Scandinavia is on a geographical basis, and the unions, as such, are not represented.

The British Trades Union Congress, unlike most of the individual national unions affiliated with it, maintains a position of formal neutrality in politics. The top Scandinavian labor federations, on the other hand, identify themselves with the socialist parties and put the weight of their organizations (including financal support) fully behind socialist political party campaigns. In Denmark, where there is no system of bloc union affiliation with the socialist party, the national unions make heavy financial contributions directly to the party, and this includes the Danish Federation of Trade Unions, which also contributes directly.

The 1941 constitution of the Swedish Federation of Labor (LO) calls upon the union movement to cooperate "in the development of a society based upon the principles of political, social and economic democracy." The constitution of the Danish Federation of Trade Unions pledges that organization "to cooperate with the Social-Democratic Party in order jointly to further labour legislation."[22]

Needless to say, even in countries where the system of contributions from union members is on an individual basis, the parties are nevertheless sensitive to union power. Representation to the party congress, selection of party candidates, the party executives—all reflect the need to assure effective union representation in these processes.

This is true, for example, even in countries like Austria where the earlier prewar formal party-union relationships no longer exist, and most contributions tend to be via direct payments of members dues to the parties.[23] The problem of coordinating union and party policies, to the extent necessary or possible, becomes increasingly acute. With the spread of national planning and the related drive to establish national wage or income policies in Western Europe, coordination becomes particularly critical.

By and large, one can find numerous instances in which socialist parties afford formal, significant representation as party executives to a few top trade union officials (who may or may not be members of the parliament). On the other hand, party representation on the top union executive level is extremely rare, though in the case of Denmark the labor federation and socialist party do provide two members each for such an interchange.

Trade unions are much more sensitive and jealous about guarding their independence than is the party, which, of course, normally seeks to encompass the ready-made constituency that trade union membership constitutes.

The British unions, Labour Party, and the cooperatives have established a National Council of Labour to expedite cooperation among the three segments of the labor movement. It serves, however, more as an information center than as a real policy-coordinating body. When it comes to serious policy consultation, informal connections between union and political party leaders appear to be much more important.

General trends in party-union relationships are difficult to divine, but one can, perhaps, cautiously state that ties seem to be loosening. For example, in the Netherlands, Germany, and Austria the union-party institutional links that existed before World War II have been severed, at least in a formal sense. The French socialist party and the socialist-"tending" French labor movement, Force Ouvrière, seem farther apart than before; in any event, they have never been formally united. But in the case of The Netherlands, Germany, and Austria, one must note the continued strong attachment of the key union leadership (and the bulk of the rank and file) to the respective socialist parties in their countries. Top trade union leaders sit in Parliament as socialist members and play active roles in the parties.

The leadership of the Swiss Federation of Trade Unions, which has a long and clearer tradition of political neutrality, has taken the opportunity to stress its independence of any political ties in the post-World War II period, with the comment that "more than ever, it [the Federation] intends to determine its position itself, in all independence. . . . The Swiss labor movement is neutral from any religious viewpoint and independent in political affairs."[24] Even in this case, however, personal, socialist ideological ties between party and union leaders and members are important.

In Britain there have been occasional signs that a few top union leaders might welcome loosening their ties to the British Labour Party, but in the recent (1964 and 1966) elections the unions again closed ranks strongly behind the party.[25]

By reason of continued ideological carry-over from the past, and by reason of mutual interests and needs, most of European labor can still be best understood as a comprehensive, encompassing movement, rather than as separate labor unions, parties, or cooperatives.

European Unions Are Still Part of a Movement

Certainly in the mind of a worker in any of the European countries that we have been surveying in the past few pages, the labor movement still conjures up a "complex" of socialist party, his union, and probably some related cooperative associations. His affiliation with or "dedication" to this complex is less intense than was his father's, and the complex itself, although still broadly extant in most countries, seems less consolidated.

Labor complexes vary considerably in solidarity from country to country. Scandinavian countries have the greatest degree of continuity in relationships between party and union. Here, as one top leader once remarked, you have two major movements, a labor party and a labor union, that have the same members but two slightly different top layers of leadership. In Norway, although the Labor Party was in power for many years during the past two decades, the two sides of the labor movement managed to maintain a balance. While the union continued to press on the industrial side, it adjusted its wage thrust to the needs of the joint relationship. A leading Norwegian union officer characterized the relationship as follows:

The organizations which are represented here are a good expression of the breadth of the Norwegian labor movement, and the good open cooperation which exists between these organizations gives us the possibilities of a progressive policy. There is a steady attempt to sow suspicion and to construct a situation of opposition between these two organizations (the Trade Union Federation and the Labor Party). . . . I am, however, pleased that the trade unions have had a horizon which has been wider than that which is concerned with . . . wage negotiations. It is clear that this is the main task, but it is not enough. The significance of a strong, united and free trade union cannot be overestimated. It is fundamental to democratic society. We hear often that the LO is directed from the government. But just as often it is said that it is this organization (the trade union federation) which in reality decides all that is done by the Party and by the government. *The actual situation is that these two organizations through tradition and mature consideration have divided the labor tasks between themselves. This our opposition clearly cannot understand.*[26]

Much the same kind of relationship prevails in Sweden and to a considerable extent in Denmark (to some extent also in Finland, which we have not included in our "definition" of Western Europe).

A great deal has been written about the steady, rather "even" character of the development of labor relations and social legislation in Scandinavia. This development has been favored, of course, by somewhat special social and political circumstances as compared with the rest of Europe. A joint official account of Scandinavian social and labor patterns has called attention to the absence of religious or national strains, the more homogeneous character of the populations of the Scandinavian countries, the lower pitch of class differences, and so on.

Undoubtedly the homogeneous character of these countries and the absence of any serious national and religious antagonisms have been among the most important factors. Similarly, the lack of any sharp class differences, in connection with the predominance even in our day in both industry and agriculture has considerably facilitated understanding between employer and worker. To this should be added the deeply rooted understanding of the benefits of teamwork which has provided the basis of orderly progress. . . . Credit must finally be given to the leaders of both workers and employers who generally have been social-minded, responsible, and far-sighted personalities.[27]

How relative the term "labor movement" can be is indicated by a comparison of the Scandinavian labor movements with those of Britain and the United States. Compared with the "collective purpose" of, for example, the Swedish LO, the British movement has been called less of a trade union movement than a collection of trade unions. But when we look at the U.S. labor movement, we realize that the important and continuing relationships between the British unions and the Labour Party, as well as the major economic policy role and activities of the Trades Union Congress itself, give to British labor a "movement" character that goes well beyond any strong sense of central purpose among the American unions.

Lack of a strong central purpose remains true of the American movement despite the fact that in the past two decades, and especially since the merger of the American Federation of Labor and the Congress of Industrial Organizations, on broad economic and social policy legislation issues the AFL-CIO central headquarters plays a much greater role than in the past. Nevertheless, the lack of a shared ideology—indeed of any common sociopolitical ideology—still leaves most AFL-CIO affiliated national unions as basically "bread and butter," collective-bargaining-oriented institutions, with relatively less consciousness of overall movement.

Among the countries of Western Europe the intensity of socialist-labor "movement" feelings or direction varies. Austria presents a situation where informal, interlocking relationships between union and socialist party officials are very close. The "togetherness" of the Austrian labor complex is not as great as Sweden's or Norway's, but does approach it, despite the official, formal separation of the union movement from party politics in the post-war period. This same formal separation in Germany, on the other hand, has left a relationship between unions and parties that is looser than in Scandinavia or even in Austria.[28] The situation in the Low Countries varies and is complicated by the importance there of plural unionism (religious as well as socialist-oriented unionism).

Overall, however, the "labor pattern" of Western Europe, especially in comparison with the United States, is still best understood in the sense of a "movement"—a movement that has changed greatly in this century, however.

N O T E S

1. Alan Bullock, *The Life and Times of Ernest Bevin* (London: Heinemann, 1960), Vol. I, pp. 242–245.
2. *The New York Times,* April 19, 1963.
3. *The New York Times,* October 4, 1964.

4. "Basic Principles in S.P.D. Home Policy, Second Part of German Social Democratic Party's Programme for Government," *Socialist International Information,* London, February 6, 1965, p. 22.

5. "The Basic Program of the DGB and its Impact on German Society", *AFL-CIO Free Trade Union News,* March 1964, p. 6; and Ludwig Rosenberg, DGB President, "Broader Outlook for German Labour," *Free Labour World,* Brussels, April 1964, pp. 18–22.

6. Burkhart Lutz, "Les Syndicats Allemands Au Début des Années 60," *Sociologie du Travail,* January–March, 1964, p. 75.

7. *Free Labour World,* July–August 1964, p. 30.

8. *Labour Party Annual Conference, Main Speeches,* Blackpool, November 28–29, 1959, p. 6.

9. The issue was also complicated by the fact that a move to commit the Labour Party to a program for unilateral nuclear disarmament climaxed at this moment. As a consequence, voting patterns at the party's 1960 Congress became quite jumbled.

10. Walter Galenson, *The Danish System of Labor Relations* (Cambridge, Mass.: Harvard University Press, 1952), pp. 45–46.

11. I have dealt with this in my "Trade Union Research Departments and the Function of Forward Planning," *Trade Union Information,* No. 29, (Paris: European Productivity Agency of OEEC, 1959), pp. 32–34.

12. Sidney and Beatrice Webb, *The History of Trade Unionism* (London, New York, Toronto: Longmans Green, 1950), p. 703.

13. Martin Harrison, *Trade Unions and the Labour Party* (London: G. Allen, 1960), p. 264. Even these figures far overstate true union strength in the Parliamentary Labour Party, since many Labour members of Parliament are affiliated with unions only as ordinary members and have no serious institutional role in the union movement.

14. Jean Blondel, *Voters, Parties and Leaders, The Social Fabric of British Politics* (Baltimore: Penguin, 1963), esp. Chaps. 4 and 5.

15. We are not including the communist labor movements of France and Italy whose relationships, financial and otherwise, with the communist parties of these countries are quite different.

16. Maurice Duverger, *Political Parties,* 2d ed. (London: Methuen, 1959), pp. 1–17.

17. In Britain, Sweden, and Norway, individual union members can exercise their option to "contract out" of being affiliated with the labor party by signing cards indicating this preference. Their unions, in turn, affiliate with the party and make financial contributions only on behalf of members who have not contracted out. A number of the more conservative British unions, including a few catering to white-collar and civil-service workers, are not even affiliated with the Labour Party.

18. Harrison, *op. cit., passim.*

19. James Jupp, *Australian Labour and the World* (London: Fabian Research Series 246, 1965), pp. 30–31.

20. *Ibid.,* p. 9.

21. *The Guardian* (Daily), May 14, 1965. D. W. Rawson argues that in the contemporary period, Australian labor party parliamentary leaders have been more independent than the structural dependence of the party upon the unions would otherwise suggest. He notes that it is risky in terms of public reaction, for the unions to force out parliamentary leaders with whom they disagree; moreover, the unions are rarely united "among themselves as to what the party should do or who should lead it." See his chapter in P. W. D. Matthews and G. W. Ford (eds.), *Australian Trade Unions* (Melbourne: Sun Books, 1968).

22. Paul Malles, *Draft Paper on Certain European Trade Union Movements and*

their Relation with Social Democratic Parties (Florence, Italy: ICFTU-UNESCO East West Seminar, May 24–30, 1959), pp. 4–5. (Mimeographed.)

23. The actual arrangements are often quite complex. In Austria, for example, although the Austrian Federation of Trade Unions (ÖGB) and the Austrian Socialist Party are independent of one another, informal machinery exists within the trade union federation to insure a flow of financial support to the party. A flow is also assured via Catholic union members to the Catholic Party and for Communists to the Austrian Communist Party. The ÖGB has, however, a socialist majority by far, and its most critical political link, though "informal," is with the Socialist Party.

24. *Le Syndicalisme Libre en Suisse,* Robert Bratschi (President of the Swiss Federation of Trade Unions) ed., (Geneva: Editions Radar, 1953), pp. 36–39.

25. For a rather pessimistic statement on future relationships between party and unions in Great Britain, see Harrison, *op. cit.,* pp. 335–350. This was, however, written during the long period when the Labour Party was in the opposition. Events of 1964 and 1965 seemed to suggest that there is nothing like the prospects of political victory to heal old wounds. With the Labour Party's return to power in the midst of a serious economic crisis necessitating a restrictive wage policy, however, new tensions did arise between some party and union leaders in 1966, 1967, and 1968.

26. Quoted in Bruce Millen, "The Relationship of the Norwegian Labor Party to the Trade Unions," in E. M. Kassalow (ed.), *National Labor Movements in the Postwar World* (Evanston, Ill.: Northwestern University Press, 1963), Chap. 5, pp. 124–125. [Italics added.]

27. *Freedom and Welfare, Social Patterns in the Northern Countries of Europe,* George Nelson, ed. (sponsored by the Ministries of Social Affairs of Denmark, Finland, Iceland, Norway, and Sweden, 1953), p. 141. Despite its official sponsorship, this book brings together a great deal of useful material on social developments in Scandinavia.

28. Nevertheless, in a statement to the Social Democratic Party Congress late in 1964, Ludwig Rosenberg, President of the German Federation of Trade Unions-DGB (after reasserting the union's political independence) could declare, "Trade unionists . . . would . . . follow the deliberations of the Social Democratic Party with the closest attention since they were bound together by a century of commonly shared democratic tradition." He added that, just as a unified trade union movement had emerged, so "there had grown from the Old Workers' Party a great People's Party." And the union and the party still waged a kind of "joint struggle for a world in freedom and social justice." *DGB News Letter,* January 1965.

IV

Western Labor Movements: Integration into Society

DURING THE LAST SIXTY OR SEVENTY YEARS the Western European labor complexes have undergone great changes. A dedicated socialist of 1900 would hardly recognize or "accept" the socialist character of today's Western labor movements. Yet, from the vantage point of hindsight the transformation seems to have had an almost inexorable logic.

Although committed at the outset to make a revolutionary change in their societies, the various labor movements in time opted for, or were drawn into, day-to-day, step-by-step forms of change. The revolutionary goals came to be pursued via essentially peaceful channels, such as legislative social reform, collective bargaining, or cooperative association. The very channels that were chosen, or "forced" upon, these movements ultimately changed their character—but the impact of the movements in turn also radically changed their societies. Before this Western experience is optimistically extrapolated to labor movements in other parts of the world, at least a few of the "favorable" forces that helped to "guide" it should be recalled. One need mention only the unique Western political evolution that culminated in parliaments and wide suffrage rights, the economic breakthroughs of the late nineteenth century, the fact that there were not in existence already industrialized countries with high living standards to fan the expectations of the masses of the poor, and so on.

On the political side Adolf Sturmthal has remarked that if one can talk of a "present crisis of European labor" today, in that its traditional political thrust may be less vigorous, one cannot understand this crisis "without reference to the void which the attainment of its democratic objectives left the whole make-up of the movement." Social security, universal suffrage, education by the state—attainment of these "revolutionary" goals inevitably left the movement less revolutionary in the political field.[1]

Union activities in collective bargaining probably had an even more "pacifying" impact upon labor movements. Acceptance of the process of collective bargaining along with written labor-management agreements meant a relative softening of "class warfare"—an acceptance that was often opposed by the left wing of the labor movements fifty or sixty years ago. Yet the very victories won in these agreements, in terms of steady improvements in wages and working conditions, made any resistance to this process seem absurd to the great majority of workers and members of the labor movement complex.

Other union programs also contributed to this process whereby the working-class movement began meshing with the very society it had talked in earlier years of overthrowing. Quite commonly unions came to establish their own mutual-benefit funds (in the 1880s and 1890s) to help carry their members through periods of unemployment and illness. In Germany, development of the union unemployment-insurance systems (each union had its own) again illustrates the tugs and strains between revolutionary and reformistic tactics.

The more revolutionary-minded in the German labor movement opposed the union insurance systems on the grounds that unemployment benefits would weaken revolutionary spirit during out-of-work periods. They felt that the workers should not bear the costs of unemployment, which was caused by capitalism. Furthermore, they felt that these benefit funds would raise union dues and build huge union treasuries. The popularity of these benefits among union members (not only in Germany but elsewhere as well) and the strength they added to the unions' collective bargaining position easily overcame these objections.[2]

Increasing Integration of Unions into Society

Before World War I, the unions in country after country came to demand that union funds be supplemented by state financial contributions. "Bourgeois" governments usually went along with these demands. Occasionally middle-class politicians were far-sighted enough to see how this concession could have a moderating influence on union development. For example, Lloyd George and Winston Churchill, leaders in the British Liberal Party's Asquith government (1908-1916), sensibly decided, when setting up the social-insurance system, not to attempt to weaken or destroy the pattern of benefits in friendly societies and in trade unions. They preferred to make the societies and unions the agents or "approved societies" for the operation of the state system. The Liberal Party leaders "took care to placate the unions, because they wanted the support of their M.P.'s in the Commons debates and the continued backing of the trade-union vote at future general elections." Strengthened by these functions, the unions experienced "a rapid expansion of membership."[3]

Moreover, the unions found themselves, as a result, integrated into the very state apparatus that they, as part of the socialist complex, were still dedicated to changing drastically, if not overthrowing.

This direct union control over, or participation in, the management of parts of the social-insurance system still exists in many European countries. It has great advantages in strengthening the bond between members and their unions, even or especially in periods of unemployment. This situation is in contrast to that in countries like the United States, where union membership losses are most severe during periods of long unemployment. Norway during the 1930s affords an example of increased union cohesiveness: "The prevailing Ghent system [as the combined union-state unemployment funds came to be called] of unemployment insurance, whereby benefits were paid out through union insurance funds, was also a factor in preserving the integrity of the unions."[4]

The American labor movement had drifted from its European counterparts in the periods before and after World War I. How far it had drifted is indicated by the official attitude of the AFL toward a government system of unemployment compensation. During the very years when European labor was integrating its own private unemployment-benefit systems with government social-insurance systems, President Samuel Gompers, on behalf of the AFL, sharply opposed any government unemployment-insurance system. He argued that it was really "not insurance against unemployment but is [only] compensation for lack of employment." His more "fundamental objection" was

that as soon as there is established a so-called unemployment insurance . . . the working people place themselves under the guardianship of the government of the country . . . labor . . . would be subject to the regulation and discipline of the government. . . . The whole of activity to organize, to assert and to live our own lives would be subject to every petty high official of the government.

Gompers also contended that unemployment insurance would compel the workers to carry "industrial passports"—books to show where they last worked and why they were out of work.[5]

Aside from traditional antigovernment feelings, many federation leaders also felt that social legislation would reduce the workers' desire to join unions. As late as the 1932 AFL Convention, John Frey, opposing unemployment insurance, argued,

"If you feed lions cooked meat they are not going to roar. If you want the lions to roar you will have to hold meat under their noses, and then they will roar. The only way to get wage earners interested in the trade union movement, and make it a driving force is to convince them that . . . it is only through the strength, the fighting strength of that economic organization that you are going to get higher wages and shorter hours.[6]

We are once more confronted, particularly in the era before mass unionism in the United States, with the almost exclusively members-only philosophy of the American union movement. The European unions, as part of a labor complex identifying itself with the whole of the European working class, found it more "natural" to support government-sponsored social security, government regulation of the length of the work week, and so on.

Today it would be difficult to find the same major differences between the positions of American and European unions. Differences that persist on how best to support or regulate welfare plans or hours of work generally stem from pragmatic judgments as to what will work best (i.e., government action or collective bargaining). They also stem from historical accident; for example, a route that was chosen at a particular moment may continue to be followed simply out of habit.

World War I Period of Accelerating Union Integration

The process of European union "integration" was accelerated during World War I when in a number of countries union officials (as well as socialist party leaders) joined in coalition government and/or otherwise supported a variety of government war activities. (Not surprisingly, wartime periods have generally opened many new doors for trade unions in the Western world, inasmuch as their special support is sought at such times of crisis.)

The World War I years stand as the watershed between the earlier revolutionary phase and the practical reformistic phase of European labor movements. Most of these movements had in actual fact, if not in theory, moved well toward reformism before 1914. But to make the movement more visible it took the events surrounding the war, as well as the emergence of a new, committed, revolutionary type of movement, which stood clearly to the left of the socialist complexes: world communism. This was true by 1918 and 1919 even though in several cases many official socialist party doctrines and platforms were not fundamentally changed for at least a couple of decades.

The way in which an older ideology can live on, however, was again well exemplified in the German labor movement. Under the Weimar Republic the German trade-union movement fought for the right to participate in economic and industrial decision-making on an equal basis with management. A comprehensive agreement was signed with the employers' federation in November 1918 and covered a whole series of industrial relations and economic policy-making areas. Laws were passed shortly afterward to help accomplish these very goals.

By act of the government, works councils to represent the employees' interests were to be established in each enterprise employing over fifty workers. Written union-management agreements were to be given the force of legislation by government extension of their terms to all (even unorganized) workers in a given industry. District Economic Councils and a National Economic Council consisting of workers and management representation were also to be established. "Social and Economic bills proposed by the government were to be submitted to the National Economic Council for its approval and it was also entitled to propose such bills itself. The Labour and Economic Councils might be granted controlling and administrative powers in the spheres allocated to them."[7]

At no other time in the Western world has such a total plan been proposed for integrating the labor movement with management into the ongoing economic and political structure of society. Yet an official (pre-Hitler) history of the German labor movement could still defend the "revolutionary" nature of German unionism: "But the fact of their [the unions] thus constituting a factor in such administration does not alter their intrinsically *revolutionary* character, it does but increase the efficiency of their work."[8]

One need scarcely add that this very elaborate structure did not work out the way in which the German unions were envisioning it in 1918 and 1919. Union power was not extended into the society to the extent they had desired.

On the other hand, in other countries, and especially after World War II, various social- and economic-planning bodies have been established, and unions are well represented on them. While they may not always play the decisive policy-making role that the planning-minded labor leaders hope for them today, they are significant. Certainly in terms of "completing" the long process whereby an outside "revolutionary" force becomes integrated into its own industrial society, their role is noteworthy.

Direct union representation on these economic- and/or industrial-planning bodies today reinforces a more "independent" stance of the unions as far as relationships with their "brother" parties go. Often the unions come to prize their role in these politically "neutral" bodies, on which they share representation rights with management, and possibly with other private economic groups. They may resist encroachment, even by a socialist government, upon the activities of these planning bodies.

For example, the British Trades Union Congress (TUC) has not been completely happy with some of the moves made by the Labour Party government (1965) to circumscribe the activities of the country's central industrial-planning body, the National Economic Development Council (NEDC), on which TUC representatives serve jointly with management. Resistance against this kind of encroachment from government, even from a socialist government, was anticipated, to a degree, by TUC representatives at an informal meeting held by the Ditchley Foundation in 1964. The meeting was devoted to a discussion of planning and economic policy and took place almost on the eve of the national election, in which a Labour victory was expected. Top level TUC leaders (including several members of the TUC General Council as well as some of the TUC representatives on the NEDC) stated: "The central planning agency, the N.E.D.C., must maintain an independent status with its own staff if it is to make meaningful recommendations to government and industry."[9]

Other outstanding examples of union participation with management (and sometimes with public or government representatives) in important economic-planning or control bodies in Western Europe include: The Labor Market Board in Sweden, which has far-reaching powers over the government's labor market operations, including the timing of private investment decisions; French unions in the National Economic Council, which plays an important role in the national economic-planning mechanism as well as in the preparation and clearance of social legislation to be presented to the parliament; Dutch unions in the Labor Foundation and the Social and Economic Council, which pass on wage and price changes; and Austrian unions both in the Joint-Wage Price Commission, which controls wage and price movements, and in the Chambers of Labor, which, among other things, helps prepare and pass upon any proposed changes in the social legislation field.

All of these examples (and similar ones could be cited in other countries) indicate the ever-increasing integration of these movements into the vital decision-making processes of their societies. Most began after World War II, although a number date back to the twenties.

These new institutions, and the role of the unions, are part of a European-wide trend in which state planning is gradually substituting a kind of collective-bargaining economy for the free market. Gunnar Myrdal has observed that many general price and wage agreements now "are made after multilateral collective bargaining" among a nation's various economic groups. Myrdal concludes that in "the interest of equity" all substantial economic groups in an industrialized society are virtually driven to develop bargaining forms in order to participate in the process. Although Myrdal's generalizations are based primarily on Sweden, where this "bargaining" is well advanced, similar trends obtain everywhere in Western industrial society.[10]

In the United States, the President's Advisory Committee on Labor-Management Policy was a good example of this tendency to draw private groups into the governmental decision-making process with respect to economic policy. Originally set up in the limited industrial relations field, this committee was used by President John F. Kennedy and later by

President Lyndon B. Johnson to help shape, and gain acceptance for, some of the provisions of the major tax cut that was finally enacted in 1964.[11] Since the formation of this committee, union and management representatives have been appointed to national ad-hoc committees designed to make policy recommendations concerning East-West trade, the Negro ghettos, and other critical aspects of American life.

In the light of these trends in decision-making processes affecting major social and economic policies in Western industrial societies, the future for collective action and bargaining, as well as for unions, seems well assured. Logically, representational forms should spread to as yet unorganized groups as they come to appreciate the need for representation. Whether, however, the same union federations, with the same relationships to political parties, will prevail among the new groups is another matter.

A keener appreciation of the general process of union integration can best be obtained from a survey of the Swedish labor movement and labor system as it operates today.

Sweden: Model of Labor Integration?

For several reasons Sweden's union movement and industrial relations system have become almost a model of the pattern of labor integration in the modern welfare state. Indeed, Sweden's labor institutions seem to be so "advanced" that the country has become the object of unusual study by a number of European and American union, management, and government groups. These groups are in search of clues to improved labor relations, a higher degree of unionism (in the case of the unions), and better manpower policies. For example, British and American unions have sent study delegations to Sweden. At the same time, top Swedish union, management, and manpower advisers have frequently been invited abroad to explain the Swedish "way."[12]

The United Automobile Workers union sent a special mission to Europe to study the structure and practice of white-collar unions in Sweden (and a few other countries in Europe) in 1959. This mission sought to improve the UAW's techniques in this field of unionism where European unions, especially Swedish unions, had been more successful. (See *Report on Special Mission to Selected European Countries to Study White Collar Organization, Submitted to U.A.W.* by Victor Reuther, Robert Shefal, and Irving Bluestone, July 1959. Mimeographed.) A U.S. Congressional Committee and a Presidential labor-management and public advisory body invited the heads of the Swedish manual workers' union federation and the employers' federation to the United States for meetings in the early 1960s. The Secretary of Labor and a number of other top officials of the U.S. Department of Labor visited Sweden before the extensive new manpower training program was launched in the United States in the early 1960s. A top expert from the Swedish labor market board was brought in to advise and work with United States labor department officials. Other teams of trade union leaders from Western European nations also visited Sweden. Of course there have been many union missions to the United States (and to other European nations and to the Soviet Union) from both developed and underdeveloped countries. In the latter there is a widespread desire to travel and to study institutions in advanced countries. It is fair to say that so far as Western countries are concerned, Sweden, despite its small size, has been *the* major study model in the labor field in the past decade. Before World War I it was German unionism, and in the first ten years or so after World War II it was American unionism.

Before presenting a brief survey of the Swedish labor integration pattern, it should be emphasized that only the most naive person would take any one country as a simple model to follow or would use such a model to predict the future. Moreover, Sweden is small (around eight million people) and has many special characteristics. From another viewpoint, however, some of these special characteristics may account for its value as a "model," in certain respects, toward which other countries may be trending in the labor and related social fields.

Not the least of Sweden's advantages, which it shares with other small countries such as Switzerland, Austria, or the Netherlands, has been Sweden's ability to operate under a system of proportional representation in choosing its central legislative body. This system in turn seems to give most citizens a keener, more democratic sense of participation and integration in the political processes of their own societies.

Compared with most other European nations from a longer term historical viewpoint, Sweden also seems to have benefited from the fact that feudalism was less deeply implanted in the country and was eliminated at a relatively early period in Swedish history. This made for a smoother development of modern political institutions.

Turning to more immediate, special, or unusual forces that have shaped the nation, one immediately notes that the Swedes avoided the disruption (especially the social disruption) of World Wars I and II. Sweden was also the first nation to seize upon and employ the modern concepts of fiscal planning for full employment. As a consequence, their unions and industrial relations institutions have been operating longer in the kind of social and economic atmosphere that is now common in the rest of Western Europe and (to some extent) in the United States. Presumably, however, a strong economy and the absence of intra-European war will continue to be the norm in all the West in the future.

It has been argued that Sweden, from the viewpoints of ethnic and religious forces, is a more homogeneous nation than most Western European nations. This homogeneity has presumably made possible a steadier course in the pursuit of mature industrial relations.[13] On the other hand, with religious conflict declining, with population more generally settled, Western Europe may also be moving toward greater homogeneity. A possible counterforce to this homogeneity is the increase of labor migration that has been encouraged by European economic integration, as well as the heavy demand for labor from Southern Europe (and Turkey) generated by European economic expansion in Northern and Western Europe. In the case of the United States, the race problem is an example of a disintegrative social force as opposed to other integrating forces that are operating in the economy.

With these broad, generally similar trends as well as those factors which are more exceptional to Sweden in mind, a brief survey of that country's industrial relations system is presented as a kind of advanced integration model.

Unions and Management: Industrial Relations in Sweden

Sweden is probably the most highly unionized society in the West. Successively, its manual workers, then its white-collar workers, and more recently its high level professional employees have been unionized to a relatively high degree—over 90 percent in the case of manual workers, well over 70 percent for "routine" white-collar employees, and better than 60 percent for professional employees.[14]

Employers, too, are tightly bound in associations or federations. As a result it is generally easier for unions to obtain recognition and bargaining rights on a wide scale. Indeed, for some years now major wage negotiations have been conducted at an all-industry level between the top union and employer federations.

The impact of the high degree of unionization upon important Swedish economic institutions has been considerable. Through officially designated representatives, Swedish unions probably play as wide and effective a role in public life as any union movement in the world. The fact, of course, that a Social Democratic government took power in 1932 and is still there (at this writing, 1969) has helped extend labor's role.

As for collective bargaining, Sweden appears to be one of the first countries where basic accommodation between employers and unions took firm and explicit hold. This occurred in the late 1930s following a period of unrest and a critical strike in the construction industry. In 1938-1939 a basic agreement (the famous Saltsjobaden accord) between the top manual workers' federation, LO, and the Swedish Employers' Confederation, SAF, led to a clear-cut acceptance of a permanent, institutional relationship between them. Under this agreement, the right of managements to manage is clearly accepted, as is the permanent character of unionism.[15]

This firm institutional relationship has grown steadily in the past thirty odd years. While all is not harmony in Swedish labor relations, it is hard to imagine trade union leaders in many other countries making a statement about employers like the one that LO President Arne Geijer issued recently:

New generations of management executives and representatives have grown up, different from those who formerly controlled industry and enterprises with patriarchal authority. They are generations with a humane and social attitude toward their employees. Company leaders who are prepared to penetrate more deeply questions which concern cooperation at places of work and on the labour market, company leaders who regard it as an asset to have a constructive exchange of ideas with employees and their union representatives. These generations have developed side by side with the general process of democratization during a period of time which dates so far back that today middle-aged people cannot remember the days when companies were almost exclusively run according to patriarchal methods.[16]

This employer-union relationship is based, in part, on a mutual desire to avoid as far as possible governmental intervention in industrial relations questions. (Related as they are to the Social Democratic Party, from time to time the unions have, however, moved along the *legislative* route to effect gains in benefits or in working conditions.[17]) Serious strikes have become relatively rare.

A special Labour Market Council was set up by the 1938 agreement to dispose of certain top-level disputes arising out of established bargaining relationships—disputes, for example, that involve third parties, threaten essential public services, and grow out of certain job-security problems involving layoffs and reemployment. Moreover, the disputes that come before the council are the kind that crop up regularly in industrial relations. They must be dealt with quickly and often require delicate handling. Long-term problems, which require lengthy deliberation, are the responsibility of the committee that drew up the basic agreement.[18]

Swedish Union-Management Cooperation Extends to Many Areas

The extensive joint voluntary action that unions and management achieve can be illustrated by referring to the works councils, whose purpose is to enable workers to contribute to and participate in the improvement of production. These works councils are based on a private agreement between the employers' association and the largest labor federations (manual and nonmanual). (On the Continent outside of Scandinavia, works councils are invariably a product of legislation.)

National agreements between the top labor and management federations broadly control such matters as the introduction of time-and-motion studies and aspects of vocational training. In time-and-motion studies, an important part of the training of union officials in these techniques is carried on jointly with the employers' training institute. Both the teachers and the course content are the same for union and for management trainees.[19]

In a few instances cooperation on some aspects of wage-setting involves joint action by unions and management in the collection of wage material to be used in bargaining.

A permanent vocational-training committee and office was established by the LO and the SAF in 1947. This body investigates the need for additional vocational training, controls apprenticeship programs, and closely follows all other vocational matters.[20]

Union Role in Social, Economic, and Manpower Planning

It is beyond the industrial relations area, however, where the wider integration of trade unions in Swedish economic life manifests itself most strikingly. They are involved in the country's long-term planning process; they have direct, operational responsibility for policy-making in the manpower field, they also administer unemployment insurance in many industries.

Swedish unions run unemployment benefit funds that cover more than half the country's employees. The funds are financed by members' contributions and state grants. Membership is open to all employees, union and nonunion, in the trade or industry that a particular fund covers. For union members, it is virtually compulsory to participate in these funds. Although administered by the unions, the funds are established on a legal basis that separates them from the regular union structure. In a sense the unions function in this area as government instrumentalities.[21]

Union unemployment funds are run by fund members themselves, under broad government supervision. Each trade or industrial group chooses its own delegate assembly, which sets general policy and also elects a governing board. The local branches are run by the accountants of the trade unions.

Government supervision is provided by the National Labor Market Board, which appoints a member to the governing board of each individual unemployment society.[22]

In the area of management of the economy, Swedish unions participate in the government's long-term planning projections and on the National Labor Market Board, which has great influence on shorter-term economic policy.[23]

Actually, when it comes to long-term planning and policy, one must turn to countries like France or The Netherlands, where such planning is practiced more than in Sweden, to see the fuller participation and integration of the unions in this type of activity.[24] In France, a top-level economic and social council, with a vocational type of representation (unions, employers, farmers, etc.) passes upon top planning policy as well as on major social and economic legislation that is proposed by the government. France's Economic and Social Council functions like a special legislative chamber. It becomes an important forum to influence policy on matters such as European integration, trade or energy policy, or housing.[25] Even when this council has not been fully effective in its operations, it has provided the unions a great national forum.

French unions also play a major role in implementing the national plan itself. They participate in the work of the approximately thirty modernization or industry committees that set targets for investment, exports, and like matters.[26]

On occasion, however, representatives of French unions may be boxed out of certain discussions in particular industry committees, when business representatives plead that "business secrets" are involved. Unions also complain that public officials and business groups, on some issues coming before the committees, have had "the real discussion . . . beforehand."[27] Inexperience or lack of adequate staff support may hinder union leaders in maximizing their roles in these new mechanisms; but time is likely to improve their performance. More extensive union education programs may help fill this gap in the future. It does seem that Scandinavian unionists, who have had the benefit of more extensive workers' education training programs, seem better equipped for the new and changing tasks confronting organized labor.

To return to the discussion concerning Sweden: The unions, along with other groups, do have a powerful influence on short-run economic policy through the Labor Market Board. The latter consists of ten members, including a director general and his deputy, along with eight other members, including four from the trade unions (two from the manual workers federation—LO, one from the white-collar federation—TCO, and one from the federation of professional employees—SACO), two from the employers, and one each representing female labor and agriculture.

This board has power over all labor market policies and operations (including the employment offices around the country) and control of certain public works programs. As it judges the economy, the board passes upon training programs and the awarding of grants to trainees; it also passes upon travel and "settling in" allowances for workers who move as a consequence of labor market policy. The board also can provide special training programs for the disabled and special work programs for those who are too old for the rigors of regular work. There are counterparts to the national board in the twenty-five counties of the country; unions are also represented on these bodies, which help carry out national manpower policy.[28]

The board meets periodically with top economic agencies and officials of the government to judge the prospects of the economy. It is empowered to authorize public works programs when it deems these necessary to offset any economic downturn. It also controls the so-called special investment reserves fund of the government. By means of tax concessions, Swedish legislation encourages corporations to leave part of their earned profits on reserve. These are "released" to the corporations, tax free, when there are deflationary tendencies and the government judges that investment should be encouraged to offset them. The general policy, then, is to damp down private investment during a boom and to increase it during a down-turn.[29]

The Labor Market Board, as can be readily seen, has far-reaching powers. The unions' heavy representation on this body insures a large and direct role for them in Swedish economic policy-making. The extensive labor market activity that is so central to Sweden's full employment policy was initiated largely as a result of pressure from economists working for the trade unions. In this instance, the unions, far more than the party, were responsible for developing this aspect of socialist economic policy.[30]

The wide role of Swedish unions in the country's economic life has also found reflection in the highly professional economic and technical reports the LO has released from time to time since 1941. These have dealt with full employment, the structural problems of the labor market and economic policy, and the problem of technological change.[31]

Clearly, unions in Sweden are no longer outside the society. Indeed, they are a fundamental part of its power and policy-making structure. Integration does not imply, of course, that labor movements do not take positions in conflict with other groups on basic social and economic questions. These questions, however, by tacit agreement of all sides, are to be worked out within the existing socio-political framework.

Even this degree of integration can be exaggerated, however. The program of the Social Democratic Party, presumably subscribed to by the mass of LO union members and leaders, declares:

The capitalist system has shown itself incapable of releasing and utilizing to the full the available resources for the people's essential needs. . . . The hallmarks of present-day capitalism are cartel agreements and other arrangements determined by considerations of profit. . . . Important human needs have been neglected where the expectation of profit was too low to provide sufficient incentive to entrepreneurs.

Just what is to be substituted for the capitalist *system* is less clear in the program, which remains essentially pragmatic and specific. Thus, complaint is made that "competition" is insufficient, in that it "is far too little directed towards lowering prices. Concentration of power in private hands has in many cases also impeded the establishment of new potentially efficient enterprises." This sounds like a plea for more effective capitalist competition; on the other hand, the program declares, "The competitive spirit which is a feature of capitalism has at the same time helped to create psychological problems for many people." In the end, no special plea for public ownership is made; the party program declares it "will choose those forms of enterprise and ownership which best serve material progress and human welfare." And, "Whether economic activities are based upon private ownership or various forms of public ownership, they must be coordinated in a planned economy to prevent labour and material resources from being wasted by lying idle or by inadequate use of their productive possibilities."[32]

The spread of the integrative process is true of Western labor movements generally, although the degree of integration varies greatly. Whether all Western labor movements will evolve into something approaching the very high state of organization and integration found in Sweden is impossible to forecast; but that the integration process is a general one cannot be denied.

The United States is an interesting case in this respect. As already suggested, the use of high level representative commissions with union participation has gained a prominent place in American life. The coming years may disclose whether this type of group participation and decision making in the United States will move from an ad hoc character to more permanent forms with some sort of a national social and economic council composed of representatives from the public, unions, management, and other economic interests. The greater geographical size and population of the United States, the relative absence of a tradition of collective action, and the complexities of a federal-state system have tended to produce a slower trend, as compared with most of Europe, toward group-integrated forms of social and economic planning.

NOTES

1. Adolf Sturmthal, "Some Thoughts on Labor and Political Action," *Relations Industrielles,* July 1962, p. 249.

2. Selig Perlman, *Theory of the Labor Movement* (New York: Augustus M. Kelley, 1949; first printing, 1928), pp. 90–91. Also see Richard Seidel, *The Trade Union Movement of Germany,* No. 7–8 (Amsterdam: International Federation of Trade Unions, 1928), pp. 47–49. This gives a description of some of the debate on this issue within the German movement, which finally led to a formal national union decision by the annual congress in favor of encouraging the creation of such funds.

3. Henry Pelling, *A History of British Trade Unionism* (Middlesex: Penguin Books, 1963), pp. 128–129. For a description of union participation in the administration of a national unemployment insurance plan as it operated in Britain in the 1920s, see W. Milne-Bailey (ed.), *Trade Union Documents* (London: G. Bell, 1929), pp. 478–480.

4. Walter Galenson, *The Danish System of Labor Relations* (Cambridge, Mass.: Harvard University Press, 1952), p. 175.

5. Remarks by Samuel Gompers, 1921, quoted in *American Federation of Labor, History Encyclopedia Reference Book,* (Washington, D.C.: American Federation of Labor, 1924), Vol. II, p. 300 Gompers expressed similar opposition to federal unemployment insurance before a senate committee in 1919. *Ibid.* On old-age pensions, the AFL in these years took a more balanced position. After refusing to permit its executive council to help "establish a system whereby employees in private employment may have assistance in making provision for old age," the federation in 1922 came out in support of a federal pension system that would be based upon the principle of regarding all aged, retired workers as members of a special "home guard" of the U.S. Army. *Ibid.,* pp. 209–211. This complex proposal was aimed at circumventing constitutional objections to federal pension legislation.

6. Quoted by Michael Rogin in "Voluntarism: The Political Functions of an Antipolitical Doctrine," *Industrial and Labor Relations Review,* July 1962, p. 532. By 1932, however, the AFL position as a whole was changing, and that year's convention endorsed an "unemployment relief measure . . . to be used in supplying aid to those who were in distress caused by unemployment." Succeeding conventions came out explicitly in favor of an unemployment compensation system. See *American Federation of Labor . . . Reference Book, op. cit.,* Vol. III, Part II, pp. 2334, 2338–2339.

7. Seidel, *op. cit.,* pp. 89–97.

8. *Ibid.,* p. 99. (Italics added.)

9. *Communiqué, The Ditchley Foundation, Anglo-American Trade Union Conference,* June 6–9, 1964, p. 2. (Mimeographed.) For a brief summary of this communiqué, see the *Monthly Labor Review,* U.S. Department of Labor, August 1964, pp. 925–927.

10. Gunnar Myrdal, *Beyond the Welfare State* (New Haven: Yale University Press, 1960), pp. 43–46.

11. Jack Stieber describes this aspect of the committee's work in "The President's Committee on Labor-Management Policy," *Industrial Relations,* February 1966, pp. 11–14.

12. For reports on the visits to Sweden, see *Sweden—Its Unions and Industrial*

Relations (London: Trades Union Congress, 1963) and Jack Cooper (a top TUC leader and member of the TUC mission), *Industrial Relations: Sweden Shows the Way,* Fabian Research Series, 235 (London: Fabian Society, 1963).

13. It has also been suggested that the path of industrialization in Sweden was relatively more gradual, as compared for example with Norway, and that this also made for less friction between labor and management in industrial relations development. See Walter Galenson (ed.), *Comparative Labor Movements* (Englewood Cliffs, N.J.: Prentice-Hall, 1952), Chap. 3, "Scandinavia."

14. The best detailed single description in English of Swedish unionism and collective bargaining is T. L. Johnston, *Collective Bargaining in Sweden,* (Cambridge, Mass.: Harvard University Press, 1962). I have drawn on this and other references, as indicated. I have also had the good fortune to visit Sweden a number of times. Her various labor, management, and government officials have been more than kind to me. I have also benefited from my friendship with the various labor attachés who have served in the Swedish Embassy in Washington, D.C.

15. A similar agreement was reached in Denmark in 1899, and a famous basic agreement was concluded in Norway in 1935. It is difficult to find any parallels to these in other Western European countries. It should be noted that in Sweden, at least, labor-management relations were rather firmly grounded before the 1938 agreements. This was not true of most other countries.

16. Quoted in *LO Series III Information to Foreign Countries,* June-July 1966.

17. The Swedish manual workers' union federation (LO) and the Social Democratic Party are part of one labor complex. The statutes of LO, dating from 1909, still provide that "the Social Democratic Labor Party is the natural bearer of the political aspirations of the trade union movement." Members of the executive board of LO are elected members of the party executive committee, and "It is an unwritten rule that the president of LO is sent to Parliament as a representative of the Party." *Trade Unions in Sweden,* (Stockholm: LO, 1961), pp. 43–45.

18. Johnston, *op. cit.,* p. 175.

19. *Trade Unions in Sweden, op. cit.,* p. 23.

20. *Ibid.,* pp. 25–27. The process of "integration" works in different ways in different countries. In Great Britain, to expedite vocational training, the Industrial Training Act of 1964 establishes Industrial Training Boards, composed of union, management, and governmental officials, for individual industries or groups of industries. These boards, when empowered by the vote of their *union and management members only,* levy a general tax on *all* employers in an industry, to pay the costs of employee training. This tax is rebated to the extent that employers undertake authorized training programs. *Industrial Training Act 1964,* (London: HMSO, 1964), and J. P. de C. Meade, *The United Kingdom Industrial Training Act 1964: An Example of Shared Responsibility* (Paris: Organization for Economic Cooperation and Development, 1966).

21. George R. Nelson (ed.), *Freedom and Welfare, Social Patterns in the North Countries.* Sponsored by the Ministries of Social Affairs of Denmark, Finland, Iceland, Norway, and Sweden (Denmark, 1953), pp. 412–420.

22. In France and several other European nations, unions participate in top-level boards that lay down the broad policy and administrative guidelines of the various social security systems, including health, old-age pensions, unemployment, and family benefits.

23. There is no single, readily available description in English of the philosophy and development of Swedish socialist planning. One can, however, consult the nineteen-page English summary appendix in Leif Lewin's *Plannhushållnings debatten* (Stockholm: Almquist Wiksell, 1967), pp. 523–541. A useful description of the

evolution of Swedish *economic policy* under socialist government is contained in Chapter 5 of Erik Lundberg, *Instability and Economic Growth* (New Haven: Yale University Press, 1968).

24. In the case of France, the largest of the trade union federations, under communist control, has participated in the planning process with very limited commitment. Generally, integration of French unions into the current society is less than in other Western European nations. The planning process in France, and labor's role in it, is nevertheless an interesting example of one way in which the integration process can work out.

25. Paul Durand, *La Participation des travailleurs à l'organisation de la vie économique et sociale en France* (Luxembourg: Communauté Européene du Charbon et de l'Acier Haute Autorité, 1962), pp. 26–28. Also see Guy Caire, "Participation by Employers' and Workers' Organisations in Planning," *International Labour Review,* December 1967, pp. 557–580.

26. Jean-Jacques Bonnaud, "Participation by Workers' and Employers' Organisations in Planning in France," *International Labour Review,* April 1966.

27. Andrew Shonfield, *Modern Capitalism* (London: Oxford University Press, 1965), p. 232, quotes G. Mathieu on some of the difficulties confronting trade unionists in this work. In similar committees in British planning under the National Economic Development Council, British unions may have fared slightly better, perhaps due to their greater industrial strength. On the reaction of some French union officials, and for other aspects of the unions' role in the planning process, see *International Trade Union Seminar on Economic and Social Programming, Supplement to Final Report* (Paris: Organisation for Economic Cooperation and Development, 1963), p. 14; and also see *Final Report,* (same seminar), (Paris: OECD, 1964).

28. For a useful summary of the work and power of the National Labor Market Board, see *Unemployment Programs in Sweden,* Paper No. 5, Joint Economic Committee of the Congress of the United States (Washington, D.C.: U.S. Government Printing Office, 1964). Unions and employers are represented on other boards that exercise policy-making power in important social and economic areas such as education, social welfare, and others in Swedish life.

29. *Ibid.*

30. On the special contributions of LO union economists Gösta Rehn and Rudolph Meidner in shaping economic policy in Sweden in the post-World War II decades see Assar Lindbeck, "Theories and Problems in Swedish Economic Policy in the Post-War Period," *American Economic Review,* Part 2, Supplement (June 1968).

31. Other reports have dealt with less purely economic matters, such as industrial democracy and the role and responsibilities of the trade-union movement in modern society. The following major economic reports have been translated into English: *Trade Unions and Full Employment* (Malmo: LO, 1953); T. L. Johnston (ed.), *Economic Expansion and Structural Change* (London: Allen & Unwin, 1963); S. D. Anderman (ed.), *Trade Unions and Technological Change* (London: Allen & Unwin, 1967).

32. The text of this programme, adopted in 1961, appears in David J. Saposs, *Case Studies in Labor Ideology, Monograph No. 1, The Nordic Countries—Denmark, Finland, Iceland, Norway and Sweden* (Honolulu: University of Hawaii, 1964), pp. 75–77.

V

Today's Changing Working Class and Union Member

SINCE THE END OF WORLD WAR II, or at least since the early fifties, the attitudes of the worker including his attitude toward his union have naturally been affected by the increasing integration of his union and his party complex, the rapid spread of affluence among large sections of the European working class, the relative stability of employment, the strengthening of the "Welfare State," and the upward equalizing of educational attainment.

Affluence and the Changing Worker-Union Relationship

One British writer argues that in postwar England the net effect of these changes, especially the economic ones, has been to produce a new self-centered family type among factory workers—workers with a greater sense of acquisitiveness, a strong taste for consumer durable goods (homes, television sets, and automobiles), and the like. The older sense of class or group solidarity is breaking down, individualism (and family centeredness) is on the rise, and "working class life finds itself on the move toward new middle-class values and middle-class existence."[1]

According to a study done on Netherlands unions and their members by Mark Van de Vall, the simultaneous changes going on in the workers' world and in the union world (union changes were outlined in Chapter IV) have over time led to an important change in what the worker expected from his union. With the establishment of the Welfare State, which is now taken for granted, workers look upon the union less and less for traditional collective services, and more and more as an instrument to serve personal needs. Van de Vall records the growing impression

that whereas the proletariat in the 19th century class society struggled to establish a new social order through collective effort, the generations in the

20th century welfare state seek to improve their position in the existing social order by individual action. They are therefore less guided by traditional sentiments of collective solidarity . . . the young worker's attitude to his union is a "Verbraucherhaltung," i.e., that of a consumer who accepts the advantages without much enthusiasm or idealism.[2]

According to another Dutch writer, who is a trade union officer, the worker's changed view of the union's role is also due to the very integration of the union in the society. Union members' sense of conflict and participation in conflict keep decreasing, and more and more of the critical union work goes on in government bodies or committees. The union becomes a remote entity to its members:

Some of the work done by unions has become "invisible," firstly because the general interest and that of the workers now coincide more closely, and secondly because the committee system (which imposes a certain degree of secrecy) has meant that much of the leadership's work can no longer be apparent to the rank and file.

The writer also notes the increasing specialization and expertise called for in modern trade union work; this also isolates the member from the official and the union.[3]

These analyses, based on Dutch union experience, are interesting, and they delineate a set of trends that are doubtless at work in union situations in other countries. They are in a sense a kind of obverse aspect of the integration process discussed in the preceding chapter. One can hardly expect members to maintain the same pitch of feeling about their unions when the unions themselves no longer face serious threats to their existence. As indicated, these trends are discernible in other countries, but in the Netherlands they also reflect some conditions peculiar to the Dutch social scene. The postwar economic reconstruction needs of the Netherlands were in some respects the most difficult in Europe because the country lost its colonial empire so abruptly. The process of integrating the labor movement into the state machinery probably went farther (and faster) there than anywhere else, except possibly in Austria (which was also affected by very special postwar conditions). It should be remembered, however, that complaints about membership indifference and "bourgeoisification," and also complaints about the difficulty of unionizing young workers, are not new. They have echoed for decades in European social democratic and union history. What then are we to make of the conclusions of Van de Vall and de Bruin? If we appraise these conclusions with caution, we will take them as only *one* reason why there is a change today in the attitudes of members of unions in Western Europe.[4]

Changes in the Working-Class Way of Life

The findings of a writer like Zwieg must also be taken with caution, but for different reasons. It is clear that workers, like their unions, are changing in a dynamically expanding industrial world. But this does not mean that they are evolving into a middle-class style of life or toward "typical" middle-class values. That this is true is suggested by interesting studies of the working-class subculture or style of life, which have been made in both the United States and Britain in recent years.

Manual workers, for example, still place a relatively greater premium upon security than promotion (unlike middle-class groups). This does not mean they are less money-minded or less desirous of accumulating appliances, a home, and the like. Rather, the difference lies in an emphasis on "getting by" well, rather than "getting ahead." One survey, for example, found that "a majority of manual workers thought it more important for the government to guarantee every person 'a decent and steady standard of living' than to make 'certain that there are good opportunities for each person to get ahead on his own.' Business, professional and white collar groups disagreed; they rated 'opportunities' much higher." Other studies found that manual workers generally showed little interest in advancement, even to the position of foreman. S. M. Miller and Frank Riessman have argued that even today, in the era of mass college education, a typical (manual) working-class family does not aspire for a college education for its children, at least to the extent, which is almost universal, in the middle class (white-collar workers, professionals, management, and owners).[5]

Only a few years ago I had occasion to discuss the subject of a college education with a small group of well-paid local officers of a steelworkers' union. The group confirmed the Miller-Riessman thesis, but in a curious way. Several of the men remarked that five or ten years ago they would have been rather indifferent to the idea of a college education for their children. They had frequently observed that many of the college graduates who worked "around" them were paid relatively modest salaries, compared to their own. Today, however, they had become convinced of the need for a college education for their children. The way jobs were changing, if these children were "to make good money," college was important. However, even this more "positive" attitude toward the value of education is not really "middle class." In a "typical" middle-class family the emphasis would be as much or more on the higher social status a college degree confers, on the kind of a job a college degree can lead to. This of course contrasts with the more limited monetary "calculus" of the working class "type." I intend no generalizations from my conversation with the union officers, but it can be cited as interesting supporting evidence.

Studies of British manual working-class attitudes confirm that security is rated higher than the middle-class goals of status and advancement. These studies also point out that there is no evidence that the working class is being accepted into the social network of clubs, communities, neighborhoods, and other longstanding middle-class institutions. A shift from a working-class to a middle-class way of life must involve a great deal more than merely changed economic circumstances. David Lockwood recalls Friedrich Engels' complaint in 1889: " 'The most repulsive thing here is the bourgeois respectability which has grown deep into the bones of the workers.' "[6]

Recent surveys suggest that today's more affluent British manual worker may be less acutely class conscious, but he does not seem to waver in his support either of his union or the British Labour Party.[7]

In other countries for which we have evidence, the same state of affairs seems to exist. In Germany, for example, Richard Hamilton has found that there is a considerable difference between the working-class and middle-class "style of life" even at the same income levels. Aside from different class values concerning "status," cultural interests, and the like, Hamilton argues that among workers even the "achievement of a middle-class income level does not lead to political conservatism."[8] In the case of the French worker, Serge Mallet's studies seem to argue a somewhat substantial change in his outlook and style of life, bringing him closer to other classes in the society.[9] France is a special case, however, and what Mallet is describing may be no more than a reduction in the "alienation" that has seemed to characterize the working class in Latin countries.

In the United States, the relative income gains among at least some sections of the manual work group, most notably the skilled workers, may well lead in the long run to a significant change in their way of life. Such is the argument of Gavin Mackenzie, who also notes that, in the absence of a feudal-class tradition, and given "the prevailing ideology of equality . . . the probability of embourgeoisement may well be greater in the United States than in Europe."[10] Mackenzie also believes that the influence of an ever-growing number of working women, most of whom will be employed in nonmanual jobs, can lead to changes in the style of family life, even where the male household head is in a manual occupation.

Kurt Mayer argues that the enormous economic and social transformation of the present age cannot but shake the old markings and categories, of class lines. The proof, he finds, is fairly obvious; for one thing, he quotes the British sociologist T. H. Marshall, "It is both remarkable and slightly ludicrous that it should prove necessary to carry out the most elaborate research in order to discover what the shape of the class structure is in modern society." In contrast, "To past generations it constituted the 'social order' by which their lives were, and should be governed." Marshall concludes, on this point, that modern class definitional problems "arise from the gradual replacement of a simple, clear, institutional structure by a complex, nebulous, informal one."[11] Mayer does go on to note that class definitions are additionally complicated, in the United States and Britain particularly, by the persistence of a poverty "class" in the midst of a general, growing affluence in both societies.

Union Membership Trends

That today's worker is less militantly class-conscious than his father or grandfather can hardly be challenged. Nor can we challenge the fact that his union plays a changed role in today's society.

Whether union membership is in any important sense "fading" is another matter. Whether a membership "crisis" in unions is really occurring is open to serious question.

While we lack any useful, scientific, long-term studies of union membership trends to test the crisis theory with respect to membership loyalty, such data as we do have do not suggest a crisis. Broadly speaking, by comparison with prewar union membership figures, practically all European labor movements have done well. (Of course, gross membership figures do not tell us about possible shifts in the loyalties of individuals or groups.) Even more significantly, if one compares trends in the past ten or twelve years, the unions, again, are not doing badly—as Table 1 shows.

Every major labor movement shows some gains in these years, and in the few cases where the gains seem small, this is sometimes because even by 1953 the "density" of union membership was already quite high in some countries (i.e., a relatively high proportion of the potential members was already organized by 1953).

It is true that if one compares union membership figures with total employment since 1953, the trends become less favorable in some countries where employment has grown at a more rapid rate than union membership. Germany is an outstanding example. Generally, however, even this does not represent failure of the unions to hold their membership position. More often it reflects a change in employment *to,* and especially rapid expansion *in,* sectors that have not been as well unionized—such as white-collar or nonmanual work and professional employment. (In Germany, the task of unionizing new workers has also been complicated by the heavy inflow of foreign workers from Turkey, Spain, Italy, Greece, and elsewhere.)

A study of British unions points out that "the industries now suffering serious structural decline—especially coal, railways and shipyards—are the ones which were basic to the British economy when our trade union movement established itself and which through their high levels of union membership have been the pillars of the union movement." Shifts within industries from blue-to-white-collar work (traditionally less well union-

TABLE 1. *Union Membership Trends in Western Europe**

Country and Union Federations	Membership (000)		
	1953	1963	1966
Austria			
Austrian Trade Union Federation (ÖGB)	1,320,000	1,518,000	1,543,000 (1965)
Belgium			
Belgian General Federation of Labor (FGTB)	670,000	703,000	770,000 (1967)
Confederation of Christian Trade Unions (CSC)	640,000	706,000	872,000
General Federation of Liberal Unions of Belgium (CGSLB)	40,000	119,000 (1962)	
Denmark			
Federation of Danish Trade Unions (FDTU)	688,000 (1955)	818,000	835,000
Federation of Civil Servants and Salaried Employees (FTF)	103,000 (1955)	125,000	143,000
Germany (West)			
German Trade Union Federation (DGB)	6,070,000	6,431,000	6,537,000
German Salaried Workers' Union (DAG)	380,000	432,000	477,792
German Association of Civil Servants (DBB)	500,000 (1950)	680,000	703,000 (1965)
Great Britain			
Trades Union Congress (TUC)	8,088,000†	8,315,000†	8,787,000†
Netherlands			
Netherlands Federation of Trade Unions (NVV)	454,000	530,000	556,000
Netherlands Catholic Workers Federation (KAB)	347,000	430,000	432,000
National Federation of Christian (Protestant) Workers (CNV)	191,000	229,000	237,000
Norway			
Norwegian Federation of Trade Unions (LO)	522,000	550,000	575,000

TABLE 1. (*Continued*)

Sweden			
Swedish Federation of Labor (LO)	1,338,000	1,547,000	1,607,000 (1967)
Central Organizations of Salaried Employees (TCO)	310,000	466,000	577,700†
The Swedish Confederation of Professional Associations (SACO)	37,874	65,000	93,000 (1967)
Switzerland			
Swiss Federation of Trade Unions (SFTU)	401,000 (1954)	451,000	444,000
Swiss Federation of Employees' Societies	80,000 (1954)	116,000	121,000†
Swiss Federation of National-Christian Trade Unions (SFNCTU)	70,000	93,000	93,000
Swiss Federations of Protestant (Evangelical) Trade Unions (SFPTU)	16,000 (1954)	14,000	15,000

* These estimates are based on different sources, but in most cases these are official figures reported by the unions themselves, by the countries, or by the labor ministries. The figures between countries, and even within countries, are not always comparable. Some unions include retired members in their count, others do not. France and Italy are excluded since their union membership figures are not reliable.

† There are, of course, unions in addition to those listed, but their membership in practically all instances is relatively small. In Great Britain, for example, total membership at the end of 1966 was 10,111,000. Several of the still independent unions and associations in public employment in Britain were giving serious consideration to affiliation with the TUC in the spring of 1968. The German Federation of Christian Trade Unions, not listed in this table, had a membership of around 230,000 in 1965. On January 1, 1968, the Swedish TCO lost its affiliate, the Foremen's union, which has a membership of around 54,000 members. The figure listed, however, does not reflect this loss. The Swiss Federation of Employee's Societies is a white-collar federation with fraternal ties with the SFTU.

ized) has also acted unfavorably upon British union strength. Even in the case of Britain, however, union density (proportion of total employment) has been fairly constant over most of the postwar period. From 1948 to 1958, for instance, union membership relative to employment declined only 1 percent, from 44 to 43 percent.[12]

Similar forces have been in operation in the United States. Industries of traditional union strength (mining and railroads most notably) have been in decline, and the relative shift from blue- to white-collar work, along with the general growth of government employment, has been very sharp.[13]

American union membership between 1956 and 1964 actually showed a decline from 17,490,000 to 16,841,000. The decline was due, to repeat, to relative shifts of employment from industries of traditional blue-collar union strength to those where white-collar employment was higher, rather than to serious defection of union members. By 1966, U.S. union membership had begun to grow again, and it reached an all time high of 17,892,000. As a proportion of total nonagricultural employment, however, union membership was still declining in 1966. It was only 28 percent of this total in 1966, as compared to 33.4 percent in 1956. In other words, employment growth was still outpacing union membership growth.[14]

Illuminating figures are provided by examination of membership trends within the AFL-CIO, which constitutes over 80 percent of total U.S. union membership. This body, which also experienced a period of stagnation in the late fifties and early sixties, has recently begun to grow again. In the last decade the largest relative share of this growth has come in the government sector; but in any event the stagnation in U.S. union membership growth seems to have come to an end.[15]

Comparisons as to the percentage or degree of union organization between different countries are difficult to make. Such factors as legal restrictions on who can join a union, the process of union recognition, and the structure of the labor force vary greatly from country to country. Even the definition of what is a recognized union can differ. Are independent civil service or nonprofit associations that do some bargaining but reject the title union, significant in the United States and Germany, to be counted as unions? Taking these severely limiting factors into consideration, it could be said that as a percent of the total nonagricultural labor force in the 1964–1965 period, the degree of union organization in Austria and Sweden was between 65 and 70 percent, with Denmark and Norway over 60 percent. The organization was as follows: in Belgium a little over 50 percent; close to 45 percent in the Netherlands; over 40 percent in Great Britain; in Germany about one-third, with the percentages for France and Italy much lower.

For the United States, on a roughly comparable basis, union membership was close to 30 percent of the nonagricultural labor force. These gross figures, of course, conceal the fact that in the United States the degree of union organization among manual workers in such industries as basic steel, automobiles and railroads is over 90 percent. The economic "hitting power" of American unions is consequently greater than the comparatively modest total percentage of organization might suggest.

Voting Trends: European Labor and Socialist Parties

An analysis of trends among European labor and/or socialist parties in a number of Western European countries in the past twenty years attests to the general stability and cohesion of "labor" strength. Table 2 shows the percentage of the vote polled by various European labor and/or socialist parties in general national elections during the post-World War II period.[16]

Generally speaking one must be impressed by the steadiness of

TABLE 2. *Percentage of Vote, European Labor and/or Socialist Parties*

Austrian Socialist Party	1949	38.8
	1953	42.1
	1956	43.0
	1959	44.8
	1962	44.0
	1965	42.6
Belgian Socialist Party	1949	29.7
	1950	35.6
	1954	37.3
	1958	36.7
	1961	36.7
	1965	28.3
	1968	27.1

(The Belgian Communist Party polled 7.5% of the national vote in 1949, which fell to 1.9% in 1958, rose to 5.4% in 1965, and was 3.3% in 1968. The total of the Socialist and Communist votes would represent a much steadier figure than the Socialist vote alone. In recent elections both the Socialists and their principal opponents lost votes to "extremist," regional, language-oriented parties.)

Dutch Labor Party	1948	25.7
	1952	29.0
	1955	29.4
	1957	32.6
	1959	30.4
	1963	28.0
	1967	23.6

(Practically all of the major Dutch parties suffered losses in 1967 to a new, as yet undefined group which seems to have had particular appeal to younger people.)

German Social Democratic Party	1949	29.2
	1953	28.8
	1957	31.8
	1961	36.2
	1965	39.3

(Although the German Social Democratic Party has made steady gains in the national elections of the past twelve years, some of these have been due to the disappearance of small parties. The principal opponent of the Social Democrats, the Christian Democratic Party, polled 47.6% of the national vote in 1965 as against 31% in 1949.)

British Labour Party	1945	47.3
	1950	46.4
	1951	46.1
	1955	46.4
	1959	43.8
	1964	44.1
	1966	47.9

TABLE 2. (*Continued*)

Danish Social Democratic Party	1947	40.0
	1950	39.6
	1953	40.4
	1957	39.4
	1960	42.2
	1964	41.9
	1966	38.3
	1968	34.2

(The Peoples Socialist Party, a left, pacifist socialist party, gained 10.9% of the vote in 1966, an increase of 5.1% over 1964, when it campaigned nationally for the first time. Both socialist parties fell in the election of January 1968, the Peoples party to 6.1%.)

Juan Linz's study of "Cleavage and Consensus in West German Politics," in Seymour M. Lipset and Stein M. Rokkan (eds.), *Party Systems and Voter Alignments, Cross-National Perspectives* (New York: Free Press, 1967), indicates that the Christian Democrats seem to receive working-class support on the order of close to two-thirds of that polled by the Social Democrats. Although there is one dominant labor union federation, the DGB, in the political field, the Catholic Church appears to be an important force in influencing Catholic working-class votes. Catholic forces, including those in the Christian Democratic Party, have not moved in the post-World War II period to throw their real support to the tiny Christian labor movement in Germany. The DGB leadership, in turn, has practiced at least formal political neutralism.

Norwegian Labor Party	1949	45.7
	1953	46.7
	1957	48.3
	1961	46.6
	1965	43.3

(Socialist Peoples Party, a left socialist party, campaigned first in the 1961 election, polled 2.4% of the vote, and won 6.0% in 1965. Totaling the two socialist parties would yield an even steadier vote.)

Swedish Social Democratic Party	1948	46.1
	1952	46.1
	1956	44.6
	1958	46.2
	1960	47.8
	1964	47.3
	1968	50.1

Swiss Social Democratic Party	1947	26.2
	1951	26.0
	1955	27.0
	1959	26.3
	1963	26.6
	1967	25.9

socialist party voting in post-World War II Europe. It is true, however, that in the past few years some unfavorable trends have occurred in Scandinavia, hitherto a strong point of socialist strength, where Danish and Norwegian socialist national governments have fallen. On the other hand, the Swedish Social Democratic Party, still ruling nationally, lost some strength in local elections in 1966 but overcame a formidable challenge in the 1968 national elections to gain a clear majority of the vote. Recent declines in the Netherlands and Belgium are also hard to evaluate, although they may be due primarily to temporary disturbances in normal voting patterns.[17]

Admittedly, without a closer study of these figures, country by country, it is difficult to ascertain whether the base of socialist voting strength has continued to lie among workers. From general observation, however, one would judge that European socialist parties have received steady support from union members. This seems to be true even though these union members have had substantial increases in real income. Even more surprising, perhaps, has been the parties' ability, in the face of the rising relative importance of white-collar and technical groups in the population, to maintain their voting percentages. This reflects, in most instances, the ability of these parties to broaden their appeals and their image.

Actually, as far as the working class is concerned, the rise in real incomes may, to a degree, protect the vote of the socialist parties in some countries. One inquiry suggests that in Germany, Denmark, and Sweden, for example, the conservative parties draw working-class votes most successfully from the more disadvantaged, less well-paid workers. A close correlation seems to exist between higher levels of workers' family income and their support for socialist parties. In France and Italy, on the other hand, socialist and communist votes seem to be in inverse relationship to workers' income levels—that is, the parties of the left score more heavily among lower paid workers.[18]

Finally, if, as seems true, workers in larger, more modern enterprises tend to vote more consistently for the labor left than those in smaller firms, this too should help the labor movement, including the trade unions.[19] This assumes, of course, that for at least some years to come European industrial development will tend to eliminate more of the smaller, more obsolete factories and firms.

Unions and Members Today: Some Concluding Remarks

It cannot be questioned that important changes are taking place within the modern-day working population and particularly within working-class institutions and unions, and even more especially within parties. What can be questioned is whether any important defections are occurring. And what remains to be defined is the character of the change in Western Europe.

In Western Europe today, labor movements are certainly less revolutionary sounding, and, indeed, judging especially by the labor parties, they are clearly less "class"-oriented. The labor parties, especially, have been trying to transform themselves into broader social movements, appealing to more groups in the population as they strive to win or maintain power in their respective countries.

Politically, these movements are consciously seeking to picture themselves as "social" rather than "class" forces. We have already referred to this. For example, we might mention the deliberate effort of the Austrian Socialist Party to cast itself in the public role of a broad social rather than a narrow class movement:

Since 1945, however, the leadership has been intent on achieving this goal without attempting to square this policy with traditional socialist ideology, and has put increased stress on the "national" rather than on the "working class" character of the movement. The elimination of Arbeiter (Worker) from the name of the Party was an early indication of this change.[20]

In his effort to broaden the appeal of British socialism, Harold Wilson, leader of the British Labour Party, has been trying to reformulate socialism today as standing for the application of science and technology to modern problems of government and the economy.

Describing a newspaper interview in 1964, Wilson remarked that when he was asked "what above all I associated with Socialism in this modern age, I answered that if there was one word I would use to identify modern Socialism it was 'SCIENCE.' " In key party Congress speeches Wilson has revealed, says *Socialist Commentary*, "how labour was to embrace the new race of scientists, technologists and technicians in an exciting future . . . Wilson developed his theme of the supreme need for more universities, more scientists, and more drive to expand and modernise industry."[21]

With the achievement of so many of labor's goals, such as (1) comprehensive social security, (2) machinery to accelerate the production of worker and lower-middle-class housing, and (3) higher wages and job security, the current broadening of socialist party programs is a political necessity—as much a necessity as the downgrading of traditional goals like extensive nationalization of industry. The net effect, of course, is to produce a type of democratic social-reform party, in place of the old class-oriented structures. This has been a logical enough evolution, for as one perceptive student wrote as early as 1923, in what was probably the first (and one of the few) comparative surveys of Western European labor movements: "The tendency of modern Socialism towards democratization is remarkable. In fact Socialism is gradually changing from a *class movement into a social movement*."[22]

While it is difficult to generalize as between union movements, there may be some evidence that new ideas and programs are more easily accepted in labor federations where the union's brother organization, the labor or socialist party, has had a role or share in governing the country over a long period. For example, there was a constant stream of concerned criticism (some of it self-criticism) directed at the British *Trades Union Congress* during the 1951–1964 period when the Labour Party was not in power. Such attacks are not leveled against the relatively strong and high-prestige union movement in Sweden where a socialist government has ruled since 1932. Nor do such attacks occur in Norway and Denmark, where socialist governments have been the general order of the day most of the time since World War II.[23]

The trade unions, because they are so solidly and largely based on the manual working class, often have a more difficult time than the parties in making this transition toward accepting new ideas. They are under less immediate pressure to make "adjustments," since they have been appealing for the most part to a fairly consistent, even if *relatively* declining, clientele.

Because of their occupational positions, manual workers, as compared with other groups, may have more difficulty in coping with the new economic society and technology in postwar Europe. In turn they may be less receptive to, or have less understanding of, the new policies needed to cope with these changes. Allan Touraine says that this has been the case in France, where technicians and very highly skilled workers, who are closer to the new technology, have a much livelier awareness of new policy needs. Because they are less receptive and understanding, manual workers may slow down the evolution of necessary policy changes in the labor-union federations that they dominate.[24]

Where the main line of union organization has been closely confined to (or has been successful primarily among) limited manual-worker groups, the movement runs the danger of falling into a kind of isolation. It can be isolated from the new, rapidly expanding white-collar forces on the one hand and, on the other, from a large mass of low-paid, hard-to-organize, nonservice workers. To some extent this has happened in the United States (and perhaps Britain), where union density is low compared, for example, with that of the Scandinavian or Austrian union movements. Under these conditions the union movement may be in danger of ceasing to be the engine for social innovation that it has been in the past. This would tend to be the case as the mass character of the movement declined in the modern, integrated welfare society of today. Needless to say, this is a slow process and hard to measure.

A comparison of Germany and Austria yields some support for the influence of these factors on union outlook and development. The major union movements in both these countries were somewhat depoliticalized in the post-World War II period, in that official ties with the socialist parties were broken. Informal ties have been maintained, however, and in the case of Austria the party-union cooperation, especially at the top officer level, is still close.

The Austrian Socialist Party has shared political power most of the time since World War II, and union officials have held important government posts. This seems to have been a factor in keeping the Austrian Federation of Labor from falling into the kind of stagnation that has somewhat disturbed the German Trade Union Federation (DGB). The much greater density of the Austrian union movement—and the large nonmanual membership (compared to Germany) relative to the total work force—may also have kept it a more central and moving force in society.[25]

Here again, one of the variables seems to be the fact that the Austrian Socialist Party has been ruling in coalition during most of the post-World War II period.

As for other European countries, it is more difficult to generalize on this theme. And I quickly add that even in the cases of Britain, Scandinavia, Germany, and Austria many other factors must be introduced for a complete explanation of union "health" in these years. But it would seem that the assumption of government leadership and responsibility that goes with a socialist party government may help or compel the union side of the socialist complex to face problems of policy and structure more squarely—problems that might otherwise be put off. Needless to say, any labor movement has certain obvious advantages—for instance, in membership appeal—when "its" government is in power.

The acceptance of a national wage policy by the British Trades Union Congress, once the Labour Government came to power late in 1964, is an example of facing a problem more "squarely." Whether an incomes policy was good or bad, or workable, it certainly had become widely believed in Britain that the establishment of an incomes policy was necessary to help overcome the nation's balance-of-payments crisis. Yet the unions would hardly have accepted this, even temporarily, if a Labour government had not been in power. Even under a Labour government the unions have chafed and threatened to go their own way.

To mention again the general pattern of loosening (though not necessarily severing) party-union relationships, which we have found characteristic in a number of countries after World War II, it can probably be judged a logical one. The pluralistic, bargaining type of society that we have been describing (Chapter IV) demands that key bargaining institutions (whether unions, professional groups, farm or business organizations) retain much of their own particular character and identity, as opposed to governments, even as they participate in wider economic and social synthesis decision making.

Predictions about further changes in working-class outlook and life style are hazardous to undertake. It is even more hazardous to predict the effect of such changes upon labor unions and labor parties.

For example it is almost surprising how little the impact of automation and major technological change, has changed traditional union forms and·outlook to date. This is probably because any dislocating effects have largely been offset by the relatively good employment conditions that have prevailed in most Western countries for the past two decades. In part the seeming lack of change in unionism may also stem from the fact that many of the newest unionists, such as professionals, white-collar workers, and public employees, are often in newer unions that lie outside the older, large federations. Any important differences in outlook and attitudes which these newer union groups may have are as yet having no serious impact upon the federations. In the long run this occupational change in the labor force and the nature of union membership is almost certain to have significant repercussions on the policies of the entire labor movement.

Again in the long run, and perhaps not so long in the United States, the more secure economic environment already referred to may well help undermine some traditional union attitudes. There already is some evidence that today's younger worker, having experienced nothing but a fairly good job market in his life, may be less interested in the traditional forms of security and more interested in income now. In addition, many of these new workers may also have more interest in programs that increase their mobility and promotion prospects. This is somewhat in contrast to the older worker and most union leaders, who are drawn from the older worker group. The latter group is more likely to be influenced by memories of the great insecurity in employment and income experienced in the pre-World War II era.[26] In another ten years or so, the work force will be overwhelmingly drawn from those who joined it after World War II. The effects upon union policy could be considerable.

N O T E S

1. Ferdynand Zweig, *The Worker in an Affluent Society* (London: Heineman, 1961), *passim*.

2. M. Van de Vall, "Trade Unions in the Welfare State as Seen by Their Members," *Trade Union Information*, No. 38 (Paris: n.d. *ca.* 1962), pp. 3–8.

3. J. J. de Bruin, "The Trade Union Movement in a Society in Process of Organization," *Trade Union Information, ibid.*, pp. 9–13. On the gap between leaders and union members in The Netherlands, also see G. Kuiper, "Dutch Trade Unions and Sociological Research: Some Recent Studies," *Sociologica Nederlandica* (Winter 1966–1967), p. 43. A former union functionary has written complainingly that the membership has less and less to do with union bargaining, and he also complains about the way in which dependence on experts (for pensions, health plans, etc.) in labor-management negotiations is reducing the membership's role in American union life. See George W. Brooks, *The Sources of Vitality in the American Labor Movement* Bulletin 41 (Ithaca: N.Y. School of Industrial and Labor Relations, Cornell University, 1960), pp. 25–27.

4. An Australian scholar has observed that in his country the "acceptance of full employment as a permanent feature in our economy" has tended to obscure "the classic purposes of unionism . . . the lifting of the economic standard of the membership and secondly the protection of the individual unionist against arbitrary action by his employer." With full employment assured, workers are no longer fearful of employer reprisals because other jobs are to be had. He does find that as greater security and benefits are extended to the manual worker, the white collar employee feels his traditionally "social and economic position" is slipping. As a consequence, unionism grows as a force in white collar or nonmanual employment, even as it declines, to some degree, among manuals. I. G. Sharp, "Trade Unionism in 1967," *The Journal of Industrial Relations*, March 1968.

5. S. M. Miller and Frank Riessman, "The Working Class Subculture: A New View," *Social Problems*, Summer 1961, and by the same authors, "Are Workers Middle Class?" *Dissent*, Autumn 1961.

6. David Lockwood, "The 'New' Working Class," *European Journal of Sociology*, 1961, pp. 248–259; and John H. Goldthorpe and David Lockwood, "Affluence and the British Class Structure," *The Sociological Review*, July 1963, pp. 133–163.

7. On the current situation see a new study, in depth, of industrial workers in one major British industrial center by John H. Goldthorpe, David Lockwood, Frank Bechhofer and Jennifer Platt, *The Affluent Worker: Industrial Attitudes and Behavior* (Cambridge: University Press, 1968). It seems to point to some continued "separateness" of the working class, with a sense of alienation as regards their work despite relatively good pay and very low participation in trade union affairs. On the political attitudes of the workers covered in this relatively new industrial center, see the same authors' *The Affluent Worker: Political Attitudes and Behavior* (Cambridge: University Press, 1968).

8. See Richard Hamilton, "Affluence and the Worker: The West German Case," *American Journal of Sociology*, September 1965, pp. 144–152.

9. See *La Nouvelle Classe Ouvrière*, Editions Du Seuil (Paris, 1963), especially the Introduction and Chapters I and II.

10. Gavin Mackenzie, "The Economic Dimensions of Embourgeoisement," *The British Journal of Sociology*, March 1967, p. 42.

11. Quoted in Kurt Mayer, "The Changing Shape of the American Class Structure," *Social Research*, Winter 1963, p. 459. Also see Mayer's useful short volume, *Class and Society* (New York: Random House, 1955).

12. *Trade Unions in a Changing Society*, PEP (Political and Economic Planning), No. 472 June 10, 1963, p. 187; and *Trade Union Membership*, PEP, No. 463 July 2, 1962, p. 156. For the longer period 1948–1964, Guy Routh estimates that the density of British manual unionism declined from 53 to 51%, while white-collar density rose very slightly. See his chapter on British white-collar unions, Adolf Sturmthal (ed.), *White Collar Trade Unions* (Urbana: University of Illinois Press, 1966).

13. As this has affected U.S. union membership, see my chapter in Sturmthal, *op. cit.*, and my article "Canadian and U.S. White Collar Union Increases," in the *Monthly Labor Review*, U.S. Department of Labor, July 1968.

14. *Union Membership Hits All Time Peak in 1966*, News from U.S. Department of Labor, September 4, 1967.

15. See *The Report of the AFL-CIO Executive Council, to the Seventh Convention, AFL-CIO*, Bal Harbour, Florida, December 7, 1967 (Washington, D.C.: American Federation of Labor and Congress of Industrial Organizations, 1967), pp. 35–38.

16. The general source for these tables has been *SII*, the semimonthly publication of the Socialist International, London. For the period prior to 1951, and in

one or two other elections, we have consulted newspapers or journals, in instances where the data was not available in *SII*.

17. The tone of the preceding analysis of the current status of European socialist parties may be a bit too optimistic. Possibly, along with *all* major existing parties, European labor and socialist parties in some countries may be challenged by a new generation just coming of age in the new, affluent Europe. Such seems to have been the case, in part, in the Dutch election of early 1967 (see "The Challenge Dutch Labour Faces," *SII*, April 15, 1967). Moreover, with the possible exception of Great Britain, Norway, and Sweden, the labor-socialist parties seem to be "stuck" at a percentage vote of from 25 to 42%, with little prospect of going beyond this. This, in turn, means they usually must rule as a coalition; but this has been true for many decades and is probably, by now, part of the socialist way of life in a multi-party (as opposed to a predominantly two-party) system.

18. Mattei Dogan, "Le Vote ouvrier en Europe Occidentale," *Revue Française de Sociologie*, 1960, I, 32–34. Working class is here defined to include *manual* workers in industry, transport, and mines, but not in agriculture.

19. *Ibid*. In this interesting monograph Dogan suggests many other factors that affect working-class voting patterns in European countries.

20. Kurt L. Shell, *The Transformation of Austrian Socialism* (Albany: State University of New York, 1962), p. 46.

21. *Socialist Commentary*, August 1964, p. 38. Also see Leslie Smith, *Harold Wilson*, (London: Fontana Books, 1964), pp. 192–193; and Harold Wilson, *Purpose in Politics*, Selected Speeches by Harold Wilson, (Boston: Houghton Mifflin, 1964), especially Speech Opening the Science Debate at the Party's Annual Conference, Scarborough, 1963, pp. 14–28.

22. B. G. de Montgomery, *British and Continental Labour Policy* (London: Oxford University Press, 1923), p. 284. (Italics added.)

23. On the critique of British unions see, for example, Michael Shanks, *The Stagnant Society* (London: Penguin Books-A555, 1961), esp. Chaps. 4 and 5. Also Eric Wigham, *What's Wrong with the Unions* (London: Penguin Books-S196, 1961). Numerous articles in the *Economist, New Statesman*, and the *Sunday Observer* also attest to the "concern" about the British union movement. Some of these criticisms of the trade unions have continued under the Labour government. For the other side of the argument (namely that trade unions have become too consensus minded, not militant enough, and too easily manipulated by government), see Robin Blackburn and Alexander Cockburn (eds.), *The Incompatibles: Trade Union Militancy and Consensus* (London: Penguin Books, 1967).

24. Allan Touraine, "Management and the Working Class," *Daedalus*, Winter 1964.

25. In the face of membership stagnation, however, DGB unions have had a very considerable influence on the strong upward movement of wages in Germany in recent years. See Burkart Lutz, "Les Syndicats Allemands Au Début Des Années 60," *Sociologie du Travail*, January–March 1964, pp. 63–79.

26. Several years ago the writer, while teaching at a union training institute, was caught between opposing sides arguing the merits of union agreement clauses protecting seniority. Two young workers from the lithography industry, employed in shops which had known nothing but expansion as long as they were employed there, almost seemed mystified by the concern about seniority provisions. They simply couldn't fathom the importance that older auto, rubber, steel, and textile unionists were giving to negotiating seniority clauses to provide orderly procedures for layoffs and rehiring in American industry. It is difficult to believe that the new sense of freedom and protest so common in the current generation of college students in so many countries will not have some significant counterpart in tomorrow's work force.

VI

Deviations from the Pattern: French Trade Unionism

As we have already indicated, labor movements in some European countries did not undergo the process of integration that we have been describing. Union development in the so-called Latin countries of Southern Europe, France, Italy, and Spain has followed somewhat different lines.

The bulk of the working classes in these countries, to use the contemporarily popular "Marxist" term, remains to a significant degree "alienated" from the mainstream and the institutions of their societies. In France and Italy this is manifested by the fact that communist-led trade unions and political parties are present in, or dominate, main sections of the working class. (Spain belongs with France and Italy in the context of this chapter, but on the basis of its pre-Civil War history. Under the Franco dictatorship, the problem is quite different.) Working-class alienation is also manifested by the failure of these societies to develop a mass, *continuously effective* trade-union movement of the type that emerged well before World War II, as the industrial representative of the working classes everywhere else in Western Europe.

The reasons for the continued alienated state, even to the present day, of the French and Italian working classes are, of course, deeply related to the social, economic, and political histories of their countries. Moreover, although the patterns of labor development in these countries differ considerably from one another, the similarities suggest many common social, economic, and political influences.

Needless to say, the French and Italian working classes are hardly as revolutionary or as alienated as they appeared to be several decades back. George Lichtheim has suggested that the highly bureaucratized French Communist Party, in a certain ponderous way, is helping the integration of French workers into modern industrial society in a far better way than pre-World War I anarcho-syndicalism.[1] Anyone familiar with unions and working-class political parties must still see a clear-cut distinction, however, between the Latin union patterns and those elsewhere in Western Europe, the United States, Canada, or in "Western"-style countries such as Australia and New Zealand.

We shall here confine our analysis primarily to the French pattern, with only corroborating references to Italy (and to a lesser extent, Spain). With respect to the differences between France and Italy, while French economic development until the past two decades can be said to have been behind in relation to that of Germany or England, Italy was so far behind Western Europe in general that until recent decades it was virtually a less-developed nation. Working-class alienation or "leftism" is in some ways, therefore, a less complex matter to explain in Italy than it is in France. This conclusion presumes that as Italy catches up economically its labor unions and parties will probably fall in more closely with the general pattern of European development.

Our main purpose at the moment is to point up—and, for clarity, perhaps even overemphasize—the ways in which France is an exception to the general pattern of Western European union development. In many technical aspects, French unionism cannot with complete accuracy be treated separately from industrial relations to the degree we do here. For broad analytical purposes, however, such treatment can be justified.

Persistence of "Leftism" in French Labor

One of the first things that strikes any foreign observer of the French labor scene is the remarkable persistence within it of leftism. In this respect, taking just the post-World War II years, it is amazing how little workers seem to change despite great prosperity (from the 1950s on), great political upheaval (the struggle against the Marshall Plan by the communists, which split the labor movement in 1948), and the like.

Table 3 shows the percentage of votes cast for candidates of each of the trade-union federations in elections in which workers selected their representatives to the governing boards of the social-security administrative bodies in France. The unions that put up candidates are the Confédération Générale du Travail (CGT), communist-dominated; the Confédération Française des Travailleurs Chrétiens (CFTC), identified here as the Christian workers union movement (in 1964 this federation changed its name and dropped any formal "Christian" references from its constitution; it will, however, hereafter be identified by its new title Confédération Française Democratique du Travail—CFDT); Force Ouvrière (FO), the free trade-union movement, sometimes described (not too accurately) as socialist-oriented; Confédération Générale des Cadres (CGC), nonpolitical union of Technicians and Supervisors, and the Mutualité, labor-oriented insurance societies.

TABLE 3. *Social Security Elections (1950 and 1962)*
Percentage of Votes by Worker Groups

	1950	1962
CGT	43.5	44.3
CFTC	21.3	21.0
FO	15.2	14.7
Mutual Insurance Societies	11.1	8.7
CGC	—	4.6
Miscellaneous	8.9	6.6

SOURCES: 1950 election: Val R. Lorwin, *The French Labor Movement* (Cambridge, Mass.: Harvard University Press, 1954), p. 179; 1962 election: Eugène Descamps, *Évolution et Perspectives,* Rapport Présenté au Congrès Confédéral Extraordinaire de la C.F.T.C. (Paris, 1964), p. 90.

Even in the greatest era of economic expansion in French history, with the working class entering the automobile and appliance age, the leftist outlook of French workers is quite unchanged—just as it was unchanged by the death and subsequent exposure of Stalin and by the discrediting of communism that seemed to occur after the Soviet invasion of Hungary. Moreover (to anticipate a possible "explanation"), the French Communist Party has changed relatively little in the past decade as compared, say, to the Italian Communist Party which has "modernized" its programs and appeals considerably. We shall be discussing trade-union development primarily; but it should also be noted that the French Communist Party has been more "traditional" and always more "slavish" in accepting Moscow leadership than any other mass communist party. While many factors enter into the explanation of the cautious, almost conservative conduct of the French communists in the face of the near-revolutionary situation that occurred among workers and students in the mass strikes of the spring of 1968, among these explanatory factors seems to have been Moscow's general satisfaction with President de Gaulle's foreign policy and its fear of what type of a regime would succeed, if he was overturned.

Clearly, we have the task of explaining a phenomenon that has deep historical roots. And as with most historical problems, its origins are interrelated. To set forth and to examine these origins is necessarily a somewhat arbitrary matter; however, the fact that they are interrelated must be kept in mind.

Political Development

French labor (including French unionism) has been cast into a left mold of thought and action by a converging set of political forces and institutions.

Europe's revolutionary tradition has, naturally enough, burned most brightly in France, the home of the modern revolution. So great and cataclysmic was this change, so far-reaching its influence upon all Europe, that it was more "natural" for many sectors of French society, especially the working class, to come to regard revolution as the normal instrument of social change. Any would-be left-wing labor leaders—socialist, anarchist, or communist—can always call upon the revolutionary tradition to rationalize a modern-day revolutionary program.

Contrast this sharp decisive event, the French Revolution of 1789 and its impact upon modern political development with the slow, gradual evolution of democracy and social change that characterized Great Britain or Switzerland.

Although the French Revolution is sometimes regarded as the touchstone of modern European liberty, political scientists such as Hans Khon and Karl Jaspers have pointed out that the revolution came out of traditions of absolutist monarchy and the feudal system. The revolution, while it "desired liberty and reason," at the same time was based on "despotism and force." To the extent that "it makes us think that the world as a whole can be established by force or reason alone, instead of on the rational transformation of historical values and order," democracy in France was and is less stable, less firmly rooted than in England or Switzerland.[2]

Also, the revolution twisted France from a monarchistic, absolutist centralism into a highly centralized republican state. In fact, the French government since Napoleon I has tended to be even more centralized than the *ancien régime*. Local self-government was permanently crippled, and the critical opportunity for people to relate locally and more directly to democratic governmental processes has been almost entirely lacking.[3]

In turn, the central state came to be looked upon as an all-powerful patron. The manner in which it acted under these conditions, and the way in which it became discredited in the eyes of the masses, is well described by Richard Lowenthal:

The absence of effective self-government has its counterpart in the system of local political clienteles. What cannot be obtained as a right through the Commune, local government, must be obtained as a favor from the Central Government. The parliamentarian who cannot control the bureaucrat but may overthrow the Government must be appeased by many favors to his constituents.

Most of these favors took the form of special privileges for the rising capitalist groups. Lowenthal adds:

Along with tariff protection, a host of privileges have been granted to cartels and monopolies, often headed by hereditary bourgeois "dynasties" with family members in Parliament. Up to 1914, the biggest fortunes in France, with few exceptions, were not made in industry, but in operations of *haute finance* depending on Government favour. At the same time, the bulk of public revenue came from the pockets of the poor in the form of taxes on mass consumption.[4]

It is not surprising that these conditions made the French citizen profoundly cynical toward his state. (Lowenthal also notes that these same conditions prevailed in Italy.) While the democratic state came to be regarded as the "expression of society" elsewhere in the West, in France it came to be regarded "as a parasite in society. The attitude of the upper classes, except in emergencies—and at the end also in emergencies —was one of cynicism and irresponsibility. Permissible resistance to the State ranged from ordinary tax fraud to anarchism."[5]

As a consequence, most trade-union movements in the European Latin countries grew up with antigovernment philosophies, notably syndicalism. While the other European labor movements, with close cooperation between unions and socialist parties, went forward to transform their societies, "the syndicalist counter-society of the Latin countries failed to grow"; social reform lagged, thereby keeping the worker alienated and outside the main workings of his society. In the development, for example, of a modern social-security system, France lagged well behind virtually all of its Western European neighbors.

Suffrage was attained in France in 1848 and was maintained thereafter (except for 1850–1851). Attained at an early date as compared with other European countries, and under the governmental circumstances described above, it seemed, curiously enough, only to reinforce the cynicism of the workers toward the state, which remained very unresponsive to their needs and desires. A similar situation in Spain, according to Hugh Thomas, led to a similar labor philosophy of syndicalism and to an antistatist, antipolitical posture:

. . . Universal male suffrage was nominally introduced in 1890. But the results of the election were always faked through the agency of the local political bosses, the "caciques." The mass of the people in Spain thereupon came to look upon the parliamentary system as a means of excluding them from all political articulation. This was one reason for the spread of syndical ideas throughout the working classes . . . for the Anarchists of the CNT [Spanish Federation of Labor] the regime was something unclean.[6]

Additional political factors in France intensified the antiparty, antiparliamentarianism of French workers and unions. During the crucial closing years of the nineteenth and early twentieth centuries, the French Socialist Party was deeply divided into several warring factions. This violent party factionalism also disrupted trade-union organization and turned many union leaders against cooperation with any political party.

Times seem indeed to have been "out of joint" as one views French labor's political development. Caught up in disgust with the faction-ridden Socialist Party, already under the influence of syndicalist philosophy, the French unions affirmed their antistatism and antipartyism in the famous Charter of Amiens in 1906. This charter was not simply a declaration of political neutrality, "but a declaration of distrust with regard to all political organization." The same philosophy barely accepted collective agreements and also saw "all social legislation as a poisoned gift."[7]

As the Socialist Party finally began to achieve unity in the period before World War I, some of its leaders looked to an alliance with the central labor federation, the Confédération Générale du Travail; but the leadership of the latter (over the objections of some reforming socialist elements within it) scorned such a political alliance, as they recalled the disruptive factionalism of the party in earlier years. It need hardly be said that the fate of this proposed pattern of party-union cooperation was in sharp contrast to what had long since become the general trend elsewhere in Western Europe.

During the 1920s reformists (as opposed to revolutionary syndicalist elements) gained control in the CGT most of whose revolutionary extreme leftist forces had moved into a new communist-controlled union movement. These reformists sought to bring about a wide political democratic left alliance (Cartel des Gauches) centering on the Socialist Party and the Radical Socialist Party (a left-tending, middle-class party in this period). At this point, however, the Socialist Party was now in its classical stand of nonparticipation in bourgeois governments, and it refused to participate in such a new democratic alignment. Once more hopes were frustrated for far-reaching democratic social reform that might have helped integrate the French working class more fully into society.[8]

Politically Divisive Effect of Church Policies

The very decisiveness of the French Revolution, its sharp break with the past, made it impossible for numerous groups and institutions in French society to digest it.

During the nineteenth century, the revolution was a positive, shining source of inspiration among French workers. But among the upper classes and the Catholic Church it was an object of scorn and dislike.

As for the Church, its resistance in France to "democracy" and social reform around 1848 deepened the anticlericalism of large groups of workers.[9] Moreover, while it was not and is hardly the monolith it is sometimes made out to be, the Church in the nineteenth century in France, as compared with, say, Belgium, was more resistant to modernism and contributed to the already abundant divisive forces in French life.[10]

In one other important respect the state-established and state-supported Church seems to have brought the working classes to a more lasting revolutionary, apocalyptic outlook—and not only in France but in other countries as well. Writing of Italy, Maurice Neufeld notes that the misery of the Italian workers produced a reaction of intense frustration and, against a background of apocalyptic religion, bred a philosophy of apocalyptic revolution:

When an atmosphere of religious authoritarianism hovers over the orthodoxies which support these evils [social and economic], then countervailing doctrines of universal, apocalyptic solutions to economic and social distress find it possible to enjoy easy acceptance. Inured to dependence, Italian workers would receive such revelations from above as in the natural order of affairs. . . . With simple faith learned from their traditional religion, they believed implicitly that they could earn economic justice for themselves by hastening a foreordained fiery day of social judgment.[11]

Hugh Thomas argues a somewhat similar impact of the Church on the "ideology" of Spanish workers, and the relatively easy process of going from one faith (Catholicism) to another (collective revolution). He writes:

For the conversion of the working class of Spain to revolutionary ideas, the Church, which was to suffer so much in consequence, had paradoxically prepared the way. The Church's anti-commercialism, its puritan hostility to the competitive instinct, particularly of its Spanish practitioners and apologists, made the ideas of Fanelli (a Bakunin-style anarchist activist in Spain) seem merely an honest continuation of the old faith.[12]

Thomas also notes that the "religious character of Spain also made the converts to the new collectivism, as it had made the liberals, more passionate, less ready to compromise, more obstinate than other groups in Europe."

Although there are major differences between the Church in Spain and in France, Thomas' description of the religious-like passion with which political beliefs are held and defended in Spain does sound suspiciously French in character also!

Finally, common to France, Italy, and Spain where Catholicism is or has been the officially government-supported religion, is the eternal struggle for control of the system of education. The question of state support or nonsupport of church schools, particularly in France, continues to divide democratic forces in a manner that one who has not lived in the country can hardly understand. This division continues long after the Church has shifted away from its nineteenth-century opposition to democratic government and modern social and economic reform.

As we look back upon the "special" social and political forces that have molded France (and many of the forces we have been describing continue to have impact even today), what strikes us most is that they have prevented any broad social or political consensus. It is not that in other European countries there are no serious "differences" between workers and employers and between some groups of workers and the Church. But the deep lack of any general consensus about the desirable form and values of the society appears to make for a continued divisiveness in French life that we do not find in most of the other Western countries.

Anarchist Influences on French Labor Ideology

It is possible, of course, to be too institutional and deterministic about the persistent, revolutionary outlook of French labor. The somewhat fortuitous circumstance that a large number of anarchist leaders and theorists converged upon France in the last decades of the nineteenth century is not to be underestimated.

The anarchists in France in the 1880s and 1890s had the advantage of operating in a relatively free society, and they made headway. This contrasts with what happened in Germany, where the anarchists found it difficult to advance, hampered as they were by the restrictions imposed by the government's antisocialist laws.[13]

A good number of anarchists decided to enter and penetrate the new trade-union movement in France. Ferdinand Pelloutier, an anarchist leader, quickly emerged as a leading figure and theoretician of the trade-union movement. He typifies the transformation from anarchism to that peculiar brand of trade unionism, anarcho-syndicalism, that became predominant in pre-World War I France.[14]

In the background, too, was the strong influence of anarchist-philosopher Pierre Proudhon, whose intellectual impact upon nineteenth-century thought in France was stronger in many ways than that of the German Karl Marx. It is difficult, however, to say which is cause and effect here, France or Proudhon![15]

The net result was to produce a special brand of revolutionary thought among unionized workers. Unlike the mainstream of most European workers' movements, French unions turned away from the pattern of union-socialist party cooperation that led to an evolutionary kind of social reform. They hoped to achieve the new socialist society exclusively by means of revolutionary trade unionism—in short, through syndicalism. The new society would be built without state intervention (this is the usual anarchist image) and without dependence upon a relationship with political parties. Lowenthal points out that syndicalism can be revolutionary or reformist, but its antipolitical, antistatist qualities are clear-cut. During part of its early history the AFL harbored a suspicion of government intervention in social and economic affairs that smacked of syndicalism.[16]

In addition to the special political and social forces we have been describing, France's usual class barriers and sentiments (which also existed elsewhere in European society around the turn of the century) made a revolutionary type of syndicalism more probable.

Economic Forces Encourage Left Tendencies

The slow rate of capitalist development in France around and after 1900, as compared to that in other Western European countries such as Great Britain, Belgium, and Germany, also accentuated discontent among French workers.[17]

Sluggish economic growth works in two ways to keep a working class alienated from modern, integrated development. On the one hand, the society fails to meet the workers' expectations for higher income, and on the other hand it relegates the workers to employment in older enterprises, under more obsolete working conditions, with more tradition-bound employers (in France these were small family-style employers who often retained feudal notions). Such industrial conditions restrain the growth of unionism and keep it weaker. They reduce the effectiveness of working-class action for economic and social reform. As a result the working class remains less integrated in the society and becomes more revolutionary in character.[18]

The wider diffusion of property and the existence of a very large lower middle class in France tended also to produce a pervasive, petty-bourgeois, property-conscious social atmosphere in which unionism found it hard to grow. Although it is difficult to "prove," it would also appear that the French employer classes seemed more resistant on principle to modernism and unionism than employers in most other European countries. Indeed, what Neufeld writes of Italy was also largely true of France:

. . . regional diversity . . . the overwhelmingly agricultural nature of the work force . . . the obduracy of industrialists. . . . This sense of hopelessness and betrayal opened the minds of workers to every drift of revolutionary political dogma.[19]

A more rigid, tradition-bound, less compromising owner class comes up against a more revolutionary, tradition-bound working class, and the tendency is for each to be reinforced in its uncompromising philosophy.

French Industrial Structure Encourages Syndicalist Reaction

The prevalence of a small-workshop, artisan type of production in much of France well into the twentieth century provided fertile ground for syndicalist thought and unionism. Anarcho-syndicalism, with its sublime faith in the ability of unionized workers to transform their society at the workshop level through their own direct action, is singularly related to an economy of predominantly small-shop production. It rests, really, on faith in the ability of skilled, unionized workers to take over, control, and organize the country's production and the society on the basis of autonomous small shops. It should be added that the basic strength of French unionism in the pre-World War I period lay in the skilled craft workers.

One finds analogies with this state of economic development and an anarcho-syndical form of organization in other Latin countries. A study of unionism in Argentina, Brazil, and Chile concludes that:

During the first period of the history of labor in all three countries, the trade union movement existed principally among the craftsmen rather than factory workers. There was a marked tendency toward anarchist influence among the unions and toward a highly decentralized form of organization.[20]

A historian of French trade unionism has observed of syndicalism that its "ideal corresponds with a multiplicity of small workshops and offices, rather than to large factories" with the skilled unionized workers acting as the elitist vanguard for the masses. But this ideal "is against the main current of [modern] economic development."[21]

To the extent that France was backward in economic development, especially before World War I, it fostered a syndicalist kind of worker reaction. Syndicalism, too, is backward-looking in its ideal of autonomously run, cooperating workshops as the economic base for society. It shares in the general anarchist ideology of individual freedom within a more simple way of life that has little relevance to modern economic society.[22]

As modern mass production overtook France, particularly from World War I on, anarcho-syndicalism became even less relevant. The very base of trade unionism, the skilled crafts in pre-World War France, was eroded under these circumstances, for, "If craft ceases to be the real link among trade unionists, where is one to find the means of giving them the necessary cohesion?"[23] The failure of the French labor movement to provide any sort of enduring unionism for the mass of new unskilled and semi-skilled industrial workers was to be one of its distinguishing characteristics right down to the 1930s.[24] The Popular Front period of the late 1930s saw a great upsurge in French unionism among the new mass-production industries. But this upsurge consisted of the spontaneous outbreaks so characteristic of the French labor scene; it was not part of an ever-continuing stream of effective unionism.

A recent study of the Popular Front period distinguishes two main types of unionism: (1) the new industrial unionism of the large industrial sectors, which "carried more toward action than organization" and was

"capable of sudden upheavals," and (2) the unionism "of the more traditionally set wage earners, much better unionized and more stable in its
numbers."[25]

Michel Collinet has described the spontaneous way in which the
millions of new unionists acted, often without any dependence on the
older trade unions and leaders, in the wave of the 1936 mass strikes.
Much of this went on as "if the workers had no confidence in the (old)
unions . . . for them (the workers) the important conversations were
those they had directly with their employers." Often the strikers would
merely "request the local union organization for a speaker to explain
what the C.G.T. was demanding"; they would "thank him with sympathy"
and go on their own with a list of demands to the employer.[26]

The general failure to achieve successful, continuous mass unionism,
even after the widespread sitdown strikes of the 1930s, left French workers as "alienated" as ever from their society—this at the very time when
mass unionism was completing its integrating role in most of the other
countries of Western Europe. (Spain and Italy, of course, also remained
exceptions in this process of integration—but for some of the same as
well as other reasons.)[27]

Syndicalism to Communism: The Logic of Leftism

Revolutionary syndicalism, like revolutionary socialism, was largely shattered by World War I and its aftermath. French syndicalist leaders, like
socialists in other European countries, by and large succumbed to nationalist pressures. Along with the mass of workers they came to support
their country's war effort. After syndicalism "betrayed" its traditional
antiwar ideology, many French workers lost confidence in it as a revolutionary force.

The great industrial changes that were already bringing modern
factory production into France were accelerated during the war and in
succeeding decades, and syndicalism, which rested on an antique, backward, simplistic appeal, became even more obsolete.

A large part of the French labor movement now went firmly over
to reformist, socialist ideology. (This ideology had been gaining ground
among French unionists before World War I.)

But the tradition and appeal of revolution was by no means dead.
Many of the forces and ideas already referred to in this chapter were still
operative in France. Almost inevitably, the communists became the in-
heritors of the old revolutionary tradition.

While the communists formed their own political party, they were
able to capitalize on the old "revolutionary" tradition of opposition to a
government "discredited" in the eyes of many French workers. During

most of its history the French communist movement, although it runs candidates and participates in elections (which of course implies the desire to be part of the government) has posed as the would-be destroyer of the "corrupt" French republic and the government.

As might also be expected of the European country where the tradition of revolution burns most brightly, there has been a wide affinity and sympathy for the Russian Revolution. Communists have played upon this at will.

Curiously enough, the tradition of the French Revolution has also helped the communists from slipping into a position of revolutionary isolation in French politics. Basic in French democratic life has been the old revolutionary notion of "no enemies to the left." In most times of crisis, when any real or imagined threat to the republican democracy has appeared from the right, socialist or middle-class forces often seek added strength by opening their ranks even to the communist who but the day before might have been declaiming against the same democratic regime. This has served to bestow upon the communists a recurring legitimacy in French life without, however, compromising their traditional, revolutionary appeal to large masses of alienated workers.

Some of the basic beliefs of French syndicalism helped ease the transfer of workers' allegiance from syndicalism to communism. In both ideologies there is a strong emphasis upon the role of what Lenin called the revolutionary vanguard—and what syndicalist writers called the revolutionary elite—to lead the workers' revolution. In both Lenin and the syndicalists there is a distrust of the large masses of workers, who cannot ordinarily be expected to comprehend the needs and dictates of revolutionary tactics and programs. Emile Pouget, a leading syndicalist theoretician, sounds almost like Lenin in his call to this elite:

The conscious minority will act without waiting for non-class conscious masses whom the spirit of revolt has not yet aroused; as a consequence one can consider the mass as having a zero numerical force. . . . Here one can distinguish between the enormous differences in methods of syndicalism and democracy. The latter by means of universal suffrage gives leadership to the unthinking, to the retarded (or better to their representatives) and smothers the minorities who carry in themselves the real future. The syndicalist method gives a result of diametrically opposed; the drive is imposed by the class conscious activists, the revolutionaries are called to participate in the movement.[28]

Pouget sounds like Lenin in that his remarks are almost an echo of Lenin's famous *What Is To Be Done?* with its attack on the mere "economism" of the trade-union masses and his highlighting of the role of the revolutionary spirit or movement. For Lenin the task of bringing "class political consciousness . . . to the workers" fell to the party vanguard.[29]

Beyond the revolutionary vanguard concept, some of Lenin's classic formulation of the coercive nature of the state and its ultimate "withering away" under communism are what Adam Ulam has called "anarcho-syndicalist rather than Marxist." Lenin's very language has at times the tone of simplistic, anarchistic optimism as he sketches the future. Thus:

It is perfectly possible immediately within twenty four hours after the overthrow of the capitalists and bureaucrats to replace them in the control of production and distribution in the business of control of labour and products, by the armed workers, by the whole people in arms. . . . All citizens become employees and workers of one national state "syndicate." All that is required is that they should work equally, should regularly do their share of work, and should receive equal pay.[30]

The Communist International played heavily upon the "revolutionary" tone and slogans of syndicalism in hurling its appeals at European workers in the years immediately following World War I. The communists scorned the "Anglo-Saxon" unions (Great Britain and the United States) for their "non-political" and "neutral attitude towards" socialism, and because of their "concentration of efforts on immediate and concrete problems."

As for the Austro-Germanic movement, while it "was impregnated with socialist ideas from its inception," its reformist tactics soon robbed the unions of any capability of "revolutionary action."[31] But of a more revolutionary syndicalist kind of unionism, while the communists sitting in Moscow had some criticisms, they could and did declare:

Revolutionary trade unionism proclaimed—and herein lies its merit—a number of ideas which showed it to be on a higher level than the other forms of the trade union movement, and which likened it to revolutionary socialism [i.e., communism], the ideas of direct action, pressure brought to bear on capital and the State by the masses, and the overthrow of capitalism by social revolution, do great honor to the revolutionary trade unions, and constitute the practical side of their general principles.

The communists went on to add that they could also "agree with the anarcho-syndicalists concerning class aims, the revolutionary tactics to be adopted, and the direct action of one class against another."[32]

Even on those occasions when the officials of the Communist International criticized the syndicalists for failing to understand the necessity for highly centralized political action on behalf of the revolution, they could and did identify themselves with certain historic appeals of syndicalism. For example, in a letter to trade unions in all countries they scorned the "collective agreement system which meant in fact that the agreements were concluded by the bureaucratic bosses, and kept the workers covered by the agreements in chains for several years." And they insisted that unions must be regarded not "as organizations designed to win partial improvements within the capitalist system," but rather "as organizations aiming at the revolutionary overthrow of the entire capitalist system."[33]

While going well beyond the limited revolutionary trade unionism of the syndicalists, the communists could and did invoke the great syndicalist myth of the general strike, as they called upon the trade-union movement to "place in the foreground the weapon of the general strike and [to] . . . prepare for combining a general strike with armed insurrection."[34]

Standing, then, as though they were the chief heirs of the revolutionary tradition in France after World War I the communists gained a strong position and a following among the working class from which they have still not been dislodged. It is true that this was, to begin with, only a minority position, since the main body of trade unionists continued to support the old, now more-socialist-led CGT (the latter also included most anarcho-syndical groups who, after a brief flirtation with communist unionism, returned to the CGT fold by the mid-twenties).

The Popular Front embracing socialists, communists, and other left political parties in the mid-thirties had as its trade union counterpart a unification of the communist-led unions with the CGT. Communist organizers and activists proved most adept at gaining control of the largest share of new members in the mass-production industries. Millions swarmed into the CGT during the successful sit-down strikes carried on during the Popular Front government. These revolutionary-type strikes produced great, now gains for the workers and the unions, and no doubt reinforced workers' beliefs in direct, revolutionary action as the surest road to social and economic advance.

Richard F. Hamilton has laid stress on strategic position and continuity as an explanation of how a particular group gains and holds control over a working-class movement. The communists emerged from the French underground in a particularly strong position in the immediate post-World War II period and gained a predominance over the union movement which they still hold.[35]

Structural Forms of French Unionism Encourage Leftism

In pointing out that French workers transferred from syndicalism to communism, we have discussed the communist movement not only from the viewpoint of France, but also from an international viewpoint, which of course also concerns France. We return now to France and to the main topic of this chapter—French unionism.

With its emphasis upon the revolutionary spontaneity of the syndicalist elite, French trade unionism had long not only accepted but, indeed, proclaimed the virtues of loose organization, low dues, and relatively little centralization. Laudable as some of these characteristics may be, they made it much more difficult to develop fully effective, nationally powerful unions so necessary to enable workers to influence modern industrial conditions.

These same characteristics have been carried into contemporary French trade unionism. Just as they became skeptical about the centralized state, French workers also became suspicious of efforts to build centralized union power. They still insist upon low dues and often refuse to pay even these dues on a regular basis. All of this has helped to perpetuate a form of unionism that, despite its occasional sharp and effective strike thrusts, does not provide that sense of continuing representation and integration in industrial life that unionism has brought elsewhere to most Western countries.

The structural forms of French unionism have also tended to lead workers in ideological and political directions rather than toward a traditional type of union-industry relationship.

Due in part to its syndicalist origins, the foundation of French unionism has been geographical rather than craft or industrial in nature. The regional organization, the so-called *département* grouping all local unions across industrial lines, has more often been the source of power than the national union based on craft or industry. Going up the line, the national federation (the equivalent of the AFL-CIO or the British Trades Union Congress) has also enjoyed more power than most other Western movements.

Continental European union movements generally passed through an early phase (1890–1900), during which the basic power unit of labor organization was often regional rather than craft or industrial. The growth in power of the industrial or craft union at the expense of the regional unit usually coincided with the decline within the union movement itself of both political control and the more purely ideological forces.

Whether the persistence in French unions of power along geographical lines is a cause or an effect of the continuing political-ideological emphasis is a good question. But in any case, established as it is, this geographical base helps to perpetuate ideological as opposed to more purely economic and "job"-oriented unionism. Of course, in France—and also in Italy—there have been some industries where, in recent years, national unions have gained predominance, notably in the metals, chemicals, and textile fields. But overall it remains true that regional union bodies, grouping all trades and industries together, have traditionally held more power in these two countries than elsewhere in Western Europe. Included among such powerful, geographically based bodies are, of course, all the central headquarters of the various federations which they represent.

Weaker in industrial power because of their structural make-up and internal political divisions, French unions, not surprisingly, often depend upon political action to obtain some of their goals. For example, despite an antipolitical tradition, French unions think nothing of depending on the state to provide office headquarters, to extend collective-agreements protection to unorganized workers, and to regulate by statute many basic wage and working conditions.

Dependence upon political action for these objectives keeps the industrial power of the unions weak, and the cycle of political dependence tends to perpetuate itself!

It must be added, however, that despite its weakness in dues-paying membership and its general lack of continuing industrial or plant effectiveness, today's French labor movement has established a fairly important role for itself at the national politico-economic level. It participates in national economic-planning processes, conducts effective high-level negotiations with employer associations on certain key bargaining problems (e.g., unemployment insurance), and in many ways, as one American student of French labor has put it, has "a standing in French society as representative of an interest group that is recognized by employers, the State, and the general public."[36] Even since 1958, during the high-handed rule of President de Gaulle, the government has been careful and generally "proper" in its relations with the unions. This contrasts sharply with its brusque and at times contemptuous treatment of opposition political parties.

This "compensatory" high-level national role does not, however, seem to have given French workers that more immediate sense of continuous participation in industrial decision-making that elsewhere in Western Europe has helped integrate workers more evenly into their societies. One reason may be that the national role is often only consultative. As a result, French unions have been criticized for taking up too much time with ritualistic representation functions, practicing a mere *"politique de presence."*

The acceptance today of French union representation in many high government commissions contrasts with the continued, bitter resistance of many employers to having unions in their plants. This resistance reflects much of top management's continued feudalistic-familistic attitude toward property. Unions constantly report employer reprisals against their activists.[37]

Proposals to strengthen the union role and the security of union representatives in the enterprise were among the chief objectives of unions in the great strike wave which hit France in the spring of 1968. Union demands included specific recognition of the union section at the plant level; setting aside a specific place in the plant for the use of the recognized unions; protection from employer discrimination of union delegates working in the plant; payment to union delegates who lost time from work due to the handling of workers' grievances and related matters; the right to use plant bulletin boards for union notices; and the right to distribute union literature in the plants. Significant employer and government concessions were made, and the unions succeeded in negotiating agreement clauses providing some of these rights in subsequent negotiations in several industries and some individual large metalworking plants. Generally, however, it was agreed (in the so-called Grenelle protocol between unions, the French employers association, and the government) that this issue of union rights would be a matter of legislation to be undertaken by the next French government.[38] In December 1968 the De Gaulle government enacted a statute guaranteeing all nationally representative trade unions (roughly all the major federations) in enterprises of fifty or more employees, the basic union rights they sought in the 1968 strike.

The union gains made in the great strike wave of May and June in 1968, as just suggested, involved the French government as well as the employers. Indeed, the gain was something of a repetition of the famous 1936 Matignon accord, which was also reached with the help of the government (and helped end the great sit-down strikes of that year). This is typical of French union and industrial relations patterns and tends to reinforce the political orientation and dependence of the unions.

Christian Trade Unionism in Western Europe

The deeply ideological (i.e., socialist and revolutionary) character of Western European unionism in the latter part of the nineteenth century provoked, not surprisingly, counteraction by other "ideological" non-socialist forces in the society. Alarmed at the prospect of "losing" large masses of workers, the Catholic Church—and numerous Catholic lay leaders in a number of countries where Catholicism remained a strong force—groped their way toward establishing workers' organizations to rival the socialist movements. The increasing social concern of the papacy itself with "The Condition of the Working Classes" (title of the famous Rerum Novarum papal encyclical of 1891) also made the time propitious for the development of unions among Catholic workers.

The nature of these Catholic unions remained somewhat unclear in the early decades of their existence, and in some instances right down until World War I. The conservative, defensive impulse that, in most countries, had brought these new unions into existence also characterized their outlook and form. Often the early Catholic unions embraced employers as well as workers: moreover, they were largely dominated by the employers, who worked with church authorities. Protestant "workers" organizations were also established in several countries, but less frequently, and in no case have the Protestant labor movements (sometimes called Evangelical, as in the case of Switzerland) attained the importance of the Catholic unions.[39]

Responding to the needs and pressures of their worker clientele, the Catholic unions gradually shucked off their employer or middle-class influences and evolved into legitimate labor unions. As a consequence, by the time of World War I the phenomenon of plural unionism, competing labor federations, as well as competing unions at the place of work, was a fairly common factor in Western Europe outside Great Britain and Scandinavia.[40]

While the traditional socialist-oriented unions have continued to dominate most of the labor world in post-World War II Europe, there have been notable gains by the Catholic or Christian unions (as most prefer to be termed) in Belgium and the Netherlands. The Belgian Confederation of Christian Trade Unions (CSC) has actually become larger than the socialist-oriented Belgian General Federation of Labor (FGTB), although the socialist unions continue to lead the Christians in the elections in which workers select their representation on various shop and factory committees. The socialist-oriented Netherlands Federation of Trade Unions (NVV) remains well ahead of its nearest competitor (including a large Catholic-oriented federation and a substantial Protestant labor center).

A different pattern developed in Austria and West Germany, where the reorganized post-World War II federations dropped their formal ties to political parties and with few exceptions were unified to embrace all ideological and religious groups.[41]

Practically all of the pre-World War II Catholic trade-union federations had their greatest strength among white-collar and civil service employees. During the past two decades this situation has changed considerably, particularly in Belgium, where the Christian labor movement has made advances on all industrial fronts, and in France. In France, the CFDT has a greater following in private industry, especially in metals, than its major noncommunist rival, Force Ouvrière, which has come to be largely representative of unions of civil service employees.

Christian Trade Unionism in France

The French Catholic unions evolved along the general lines sketched above, although even at an earlier stage the French movement seemed to be freer from Church influence than the other Catholic labor movements. A full-scale confederation (what we in the United States would call a federation) of French Christian Workers came into being in 1919.

The temporary unity between traditional free unions (reformist-socialist and more traditional anarcho-syndicalist unions) and the communists at the time of the 1936 Popular Front exerted great pressures on Christian trade unionism in France. It survived, however, and, indeed, prospered down to World War II.

Against the wishes of some prominent religious figures, Catholic union leaders in France refused to cooperate with the Vichy government's plans to reorganize the labor movement from 1941–1943. This stand, plus the notable resistance record of important Catholic union leaders, reinforced the strength and legitimacy of Catholic unionism in France.

Once again, in the immediate post-World War II years, CFDT[42] leaders resisted unity appeals from the CGT, which had unified socialist, syndicalist, and communist-tending labor groups. The tremendous attacks of the communist majority in the CGT against the Marshall Plan for European economic recovery quickly led to a breakup of the CGT. Force Ouvrière, supporting the Marshall Plan as essential to French recovery and opposed to a series of CGT strikes aimed at bringing France to its knees, was formed by a minority breakaway from the CGT. It could now be seen that the CFDT resistance to the earlier pleas for unity had been justified.

The CFDT grew slowly but steadily in the post-World War II years, but had to contend with its own internal struggles. Gathering around the ideological leadership of the journal *Réconstruction,* a group of younger leaders pressed for the complete "deconfessionalization" of the organization to make it a rallying center for all free French labor. (The free unions are generally distinguished from communist union movements in Western Europe. Whether the Christian or Catholic unions are included in the free group depends upon one's biases!)

This deconfessionalization was accomplished in the fall of 1964, the time when remaining references to Christian principles in the constitution were dropped. More important, the name of the organization was changed to French Democratic Confederation of Labor (CFDT).[43]

Actually, as previously noted, the organization had not been confessional in the sense in which some other Catholic or Christian labor movements in Europe have retained close ties to the Church and have accepted a certain amount of social policy guidance from it.

Ten years ago, a leading CFDT official, of center-right tendency, expressed to the author his shock, when visiting American union conventions on finding them regularly opened with an invocation by a Catholic priest, a Protestant minister, or a Jewish rabbi. He declared that so close or obvious a link between the Church and his organization would simply have been impossible in France.[44]

A small part of the "old" CFTC, including an important group of miners, refused to accept the deconfessionalization, and the change of name to the CFDT, and have formed a new, rump CFTC. They have been recognized nationally by the French government.

Plural Unionism—A Weakening Force

The mere existence of the Catholic labor movement for a long time added somewhat to the plural, divisive character of the French labor movement, which, as we have observed, was already plagued by communist-socialist and syndicalist splits.

A fresh example of the confusion that plural unionism can provoke was provided in the metal industry negotiations in 1966 and again in 1967. In those years the FO took the lead in negotiating agreements with the metal industry employers' association in the Paris area; the association made certain limited concessions. The CFDT and the CGT denounced the agreements—which the FO hailed as worse than nothing.

A plurality of unions tends to weaken the industrial strength of workers. This, in turn, returns them to dependence on political parties for social and economic protection. The circle is then completed by the fact that workers (and unions to some extent) thereby become increasingly political and less "industrial." In this connection, it might be noted that the tradition of state intervention in economic affairs, whether it be mercantilism or modern "indicative" planning, is probably deeper and wider in France than in most of Europe. This has also colored the character of French industrial relations and made it more political and state-controlled than in most other European countries.

Judging by the general course of events in Western Europe after World War II, the indication is that plural unionism need not necessarily mean weak unionism. In the Low Countries and in Switzerland, for example, it has been demonstrated that cooperation can be reasonably effective even with plural unionism at the same work site. This is particularly true in the Netherlands where a joint union consultative body has functioned since 1958. In October of 1967 the three Dutch labor federations established a joint, common executive consisting of the presidents and general secretaries of each federation. The consultative committee has also issued a joint action program.[45] In the Low Countries and Switzerland, dues are paid regularly, and the unions are financially strong. This is unlike the situation in France and Italy, where competition among unions has resulted in payment of irregular and low dues and in a relatively weak financial position for the union movements.

Plural unionism seems to have been a more divisive force in France and Italy because of the presence there of strong communist labor movements (they do not exist in strength in the Low Countries and in Switzerland). The communists can usually be expected to "outdemand" the other unions, thereby forcing them almost constantly to the left. The presence of substantial communist union strength also makes most employers more wary of any serious efforts to make collective bargaining work. Class warfare on each side, then, is naturally reinforced.

The French union scene remains a clouded one. The "new" CFDT leaders obviously placed much hope in the eventual unification of all free union forces in the country. But their very deconfessionalization may have made the other major free federation, the FO, more suspicious than ever. As long as the CFDT was Catholic in its orientation, it was not a direct challenge to the FO. Today, with its new secular title and orientation, it creates uneasiness among some FO leaders. On the other hand, some FO leaders do not accept the CFDT's separation from church ties or influence as genuine.[46] The CFDT's continued affiliation with the International Federation of Christian Trade Unions is cited as evidence that the deconfessionalization movement is far from total.[47]

The FO leadership also resents the willingness of some CFDT unions and leaders to engage, as they do from time to time, in joint action with the communist-controlled CGT. The CFDT defends its tactics by citing the need to protect workers' rights in some situations by unity of action among all represented unions, including the CGT, particularly in key industrial disputes. Early in 1966 the CFDT entered into a more formal pact with the CGT to effect wider unity on economic questions. The CFDT has, however, generally sought to avoid cooperation with the CGT on political questions.[48]

While FO leadership at the top is generally successful in forestalling cooperation with the CGT, unity of action is practiced occasionally with CGT forces at the local union level, at the plant or work site, as workers confront recalcitrant employers.

The same tendency toward common action occurs more rarely at the national level. The FO did, however, join the CGT and the CFDT, as well as other union groups, in a nationwide one-day union demonstration against President Charles de Gaulle's proposal for emergency powers in May 1967. (Economic grievances were also at issue.) This suggested that if the conservative-tending forces generate enough pressure, even a new Popular Front of all union and left forces can again become a reality. The great wave of strikes in the spring of 1968, endorsed again by all three major federations, was dramatic proof of the manner in which dissatisfaction with the conservative tending de Gaulle government could promote union unity.[49]

Such a tendency toward united action has been feared by some FO leaders, who recognize that they may find their smaller forces swallowed up by the communist-controlled CGT, which, after all, does have the historic claim to orthodoxy, by virtue of name and numbers. Such a national tendency might also be encouraged by any greater flexibility or "modernization" of the CGT itself. The CFDT, with a different tradition and history (even though it has formally dropped any religious ties) is probably less endangered, organizationally, when it engages in common action with the CGT.

How difficult it is to estimate the actual strength of a labor movement like the one in France was demonstrated, incidentally, by the May 1967 demonstration. French trade-union membership at the time was probably less than 3 million (estimated on the basis of fully paid-up, year-round dues). Yet the common call by all the major federations led to a strike turnout of about 10 million, something that might have given political pause even to the de Gaulle government.[50] As we have noted, the influence of these short strikes, so characteristic of France, is difficult to measure. (Short strikes are also characteristic of Italy, although in recent years longer, collective-bargaining, issue-oriented strikes have been more common.)

Both the CFDT and the FO stand for free and independent unionism. From the viewpoint of publicly expressed programs, the CFDT leadership seems to be more explicitly and more rigidly committed to the principles of a socialist society than the FO leadership, even though almost all of the latter have a socialist background.

This is worth noting, because the usual "foreign" conception of the FO is that of a typical European socialist labor movement. Actually, in 1964 and 1965, during the political maneuvers aimed at creating a broad left-front opposition to President de Gaulle, and centered around the person of Socialist Party leader Gaston Deferre, several of the top leaders of the CFDT were seriously, if unofficially, involved—more so than many of their FO counterparts.[51] Even after this move failed and François Mitterand, a left but not Socialist Party figure, became the left opposition candidate against de Gaulle, the journals of the CFDT were more specific in their opposition to de Gaulle than the FO. While the CFDT did not endorse Mitterand in the presidential campaign in the fall of 1965 (which would have been an enormous departure from the tradition of the Charter of Amiens for any free French union body), it took a clear stand against de Gaulle and in favor of greater social democracy and similar principles. Once again, in the 1967 parliamentary elections, CFDT pressed closely to the left opposition to de Gaulle, although it avoided formal endorsement.

French unionism remains as divided as ever, and it continues in a pattern quite different from anything else in Western Europe. The communist-led CGT, despite the growth of polycentrism in the Soviet world, seems to have remained relatively frozen in its old mold, unlike the Italian Confederazione Generale Italiana Lavoro (CGIL), which shows more signs of change and movement. A great deal of labor leftism in Italy seems accounted for by that country's undeveloped state prior to World War II. Rapid economic progress in the past ten or fifteen years seems to be producing a modernizing effect, which is bringing Italian workers into a more integrated social and political position (although communist voting strength in Italy has actually increased in this same period). This modernizing effect is in advance of what has been happening in France, where, as previously noted, alienation has deeper roots.[52]

While union patterns and loyalties remain fairly frozen, some change is apparent in French industrial-relations practices. Here one senses more realism, reflecting perhaps the greater initiative of some employer groups, as well as the more pragmatic outlook of workers and local leaders caught up in day-to-day problems. The opportunities for, and indeed the achievement of, a higher standard of living for many workers in the more affluent French society of the past ten years seems to be having important effects. One writer finds that these trends are tending to integrate the workers and their local bodies into the industrial enterprises in which they are employed. The function of unionism seems more and more to be linked with its role in industrial enterprise, but these tendencies are still largely confined to new, relatively large companies and plants.[53]

From this viewpoint, the evolution of labor in France is somewhat more closely related to that in the rest of Western Europe. Whether, when, and how these trends may affect overall national trade-union evolution is a different question. The conservative-tending de Gaulle government seemed, after 1958, to have had the effect of pushing the entire labor movement leftward, and this has doubtless delayed any possible changes at the national union level. Voting data (by workers in social-security elections) cited near the beginning of this chapter certainly suggest that as far as "formal" affiliation or identification can be measured, any change in union affiliation is likely to be a slow process.

An example of limited but nevertheless interesting change can be seen from the gains recorded in recent years by the CFDT's metal workers' union, as shown in election results for union plant representatives in the always important metals industry. Table 4 gives some details, based on a survey prepared by the CFDT's Fédération de la Metallurgie.

One criticism of these CFDT figures has been that they cover only those plants where the CFDT was present and participating. In a 1967 survey of a broader group that included a large number of plants (17 percent of the total) where CFDT was not present, the results showed the federation's metal union gained 21.2 percent of the eligible voters, compared to 39.9 percent for CGT—not a radical difference from the earlier surveys.[54]

This same survey also suggests that it is particularly in the newer sectors, most notably electronics and other electro-metals, that the CGT metal federation shows weakness. Data such as this must be used cau-

TABLE 4. *Eligible Voters in Election of Plant Representatives*
(Fédération de la Metallurgie)

Year	Number of Establishments	Number of Eligible Voters	% of Eligible Voters Participating*	CGT % of Eligible Voters	CFDT % of Eligible Voters	FO % of Eligible Voters
1960	119	302,426	72.5	43.4	19.8	5.5
1961	286	482,535	72.3	41.0	20.8	5.4
1962	267	472,228	71.1	39.5	21.7	5.3
1963	423	569,773	73.2	41.3	21.4	5.5
1964	467	609,521	72.8	39.9	22.8	5.0
1965	625	704,455	72.6	38.9	23.9	5.0
1966	690	754,721	72.1	39.4	23.1	4.4

* Miscellaneous groups polled 5.1% of the vote in 1966 and from 3.7 to 5.0% in the other years.
SOURCE: "Les Elections De Délégués Du Personnel Dans La Metallurgie, Statistiques," *Bulletin du Militant, Fédération Générale de la Metallurgie, CFDT* (Paris: December 1965 and January 1967), Appendix 4 in both documents.

tiously, since it is difficult to compare the sample of plants selected from one year to the next: notice that since 1961 the number of plants in Table 4 more than doubled, though the number of workers increased less than 50 percent. The percentages gained by the various groups add up in 1966 to only 72.1 percent. In a sense then, the communist CGT, in polling 39.4 percent of the eligible vote, actually gained 55 percent of those voting, the CFDT metal union 32 percent, and so on. CFDT trade-union leaders also generally agree that change in worker affiliation in metals has taken place much more readily outside the Paris area than in great metalworking complexes. It is still too early to judge the impact of the post-1964 split in the CFDT, but the merely fractional drop in its vote between 1965 and 1966 suggests that in metals, at least, it may not be too serious.

Less comprehensive data for the chemical and rubber industries, compiled by nonunion sources, show CFDT has become an even stronger second to the CGT. In petroleum it even runs ahead of the CGT in the number of votes gained in plant representation elections, while in the glass industry it trails the CGT by a slightly larger margin than in metals.[55]

In assessing the results and trends of these surveys of voting in privately owned manufacturing plants, it is important to keep in mind that FO (which generally runs a poor third in them) does better in industries such as textile and banking. More important, FO's greatest strength continues to be among the civil servants. (FO surveys of plant elections in which its unions participated late in 1968 and early in 1969 showed it running second to the CGT, with the CFDT third.)

Perhaps of greatest importance in looking to the future of French unionism are possible changes in the CGT and the French Communist Party, which remain by far the largest working class organizations. For example, the great strike wave of the spring of 1968 almost seems comparable to the sit-downs of 1936, and the latter certainly brought about major, lasting changes in French unions and industrial relations.

During the 1968 strikes the CGT did not behave like a revolutionary organization. It prided itself on resisting what it described as irresponsible leftist tactics and demands, which it attributed both to demonstrating university students and the CFDT. At one point the CGT issued a communiqué arguing that it was its leadership and restraint, in "the complete absence of the authority of the State," which "came to reestablish order." It added that "if the people are not deprived of electricity, of water, and of bread, of milk and other necessities . . . if some trains have been able to travel . . ." it was not because "of the science of government," but rather "the will of the C.G.T. unions." It called itself, in this same communiqué, "La Grande Force Tranquille."[56]

Doubtless part of the CGT's caution in 1968 was due to purely tactical considerations. Indeed, recognizing that it was under attack from the left during and after the strike, the CGT went out of its way to argue that a truly revolutionary situation had not existed in May and June and that its own more limited demands were, therefore, correct for the times.[57]

It is possible that a new crisis might produce a new, more revolutionary turn by the CGT. This has certainly happened in the past, under communist leadership. On the other hand, the organization, did seem to betray certain highly bureaucratized qualities and responses during the 1968 crisis. These seem to suggest that its revolutionary potential, even under communist leadership, may be disappearing. However, it is difficult to believe that French labor, let alone the CGT, will fall easily into the general European labor path of reformism and integration.

NOTES

1. George Lichtheim, N.Y. Review of Books, April 6, 1967, p. 30.

2. Hans Kohn, Nationalism and Liberty, the Swiss Example (London: G. Allen, 1956), pp. 13–14. Scandinavia, and especially Sweden, may also be said to exemplify a slower, more even pattern of political and social modernization.

3. Richard Lowenthal, "Secessio Plebis," The Twentieth Century, May 1951, p. 361.

4. Ibid.

5. Ibid., pp. 361–362.

6. Hugh Thomas, The Spanish Civil War (London: Eyre and Spottiswoode, 1961), p. 14. Some of the cynical disillusion with politics, and a turn toward anarcho-

syndical ideas among many groups of Latin American workers some decades back, may have a similar origin.

7. J. D. Reynaud, *Les Syndicats en France* (Paris: Librairie Armand Colin, 1963), pp. 62–63. A copy of the Charter of Amiens can be found in Lorwin, *op. cit.,* pp. 312–313. Lewis L. Lorwin's article on "Syndicalism" in the *Encyclopedia of Social Sciences,* Vol. 14 (New York: The Macmillan Company, 1934), p. 496, is a short, useful description of this philosophy and movement.

8. David J. Saposs, *The Labor Movement in Post-War France* (New York: Columbia University Press, 1931), pp. 462, 472.

9. Carl Landauer, *European Socialism,* Vol. I (Berkeley: University of California Press, 1959), p. 211.

10. Val Lorwin, "Labor Organization and Politics in Belgium and France," in Everett M. Kassalow (ed.), *National Labor Movements in the Postwar World* (Evanston, Ill.: Northwestern University Press, 1963), Chap. 6.

11. Maurice Neufeld, *Italy: School for Awakening Countries* (Ithaca, N.Y.: New York State School of Industrial and Labor Relations, Cornell University, 1961), pp. 19, 318.

12. Thomas, *op. cit.,* p. 41.

13. Carl Landauer, *op. cit.,* Vol. I, p. 289.

14. On the links between anarchism and syndicalism in France, see James Joll, *The Anarchists* (New York: Grosset and Dunlap, 1965), Chap. VIII, and George Woodcock, *Anarchism* (Cleveland: The World Publishing Company, 1962), pp. 316–326.

15. Henry Ehrmann stresses Proudhon's lasting influence on French labor thought in his *French Labor From Popular Front to Liberation* (New York: Oxford University Press, 1947), pp. 37, 209, 210. On Proudhon's special influence on France, see also J. Hampden Jackson, *Marx, Proudhon and European Socialism* (New York: Collier Books, 1962), Chap. 9.

16. Lowenthal, *op. cit.,* p. 358. It has been argued that the American Federation of Labor, especially during the latter half of Gompers' leadership, practiced a kind of *reformist syndicalism.* It came to have a deep suspicion of government action or any serious ties with political parties. By the late 1920s its suspicion of government and its reliance on union action led to opposition to most forms of social-security legislation. This statement should be qualified, however, by noting that this "philosophy" or attitude toward government was not accepted by all AFL affiliates. The railway unions within the federation had long since come to accept and, indeed, depend upon government intervention and regulation in industrial and labor matters. The substantial commitment of many local building-trade unions to local-level political action also constitutes a qualification.

17. Val Lorwin, "Working Class Politics and Economic Development in Western Europe," *American Historical Review,* 1958.

18. See Seymour Martin Lipset, *Political Cleavages in Developed and Emerging Politics* and *The Changing Class Structure and Contemporary European Politics,* Reprints No. 244 and No. 223 (Berkeley: Institute of Industrial Relations and Institute of International Studies, University of California, 1964). The economic historian Alexander Gerschenkron doubts that the small family firm was much more prevalent in France than in Germany in the first decade of the twentieth century. See his *Economic Backwardness in Historical Perspective* (New York: Praeger, 1965), pp. 63–64.

19. Neufeld, *op. cit.,* p. 318. Regional variations, while not quite as great in France, were probably more serious there than in most of Western Europe. The regional discontinuities make it more difficult to achieve any smooth economic and political evolution.

20. Robert Alexander, *Labor Relations in Argentina, Brazil and Chile* (New York: McGraw-Hill, 1962), p. 379.

21. Georges Lefranc, *Le Syndicalisme en France* (Paris: Presses Universitaires de France, 1953), p. 36.

22. Woodcock, *op. cit.*, pp. 27–28.

23. Lefranc, *op. cit.*, p. 39.

24. Organization was extended to thousands of *government* workers, and this group became one of the main sources of strength for French unionism after the 1920s. Saposs, *op. cit.*, pp. 281–288.

25. Review by Theodore Beregi of Antoine Prost's *La C.G.T. à' l'Epoque du Front Populaire* (Paris: 1964), Armand Colin, in *Force Ouvrière*, October 27, 1965.

26. *Esprit du Syndicalisme* (Paris: Les Editions Ouvrières, 1951), pp. 112, 114. In the great wave of sitdown strikes in the United States during the same years, it was fairly common in such centers as Detroit for local union headquarters to receive calls from groups of workers around the city, informing officials that "we are sitting down here, you'd better get somebody over!"

27. The American Federation of Labor was unable to extend continuing unionism to the mass of production workers who came into the U.S. labor market during World War I and the 1920s. This inability left the American labor movement a crippled minority force by the early 1930s. The wave of mass unionism, which took place within AFL as well as CIO unions beginning in the middle 1930s, changed all this.

28. Quoted in Jean Montreuil, *Histoire du Mouvement Ouvrier en France* (Paris: Aubier, 1947), p. 228.

29. See V. I. Lenin, *What Is To Be Done?*, especially Chap. II, "The Spontaneity of the Masses and the Consciousness of the Social Democrats" and Chap. III, "Trade Unionist Politics and Social Democratic Politics" (Moscow: Foreign Languages Publishing House, 1952; original edition, 1902, and various later editions). Lenin, of course, was to stress the role of the working class vanguard, so similar to Pouget's elite, even more clearly in *The State and Revolution* (Moscow: Foreign Languages Publishing House, original edition, 1917, and various editions later). The writings of Lenin and Pouget from about 1900 to 1910 may well have been independent of one another.

30. Quoted in Adam B. Ulam, *The Unfinished Revolution, An Essay on the Sources of Influence of Marxism on Communism* (New York: Random House, 1964), pp. 192–193. It is true enough that the subsequent actions of Lenin and the Soviet State were to disillusion temporarily mesmerized anarchists, but there was a striking similarity of style and diction between the Bolsheviks, particularly Lenin, and the anarchists of an earlier era. As Ulam suggests, this is probably attributable, in part, to the relatively backward state of Russia in the first decades of the twentieth century.

31. *The Trade Union Movement in Soviet Russia* (Geneva: International Labour Office, 1927), pp. 4, 5. The book quotes resolutions and statutes adopted by the First International Congress of Trade Unions, which was held in Moscow.

32. *Ibid.*, p. 5. For a later Soviet critique, but one still based on the pros and cons of anarcho-syndicalism, see A. Losovsky, *The World's Trade Union Movement* (London: National Minority Movement, 1925), pp. 14–17, 251–255.

33. "Extracts from Letter of Executive Committee of the Communist International to Trade Unions of All Countries," in Jane Degras (ed.), *The Communist International, 1919–1943, Documents* (London: Oxford University Press, 1956), Vol. I, 1919–1922, p. 88.

34. *Ibid.*

35. Hamilton contrasts this with the case of Belgium where moderates were in

strategic control of the unions after World War II. In both countries the real income of workers has mounted substantially in the post-war period, and in each case the leadership in control of the "ports of entry" of workers into the labor movement, communists in France, noncommunists in Belgium, has maintained its strength. Richard F. Hamilton, *Affluence and the French Worker in the Fourth Republic* (Princeton: Princeton University Press, 1967), esp. Chap. XII.

36. Frederic Meyers, "The Role of Collective Bargaining in France: The Case of Unemployment Insurance," *British Journal of Industrial Relations,* November 1965.

37. See, for example, the cartoon article, "Les Inconnues Libertés syndicales dans la maison" ("The Unknown Trade Union Liberties in the Enterprise"), *Syndicalisme,* May 1967. These cartoons refer to specific cases in recent years, such as actual physical assault upon a union steward in firms like Citroen, isolation of union militants in other plants, constant layoffs of other union activists, and similar incidents. Resort to the Ministry of Labor or other tribunals frequently brings redress, but the incidents pile up, and the government agencies take a long time to make their awards. For a recent study of the obstacles confronting French unions at the level of the work place see Hubert Lesire-Ogrel, *Le Syndicat dans l'entreprise* (Paris: Editions du Seuil, 1967).

38. *Le Monde,* May 28, 1968 and June 11, 1968. Later eruptions during the strike crisis seemed to indicate that it was the non-Communist labor Federations (FO and CFDT) which seemed to be placing the greatest stress on making advances in the area of trade union rights and presence in the plant. See, for example, *The New York Times,* June 18, 1968.

39. A useful and very sympathetic account of the rise and development of Christian workers organizations in Europe from their beginnings down to the early 1950s appears in Michael Fogarty, *Christian Democracy in Western Europe, 1820–1953* (London: Routledge & Kegan Paul, 1957), esp. Chaps. XV and VI. Of general interest, too, is William J. McIntire's *The International Federation of Christian Trade Unions: Analysis and Prognosis,* a paper presented in June 1962 to the special Research Seminar on Comparative Labor Movements conducted by the National Institute of Labor Education, as yet unpublished. There are, of course, studies of the movements in the individual countries. For France, in the modern period, the most significant work is Gerard Adam, *La C.F.T.C., 1940–1958* (Paris: Armand Colin, 1964). For the recent history of the CFDT, including its confessionalization, see Adam's "De la CFTC à la CFDT," *Revue Française de Science Politique* (*February* 1965), 87–103.

40. In Chapter VIII we shall indicate how plant or work-site-level representation has developed in many of these same countries outside strictly union channels. The persistence of plural unionism helped create such an extraunion system, out of the sheer necessity to develop some effective form of representation at the plant level that would not necessarily bog down in competing union rivalries and ideologies.

41. Informal ties, particularly with the socialist parties, as we have noted in Chapter III, continue to exist in Germany and Austria. There has been a modest revival of Catholic unionism in West Germany, but it amounts to only about 3% of the German Federation of Trade Unions (DGB). It remains insignificant beside the Catholic minority faction in the DGB and shows no serious signs of growth. *Labor and Press Information,* August 1965, published by the International Federation of Christian Trade Unions, reported the German Christian Workers Union membership as 234,730 as of December 31, 1964. The DGB reported a membership at that time of 6,485,471.

42. The reader is again cautioned that we are using the Confederation's new initials. It was the CFTC up until 1964.

43. The lasting influence of syndicalist ideology on French trade unionism can

even be seen in the new principles and programs adopted by the CFDT. In defining its beliefs, the CFDT leadership states, among other things: "The end objective is the emancipation of workers by their own action, by the medium of trade unionism. Trade unionism is a means of liberating ["liberation"] the world of work ["monde du travail"]." Others among the new principles emphasize democratic socialist ideals and the problems of worker alienation, but to a degree the overtones and slogans of syndicalism also live. See *Evolution et Perspectives, op. cit.,* p. 64.

44. Such influence as the Church exerted no doubt depended on more informal relationships between Catholic union leaders and Church leaders. In a sense, much the same can be said of relationships between socialist political figures and socialist-oriented unions in a few countries. To repeat, however, in one or two countries Church leadership on some social policy issues is accepted by Catholic unions.

45. For the program, see *Programme of Action, Consultative Body,* Netherlands Federation of Trade Unions (NVV), Netherlands Roman-Catholic Trade Union Centre (NKV), Protestant Christian National Trade Union Centre (CNV), February, 1967. It is stressed that the new body and the joint action program "does not mean that the independence of the three trade union centres will be abolished . . . but the influence and strength of the Dutch trade union movement as a whole will certainly be increased. . . ." (*Information Bulletin No. 95,* NVV, October, 1967.) The high degree of cooperation between the three labor federations in the Netherlands is described in an execellent study of that country which appeared after ours was in galleys. See John P. Windmuller, *Labor Relations in the Netherlands* (Ithaca, N.Y.: Cornell University Press, 1969). Windmuller, citing surveys that show most union members are now sympathetic to the idea of organic unity between the three labor federations, believes the present coordinating body is a prelude, "Until organic unity comes—as some day it surely will. . . ." By way of contrast, the renewal of consultation meetings between the CFDT and the FO in France, early in 1969, seemed once again to reveal differences rather than similarities between the two noncommunist federations.

46. See André Bergeron, "Where Are French Christian Unions Heading," *AFL-CIO Free Trade Union News,* July 1964, p. 2.

47. In the spring of 1968 the CFDT union affiliate for the metalworkers was accepted into membership by the International Metalworkers Federation (IMF), a world association of metal unions including those in the United States (the United Automobile Workers, The United Steelworkers, The International Brotherhood of Electrical Workers), those in Great Britain, Germany, Sweden, and others. The IMF is closely related to the International Confederation of Free Trade Unions (ICFTU, Brussels headquarters, which includes the AFL-CIO, the British TUC, the German DGB, the Swedish LO, and other free union federations in Western Europe, Latin America, Asia, and elsewhere). Its acceptance of the CFDT metalworkers is a noteworthy step. At the same time, this CFDT metal group cut its ties with the Christian international association of metal unions. These actions, taken with the obvious approval of top leaders of the CFDT itself, suggest a desire to carry deconfessionalization further. Under pressure from the CFDT, as well as some of its African affiliates, the IFCTU changed its name to World Confederation of Labor (WCL) and removed almost all references to religion in its constitution at its October 1968 congress.

48. For CFDT views on this subject and a defense of its unity-of-action agreement with the CGT, see "Réflexions sur les perspectives d'action," *Syndicalisme,* Nos. 1 and 2 (January 1966). An FO rejoinder is to be found in its *Magazine,* February 1966, under the title "Où Allons-Nous?"

49. The joint strike action of May 1968 also produced some serious strains and cracks in the CGT-CFDT relationships. The CFDT warmly supported the uni-

versity students' strikes and demonstrations which helped to touch off the strike wave among millions of workers later in May. The CFDT found itself under attack from the CGT, as the latter took a more conservative position on the students and on other aspects of the total strike situation. For the bitter reactions of the CFDT to CGT attacks, see "La CFDT generait-elle à point la CGT?" *Syndicalisme,* June 20, 1968.

50. Estimates of the response to the strike call come from several sources, including the *Press and Radio Service,* International Confederation of Free Trade Unions, May 25, 1967. The response to strike calls in the spring of 1968 was also very strong.

51. Given the earlier history and background of the CFDT, however, it is likely that its *membership* is less socialist oriented than that of FO.

52. The same lesser flexibility is evident in the French Communist Party as compared to its Italian counterpart. As far as the union federations are concerned, the presence of a significant socialist minority within the Italian CGIL has for many years helped to compel it to pursue a more supple policy than the French CGT. Thus, the CGIL adopted a more "nuanced" policy than the CGT toward the common market, collective agreements, etc. On recent changes in the communist labor movement I have been helped by Gino Guigni's *The Italian Communist Labor Movement Today,* paper presented to the University of Wisconsin Seminar on Comparative Labor Movements (Madison, Wisconsin, and Washington, D.C., February 1966. Mimeographed; to be published). For an interesting comparison of the occupational composition of the French and Italian Communist Parties see the chapter by Mattei Dogan "Political Cleavage and Social Stratification in France and Italy," in Seymour M. Lipset and Stein Rokkan (eds.), *Party Systems and Voter Alignments, Cross National Perspectives* (New York: The Free Press, 1962). Dogan's study indicates that the French Communist Party is based more upon the working class, both as regards party membership and electoral support, than is the Italian party. The latter has a larger percentage of its support among agricultural workers and tenant farmers. Moreover, the agricultural section of the Italian Communist Party is its most rapidly growing one. Dogan attributes this agrarian turn to the communists to the problems engendered by the rapid economic development of Italy in the past two decades. According to Dogan the working class base of the Italian Socialist Party is much larger than is the case in France. The angry reactions of French Communist Party and union leaders to the Soviet invasion of Czechoslovakia in the summer of 1968 may presage a more independent Communist line in France in the future.

53. Pierre Belleville, *Une Nouvelle Classe Ouvrière* (Paris: Réné Julliard, 1963), esp. Chap. VIII. Also see Serge Mallet, *La Nouvelle Classe Ouvrière* (Paris: Editions du Seuil, 1963).

54. *Ibid.,* January, 1968. Material from other nonunion sources seems to bear out the general validity of these CFDT surveys.

55. National Foundation of Political Sciences, 1968.

56. *Le Monde,* May 23, 1968.

57. An interesting major statement, in English, of the CGT's summary view of the May-June strikes, is contained in the translation of the report of its General Secretary to a two-day meeting held on June 13–14, 1968. See "Report Presented by George Seguy," *Trade Union Press* (WFTU), June 1968, pp. 2–8.

VII

Comparative Industrial-Relations Systems

INDUSTRIAL-RELATIONS SYSTEMS are shaped on the one hand by the interaction of unions and management and, on the other, by the intervention of the state.

In the United States government intervention has mostly been confined to regulating the framework of collective bargaining; the determination of substantive issues has been left in great part to management and labor through the collective agreement.

In Europe the situation is different. Government's role is greater. The party-union character of European labor movements, as well as the older tradition of state intervention in economic life, has produced an industrial-relations system in which legislation is regarded as a "normal" means of determining wages and working conditions—as normal as the device of the collective agreement between management and labor.[1] Not so in the United States, where union labor has concentrated almost exclusively upon collective bargaining. Here the collective agreement has been looked to as *the* guarantor of wages and working conditions. The rise of mass unionism in the United States modified this nonstate outlook slightly, but it is still widely prevalent. Since the thirties, American unions have come to accept the state's role in enforcing the recognition and bargaining rights of unions; but the unions still stress their own "private" negotiations with management concerning the determination of actual working conditions.

Finally, by way of introduction to this chapter, it should be added that European unions have been able, until now anyway, to count upon the traditional, ideological loyalty of workers, and in a way unknown in the United States. As a result European unions have not placed as much stress as American labor on the negotiation of closed or union shops, the checkoff, and other union security measures.

Attitudes Toward Collective Agreements
in Europe and America

Attainment of written collective agreements with employers became a major objective of most American unions early in modern labor history. In this early period such agreements were often frowned upon—in any event they were accepted more slowly—by many European union movements, which considered them an undesirable form of class collaboration. For example, in 1896, the Leipzig trade council, part of the German labor movement, took action against the local printing trades union for signing a wage agreement with employers. However, the national labor body overruled the Leipzig council.

In France, the persistent hold of anarcho-syndicalist philosophy over much of the labor movement, accompanied by an unyielding "revolutionary" attitude toward employers, kept opposition to written agreements alive in some sections of the French labor movement right up to World War I. Afterward, during the 1920s, the communist wing of the French labor movement continued to "be hostile in principle" to the class collaboration symbolized by written agreements. In 1936 the Popular Front policies and legislation (including the law of collective agreements) gave written agreements a strong boost and reduced communist opposition to them. But employer resistance and the weakening—indeed the elimination—of the French labor movement in World War II really means that significant experience with written agreements is only a recent development in France. After World War II collective agreements came to be widely accepted. But opposition continued. For example, take the case of the free union federations, which began to negotiate some agreements that were limited to a single enterprise (in contrast to the prevailing type of agreement, which involved a particular area or industry). The federations negotiated these agreements in order to maximize the advantages that could be gained at wealthier companies. But the communist-controlled Confédération Générale du Travail denounced the agreements as class betrayal. Under pressure from its members, however, the CGT came to accept them.[2]

Similar opposition to plant or company agreements was voiced in Italy—by the communist-controlled Confederazione Generale Italiana Lavoro (CGIL) in 1954–1955. But within a year it, too, had "reversed itself after mounting stress within its own ranks." In fact by 1966 the CGIL was claiming that it had the initiative in negotiating trade-union agreements at "the level of the factory, or a group of factories." Such agreements took advantage of the fact that opportunities existed with the more prosperous firms to obtain agreements that brought wages higher than were provided for by industry-wide agreements.[3]

In the United States, however, the AFL and its leaders like Samuel

Gompers had looked to the written agreement virtually from the outset as a cornerstone of union action and philosophy. Opposition to collective agreements did come from the revolutionary syndicalist Industrial Workers of the World (IWW), which, not surprisingly, denounced them as a form of class betrayal. But IWW influence was concentrated in only a few industries, mostly before World War I, and their opposition to collective agreements had no lasting impact. In U.S. industrial relations, the execution of a written collective agreement has come to stand as the single best test of good faith in bargaining.

In countries like England and Sweden, as might be expected, the acceptance and execution of written agreements followed a path of evolution similar to that in the United States: By the turn of the century agreements were widely accepted as highly desirable and important goals of union action.[4]

It would be fair to say that today all Western European labor movements fully accept the written collective agreement. Indeed most of them are seeking to enlarge its scope and character, often against the opposition of employers.

Scope of Collective Bargaining More Restricted in Europe

Since legislation plays such an important role in regulating many aspects of industrial relations, a number of bargaining items that are critical in America have been largely removed from the scope of union-management agreements in Western Europe. A good example is paid vacations, which are regulated by legislation in Western Europe, except in the United Kingdom and to some extent in the Netherlands.[5] It has become common in European collective bargaining, however, for the parties to treat state provisions regarding paid vacations (or paid holidays) as minimums and to negotiate benefits in excess of these minimums in their collective agreements.

Other typical instances where legislation is used to regulate items that are left to collective bargaining (or employer initiative) in the United States include notice of and protection against layoff (in several countries), health and hospital insurance (almost a universal function of social security systems in Western Europe), and so on. Pension and retirement systems are largely a state function in Western Europe and there is little counterpart to the multibillion-dollar private complementary pension systems that have developed within the American collective bargaining system.[6]

European labor and management are beginning, however, to include in their collective agreements more of the fringe benefits so common in U.S. collective bargaining. In France in the past half-dozen years, the unions have negotiated nationwide agreements with the employers' associations (in the private sector). These agreements provide a special unemployment benefit system as well as a complementary pension plan. Dutch and German unions have been developing, and in a few cases have negotiated, joint profit-sharing and investment programs as part of their labor-management agreements. These programs are significant both in terms of fringe benefits and as evidence of the erosion of traditional, doctrinal opposition to capitalism.[7]

The broad generalizations about differences between U.S. and European collective-bargaining agreements with respect to fringe benefits, however, still hold.

There are several reasons for the sharp differences between the United States and Europe in collective bargaining. European social-security systems were begun, and then broadened to cover more risks, at a much earlier date than in the United States. Since Europe's culture is historically less committed to individualism, it is not surprising that it has a long tradition of state intervention on behalf of family security and the poor.

In the United States, the rich and interesting structure of fringe benefits under collective bargaining, such as health and hospital insurance, supplementary pensions and unemployment insurance plans, were and are, in some respects, a reflection of U.S. labor's inability to make a big enough breakthrough on the legislative front. Indeed, when supplementary pensions were first being won in the mass-production industries of the United States, in the late 1940s, some key labor leaders believed that this was but a prelude, a tool to break down obstacles to an improved *legislated* social security system.

The author can recall attending a meeting of top CIO leaders early in 1950, shortly after private pensions had been won for the first time for industrial workers in the steel and automobile collective agreements. It was widely anticipated at this meeting that these bargaining developments would quickly lead to major changes in social security pensions—and there was little anticipation that the private pension would ultimately come to be almost as important as social security for workers in industries such as automobiles or steel. There was a common belief, for example, that large employers in the automobile and steel industries would join the struggle for major changes in the social security law, to relieve themselves of the heavy costs of private pension systems.

One top union leader suggested that the lesson that had just been learned from bargaining for pensions in automobiles and steel would now have to be applied to unemployment insurance. In other words supplementary unemployment benefits—the so-called guaranteed annual wage—which were later negotiated in steel, automobiles, rubber, and a few other industries—were then being looked upon as a device that would ultimately effect, via legislative action, major improvements in the unemployment compensation system.

Needless to add, by the 1960s collectively bargained benefit systems in the United States have developed their own logic and rationale, have spread to many more industries, and in some ways have become almost a substitute and certainly a permanent complement to the public systems. And it should be added that only rarely have American union leaders "jockeyed" back and forth, even in their minds, between bargaining and legislation, for these two areas are regarded as quite separate and distinct in American labor life.

Bargaining and Legislation: Alternative Routes of European Unions

European unions very consciously view and employ legislation and collective bargaining as alternative routes. Given the deep political involvement of workers' movements in Europe, the choice of which road to take can become a tactical one. When, for example, several years ago in Sweden a major overhaul in the pension system became a key goal of the Swedish Federation of Trade Unions (LO), tactical reasons helped dictate the choice of a legislative route. Since the Social Democratic Party was in control of the government, the choice to continue to pursue pensions by the legislative route was a natural one.

Action taken by the British Trades Unions Congress to establish severance-pay protection for laid-off workers is a striking example of the way in which a Western European labor movement can sway between a legislative and a collective-bargaining approach to a problem. In 1963 the TUC's General Council proposed that agreements with employers "should provide severance payments compensation for loss of job when workers are discharged because work is no longer available."

At that time TUC seemed to oppose the idea of establishment by the government of a "national redundancy fund" out of fear that this "might result in the Government making no increase in either unemployment or sickness benefits."[8] ("Redundancy" is the British term for the American term "layoff.")

Apparently, also, the TUC was choosing the collective-agreement route because "no legislation" establishing severance benefits in private industry appeared to be "imminent" in 1963 and 1964 under the Conservative government.[9]

The victory of the Labour Party late in 1964 altered this situation. The TUC and the Ministry of Labour promptly set to work and drafted a new bill to establish "compensation for redundancy as a legal right." A national "Redundancy Fund," financed by employer payroll tax payments, was provided by the bill and covered "all employees between 18 and 65 (60 for women) who work 21 hours a week or more . . . [and] have had a minimum of two years' service." The scale of payments varied with the service and age of the worker as follows:

Age 18 to 21, ½ week's pay for each year of service; 1 week's pay, age 22 to 40; 1½ weeks' pay, age 41 to 65 (60 for women), with "reckonable service" limited to 20 years, and earnings above 40 pounds a week not taken into account.[10]

In this case the unions' desire for redundancy payments coincided with the Labour government's desire for programs that would encourage mobility of labor from overmanned companies and industries to sectors of the economy that were short of labor. In the process, a national legislative approach to what ordinarily might have been regarded as a private union-employer matter became feasible.

Such a shifting back and forth between direct, industrial collective-bargaining action and a legislative approach is virtually inconceivable in the United States. U.S. labor has evolved a long way from the stage when it officially opposed federal action even for social security protection. But private bargaining and federal action are separate areas of operation in the minds of American union leaders. In addition, the very nature of American politics and the political system, as well as union labor's relation to this system, do not provide the kind of flexibility that would make possible a shift between a legislative and a collective-bargaining approach to basic social problems.[11]

In a country like France, where party-union relationships are less formal, conflict can develop on occasion over which of the alternative routes, legislation or collective bargaining, is preferable. In 1956 the free French unions (the socialist-oriented Force Ouvrière [FO] and the Christian Trade Union Federation [CFTC]) succeeded in negotiating a new three-week vacation plan with the management of the Renault Company. This marked an advance of one full week over the plan provided for by legislation.

The free unions (so-called in France to distinguish them from the communist-controlled CGT) prepared to exploit this breakthrough by making the same demand of other employers. Much to their consternation the socialist-led government promptly amended the existing legislation to universalize the three-week vacation for all eligible workers. Competition for the workers' allegiance had led the Socialist Party to make a move that deprived the unions of their temporary tactical advantage over both the employers and the communists. Several top CFTC and FO leaders privately expressed their anger at the government. Generally, however, such competition between a socialist party or government and the trade unions are not likely to occur in other Western European nations where relationships are closer and more integrated.

In the United States, collective bargaining inevitably evokes more tension in industrial relations and often leads to more serious strikes. This is because so much more is typically packed into an American collective agreement and because progress along a legislative route to a social objective is so often a much slower, more tortuous, and much less certain process. One European union official speaks of "the more violent method of collective bargaining adopted by the American Trade Unionists, who can reckon only on themselves."[12]

Major economy-stopping strikes arising out of purely industrial or collective bargaining problems—such as those by steelworkers, automobile workers and longshoremen—which continue to rock the United States once or twice a year, have almost no counterpart today in most of Western Europe. There are a number of reasons for this, but the very scope and character of the collective agreement in the United States doubtless helps keep industrial relations at a much higher level of tension in this country.

Differences Between European and American Bargaining

As European bargaining relationships and agreements have evolved, they reflect, besides those already discussed, key differences from those in the United States. Perhaps the most critical influence in this respect is the nature of employer organization in Western Europe. America's greater force of competition, its greater geographical diversity, and the presence of more large key companies in the mass-production industries—all these have led to agreements of the type that are negotiated between a single employer and a union or, at the most beyond this, agreements between a union and a group of employers in a fairly restricted geographical area, such as a metropolitan complex.

Compared with the United States, Western Europe has a long-established tradition of cooperation between employers (which dates as far back as the Middle Ages), less intense competition, and relatively few key large companies. As a result, these factors, when viewed in relation to the employer, have tended to favor a broad industry-wide approach to collective bargaining and the negotiation of the collective agreement (industry-wide, that is, for at least a given area of a country). As for the unions, broader sentiments of working-class solidarity have tended to lead them down the road to industry-wide types of agreements. The idea of American unions to concentrate the "attack" upon the more affluent company or companies has not been much in evidence in European bargaining. To some extent Europeans have been aware of the consequences of such an approach: that it would tend to protect the marginal or least efficient producers and would set wages and other standards at levels that failed to take advantage of the stronger firms' ability to pay. In the interests of broader solidarity and in the desire to maximize protection, they willingly chose this road to industry-wide types of agreements.

European Employer Associations and Unions Encourage Broad-Base Bargaining

In most instances unions in Europe that favor industry- and/or area-wide bargaining have been aided and abetted by the fact that bargaining *through* their associations and general dependence upon them *for* policy guidance is also a norm for most European employers.

Employers have a long tradition of forming associations to perform jointly a variety of economic functions, often in conjunction with the state. This "will" to association was reinforced in several countries at the turn of the century when trade unionism began to make its impact. In Sweden, for example, as a student of its collective-bargaining system writes, "Employers' organizations . . . have been formed as a defence mechanism against trade unionism." The famous Swedish Employers' Confederation (SAF), which has since taken on other important economic functions, had its origin in 1902 in the need to bargain with and resist union "whipsawing" tactics.[13]

In Germany, the Central Federation of German Manufacturers, which was already functioning for other purposes, created a special association in 1904, the Central Administration of Employers' Associations, as an agency for combating labor. Other employer groups were formed in succeeding years and, as in the case of Sweden, their general purpose was to present a common bargaining front to the unions.[14]

The British engineering industry is another interesting example of the employers' propensity to favor association bargaining. (Incidentally, there is no exact American equivalent to the British engineering industry; the nearest to it would be all metal-fabricating industries except shipbuilding.) Shirley Lerner writes:

In the nineteenth century the local craft unions which catered for journeymen within a given district tried to enforce their own district standards on individual employers. This practice encouraged employers to unite into district associations to prevent the bidding up of wages. Therefore, when collective bargaining replaced the autonomous trade union regulation of wages, the district wage rate, rather than the factory wage rate, became the paramount bargaining issue. Later, when national trade unions and national employers' associations entered into negotiations, the district wage rate grew less important and was subordinated to the national wage rate.

British engineering employers came to view attempts by workers "to negotiate at the factory level as a gross interference with the prerogatives of management. . . . the prevention of such negotiations was often the main reason for the existence of some employers associations."[15]

Once created, employer associations that are devoted to bargaining, especially those on the Continent, have often become more centralized and at least as effective as their union counterparts in making policy decisions concerning bargaining. They have assumed control over strike decisions, the settlement of key disputes, and other matters of basic industrial relations.[16]

The structure of most European unions also contributed to the growth of broad association and/or industry-type bargaining as opposed to plant- or company-type bargaining. Local unions at a given place of work, in the American sense of the local union, are largely unknown in Western Europe. Between the workers and the national union headquarters usually stands a geographical branch that unites members on the basis of their place of residence instead of on the basis of their particular work site. Unions are therefore in a better position to negotiate with employers in terms of districts or of the entire nation.

We might note at this point that some large European corporations, especially in the metal industry, have tried to achieve greater autonomy from associations in their industrial-relations policies.

Both unions and employer associations in Western Europe, as well as governments, have always realized the importance to them of exports. This also helps to explain why association-bargaining involves particular concern for the marginal producer. In an economy where a country has to export 15, 20, or 25 percent of its national product to live efficiently (and this is typical of Western Europe), consensus is probably easier to achieve than in the United States, where less than 5 percent of gross national product flows into exports. The fear of driving *any* employer out of business carries much weight in a more "exposed" economy.

Union Recognition and Extension Easier in Europe

The structure of association-bargaining and recognition tended to make the problem of union recognition somewhat less critical in Western Europe than in the United States, once unionism got well under way. Even today, in the well-unionized mass-production industries of the United States, when a large unionized company opens a new plant, the union (or unions) must undertake a special organizational campaign to win its rights to bargain in that particular plant. In Europe, on the other hand, when a new plant is opened by either an old or a new employer in an industry where an association-wide agreement is already in effect, the employer is under pressure from both the employer association and the union to recognize the union and to accept the terms of the agreement.[17]

Broad union-employer, association-wide relationships tend to strengthen the institutional position of trade unionism, whereas in the United States each relationship with an employer must be jealously defended. The European employers' association itself develops a "stake" in the institutionalization of relationships with the union. It makes it much easier, for example, to extend union benefits and, to a degree, to enlist union membership among smaller employers, who are ordinarily fairly difficult to organize in American industry.

The only analogies in the United States are in highly competitive industries and/or industries dominated by many small employers (e.g., the ladies garment or building industries), where employers seem to share the unions' desire to extend unionism and the collective agreement as a means of curtailing potentially "unfair" competition. These, however, are exceptional situations in the American labor relations system.

Employers and unions in a number of Western European countries have pursued their bargaining systems to their full and logical conclusion by jointly supporting *legislation* that is designed to extend the terms of negotiated collective agreements to unorganized employers. This has become quite common in Western Europe.

Under such laws, typically (but of course with variations from country to country), if an agreement is judged to cover 50 percent of the workers in a given industry or occupation, the state can extend the terms of the agreement to cover the entire trade or occupation. The decision generally lies in the hands of the ministry of labor. Laws to extend the terms of collective agreements operate in France, Belgium, the Netherlands, Germany, Austria, Switzerland, and Luxembourg.[18]

These laws, however, have no real counterpart in Scandinavia, where the high degree of union organization would make them irrelevant or unnecessary, or in England, where the reason lies in a greater tradition of voluntarism.

Promotion of legislative systems to extend collective agreements and broad industry-wide bargaining, which has been so common in Western Europe, also reflects the more "inclusive" character of European labor movements—inclusive in the sense that labor movements work more toward the benefit of the working class as a whole, as well as toward the interests of individual unions. All unions are, of course, immediately concerned with their members' interests. In America, however, with its lesser class consciousness, unions have developed in the direction of exclusively concentrating their collective-bargaining efforts upon their members' immediate needs and interests. To the degree that European unions have traditionally been influenced by concern for an entire class—the working class—their agreements and tactics have had a more inclusive character. They have tended to be less *exclusively* devoted to the interests of members only and, therefore, willing to accept institutions and practices which seemed to afford wider protection to larger groups of workers, including those working in less profitable firms, and even in unorganized firms.

To some extent these wider considerations have eroded in the past decade, primarily because industrial development has been at a more dynamic pace and because wage levels have increased sharply. Defensive instruments like the extension of agreements to prevent unfair competition and to achieve broad solidarity protection become less relevant in rapidly expanding economies.

During the past ten years or so, resort to extension of collective agreements has become less common, even in the countries where legislation permits it. This is the result of several developments; the principal one, perhaps, is that many individual companies now frequently give workers more than industry- or association-wide agreements require. Extension of agreements as a protection against unfair competition often become unnecessary.

The declining practice of extending agreements also results from rising union concern about the problem and difficulties of unionizing unorganized workers. Growing affluence and the institutionalizaton of unions and labor parties seem to be reducing the more or less automatic propensity of workers to identify with and join traditional class institutions like unions. To the extent that the extension of agreements brings union-negotiated benefits to unorganized as well as to organized workers, they reduce the pressure on unorganized workers to join unions and pay dues. For this reason the Swiss unions, for example, now seem less anxious to use legal machinery to extend agreement terms to protect nonunionized workers.[19]

As another example, the German Federation of Trade Unions (DGB) has unequivocally stated in recent years that it is only in very rare instances "that its affiliated unions ask to have an agreement extended." In explanation the DGB states:

The reason why, in general, Trade Union members reject an extension of contract is their view that the normative provisions of collective agreements should be applicable to, and have the force of law, only for organised workers. It is the endeavor of Trade Union organised workers to exclude unorganised workers from the benefits deriving from collective bargaining. In the conviction that the successes achieved through collective agreements are made possible only by Trade Unions with a strong membership and sound finances they reject the idea that the unorganised should share the benefits without making any contribution.[20]

Union Recognition and Union Security

As already indicated, the establishment of union recognition among workers at a given work site is generally a less formal matter in Western Europe than in the United States. Nowhere can one find anything like the very elaborate system of the U.S. National Labor Relations Board, with its conduct of elections and the certification of sole and exclusive bargaining rights to unions that gain a majority in such elections. Generally recognition in Western Europe flows from the negotiation of a broad agreement with an employer association. Some legislation exists to protect workers from employers' antiunion acts, but nothing to compare with the complex body of administrative law developed under the National Labor Relations Board.[21]

This is partly because European employers seem to have accepted unions and their institutional role to a degree still not known in the United States.

Given these conditions, as well as the class and ideological background of the European labor movement, it is not surprising that in European labor relations, as compared to the United States, there has been much less emphasis upon the negotiation of union security clauses (collective-agreement provisions in one form or another that make affiliation with the union and/or dues payment a condition of employment).

To attract loyal members European unions have generally been able to count upon a deeper and more abiding sense of class consciousness among workers than have American unions (for reasons outlined in Chapter I). Union dues payment appears more "natural" and "automatic" to European workers. Moreover, given the depth of commitment to a particular ideology (socialist, communist, or religious), a union might be loath to compel a nonbeliever in the union theology to join, pay dues, and participate in its activity. Also, unions have found it objectionable, especially in the days when class consciousness and a sense of class conflict ran deeper, to look to the employer to have workers adhere to the union, as would be provided under collective-agreement terms.

Much the same conclusion could be drawn in connection with the emphasis placed by the typical American union upon seniority clauses and provisions in collective agreements. The European union leader may not have felt the need for this kind of special protection against possible arbitrary layoffs or promotions. Walter Galenson, writing of Norway, says that the general acceptance of trade unionism "renders seniority in hiring and discharge as largely superfluous as a union security measure." Similar considerations render union security clauses, such as the closed shop, largely unnecessary in Norway.[22]

To these factors cited by Galenson one should add that a class-oriented union movement, in any country, dislikes the role of helping to determine who will be laid off and who will be retained (by means of seniority clauses in the collective agreement). Even in the recent past, for example, several important unions—we are here speaking of Britain—simply turned their backs on questions of redundancy (layoff) and sought to deny its existence. They preferred this to developing a union policy to deal with them. William McCarthy writes, "The Amalgamated Engineering Union insists that redundance in any form must be opposed. This means that its officials cannot raise the problem of job security in all its aspects until an employer is threatening members with the sack."[23]

This lack of effective policy in Britain has not, however, been confined to any one union. A Ministry of Labour survey completed early in 1963 revealed that "five out of every six workers in manufacturing did not even have the protection of a published redundancy policy." Where policies were found, less than 10 percent were incorporated into agreements signed with unions. The General Council of the TUC, in 1963, somewhat belatedly urged upon the Ministry the need for "a rapid and wide extension of agreements and procedures especially in the private sector" to establish redundancy procedures, compensation for loss of work, systems to transfer workers to other positions, the protection of "superannuation" rights during layoffs, and so on.[24]

Generally, in Western Europe, seniority is given some consideration when layoffs are to be made, but factors like family responsibilities, degrees of skill, and the like may count for as much or more. Seniority seems to play a very limited role, or no role at all, with regard to promotions in Western European industrial relations.

As a final point, though, it should be noted that in the past European employers have been much less prone to lay off workers when short-term cyclical downturns occurred. Government policy has often been unsympathetic to such layoffs, and lingering traditions of employer paternalism have also been a consideration. To the extent that such traditions and considerations have governed or limited employers, there has been less need for seniority systems and other devices to control layoffs under collective bargaining.[25]

With the foregoing as background, one must add that in some ways the inclusion of detailed seniority provisions in collective agreements made in the United States, as contrasted with their absence in European agreements, also reflects the greater economic-industrial power and job control of American unions. Let us look at an example of the lesser control of European unions. The Swedish Federation of Trade Unions (LO) is probably as well organized as any union movement in the world. Yet as late as 1961, in a special report on *The Trade Unions and Industrial Democracy* to its congress (Americans would say "convention"), LO could note:

The employer's right to discharge as he sees fit still prevails in Sweden in contrast to the situation in several other countries where instead there is protection against being discharged. . . . The Committee now considers the time appropriate to remove the free right of termination of employment from the collective bargaining system. Instead protection against being fired should be established which would require the employer to show objectively acceptable reasons for a termination or a dismissal.[26]

The report went on to propose that the special Labor Market Council (composed of union and employer association representatives) should act as "an arbitration committee with the right of making a binding decision in a dispute." The same report also called for the strengthening of the seniority principle "in terminations or layoffs because of lack of work."

It is evident that even the strongest of European unions still lacks the full presence and strength at the workshop that is characteristic of American unionism and bargaining. This is true despite the fact that the impact of the Swedish labor movement on its society—whether through union, party, or cooperative organization—is greater than the total impact of its American counterpart on American society. As already suggested, European union efforts to bolster their strength at the job level—including those in Sweden—have been growing. In the spring of 1968 the Swedish metalworkers announced that they had made a breakthrough in the field of trade union representation at the work place. At the Sandviken Steelworks—one of the largest plants in Sweden—company management had agreed informally to pay the wages of six full-time trade union representatives (workers in the plant) who were presumably to handle grievances and related matters. Until this informal agreement (and it has not yet been incorporated into the collective agreement), union representatives anywhere in Sweden only rarely received company compensation for time lost from their jobs while handling grievances.[27]

A postscript vis-à-vis the Swedish LO should be added here regarding the layoff or discharge of workers. The 1964 negotiations between LO and the Swedish Employers' Confederation modified the right of management "to hire and fire . . . so that a dispute over the dismissal of a worker who has been employed for at least 9 months and has reached the age of 18 years must be submitted for arbitration to a joint LO-SAF council, which can award damages to a worker if it finds the dismissal unjustified."[28]

The recent experience of Swedish labor with the problem of layoffs and subsequent compensation is by no means unique. The Norwegian Federation of Trade Unions took a similar step, in its 1966 negotiations, to obtain severance pay for the first time. Serious layoff threats in the metal industries of Germany and the Netherlands in late 1966 and early 1967 led the large metal unions in these countries to take new measures to protect their members against layoffs.[29]

Provisions for payment to union stewards for time spent on grievances, arbitration of dismissals, and severance pay for workers when operations are shut down are to be found in innumerable union-management agreements in many mass production industries in the United States.

Changing Attitudes of European Unions Toward Union Security

The high levels of employment and the greater degree of worker affluence in the past decade have led some European labor movements to reconsider the need or desirability for some form of union security in their collective agreements. As unions become increasingly integrated into industrial life, as the spirit of class conflict declines, many workers seem to be shifting away from their prewar position of automatically paying union dues. The American phenomenon of the "free rider," or nonpayer of dues, appears to be growing in some Western European countries. The issue of checkoff and/or other forms of compulsory union affiliation is, therefore, coming in for increasing discussion in Western Europe.

Proposals to deal with the nonpayer of dues include one made by some French trade union leaders that all employees, whether or not union members, be required to make a regular financial contribution to a union of their choice to help defray the costs of negotiating the collective agreement that protects them. (This is similar to the arrangements under the so-called agency shop in the United States and Canada, which requires nonunion members to pay dues or some equivalent to help support the costs borne by the unions.) Similar proposals have been made elsewhere in Europe, including Germany.[30]

In Switzerland, the unions have obtained the equivalent of this support, under an act passed in 1956.

The following events led up to this legislation. Prior to 1950 the closed shop existed, to a limited degree, in Swiss collective agreements. The validity of the closed shop or other forms of compulsory unionism was however, struck down by the Swiss supreme court in 1949. The unions thereupon turned to negotiating agreement clauses that required a worker to contribute payments to the union that had negotiated on his behalf. The courts upheld this, but set careful limits on such payments

COMPARATIVE INDUSTRIAL-RELATIONS SYSTEMS

(usually 50 percent or less of the regular dues), on the grounds that the member was not enjoying all the benefits of union membership.

The court's action was subsequently followed by legislation in 1956, which explicitly authorized the negotiation of clauses in collective agreements that could require "contributions of solidarity" to be paid by nonmembers. The amount of these contributions was to be determined by the courts. The contributions are to be used only to defray "costs for the execution and application of collective agreements or for welfare or other purposes benefiting all workers in the bargaining unit."[31]

In Belgium, the reaction of the unions to the signs of losses in membership and dues payment has been quite different.

In this country, as in others, the gradual integration of the unions in the social order, the general development of labor peace, and the "disappearance of violent struggles has led to worker disaffection vis-à-vis the unions, whose utility no longer seems so immediate."[32]

Belgian unions continue to oppose the closed shop or other forms of compulsory unionism. To counteract the free-rider problem and, in the words of a delegate to the Belgian Christian trade union convention, "to put an end to the present system of favoring parasites," Belgian unions have developed a special bargaining program. In a growing number of industries they have negotiated special benefits (usually an annual bonus) that the employer pays only to union members. The amounts have varied from industry to industry, and in general they tend to be modest. The precedent, however, seems significant.[33]

Proposals to restrict certain benefits won by union negotiations to union members only have received serious consideration in Germany and Switzerland. An assembly of German lawyers, for example, concluded that "collective agreements made by a union solely for its members are legally admissible." In some labor cases the judges have dismissed claims by German workers who, when questioned, say they are not union members. In Switzerland a leading labor jurist has also defended "differential treatment" of trade unionists and unorganized workers. He recommended that, as certain fringe benefits are extended under union contracts, they be restricted to union dues payers:

. . . Where overall labour contracts come about, lines must be drawn; hence differentiation between parties to the overall contract and non-participants is nothing unnatural, but on the other hand is perfectly understandable and close at hand. Not only does legislation draw the line; the outsider himself draws the line between himself and the community effects of the contract. Parties to the contract, for their part, must be consistent. To enjoy benefits won at no personal cost is not right.[34]

In the Netherlands, the union approach to a more equitable solution to the matter of dues payment by members and nonmembers has been more oblique, but it seems to reflect the same basic uneasiness about the "advantages" of the nonmember. Instead of putting pressure on nonmembers to join unions in order to offset the burden of dues-paying members, the three Dutch federations (Catholic, Protestant, and socialist) have "proposed the creation of special funds in the various industrial branches, to be financed by the enterprises." These funds are to "be used for the participation of trade union members at educational training courses, for the financing of scientific research of the trade union movement or for the repayment of a part of trade union fees to the individual member."

Agreements have been reached in some Dutch companies to carry out these objectives, but many employers objected to "the proposal for repayment of trade union dues." After some negotiation, however, this objection was rejected in principle by the unions, and they have continued to seek establishment of these funds, inclusive of "the possibility of repayment of affiliation fees to trade union members."[35]

In Britain closed (union) shops have existed in a number of industries for some years;[36] they are not common, but they are increasing. Key unions such as the National Union of General and Municipal Workers and the Electrical Trades Union now openly campaign for the checkoff in their agreements. Other unions seem to be giving the matter increasing, sympathetic consideration.[37]

The General Secretary, Jim Conway, of the Amalgamated Engineering Union, following a visit to the United States late in 1965 expressed cautious interest in the union shop and the checkoff as he had observed them here. He was concerned that the checkoff might make the union "a tool of the management or it might become slack and bureaucratic, but I saw no sign of this happening in the U.S.A."[38] When, however, Conway and other leaders later proposed that the AEU formally change the union's constitution to permit the checkoff system, it was rejected in a very close vote by the organization's Rules Revision Meeting.[39]

The checkoff system has grown most rapidly in Britain among civil servants and publicly owned industries such as coal, and others. A recent survey estimates that two million trade unionists, or one in every five, are working where checkoff arrangements are in operation.[40]

The checkoff of union dues, particularly in the years to come, is likely to be a subject of growing importance in many European countries.[41]

N O T E S

1. An exception must be noted in the case of Great Britain where the system of industrial relations rests upon the principles of voluntarism, with little dependence upon state regulation. This contrasts with the countries of the Continent. One might also draw a partial distinction between such countries as France and Belgium where the traditions of Roman and Napoleonic law have helped provide a basis for wider state regulation of labor matters. In the Scandinavian countries however, the state's role in industrial relations has been a lesser one.

2. J. D. Reynaud, *Les syndicats en France* (Paris: Armand Colin, 1963), pp. 163, 180–181.

3. Maurice F. Neufeld, *Italy, School for Awakening Countries: The Italian Labor Movement in Its Political, Social and Economic Setting from 1860 to 1960* (Ithaca, N.Y.: Cornell University Press, 1961), pp. 502, 503. Also Daniel L. Horowitz, *The Italian Labor Movement* (Cambridge, Mass.: Harvard University Press, 1963), pp. 293–294. Actually, in both France and Italy plant or enterprise collective agreements have remained the exception, in most industries, and industry-wide and/or area-industry agreements are still the general rule. Metals are a notable exception in both countries. For a recent statement of the CGIL position, see *World Trade Union Movement* (WFTU), January 1967, pp. 23–27.

4. In Sweden there were in effect "as far back as 1908 . . . no fewer than 2,365 collective agreements covering 12,614 employers and 318,190 workers"—an extraordinarily large number considering the date, the size of the country, etc. Sigfrid Hansson, *The Trade Union Movement of Sweden* (Amsterdam: International Federation of Trade Unions, International Trade Union Library, No. 6, 1927), p. 39. Developments were a bit slower in Denmark and Norway because industrial development was slower.

5. "Annual Vacations with Pay," *International Labour Review*, August 1962, pp. 128–147.

6. Faced with very tight labor markets in recent years, many German companies have established voluntary pension plans, generally under employer control, to help and attract labor. G. V. Rimlinger, "Post War German Social Policy," *Industrial Relations*, February 1967, p. 195. Voluntary pension plans, sometimes confined to staff or white-collar employees, and often under exclusive employer control, are fairly common in some segments of British industry.

7. The German Construction Workers' Trade Union has developed an elaborate program for workers to "accumulate assets" through collective bargaining. To accomplish this objective, it succeeded in negotiating an agreement with construction employers in March 1965. Employers set aside a little more than 2% of the workers' hourly wage in a special fund (employees must contribute around ⅕ as much), which is invested in a form of capital assets chosen by the individual worker (securities, payments to savings associations for housing, etc.). The German Trade Union Federation (DGB) has also favored workers' accumulation of assets as a general policy for its affiliated unions. The German government has responded by exempting from taxation most of the assets thus accumulated. See George Leber, *Accumulation Of Assets For The Worker* (Berlin: Industriegewerkschaft Bau-Steine-Erden, 1964), and Herbert Ehrenberg, "Accumulation of Assets for Workers Through Collective Bargaining," *AFL-CIO Free Trade Union News*, May 1965. Leber and Ehrenberg have been officials of the Construction Workers' union.

8. *Report of the 95th Annual Trades Union Congress, September 2–6, 1963, Brighton,* p. 139.

9. C. H. Hartwell, "New Moves to Cushion Effects of Loss of a Job," *TUC release, New Series No. 145,* May 1964.

10. Ministry of Labour, News Release, London, April 1, 1965. The bill became a law in August 1965.

11. As we have suggested in the preceding section, for a brief period (1949–1950) a few top CIO leaders seemed to envisage a tactic consisting of both private collective bargaining and public legislative pressure for parts of the social security field. Generally, however, American union leaders jealously guard "their" private collective-bargaining area from any government "intrusion."

12. George Levard, *Collective Bargaining and Productivity, Final Reports of the Trade Union Seminar in Berlin, June 18–22, 1957* (Paris: Organisation for European Economic Cooperation), p. 3.

13. T. L. Johnston, *Collective Bargaining in Sweden* (Cambridge, Mass: Harvard University Press, 1962), p. 68.

14. Philip Taft, "Germany," in Walter Galenson (ed.), *Comparative Labor Movements* (New York: Prentice Hall, 1952), p. 268.

15. Shirley W. Lerner, "Factory Agreements and National Bargaining in the British Engineering Industry," *International Labour Review,* January 1964, p. 2.

16. A useful description of the labor operations of the Swedish Employers Confederation (SAF) is contained in Johnston, *op. cit.,* Chap. II. For a self-view of the same organization, see *SAF—The Swedish Employers Confederation* (Stockholm, 1961).

17. This situation has often been disconcerting to Western European branches of American firms, and they frequently hold out against such "automatic" recognition of the union and/or bargaining as a requirement for membership in an employers' association. Often they refuse to join such associations. See the author's "Industrial Relations Policies of U.S. Corporations Abroad," *Industrial Relations Research Association, Proceedings of 17th Annual Meeting, December 28–29, 1964* (Madison: Industrial Relations Research Association, 1965), pp. 88–89.

18. See Ludwig Hamburger, "The Extension of Collective Agreements to Cover Entire Trades and Industries," *International Labour Review,* XL (August 1939), 153–194. This is still the only *general survey* of these laws and their operation. Information on particular countries and laws is obtainable, of course, in the monographs on collective bargaining and unionism that are issued in individual countries. Information also appears in various issues of the *International Labour Review.*

19. Alexandre Bernstein, "Union Security and the Scope of Collective Agreements in Switzerland," *International Labour Review,* February 1962, pp. 22, 23.

20. *DGB News Letter,* Dusseldorf, January 1965, p. 4.

21. In France, Belgium, and the Netherlands, procedures do exist whereby the government extends a formal "representation" status to labor organizations it judges sufficiently representative of workers. This, in turn, permits these recognized labor federations to participate in negotiations with employers in almost all sectors of the economy. It also accords them membership on key government commissions and other public bodies. Difficulties in obtaining recognition from some employers have recently led the British Trades Union Congress to explore ways and means, including legislation, of insuring union recognition by hostile employers.

22. Walter Galenson, *Labor In Norway* (Cambridge, Mass.: Harvard University Press, 1949), pp. 205–207.

23. William McCarthy, *The Future of the Unions,* Fabian Tract No. 339 (London: Fabian Society, 1962), p. 22. The engineers laid down a new policy on "automation" in 1966 that spelled out the need for consultation and agreement between

union and management before "introduction of automation." Also, it stipulated, there was to be "no redundancy arising from introduction of automation; labor so displaced to be retained on pay-roll pending alternation work cutback loss of earnings." This new policy also calls for retraining programs, sharing of automation benefits, etc. *IMF News,* No. 31, June 1966.

24. John Hughes, *Change in the Unions,* Fabian Research Series Pamphlet No. 244, (London: Fabian Society, August 1964), p. 24. A publicly commissioned report in 1967 advised against any statutory proposals to control dismissal procedures, for the time being at least. It did urge improvement of voluntary procedures within firms. *Dismissal Procedures, Ministry of Labour* (London: Her Majesty's Stationery Office, 1967).

25. Legal protection against arbitrary dismissal or discharge for all workers, organized and unorganized, is also important in a number of European countries. This situation contrasts with that in the United States where such protection is almost totally dependent upon the collective agreement. See, for example, Frederic Meyers, *Ownership of Jobs: A Comparative Study* (Los Angeles: Institute of Industrial Relations, University of California, 1964), esp. Chap. 3.

26. *The Trade Unions and Industrial Democracy, Summary and Conclusions* from a report to the LO Congress (Stockholm: 1961), p. 3.

27. *IMF NEWS* (June 1968). In the United States, company payment for the time union stewards spend on legitimate grievance handling has been a common practice under collective agreement clauses for more than 20 years in a number of industries—automobile, aircraft, machinery, etc. In some American industries, such company payments are relatively unknown. The unions have never sought them on the grounds that this might undermine the union representatives' militance on behalf of his fellow workers.

28. *Labor Developments Abroad* (Washington, D.C.: U.S. Department of Labor, January 1965), p. 8. In the same agreement the LO negotiated severance pay for older workers who "have to leave their jobs because of closure of the plant or large reductions in manpower." *IMF News in Brief* (Geneva: International Metalworkers Federation, December 1964).

29. *Trade Union News Bulletin From Norway,* February and March, 1966. On Germany and the Netherlands, see *IMF News,* December 1966, and February 1967.

30. *French union* interest in checkoff or other union security devices can, of course, also be traced to the longstanding pattern of nonpayment of dues by French workers, with the consequent financial paralysis of French unions. There are other *individual* instances of European unions demanding some sort of checkoff from employers in recent years.

31. This description of the Swiss experience is drawn from Michael Dudra, "Middle Way Approaches to Union Security in Switzerland, Canada and Columbia," *Industrial Relations Research Association, Proceedings of Fifteenth Annual Meeting,* Pittsburgh, December 27–28, 1962, pp. 36–48. Also see the author's comments, *ibid.,* pp. 53–54.

32. Marcel Bolle de Bal, "Syndicalisme 'Integré' et Syndicalisme 'Encouragée,'" *Socialisme,* May 1964.

33. Robert A. Senser, "Special Bonuses for Belgian Unionists," *Monthly Labor Review,* August 1964, pp. 928, 929. Bolle de Bal notes that the unions were careful to obtain a legal opinion on the validity of negotiating special benefits for union members only, even if nonmembers are employed in the same enterprise. Apparently this is acceptable under Belgian law, for it is regarded as a special bonus for union members and not "damage" to nonmembers. Bolle de Bal, *op. cit.,* p. 9.

34. On Germany, see *IMF News,* No. 53, November 1966; on Switzerland, *ibid.,* No. 32, June 1966.

35. *Information Bulletin of the Netherlands Federation of Trade Unions, NVV,* No. 83/84, June 1965, p. 16. The Dutch unions, to repeat, "do not at all like to exert pressure on non-members to join the unions." Letter from J. G. van Wouwe, International Department, Netherlands Federation of Trade Unions, to the author; dated September 30, 1965.

36. W. E. J. McCarthy, *The Closed Shop in Britain* (Berkeley and Los Angeles: University of California Press, 1964), esp. Chap. 2.

37. See *National Union of General and Municipal Workers Journal,* December 1965, pp. 8, 22, for a descriptive announcement of the signing of a new union shop agreement at one important private firm and the notation that sixty local government agencies "now operate the check-off system, and these agencies represent more than 10 per cent of the population." While the Electrical Trades Union is seeking the check-off widely, as a matter of policy (see *Electron,* Journal of the ETU, July 1965), it has had very limited success, and in 1965 it was estimated that only 500 of its 300,000 members had it. (Letter from F. J. Chapple, Assistant General Secretary, October 12, 1965.)

38. *AEU Journal,* February 1966, pp. 45–46.

39. *Ibid.,* April 1968, p. 145.

40. See A. I. Marsh and J. W. Staples' study "Check-Off Arrangements in Britain: A Study of their Growth and Functions," in *Three Studies in Collective Bargaining, Royal Commission on Trade Unions and Employers' Associations,* Research Papers 8 (London: Her Majesty's Stationery Office, 1968).

41. Rudimentary beginnings of a checkoff system are provided by agreements signed in Italy in 1962 by metals unions and employers, and in 1963 by the three leading union federations and the general employers' association. Isolated efforts have been made in other countries. *The New York Times,* January 29, 1961, reported that the large Construction Workers' Union of the German Federation of Trade Unions was demanding that nonunion workers be compelled to pay the equivalent of dues to the unions—with the funds to be used to train young workers or to pay special benefits to older workers.

VIII

Grievance Settlement, Worker Representation,

Strikes, and Union Structure

THE form of worker representation at the job level and the nature of grievance procedures available to settle disputes go a long way toward characterizing a country's collective-bargaining system. This is especially true when comparing American and European unionism.

As already noted, European collective agreements are generally less comprehensive than American collective agreements, and this is partly because social legislation regulates a great many matters in Europe that in the United States are covered by collective bargaining. And since the scope of bargaining is smaller in Europe, there is less need there for strong grievance procedure systems in industrial relations. In some countries there are labor courts, which further reduce the need to include strong grievance provisions in collective agreements.

Aside from social legislation, the area of collective bargaining in Europe tends to be limited in other respects, as compared with the United States. In a few countries the setting of piece rates, arranging the order of layoffs or new job assignments, or determining the vacation period—these and other matters tend to be the *sole* prerogatives of management. Where management must consult the workers, often it is not the union that is consulted, but a special plant committee—a committee created not by, but outside, the collective agreement.

One reason why collective agreements are more limited in scope in Europe is that labor there has long sought to extend the power of the worker into management. The long struggle for "workers' control" or worker management of industry has doubtless drained off some of the union energy that might otherwise have gone into the struggle for job control so prominent in American labor history.

The very structure of European unionism reflects a different approach to the importance and problems of worker representation at the plant or job level. European union structure also reflects, in most instances, a long and complex history, during which there have been only rare opportunities to "rationalize" union institutions.

Grievance Procedures in American and European Labor Systems

It is not surprising in the light of the foregoing factors that "grievances are raised much less frequently in most European countries than in the United States."[1] Again, European agreements do not spell out in the same detail the steps in the grievance procedure the way most American agreements do. They do not usually concern themselves as much with careful definitions of grievances and with what kinds of unresolved disputes can be arbitrated.

The Amercan concept of social equality as opposed to the class basis of European social action also helps account for the more aggressive character of American unionism in collective bargaining, which includes the processing of grievances. Within a class-oriented movement, as it exists in Europe, a worker may tend to "behave in a manner appropriate to one's station," in the words of S. M. Lipset. American society, on the other hand, which places such a "high premium on economic affluence and social ascent for all its members," makes it easier and more natural for workers to seek their economic aims more aggressively. Lipset adds, ". . . an open class system leads workers to resent inequalities in income and status between themselves and others more frequently than does an ascriptively stratified system. America's equalitarian value system, by more broadly and less clearly defining the range of groups with which members may legitimately compare themselves, may make for a more free-flowing discontent among workers than in Europe." This relative lack of class consciousness and the rejection of a set class position, combined with more dynamic self-interest, helps to account for the more aggressive collective-bargaining policies and grievance activities of American unions.[2] By the same token, management in the United States may have a less firm foundation for defending all its usual "prerogatives," where it lacks the support provided by a sense of class rank.

We have already indicated that the European union structure often does not provide for distinct tiers of union organization at the work site. This type of structure results in less union power at the workshop level as far as handling grievances is concerned. The typical European local union organization is established on an area-wide basis (a local union will cover an entire city or corresponding area). The next higher tier is the district, departmental, or provincial level. Above this, the top tier, is the union's national headquarters.

In a sense one could say that the typical European structure is like the typical craft-union structure in the United States, in that the local covers a given area. This contrasts with the typical U.S. industrial union structure, in which the local organization is firmly implanted in a given plant or company. But this similarity between the typical geographically based European local union and the American local geographic craft union is quite limited. Even Western European unions organized on a craft basis do not usually have as much job control and as much "penetration" of employers' establishments as American craft unions. Moreover, as already indicated, the industrial type of local union geared to a single plant, which is common in the United States, for the most part does not exist in Europe. Typically, a worker in a chemical or metalworking factory will belong to a branch of his chemical or metalworking national union, which covers a given area, usually a city. In this sense he is a union member on the basis of residence, rather than on the basis of his place of work.

In Sweden, for example, geographical union branches may be complemented at a factory by local "clubs." The club functions pretty much as the local union does in the United States, although the more centralized character of bargaining by an entire industry, or even by the nation, for general wage movements leaves the Swedish "club" with less power than the typical American local union.

Worker Plant Representation and Government-Created Committees

To a degree the European structure reflects the reduced grievance role of the union in the plant, as compared with that in the United States. But to a degree the very structure also has encouraged a system of labor relations under which potential union control over the job and job problems is weaker than in the United States.

Formal methods and systems to handle employee grievances were ultimately developed in the European labor movement, but at a relatively late date. They were often the product of legislation and date from the period following World War I. Created by legislation, these systems of grievance-handling often lie mostly outside regular union channels. Such, for example, is the case with the system of *délégués du personnel* (shop stewards) in France and with the works councils in Germany and Austria.

The members of these plant committees that handle workers' grievances at the shop level (the scope of their activities varies with each country's legislation) are elected by all the employees both union and nonunion, in a given plant or office. Rules governing elections are set forth in national legislation. The legislation generally provides strongest support to union-nominated candidates or union lists of candidates, but these committees, once elected, are clearly plant-linked and -based, and *at best* only indirectly subject to union control.

The legislative nature of and support for plant committees—which in the United States, Great Britain, and even Sweden are based more on the union than on legislation—may in part also be accounted for by Europe's long prevalent system of plural unionism. In pre-World War II Germany and Austria—and the same is true today of France, Belgium, the Netherlands, and Italy (to give four good current examples)—the presence of several different unions (socialist, Catholic, independent, etc.) at nearly every work site made it easier to depend upon "outside" governmental machinery to provide worker representation in the plant. Theoretically the various unions might have developed devices to effect joint representation. In practice, however, it became easier to accomplish this by means of government-sanctioned legislation and elections—elections that generally provide for proportional union representation at the plants.[3]

The net result of this evolution has been to establish systems of grievance procedure that function fairly well, but to an important extent lie outside the control of union machinery. In actual practice, one does find that in some situations, as an alternative to using the plant committees, workers can and occasionally do call upon the area union representative to handle grievances. The lines of authority are often not clearly defined. (Employees in a few countries, France is a notable case, can also call upon the ministry of labor to protect certain rights that may be violated by an employer in the plant.)

As might be expected, employers generally prefer to deal with "their own" plant committees rather than with the unions. The employer may deliberately use the plant committee to divert worker loyalty away from the union. Of the German situation Adolf Sturmthal writes: "Management is just as interested in friendly relations with the plant or works council. By strengthening the council's position, management often hopes to weaken the union, and this not always without justification."[4]

As to the French labor movement, Val Lorwin comments, "A shrewd employer may deliberately play off the plant committee against the union, by making it a substitute in workers' minds for union action." Union training programs have been intensified in order to ensure the competence of plant committee members, as well as to keep their union ties strong.[5]

Labor Courts—Final Disposition of Grievances

In the light of the primarily legal basis for worker representation in the plants or workshops of most Continental Western European countries (in contrast, for example, with the collective-agreement basis in the United States and Great Britain), it is not surprising that final disposition of day-to-day labor-mangement disputes is generally accomplished through legal rather than collective-agreement channels. This disposition is made primarily in the so-called labor courts, which are found in one form or another in all Continental Western European countries.

These courts have different origins, some having emerged after today's unions and management were well established, while others apparently arose out of needs going back to feudal or early postfeudal times.[6]

The composition of the courts varies widely, with equal representation between labor, management, and the public in some instances, and only public representation in others. In France the labor courts are bipartite; only labor and management are represented.[7]

Labor courts are usually set up outside the regular courts or as autonomous divisions within them. Their decisions are generally enforceable in the same manner as the decisions of regular courts.

Generally speaking, labor courts are empowered to deal with disputes arising out of collective agreements, labor laws, and decrees. Disputes about *rights* stem from the interpretation or application either of a law or of a provision contained in a collective agreement.

There are also disputes about *interests*, which in labor-management relations, arise out of a demand by one party for either the modification of an existing right or a claim for a new right. Disputes over interests generally do not come before labor courts, but are resolved by a test of bargaining power between unions and management, or through other established machinery. (Occasionally [Germany is an example], the government may appoint a labor court judge as a chairman of an arbitration board to settle a dispute over *new* agreement terms or some other *interest* dispute.)

Of crucial importance to union strength and position vis-à-vis these court proceedings is the matter of *who* can bring cases before the courts. In some countries those who bring cases before the courts are primarily individuals (which indicates the preunion origin of some of these courts). Indeed in France, whose labor court system is the oldest, no "collective" disputes are entertained by the courts.[8]

But the practice of completely excluding groups, particularly unions, from labor court cases tends to be the exception, rather than the rule. Usually unions as well as individuals, trade associations as well as individual employers, may bring cases before the tribunals.

The greater strength and firmer institutionalization of the Scandinavian labor movements is evidenced by the fact that individual employees generally cannot take cases before the courts in any of the three countries. Group action (basically by union representation), is required. The incentive that this gives to union affiliation in Scandinavia is, of course, significant.

On the whole the very existence of labor court systems makes dispute settlement in Western Europe more legalistic and centralized than dispute settlement in the United States. Nearly all collective agreements in the United States now provide that nearly all unresolved disputes over the interpretation or application of the agreement are subject to compulsory arbitration, on the appeal of either or both parties. This is done, however, in a private arbitration proceeding and remains a highly decentralized process.[9]

While Scandinavia is a notable exception, in most countries labor court proceedings, like the handling of grievances, for the most part "exist apart from the union itself," as Sturmthal aptly puts it.[10] Grievance and arbitration handling, which are often regarded as the cornerstones of union strength and membership appeal in the United States, simply have not had that function in most European unions.

Strike Trends—Some Comparisons

Just as the propensity to "grieve" in labor relations is higher in the United States than in Western Europe, so is the propensity to strike. Although statistics show a declining trend in strikes in the United States since the fifties (particularly if these statistics are compared with those of pre-World War II and immediate postwar years), the incidence of strikes is still generally greater in the United States. There are a number of ways to measure this incidence,[11] but Table 5, prepared by the U.S. Department of Labor, presents a good and generally useful survey of these trends in the 1956–1965 period.

Although strikes may continue to decline in the United States, it will be some time, if ever, before they drop to the generally lower levels of Western Europe.

The experience of Italy in recent years seems to deviate from the general pattern of strikes in Western Europe. The severe pattern of strikes in Italy reflects an accelerated "modernization" drive in that country's economy and industrial-relations system. The great strikes in France in 1968 (not shown in these tabulations) stemmed as much from political as industrial forces.

Despite the concern constantly expressed during the past decade about strikes in Great Britain, that country's statistical record is not too bad compared with others, such as the United States, France, Italy, Belgium, or Canada. Possibly the intensive craft type of trade-union organization in British industry means that their strikes have a bottleneck character, and shut down vital functions or processes which upset production on a wider scale than the strike statistics indicate. This suggests that comparisons like these must be made with considerable caution,

Year	United States	Belgium	Canada	Denmark	France	Germany (West)	Italy	Netherlands	Sweden	Switzerland	Great Britain
1956	641	376	291	715.0	126	93.0	492	66.0	1.5	0.8	98
1957	317	1,471	333	4.7	353	61.0	511	2.2	20.0	0.4	392
1958	466	115	631	6.0	96	44.0	442	11.0	5.6	1.1	162
1959	1,306	388	482	11.0	163	3.4	961	4.1	8.7	1.0	247
1960	354	130	156	36.0	89	2.0	581	132.0	6.6	0.5	139
1961	300	35	278	1,323.0	212	3.1	961	6.8	0.7	NA	137
1962	334	101	285	8.2	152	22.0	2,156	2.4	1.7	0.7	258
1963	282	91	179	13.0	461	90.0	1,051	10.0	8.4	32.0	78
1964	390	159	294	9.4	187	0.8	1,202	11.0	11.0	2.1	100
1965	383	25	414	129.0	74	2.3	656	14.0	1.4	0.1	127
Annual average (1956—65)	477	289	334	226	191	32	901	26	6.6	3.9	174

NA—Not available.

SOURCE: *Labor Developments Abroad,* U.S. Department of Labor, June 1967, pp. 27–29. The original sources for this table are the U.S. Department of Labor, the International Labour Office (Geneva) and the Organisation for Economic Cooperative Development (Paris). Definitions and coverage, as between countries, vary somewhat, but for overall comparisons the data are usable. Since the table may be a bit confusing, an example will help simplify it: In the United States in 1963 there were 57,081,000 people with paid hours in nonagricultural industries, and there were 16,000,000 man-days lost in strikes. The figure of 284 man-days lost per thousand persons is arrived at by dividing 16,100,000 by 57,081.

since the statistics for any country or any particular year may require some special explanation. To repeat, however, the table does have validity and usefulness as a general basis for comparison.

Legal Status of the Strike

In Western European countries today, generalizations concerning the right to strike are difficult to make, and it is even more difficult to cite specific limitations on this right. In the nineteenth century nearly every country either forbade or severely limited the right, and often severe penalties could be inflicted on strikers; but this is completely changed today. Either explicitly or implicitly, the right to strike is accorded all or nearly all categories of workers. Sometimes this right is explicitly provided for in a nation's constitution, as in France and Italy, or by statute; in other cases it flows from the right to form unions, which is provided by the constitution or a statute.[12]

Since the right to strike is so broadly based in many countries there are often no distinctions between authorized strikes and non-authorized, or so-called wildcat strikes. The latter do not have the formal approval of union officials. Unlike the situation in the United States, for example, serious punishment is almost never meted out to shopleaders of unauthorized strikes. (Punishment in some countries is not even legal.) This has been a particular source of industrial relations difficulty in Great Britain during the past decade.

Proposals to provide a legal remedy against leaders of unauthorized strikes in Great Britain were strongly advocated by a minority of the recent British Royal Commission on Trade Unions and Employers' Associations. Although a majority of the Commission rejected the plea for new legislation, the issue remains very much alive in Great Britain.[13]

Although the right to strike is extended to nearly all categories of workers, purely political strikes are generally prohibited in a number of countries. Such is the case, for example, in Germany, France, Italy, and Luxembourg.

Many countries also restrict or prohibit strikes by public employees. Occasionally a distinction is made between, on the one hand, regular civil service employees and, on the other hand, manual-worker public employees and those in publicly operated corporations (e.g., railroad or postal workers). Civil service employees may be prohibited, by law, from striking, while the others are generally permitted to strike, under certain circumstances.[14]

Often, as in the Scandinavian countries, carefully defined government mediation procedures must be exhausted before a strike is legally permissible. In Scandinavia, too, strikes may be illegal in cases that come within the jurisdiction of the labor court. In Scandinavia, when labor court procedures and jurisdiction are ignored by strikers, damage suits can be filed. Where the labor courts are devoted to the problems of individual workers and not of unions, as in France—and also as in Italy, where there is no comparable labor court system—there are fewer limits on strikes.

A collective agreement between a union and management (or an industry) usually limits the right of strike or lockout by either party. The collective agreement and its procedures for settling disputes, however, often has not had the same "sanctity" in Europe as in the United States. In some countries, for example, Italy, the parties have only recently begun to incorporate no-strike clauses in collective agreements, and so far in only a few of them. In this connection, it might be noted that the no-strike clause in the 1962–1963 agreement in the metal industry was accepted by all the unions, including the communist-dominated CGIL.

Because of legislation and traditional practice, the right of the union to strike with relative impunity seems to be more absolute in many European countries than in the United States. On the other hand, and in this context it is worth repeating, strikes are by and large less common in Europe than in the United States despite the comparatively broad legal basis for it in Europe.

The right to strike is perhaps least inhibited by law in France and Italy, and since World War II this right has been widely exercised in these countries. One-day demonstration strikes and even strikes of shorter duration, which involve large numbers of workers, are quite common. In the absence of continuous, permanently effective unionism and collective bargaining, the labor movements in France and Italy depend to an important extent on the kinds of political pressures that are generated by these short strikes.[15] It should be added that in recent years longer strikes, limited to workers in particular firms or industries and directly related to specific collective-bargaining questions, have also been common in Italy and to some degree in France.

Although generalizations are hazardous, it does appear that strikes vary inversely with the acceptance of unionism as an institution by the society, and especially by the managerial classes. The more firmly the labor movement is institutionalized and "accepted," particularly in the sphere of labor-management relations, the greater the likelihood that there will be fewer strikes. The persistently higher incidence of strikes in France and Italy as well as in the United States and Canada, as compared with Scandinavia or Switzerland, seems to support this thesis.

Programs to Strengthen Union Role in Plant Bargaining

European industry has been more dynamic in the past decade, and there has been greater concern with the need to exert more union control in the plant itself. These factors have touched off a move in several countries to strengthen the role of the union in the plant or on the job.

In France the unions, in addition to carrying on training programs for plant committee members, have agitated for extending more effective recognition to union representatives in the plant, this to be in addition to the rights accorded to the shop delegates (as they are called in France), who are elected in accordance with government legislation.

The unions called for the enactment of legislation under which each union's representative would enjoy some of the same rights and privileges of shop delegates—for example, an allowance of up to twenty or thirty hours per month (depending on the size of the plant) for work *on behalf of the employees* within the plant. The union's representative would also have other protections and privileges already accorded to the shop delegates, including protection against arbitrary layoff, and so on.

Legislation enacted in June 1966 did grant limited consultation status to union representatives in the plant, chosen from among the workers, one for each representative union. Here again we have an instance of how greater union effectiveness in the plant was accomplished by law rather than by the exercise of direct union industrial power. One of the French union leaders remarked that although they "preferred—we wish it still—that the problem of the union representative could be resolved by the collective agreement"—this route is better than none."[16] The issue of union representation in the plant was raised once again in the context of the gigantic French general strike in the spring of 1968, and some additional concessions were made by both employers and the government.[17]

In Germany, the metalworkers union has undertaken special organizing and educational campaigns in a number of important firms to exert direct influence over plant committees. The same union has also striven to reinforce the prestige of informal union committees that function alongside the works council or the plant committee.[18]

This gap in union power or structure—in other words, the relative weakness of the union at the plant or job level—is also due to the fact, as previously noted, that the collective agreement in Europe is generally on an industry-wide and/or an area-industry-wide basis. Its terms are broad and general, and local adaptation and application is likely to be through the local plant committee rather than through the union.

One more sign of changing times was the negotiation in Italy in 1962 of a new agreement in the metals industry to meet the unions' needs in this respect. The International Labour Organisation report of this agreement, the product of a nine-month dispute, is interesting:

Prior to the conclusion of this agreement, minimum working conditions in the metal trades had been established through collective agreements on a national scale. The actual conditions obtaining in individual undertakings, frequently more favorable than the contractual provisions, were determined unilaterally by management or by agreement with workers councils, rather than with the trade unions representing the workers. The unions wished to be recognized by management as bargaining partners in sector-wide and plant level negotiations covering a wide range of subjects. Management wished to retain their margin of freedom of action at the plant level, within the basic framework of the national agreements.

The unions' efforts to break into plant negotiations at the expense of management's unilateral power there, and/or at the expense of the plant councils, met with important success. The 1962 agreement provided "bargaining at the plant level may be undertaken on the specific questions of piece-work systems and rates, and production bonuses." It was also agreed that "the competent parties for such negotiations are the provincial trade unions representing the workers concerned and the regional industrial organization for the employers."[19]

This agreement was a noteworthy breakthrough for the Italian metal unions. The lack of full-time manpower at the local and provincial levels, as well as an economic setback in 1963 and 1964, prevented the unions from fully exploiting the new possibilities. In 1966, however, the metal unions once more took up the struggle to strengthen the position of the union. One demand, among others, was for the right to hold union meetings outside working hours on company premises and the use of company notice (bulletin) boards for union information.[20]

Problems of Union Structure and Bargaining in Britain

The problem of worker representation at the place of work takes a different form in British unionism and British industrial relations. Many early British unions (that continue in today's modern labor movement) were effective craft unions whose power over local working conditions was considerable.

As we have already observed, however, employers tended to shift negotiations away from the workshop to the area or region, or to the entire industry, in order to prevent whipsawing and also to curtail union power at the work site. The agreements negotiated under these conditions that covered factories, in the period before World War I, established national procedures for settling disputes, but usually lacked any provision for processing grievances within the firm or any provision for the recognition of shop stewards.[21] The structure of British unionism was, and is, ill-adapted to union work-site representation; the local organization or branch is, as on the Continent, geographically based, not plant-based. Allan Flanders believes that the problems of re-forming British union and industrial-relations structures, both at the plant and at the top bargaining level, is critical for their growth and survival, as well as for increasing the country's economic progress.[22]

During World War I the government sought to enlist more effective worker cooperation in defense production and sponsored the establishment at the plant level of joint union-management consultation committees. At about the same time, the increased strength of the workers, the result of labor-market shortages, encouraged the formation of committees of shop stewards in many large factories, especially in the engineering (metal-fabricating) and shipbuilding industries.

These shop-steward committees fought for and succeeded in many instances in winning recognition (formal and informal) for themselves in the closing years of World War I. The Engineering Employers' Federation in 1917 signed a national agreement with the group of unions that bargains for engineering workers, an agreement that laid down national procedures for factory-level negotiations.

The post-World War I depression and the depression of the 1930s weakened and sharply reduced the importance of the shop stewards in British union and industrial-relations life. During World War II, however, again under government pressure, many shop committees were established at the work site.

In the past twenty years or so, the shop-stewards movement has genuinely blossomed, particularly in the engineering industry. Its persistence and its success is doubtless due to the very real need for worker representation at the work-site level. But this general role of the shop-stewards movement has been greatly enhanced by the conditions of full employment and industrial expansion following World War II. The need of management to keep its work force and to compete in the labor market for more workers has provided a special opportunity for the shop stewards to maximize workers' bargaining strength in the plant or firm. Wage negotiations at the local level, over and above whatever is laid down in general industry-wide agreements, have taken on greater and greater importance. The function of national agreements is reduced to providing just minimum protection.

The place of the shop steward, especially in the engineering industry, has never been too well defined or fixed in the British union hierarchy. The degree to which he is subject to top union control varies from case to case. The exact manner of his election, his precise powers and role—these often remain as a sort of no man's land in British industry and union life. Yet with the great economic strength so many British firms now have and with national agreements, particularly in the engineering industry, typically providing only the minimum, the relative power of the shop steward in the bargaining process has grown enormously.

These stewards, often under left-wing leadership, have been the greatest source of strikes in Britain in recent years. Commonly they act without official union sanction. One estimate is that 90 percent of all strikes and 70 percent of time lost in strikes in these recent years are a result of unofficial action.[23]

The large share of power enjoyed by shop stewards also stems from the fact that British unionism is basically craft-organized. In a typical large automobile or appliance plant (or in most factories, for that matter), anywhere from one to two dozen unions represent the workers. Indeed, over thirty-five unions participate in the bargaining for the industry-wide engineering agreement; they do so by means of a special "confederation" that is set up along with the employers' confederation. Establishing *union* "presence" at the plant level in the face of this conglomeration is difficult, and the stewards have filled the vacuum.

Often the stewards (and unions) compete with one another at the shop level, and often, too, their strategy vis-à-vis the employer is not coordinated. A strike called by one relatively small group, led by a particular shop steward, can bring about a total shutdown in a major enterprise.

Contributing to nearly constant industrial unrest at the great Ford plant in Daggenham, England, which employs around 58,000 workers, is the presence there of more than twenty unions—a number of which have overlapping jurisdictions. One British union official, from a union *not* involved at Daggenham, has argued, "The existence of 22 separate unions in one factory makes it impossible for satisfactory negotiations to take place, and for harmonious relations to be maintained."[24] An official inquiry into the unrest at Daggenham suggested that a small council or subcommittee ought to be set up in order to by-pass the problems of trying to negotiate with so many unions. The inquiry found the existing system "frustrating and indefensible" and concluded that "so long as the twenty-one unions insist on their democratic right of representation in the executive negotiating machinery, coupled with a refusal to delegate powers to a smaller body" there was "little hope" that the negotiations "will function with proper efficiency."[25]

Industrial relations in the British motorcar industry were back in the news again in 1966 with the report of the special Motor Industry Joint Labour Council, which found that there were 600 stoppages in eight car firms in the first six months of the year, all but five unofficial. The chaotic union structure, poor negotiating procedures, and a "lack of discipline" were listed as contributory causes. The report hinted that it might be necessary to "consider legislation to enforce industrial bargains."[26] An export-crippling strike of several weeks duration broke out early in 1969 as a result of interunion differences concerning proposals to penalize wildcat strikes.

The situation in the motorcar industry is, of course, the worst in Britain, but it does point up what has been a vexing and fairly widespread problem in British trade-union life, especially in the engineering industries.[27] (The relatively rapid rate of technological change in the engineering industries aggravates labor problems in that sector as jobs must constantly be redefined and wage incentive rates changed.)

In defense of the unions on this matter of the shop stewards, one should point back to the earlier period when employers sought to shut the unions out of local plant life. Moreover, in more recent times some employers have deliberately encouraged steward groups rather than deal with "outside" union officials. The general result has been to create bargaining situations that often function beyond the control of the unions.[28]

The critical state of British industrial relations—in which the formal national agreement has become increasingly divorced from the reality of plant life in a number of industries—was a major theme of the report of the Royal Commission on Unions and Employers' Associations in June 1968. Completing a three-year investigation, the Royal Commission proposed that plant and company bargaining (as against formal industry-wide bargaining) be accorded a more central role. As has already been suggested, the focus of power in British bargaining in many industries has actually shifted to the plant and the company. It has been primarily the failure or inability of companies (the commission seemed to put less blame upon the national union bodies) to adjust their policies to this reality that has led to the present crisis in the system. To help British companies and unions make the transition to more conscious plant- and company-oriented bargaining, the Royal Commission proposed the establishment of a permanent Industrial Relations Commission. The latter would, however, depend primarily upon the voluntary cooperation of employers and unions, and the commission would have little power to force changes in the system. An examination of the Royal Commission's Report as well as several expert commentaries on it fail to make clear the exact powers or scope of activities of the proposed Industrial Relations Commission.[29] Until legislation is passed to implement any of the Royal Commission's recommendations, it will be impossible to estimate its potential influence. Two members of the Royal Commission favored granting a greater degree of legal power to the proposed Industrial Relations Commission. Any such body, even with limited power, marks a significant departure for Britain and its voluntary tradition in industrial relations.[30]

British Unions Attempt Reorganization

British unions have been trying to deal with these problems on different levels. Several unions have sought to define and redefine with care the role and function of the shop steward within the union structure. The Electricians and the General and Municipal Workers, for instance, have clearly set forth the responsibility of the shop steward to the area union official. New shop stewards' handbooks have been provided and a substantial number of short training courses are offered to educate stewards as to their responsibilities as well as to their rights.[31] Many unions are trying to improve their communication with the work site and with the members and stewards there.

At a higher level the Trades Union Congress in recent years has been giving considerable attention to the problem of effecting voluntary mergers among the plethora of craft unions (often competing) that dot its structure. Similar efforts were made in earlier periods by the TUC, but these new efforts seem to be characterized by more persistence, pressure, and imagination.[32] In 1964 the TUC persuaded the parliament to pass a new act (in a sense actually an amendment of an old act) to facilitate trade-union mergers.[33]

As the world's oldest continuous major trade-union body based on principles of voluntarism, the TUC probably and not surprisingly has the most varied and in some ways the most cumbersome union structure of all major labor movements. A British writer expects present-day technological trends to increase amalgamations among existing unions, which would be accompanied by a simultaneous strengthening of unionism at the work site. A shift in emphasis from the union geographical branch to the workshop also seems inevitable "to meet the reality of improved workshop bargaining in a high-employment economy."[34]

The recent Royal Commission report also puts great stress on the necessity for the TUC to accelerate the amalgamation process among the trade unions. It added that:

In particular it seems to us that problems caused by a multiplicity of unions organizing in individual factories would be considerably eased in a number of important industries if certain groups of craft unions could be induced to amalgamate.[35]

Some Concluding Comments on Union Structure

A final point should be made on this very complex subject of union structure. The broadly voluntaristic nature of Western trade-unionism development makes structural change a difficult matter. Unions serve a complex set of purposes and respond to many pressures. Proposals to rationalize union structure according to some abstract plan are usually directed to the improved economic functioning of the trade-union movement as a whole. But this can run head on into the interests of particular groups and their leaders, including skilled and unskilled workers, workers in individual industries, and workers seeking to gain or protect status considerations based on other than purely economic needs.

Once established, trade-union structures come to have an almost independent role in their influence on trade-union policy and evolution. Witness the great split in the American trade-union movement in the 1930s between the American Federation of Labor and the Congress of Industrial Organizations. To an important extent, the split was the result of an evolutionary process. This process began with craft unionism, a type of unionism that was necessary in the latter part of the nineteenth century if the union movement itself was to stay alive. As a pragmatic reaction to the circumstances of the time, the process evolved into a hardened "philosophy" that lacked the flexibility required to admit new and (by the 1930s) necessary forms and methods of organization. In other words, this inflexibility blocked industrial unionism in the mass-production industries. Fortunately, however, flexibility did develop, on both sides, and the split of the 1930s could later be healed. Taking an overall view of labor history, one realizes that reunifying these groups within twenty years, by 1955, was no mean feat!

In Europe, generally speaking, union movements at one time or another have expressed preference for a broad, industry-wide type of union structure, as opposed to craft organization, in order to meet the challenge of modern industrial corporate development.

This preference has grown in many countries as the need to participate in industrial- and income-planning has grown. Typical of this view is a recent statement by the Electrical Trades Union of Great Britain (a predominantly craft union, incidentally), which declared, in a special report, on December 7, 1964, "It goes without saying that if we never had a Trade Union Movement and we were now to determine for the first time a kind of structure that would best fit the pattern of our industry and the disposition of our work force, that there would be general agreement for the proposition that by and large there should be one union for each industry."[36]

As previously observed, on several occasions the TUC, with which the ETU is affiliated, has sought to effect amalgamations aimed at industrial grouping, but TUC has had very limited success.

Among the movements that have succeeded in establishing a strong, continuously effective union organization, the one in Sweden is among the few that have also been systematically successful in gradually reducing the number of national unions within its fold (by the process of voluntary amalgamation) in the direction of broader industrial grouping. That this is no particular Scandinavian trait, however, is demonstrated by the fact that the Danish Federation of Trade Unions is as craft-dominated, if not more so, as any other labor movement in the world.

To help overcome some of the rigidities of traditional union structure, the movements in a few countries also include general unions that cater primarily to semiskilled and unskilled workers in a great variety of industries and services. In Denmark, where skilled workers are divided into numerous craft unions, the large general workers' union embraces the less skilled.

The general union can be a useful device to organize small and (from the viewpoint of industrial classification) unclearly defined manufacturing and service establishments in large metropolitan centers. The relatively small size of such units may make them less attractive and more costly to unionize than industrially oriented or craft-oriented unions. The absence of general workers' unions helps account for the relatively low level of unionism in smaller industrial establishments in the United States.[37]

These factors explain, in part, the successes of the two large general unions in Great Britain. These unions have also reached out to organize large numbers of semiskilled and unskilled workers in major industries like automobiles, shipbuilding, or chemicals, as well as in the public service, where they work side by side with numerous craft unions. (The general unions occasionally establish special divisions to deal with their members' problems in particular industries, such as automobiles or chemicals.) Each of these unions, however, began with its own firm industrial base: the gas industry in the case of the General and Municipal Workers' Union and the dock and local transport industries in the case of the Transport and General Workers' Union.[38] The original "ideal," which called for the general union to unite all the less skilled workers into one union, with interchangeable cards, failed to materialize. Recently, however, these two large unions have had discussions that are aimed at bringing about closer, coordinated action between them.[39] The labor movement in the United States is well ahead of its European counterparts in one important structural respect, namely the number of full-time union officials and representatives it supports in proportion to total union membership. This reflects, primarily, the greater degree of local activity and job control exercised by American unions. These larger numbers in the United States may be partially offset by the fact that in several European countries, as previously noted, the workers' local representatives are plant employees, elected by the workers, who hold no official union positions but are reimbursed by employers for time lost. (Shop stewards in some United States mass production industries are also reimbursed by their employers for time lost on grievance handling, but these stewards are part of the American union structure.)

Both in the United States and Western Europe union leaders are elected and selected overwhelmingly from the industries whose workers they represent. This is in contrast with unions in most less developed countries, where there is much greater reliance on "outside" political or intellectual figures for union leadership.

Whatever the theoretical preferences for one union structure over another, most labor movements are usually a combination of craft and industry-wide unions. The force of historical inertia, tradition, and leaders' personalities (at the top and lower levels) usually frustrate any plans for sweeping union reorganization.

Three union movements that have established the most streamlined, industrial type of trade-union structures in modern Europe—the

German Trade Union Federation (DGB), the Netherlands Federation of Trade Unions (NVV), and the Austrian Trade Union Federation (ÖGB)—did so only in the aftermath of World War II, which had swept away their older union structures. These federations reduced the number of their national unions. In Germany they were reduced to sixteen large national union industrial structures (covering manual and non-manual workers in the same national industrial organization). In Austria they were also reduced to sixteen, with, however, one separate union among the sixteen to cover all nonmanuals in private industry. In the Netherlands they were reduced to twenty.[40] Note, by way of comparison, that there are approximately 130 national unions in the AFL-CIO and 175 in the TUC.

The postwar success of the NVV and the DGB in organizing non-manual workers in most sectors of the private economy has been only moderate. This suggests that even *their* new streamlined organizations may not be the last word in modern trade-union structure!

Trend Toward More Centralized Power in Unions

It has been suggested that few generalizations will hold about the nature and evolution of union structure, since it varies greatly among labor movements. It might be tentatively suggested, however, that in a number of European countries the growing role of the union movement in national economic, manpower, and wage planning does seem to be leading to the accumulation of greater power at the federation level.

Although most notable in Scandinavia, Austria, and the Netherlands, similar tendencies can be observed in Britain and Belgium. Whether this tendency will become generalized is not clear; but there does appear to be a certain logic in this movement, which reflects the development of more formal planning in the economic life of Western nations.

The same planning developments also seem to be pushing some of the labor movements that are highly craft-dominated into a search for methods and policies to help effectuate more mergers or amalgamations among individual national unions. This virtually becomes a necessity for effective union participation in *industrial* planning.[41]

N O T E S

---

1. William H. McPherson, *Grievance Settlement Procedures in Western Europe*, Reprint Series No. 131 (Urbana: Institute of Labor and Industrial Relations, University of Illinois, June 1963), pp. 1, 2. American observers, however, often overlook the continuing full employment situation and the tight labor markets that have

undoubtedly constrained European employers in the past ten or fifteen years, thereby reducing some of the pressure for grievances.

2. Seymour Martin Lipset, *Trade Unions and Social Structure*, Reprint No. 182 (Berkeley: Institute of Industrial Relations, University of California, 1962), pp. 79–83. The same social factors, as outlined by Lipset, may also help explain the greater resort to violence in United States labor-management history despite the higher degree of class consciousness in Western Europe. The lack of a fixed sense of class status and responsibility may reduce the inhibitions to resort to more violent conduct in both labor and management in the United States.

3. There is no really good general treatment of the structure and function of plant committees in Western European labor systems. One interesting survey of these committees as they function in France, Belgium, and the Netherlands can be found in *Sessions d'études syndicales sur les conseils d'enterprise*, Brussels, July 4–7, (Paris: Organisation for European Economic Cooperation, 1956). One difficulty is that the movement to establish plant grievance committees was merged with the movement for workers' control of management of industry in Europe, which is treated below in Chapter IX.

4. Adolf Sturmthal, *Workers Councils* (Cambridge, Mass.: Harvard University Press, 1964), p. 78.

5. Val R. Lorwin, *The French Labor Movement* (Cambridge, Mass.: Harvard University Press, 1954), p. 270.

6. The International Labour Organization states, "The common view is that the labour tribunals owe their origin to the probiviral court or *conseil de prud'hommes* [literally court of wise men], which was set up at Lyons by virtue of a Napoleonic law passed in 1806. The principle of the probiviral court consisted in merely having certain labour disputes settled promptly and without expense by a council composed of representatives of employers and workers. The idea was not entirely new. It is said that a category of persons known as *Prud'hommes* had existed already for several centuries in France, although their powers and duties had not been defined by a national law. In the fifteenth century the tradesmen of Lyons had obtained permission from King Louis XI to have certain disputes adjusted by *Prud'hommes* just as had been done in the city of Paris for two centuries. The prud'hommes are persons specially acquainted with the subject matter upon which they may be asked to give an opinion." *Labour Courts, An International Survey of Judicial Systems for the Settlement of Disputes*, Studies and Reports Series A (Industrial Relations), No. 40 (Geneva: International Labour Office, 1938), p. 3. This volume remains the basic work in the field, but a recent article by J. de Givry and J. Schregle of the ILO, "The Role of the Third Party in the Settlement of Grievances at the Plant Level," *International and Labour Review*, April, 1968, does help to amplify the earlier work and bring it up to date. These ILO studies, however, should be supplemented by reference to recent monographs concerning industrial relations in individual countries (some of which, of course, are cited in this volume), which usually contain relevant material on the functioning of the labor courts. It might also be noted that in a few European countries where authoritarian or totalitarian regimes have abolished free trade unionism and collective bargaining, the labor courts have been preserved and continue to function today, though sometimes in modified form. This, too, suggests the premodern nature and character of labor court systems in some countries.

7. Despite the purely bipartite character of the French labor courts, concludes one study, they must be credited with "a remarkable acheivement" in settling employer-worker disputes and one should be hesitant in "making simple generalizations about the French industrial relations climate." William H. McPherson and Frederic Meyers, *The French Labor Courts: Judgment by Peers* (Urbana: University of Illinois Press, 1966), p. 86.

8. In France labor disputes, individual and collective, can be taken through a variety of channels, including the Ministry of Labor, which has a special corps of inspectors who help mediate or adjudicate disputes arising out of legal interpretations or labor-management differences. As might be expected, the availability of a variety of channels often results in a weaker grievance settlement system for workers. See Lorwin, *op. cit.*, pp. 255–259, and J. D. Reynaud, *Les syndicats en France* (Paris: Armand Colin, 1963), Chap. VIII.

9. Since the end of World War II the development of commercial services, which cater to unions and management, and which collect and publish major labor arbitration decisions in the United States, has tended to give the arbitration process a more formal character, at times almost approaching the character of court proceedings in Western Europe.

10. Adolf Sturmthal (ed.), *Contemporary Collective Bargaining in Seven Countries* (Ithaca, N.Y.: Institute of International Industrial and Labor Relations, Cornell University, 1957), p. 325.

11. For an interesting comparative treatment of strike trends in different countries, see Arthur M. Ross and Paul T. Hartman, *Changing Patterns of Industrial Conflict* (New York: Wiley, 1960). Ross and Hartman make use of the strike ratio we have used in Table 5, but they also stress the ratio between (1) time lost due to strikes and (2) union membership and duration of strikes (days lost per striker). Unfortunately the tables in this work go only through 1956.

12. For an analysis of rights and limitations with respect to strikes in the six European countries forming the Common Market, see *Grève et Lock-Out*, (Luxembourg: Communauté Européene du Charbon et de l'Acler, Haute Autorité, 1961).

13. *The Times* (London), June 14, 1968. Control of unauthorized strikes and, related to it, limitation of the right to strike during the term of a collective agreement, had emerged as the major public industrial relations issues in Great Britain by the late 1960s.

14. *Ibid.*, pp. 35, 38, 39.

15. Such, for example, was the one-day strike called in France, in May 1967, to protest the proposed grant of six-month emergency powers, especially in the economic field, to the de Gaulle government. This strike, it will be recalled, was discussed in Chapter VI.

16. *Force Ouvrière*, March 31, 1965, and October 10, 1966. Also see *Syndicalisme*, March 20 and 27, 1965, and January 15 and August 27, 1966.

17. *Le Monde*, May 28, 1968.

18. Both in the French and German cases plant-committee or shop-delegate members, as previously noted, are almost always elected from union-sponsored lists. Problems of union control, however, arise from the fact that the committee members hold their positions under law and in relation to the plant, and not as part of the union's institutional structure.

19. *International Labour Review*, October 1963, pp. 417–418. For an analysis of the significance of this agreement, see Gino Guigni, "Recent Developments in Collective Bargaining in Italy," *International Labour Review*, April 1965.

20. *IMF News*, No. 12, March 1966. The call for "the deduction of trade union dues at source, following a referendum held amongst the workers," something that seemed to have been won, in principle at least, in 1962, suggests that some of the "earlier" union gains are still only on paper.

21. Shirley W. Lerner, "Factory Agreements and National Bargaining in the British Engineering Industry," *International Labour Review*, January 1964, p. 3.

22. Allan Flanders, *Industrial Relations: What is Wrong with the System* (London: Faber and Faber, 1965), and *Collective Bargaining: Prescription for Change* (London: Faber and Faber, 1967).

23. *Facts No. 408, Industrial Relations in the United Kingdom*, July 21, 1964 (release of British Ministry of Information).

24. Alan Fisher, Assistant General Secretary of the National Union of Public Employees, quoted in *The Observer* (London), March 10, 1963.

25. *Report of a Court of Inquiry of the Causes and Circumstances of a Dispute Between the Ford Motor Company, Limited, Daggenham, and Members of the Trade Unions Represented on the Trade Union Side of the Ford National Joint Negotiating Committee* (London, HMS, April 1963), p. 53. (Also known as the Jack report.)

26. *The Guardian* (Daily), December 22, 1966. For an interesting, general analysis of industrial relations in this industry see H. A. Turner, G. Clack and G. Roberts, *Labor Relations in the Motor Car Industry* (London: Allen & Unwin, 1967).

27. In the one other European movement (in Denmark) that has a system of shop-steward representation similar to that of Britain and which is highly craft-dominated, like the TUC, the shop stewards seem "consciously [to] see themselves as responsible for promoting a smooth relationship between workers and employers. This means that they find themselves in a dual role, namely, in the role of negotiator and in the role of mediator, who has to explain the views of workers and employers to the other side. In this respect they appear to differ from British shop stewards, who do not seem to be much concerned with the second role." Reinhard Lund, "Some Aspects of the Danish Shop Steward System," *British Journal of Industrial Relations*, October 1963, p. 375. Space precludes a detailed treatment of the Danish methods of worker representation at the plant level; but here, as elsewhere in most of Scandinavia, the smoother social history and relationships between classes help explain matters more than do mere formal instruments. An unofficial shop steward movement, somewhat like that in Britain, has also functioned for some time in Australia, but it has been much less significant. See Kevin W. Hince, "Unions on the Shop Floor," *The Journal of Industrial Relations*, November 1967, pp. 214–223.

28. The most recent survey of the subject is W. E. J. McCarthy, *The Role of Shop Stewards in British Industrial Relations, Royal Commission on Trade Unions and Employers' Associations*, Research Papers 1 (London: Her Majesty's Stationery Office, 1967).

29. *The Times* (London), June 14, 1968.

30. See the dissenting remarks of Andrew A. Shonfield and Lord Tangley in *Royal Commission on Trade Unions and Employers' Associations 1965–1968 Report* (London: Her Majesty's Stationery Office, 1968), pp. 282–302. The Industrial Relations Commission was formally established in March 1969. George Woodcock, retiring from his post as General Secretary of the Trades Union Congress, was named the Commission's first chairman.

31. John Hughes, *Change in the Unions*, Fabian Research Series Pamphlet No. 244, August 1964, p. 12.

32. *The Guardian* (Daily), March 23, 1965. Despite some notable progress in union organizations in recent years, there is still considerable discontent among many employers and public officials and experts about trade-union structure in Britain. The director general of the Confederation of British Industry (the principal employers' association) has called the union structure "antediluvian," and added that the "Voluntary movement [for changes in union structure] has been singularly ineffective." This same official, and he seemingly speaks for a fairly large group in Britain, has called for arming the new public Industrial Relations Commission with legal power to force union structural changes. *The Times* (London), June 14, 1968.

33. *Report of the 96th Annual Trades Union Congress* (Blackpool, 1964), p. 105. The effort to encourage union amalgamations started well back in British labor history. For an example in the twenties, see W. Milne-Bailey (ed.), *Trade Union*

Documents (London: G. Bell & Sons, London, 1929), p. 129, in which the TUC recommended movement toward amalgamations and a more industrial type of structure. With respect to the shop-stewards movement and the problem of multiple-craft unionism in industry, one can go back to B. G. de Montgomery, whose words, in 1923, sound strangely modern: "This movement [shop-stewards] is particularly strong in engineering and ship building where workers in the same establishment often belong to different crafts and unions. It is this disintegration of the workers into different crafts (rendering united action between the workers of the same factory difficult or even impossible) that has given rise to the shop steward movement . . ." B. G. de Montgomery, *British and Continental Labour Policy* (London: Humphrey Milford Oxford University Press, 1923), p. 198.

34. Shirley Lerner, "The Future Organization and Structure of Trade Unions," in B. C. Roberts (ed.), *Industrial Relations: Contemporary Problems and Perspectives* (London: Methuen, 1962), Chap. 3. The Draughtsmens and Allied Technicians Association, a key TUC white-collar affiliate heavily concentrated in the engineering industry, prides itself on having had "commendable foresight when they decided at the very outset that office committees were to form the keystone in the structure of the union. They were also right to insist that members should belong to branches according to their place of work and not according to their place of residence. There are many unions where the branch structure is divorced from the factory or office trade organisation." See "Trade Union Representatives in Workshop and Office," *The Draughtsman,* August 1963, for an interesting discussion on and some proposals for trade-union reorganization in England.

35. *The Times* (London), June 14, 1968.

36. *Trade Union Structure—Relations with Other Unions,* presented to the Electrical Trades Union Executive Council meeting of December 7, 1964. (Mimeographed.)

37. This lack of general unions and the failure to organize many small shops seems to be one reason for the lag in unionization in the United States since the mid-1950s. Amalgamated local unions and new linkages with the poverty movement may overcome this lag in the future.

38. E. J. Hobsbawm, *Labouring Men* (London: Weidenfeld and Nicolson, 1964), Chaps. 9, 10. The strategic position of the local motor transport industry seems to tempt other transport unions—for example, the Teamsters in the United States— to become general workers' unions. Recent experiments in organizing the urban poor into community unions in the United States bear some resemblance to the general union concept. See "Community Unions, Organizing the Poor, A Talk with Jack Conway," in the *Center Diary,* Fund for the Republic Journal, May-June, 1967.

39. These discussions have been looking to the provision of common research, education, legal, and other services, as well as to the settlement of jurisdictional disputes and to some coordination in bargaining. The Amalgamated Engineering Union, with 1.1 million members (GMWU has 800,000; TGWU, 1.4 million) has also participated in the discussions. Any coordination or near amalgamation of such a large union bloc would have nearly 3.5 million members and would have far-reaching consequences for the entire British trade-union movement. For instance, it might, in part, meet the problem of conflicting union jurisdiction lines, which have been so vexing in the motor car industry. *Labour News From Britain,* New Series No. 197, November 1966. For an interesting earlier discussion of such a three-way "merger," see H. A. Turner, "British Trade Union Structure: A New Approach," *British Journal of Industrial Relations,* July 1964.

40. The religious-oriented labor federations in the Netherlands did not follow the NVV in establishing industrial unions. The Catholic trade-union movement in that country has, however, begun to move in the direction of consolidation into industrial

unions, but it arouses some opposition from white-collar and supervisory employees, who seem to prefer separate unions. See, S. Th. Van Bijsterveld, "The Catholic Trade Union Movement of the Netherlands Takes on a New Appearance," *Labor* (International Federation of Christian Trade Unions), June 1964. Part of the nationalization of the Austrian movement was begun before World War II. The principal Swiss union federation has only eleven affiliates. This figure was reached over a long period of amalgamations following a plan adopted around the turn of the twentieth century.

41. In addition to labor movements already referred to as encouraging the movement toward amalgamation, one can add the very craft-conscious Danish Federation of Trade Unions, whose congress recently adopted a new report that establishes procedures to facilitate such steps—although in Denmark this may take the form of "cartels," rather than full mergers. See *Danish Labour News-LO*, Information Bulletin from the Danish Federation of Trade Unions, June 1967. In addition to Austria, Germany, and the Netherlands, which accomplished a major union reorganization in almost a single swoop, the Belgian FGTB took similar though somewhat more gradual steps after World War II.

IX

Worker Control of Industry

ANY COMPARISON of American and European industrial-relations systems is difficult because, in addition to on-the-job protection and security, European unions have also sought to establish direct workers' participation in the management of industry. The programs of most U.S. unions have not included this as a goal since the rise and triumph of the AFL. (Minority movements such as the Industrial Workers of the World, and also some socialist forces in the AFL, did advocate forms of workers' control.)

Historical Background of Worker Control Movement

The goal of direct workers' control was first inspired by socialist philosophy in the nineteenth century. It was reinforced by the famous papal encyclicals "Quadregisimo Anno" and "Rerum Novarum," which, although they expressed allegiance to the idea of private property, nevertheless sought substantial alteration in the rights and practice of ownership. Christian trade-union movements were quick to draw upon these encyclicals in their demands for worker participation in management. The philosophies of both anarcho-syndicalism and guild socialism strengthened the support for worker control.[1]

The combination of socialist and Christian thought encouraged a powerful drive to achieve worker participation in management. The impact of World Wars I and II, when governments sought to increase production and ensure workers' cooperation, added to the pressure to grant workers some share in management. Finally, the growth in several countries of modern management schools, which have stressed the positive values, both from a social and a production viewpoint, that can result from such sharing also contributed to the success of the movement in the contemporary period.[2]

The precise meaning of workers' control has never been clearly defined, and it has varied from leader to leader, movement to movement, and country to country. The goal in some cases has been nothing more than the kind of collective-bargaining job control that American unions exercise over such matters as the establishment of piece rates and the order of layoffs or job assignments. This is not unexpected in view of the weaknesses of some European unions in job-site bargaining, as described earlier in Chapter VIII. Frequently, therefore, some of the present systems of worker control include many on-the-job protection measures that are normally seen as part of collective bargaining in the United States.[3] In a deeper sense, however, the ideal of the workers' control movement has been to transform the worker from a mere management-directed and management-manipulated object into someone who shares in industrial decision-making.

How confused the meaning of workers' control can be, however—especially to those accustomed to American concepts of collective bargaining—is exemplified by developments in the Netherlands in 1966. The Netherlands Federation of Trade Unions (NVV), which had admittedly never sought much connection with the individual enterprise, decided at its national convention to remedy this weakness and to seek greater job control.[4]

The Dutch government, at the same time, was proposing legislation to provide for the inclusion of union representatives on company boards of directors. The NVV's metalworkers union, as well as the federation itself, tentatively concluded that "there was a need to build up union organs . . . on the shop floor" as opposed to moving toward improvement of works councils through legislation. The union expected "greater success from this method [strengthening the union on the shop floor] than from an attempt to extend the powers of the works council by legislation."[5]

The union also expressed dissatisfaction with the proposal to provide only minority representation on boards of directors. Moreover, the government report was criticized for providing a management veto "as regards the appointment of experts by members of the works council." It was also criticized for failing to provide an avenue of appeal from its decisions affecting workers. Clearly the NVV sees more independent "trade union work on the floor" by shop recognition, as the alternative to the works' council legislation if the latter is not substantially improved.[6]

In this section we shall deal primarily with those aspects of the workers' control movement that are designed to bring about worker participation in *managerial* activities at the work site, and not with activities, like those in the United States, that are more normally associated with collective bargaining and job control. Also, we shall concentrate upon participation in management, through systems of representation, and not with representation at the *national* industrial level or in economic-planning bodies.[7]

While a great variety of plans to provide for participation in management has been adopted in Europe (and in other areas), in many cases this machinery lies outside the regular union structure. It is therefore not surprising that, as in the case of the worker plant grievance committees elected under state laws, the worker-management councils have sometimes been used by management to circumvent the union.

In some Scandinavian countries (and in Switzerland), however, the joint councils are based upon national agreements reached between the top employers' federations and the top union federations, and union control of the workers' side is no issue.[8]

To offset the danger that the works council, or the joint labor-management committee, where it is set up by law, will be a competitor of the union, the legislation may provide for union priority in nominating candidates. The law in France, for example, states that in the first ballot for members of the councils (*comités d'enterprise*) only representative trade unions can present lists of candidates. If the number of voters in the first election is less than half of the eligible employees, there is a second ballot during which other than trade-union nominated candidates can run.[9] There is still another safeguard, in that each trade union can nominate an advisory representative to the committee.[10]

How far reaching the impact of any system of workers control can be upon the union and its role has been well illustrated in Yugoslavia. In that country workers' councils have formally been assigned the full responsibility for plant management. (This title of workers' councils is interchangeable with works councils, but it seems more appropriate in terms of the way in which the councils are structured in Yugoslavia.) Under this "self-management" system the Yugoslav union movement has found it extremely difficult to define its role in plant problems. The quest for such a definition of the relationship between the union and the self-management system is the source of great debate in labor circles in the country.[11]

While the workers' control movement has taken different forms, depending upon the conditions in a particular country, the analysis presented here will concentrate on two forms generally illustrative of the movement: Great Britain's system of joint consultation and West Germany's works council and codetermination system. Other countries will be referred to only occasionally.

Since World War I several different types of councils designed to give workers some share in management tasks, at different levels of the economy, have been undertaken in Great Britain. There are, for instance, councils at the national industry level (textiles and aircraft are examples), and there is a national productivity council to encourage improved methods and systems across all industry.[12]

At the individual enterprise level, and particularly at the plant, participation in British management takes the form of joint committees. These are set up voluntarily and have no statutory force behind them. (In a few cases, in some of the nationalized industries, the establishment of joint committees is compulsory.) Workers choose their representatives in secret elections, generally in "different sections of the works," to ensure wide representation.[13]

Management usually does not want union stewards to be chosen as worker representatives for joint consultation, lest they seek "to establish an atmosphere of negotiation rather than consultation" on managerial types of problems.[14] Union officials, on the other hand, fear exclusion of union stewards from joint-consultation committees, on the grounds that management will use the committees to by-pass and undermine union power.

Despite management's fears, there is evidence, however, that the people who are willing to accept a union role often will also accept joint-management responsibilities. Such people seem to have a stronger than average identification with the plant. One major study of more than one hundred British factories revealed that union stewards had considerably more interest and *positive* interest in worker-management consultation than rank-and-file workers.[15]

In most other European countries worker representatives on joint-management committees are provided for by, and elected on the basis of, formal legislation. The pertinent statute in France, for example, provides for 2 workers' representatives for each 50 employees, 3 for 51–75, 4 for each 76–100, and on up to a maximum of 11 if there are 10,000 employees in the establishment.[16] Management representation on the committees varies from country to country. In some instances they sit as chairmen; in others this position rotates. Management representatives are, of course, selected by the firm.

In any event, as one expert sums it up for Britain, ". . . despite the variety of procedures . . . there is common understanding that joint consultation is a rational policy for improving production, for letting the worker know what is going on, and for giving him a chance to 'speak his mind.' "[17] The reader can see in passing that this is in some ways a far cry from the original ideal of drawing the worker in as part of management. In the British system, he is consulted and permitted through his representatives to speak his mind about managerial problems. But in general his role does not go beyond this. On occasion, full meetings of particular departments may be held to consult with management, and even full plant assemblies may be convoked to consider and advise on broad managerial problems.

The range of subjects that may come before the joint consultation group can include (and this list applies to most countries that have this type of machinery):

1. Finance and business, including an explanation of company financial statements, a look at orders ahead, a view of the competitive situation in the industry and the general economic situation.

2. Production, including goals and accomplishments in the previous period, present targets in relation to orders, new methods, equipment and techniques, defective work, customer complaints, reports on worker suggestions.

3. Personnel, including changes in top management, reorganizations, turnover and absentee figures, prospective hirings and firings, opportunities for training.

4. Welfare, including canteens, washrooms, heating and ventilation, safety and health, transportation, housing, vacation plans, company athletics, benevolent funds to assist employees.[18]

Special subcommittees are sometimes established to look into and to report on particular matters, such as production and welfare.

All meetings and decisions are voluntary. Even if agreement is reached in the committee, the company is under no obligation to take action. Needless to add, if the company fails to implement decisions reached in the joint committee, the committee soon disintegrates.

It is difficult to evaluate the results obtained by these committees. Of course they vary greatly from one company to another. There has perhaps been an excessive amount of "promotion" of what may possibly be achieved by this work, and to some extent the modest results therefore seem disappointing. It seems reasonable to accept the rather cautious judgment expressed in 1963 by the Trades Union Congress when one evaluates Britain's experience with joint-management efforts:

It does not, however, seem likely that joint consultation will revolutionise work-people's attitude to work or can be regarded as more than one means among others by which the interested minority of work-people may associate themselves with the progress and development of their industries and by so doing develop themselves and help to tap reserves of experience and knowledge which would otherwise remain unused.[19]

Apparently one of the "obstacles" to fuller development of joint consultation in Great Britain is the regular negotiating machinery that unions and management have fashioned in the course of a long collective-bargaining history. This machinery serves them well for most problems. But because, historically, it is based on a certain conflict type of relationship, it may be difficult to find significant areas for consultation and positive collaboration.[20]

One can, however, find a number of successful examples in British industry where joint consultation has worked to improve production. With Britain still facing a great need for improved productivity to equalize its balance of payments, any plans aimed at improving productivity will be given new emphasis.

Meeting with the Royal Commission on Trade Unions and Employers' Associations, early in 1967, the TUC called for a change in the legislation governing corporations in order to make it easier for private companies to appoint representatives to company boards of directors. The Royal Commission rejected this proposal (a minority of the Commission favored it), on the ground that for the unionists appointed:

Such an office might expose its holder at times to an almost intolerable strain when decisions unfavorable to workers (for example on redundancy) had to be taken because they were in the interests of the company as a whole. A concurring vote by the workers' director might be unavoidable if he is to do his duty as a director, and yet could be easily misunderstood or misrepresented.[21]

The Commission noted that although trade unionists were occasionally appointed to serve on the boards of nationalized industries, they did so in their individual capacities, not as union representatives. Indeed, in the case of naturalized industry boards, union representatives so chosen were often in the process of retiring from their regular union posts.

Even this much of a call for legislation by the TUC marks an important departure from the past, when emphasis was placed almost entirely upon voluntarism in union-management relationships in the private sector. The Labour Party is also increasingly committed to the idea of extending worker participation in the management of industry, although it avoids setting forth any one formula to accomplish this end.

In renationalizing and reorganizing the steel industry in 1967 and 1968, the Party cooperated closely with the TUC in providing for worker directors on the four managing boards covering the industry. The boards have authority for "the preparation and implementation of an annual operating plan and schemes for new capital expenditure." Twelve TUC members have been appointed to the four steel boards. They are part-time directors whose full-time jobs are as employees in steel plants.[22]

While the German government acknowledges that "the demand or right of joint consultation originates chiefly with the trade unions," other forces also operated to bring it into being. For instance: "The majority of employers have become clearly aware of the bearing of favorable human relations on the development of their establishments." Additionally, "cultural impulses" in the direction of the "principle of equality, which was originally confined to the political sphere, has contributed to superseding former relationships of authority in industry, as it has in the home, at school and in other fields." The general adoption of the Christian doctrine that workers are more than hands and that "the employment relationship is a joint relationship" also contributed to the success of the movement for worker participation in management.[23]

The idea of works councils can be traced in German history as far back as 1848, when the Constitutional Assembly, meeting in Frankfort during the revolutionary upheaval of the time, called for such councils. Although a few employers voluntarily established "factory councils" or "councils of elders" in succeeding decades, the movement did not receive its next major support until the passage in 1905 of a mining law in Prussia, which provided for consultative councils with worker representation. Later on, during World War I, workers' rights for joint consultation were extended to all enterprises with more than fifty employees.

After World War I, a more extensive works-council law was passed under the Weimar Republic; it provided for councils with both bargaining and managerial functions. The law also stipulated that German workers could name two members to company supervisory boards (roughly equivalent to a board of directors in the United States).

In addition to works councils at the plant level, Weimar Republic legislation also sought to institute a hierarchy of councils on an industry-wide basis, as well as a top-level national economic council, on all of which labor and management would be represented. These higher-level councils proved to the ineffective and disappeared in the early 1920s.[24]

The advent of the Nazi regime led to dissolution of the trade unions in 1933, and the works-council system also ceased to function in the National Socialist era.

Restoration of the works councils and provision for worker participation in management were major goals of the German labor movement after World War II. A series of laws passed between 1950 and 1956 provided for employee participation in management in private and public enterprises; this participation was effected through works councils and related bodies. For the coal and steel industries a special codetermination law was also enacted.

It should be noted that Germany and most Continental countries differ from Britain in that provisions for worker participation and consultation in management rest on a legislative foundation. This participation, moreover, although established as a result of union pressure, for the most part lies outside regular union machinery.[25]

In Germany all employees eighteen years of age and older, save high-ranking officials, may vote in the works councils elections, and those over twenty-one are eligible for election to the councils. Full-time union officials are not eligible. The size of the councils vary from one member for establishments with less than twenty employees to up to twenty-five to thirty-five for very large establishments. Seats are divided between wage earners (mostly manual workers) and salaried (mostly white-collar) employees, in proportion to their numbers; but there is only one council. Management, as such, is not represented on the council, which chooses its own chairman.[26]

Council members may receive much secret company business information, and German law imposes "a special obligation of secrecy on them." Penalties up to one year in prison are possible, only on petition by the employer, "for premeditated or wanton betrayal of secrets."[27]

An extensive protection system safeguards a council member against dismissal by the employer. Ordinarily only if a complete plant closure is contemplated can he be laid off. Extreme misconduct can also lead to discharge, but this is very rare. (In France not only members, but past members and recent candidates for council positions, also have a certain amount of protection from discriminatory layoffs.) To the extent necessary, council members in Germany are released from their regular work, without loss in pay, to perform council duties. All expenses for works councils are borne by the employer. Ties between trade unions and councils are strictly informal. There are no formal election "lists," but in practice the unions do prepare slates of candidates for council elections. About 90 percent of council members are union members, although only about one-third of all German workers belong to unions. The council members, it should be noted, in all cases hold their positions because of their status not as union representatives but as employees. The council, to repeat, is separate from the union, and must "observe strict neutrality in respect of any strike conducted by the trade unions."[28]

Employers often prefer to deal with the council and a few try deliberately to divert worker loyalty from the union. Adolf Sturmthal, writing of the German situation, states:

By strengthening the council's position, management often hopes to weaken the union. . . . Cases in which councils have been used against the union are well known, and others in which councils have kept the unions from obtaining information about individual enterprises are not infrequent.

Sturmthal notes that in the course of the Bavarian metalworkers' strike in 1954, many works councils, under management suggestion, appealed to workers to stay on the job in defiance of the decision of the national union.[29]

These cases are not the general rule, however, and German unions continue to be supporters of works councils and codetermination. Some unions help to run training programs for council members. The large metalworkers' union in recent years has sought to place its relations with the councils on a more effective basis through intensive educational campaigns and by strengthening the union organization at the plant level. In some areas powerful union leadership has led to de facto union control of the councils.

In addition to works councils, the laws make provision for "economic production committees" in enterprises of one hundred employees or more. It is also provided that in all joint stock companies (corporations, excluding family-held companies, would be the best analogy in the United States) one-third of the seats on the board of supervisors (board of directors) are to be filled by workers' representatives.

Powers of the Works Council

In Germany the works council is advisory in some cases; in others its power is equal to that of the employer. If a decision cannot be reached in a dispute in which the council and the employer have equal power, the issue goes for final determination to the labor court or to a special conciliation commission.[30]

Matters in which council and employer have an equal vote include hours when work starts and ends; determination of breaks; the system of wages; incentive rates versus time rates (but the matter of determining the level of wages is left to the *unions* and management in their negotiations); settlement of piece rates; assignments of holidays and vacations; questions of work rules (e.g., signing in, reporting sick, parking places); vocational training, especially in setting up apprentice programs; the administration of welfare services *already in existence* (e.g., convalescent homes, cafeterias, company housing for workers).[31]

Most of the foregoing are areas where a vigorous American plant union also operates with powers "equal" to management, in that unresolved issues can generally be taken to arbitration. Notable extensions beyond American union activity are in the welfare services such as control over plant canteens and company vacation colonies.

Works councils also have equal power with management with regard to *bulk* personnel appointments, reassignments, or transfers—but not with respect to individuals. The council has no power over dismissals, but it must be advised, in advance, of bulk dismissals. In the case of dismissals individual employees may appeal to the labor court, and the council can join the appeal.[32]

ECONOMIC PRODUCTION COMMITTEES IN GERMAN INDUSTRY. Economic production committees have an equal number of labor and management members (4 to 8) and operate with extensive consultative and advisory functions on such matters as production and working methods; economic situation of the enterprise, including order backlogs; credit position, profit and loss statements; and other matters vitally affecting employees, as, for example, proposed mergers or new investments. The committee's power is purely advisory. Members' terms are the same as in the works council, usually two years.

There has been little enthusiasm for these committees. Employers have been fearful that they will encroach upon management prerogatives. On the other hand, the unions argue that their purely advisory status makes them too weak.[33] Not all plants of appropriate size have undertaken to establish economic production committees.

Worker Participation on Boards of Supervisors

We have noted earlier that except for the coal and steel industry, where codetermination exists, the works-council law provides that one-third of the seats on boards of supervisors of joint stock companies are to be filled by workers' votes. These men are elected directly by the workers in a secret ballot. If two or more workers' representatives are elected, there must be at least one wage earner and one salaried employee. There are no other stipulations as to workers' representatives, and in some companies union officials (i.e., full-time union employees) have been elected to these boards. It has been alleged by a number of unions, however, that many companies limit the boards to six members, to be sure that "outside" union officials cannot become members, since the first two worker members must be chosen from the plant.[34]

The unions have opposed the lack of equal representation on supervisory boards, holding up codetermination in coal and steel as a better example. In practice, however, voting on boards only rarely reflects the views of shareholders versus employee representatives. Most decisions are unanimous.

While the experiment with labor members on supervisory boards is still difficult to evaluate fully, Sturmthal comments, "It may perhaps be said that the presence of labor members on the supervisory boards so far has had neither the catastrophic consequences that many observers expected, nor the profoundly beneficial effects that others hoped for."

Certainly communications between employees and management have been improved as a result. Improved communications are particularly important to workers in a period of prosperity, when it is advantageous to have a closer and clearer view of an enterprise's finances.[35]

Criticism by unions generally concerns the problem of under-representation, and the desire for greater rather than lesser participation. The basic program of the German Trade Union Federation (DGB) demands, "Co-determination on a basis of parity for the workers must be secured in the case of all economic, social and personnel decisions. It must be made effective in all private, public and cooperative undertakings."[36]

Codetermination in Coal and Steel

The establishment of codetermination in coal and steel is related to the general workers' movement for a share in management, but it also has its own immediate history—in the 1949–1950 period. The call for codetermination in these basic industries represented a democratic updating of socialist labor thinking in Germany after the war. A certain disillusionment with the effects of "mere" nationalization, which were observable in the Soviet Union—as well as a realization that full socialization of industry was probably impossible politically—helped move socialist labor leaders toward codetermination. The move in that direction was strengthened by the fact that important Catholic and Protestant religious leaders were sympathetic with programs to humanize industry and raise the dignity of workers. In keeping with earlier encyclicals and other Christian social doctrine, many of these religious figures came to support the idea of worker participation in management. On the other hand, it is not likely that many of these leaders would have supported full socialization of industry. The Catholic influence was particularly important in helping to put the support of the leading Christian Democratic Union party behind the law.[37]

The fact that German unionists were united after 1945, in contrast to their ideological and religious divisions before Hitler, made it easier to build consensus around the codetermination concept.

Codetermination itself has two major aspects: the principle of parity between workers and shareholders as far as appointments on the supervisory boards of coal and steel companies are concerned, and the provision for a labor member on the managing boards of these companies.

Under a law passed in 1951, in coal and steel firms of 1,000 or more employees (individually owned and private trading companies are exempted), codetermination is provided in the top management of supervisory boards. (To repeat, these are the American equivalent of boards of directors. They are not full-time positions.) These boards usually have eleven members, including four representing shareholders and four representing workers. Two of the workers' representatives are chosen by the works council (one wage earner and one salaried employee), and two are selected by the central trade-union organizations. The two groups, workers and shareholders, each names an additional "independent" member, and an eleventh man is chosen by the first ten. The eleventh man must receive at least three votes from each of the two groups; when agreement cannot be reached, a mediation committee may assist in choosing him. In practice this complicated arrangement has usually given way to a system whereby both sides agree that the shareholders appoint the chairman of the board, and the employees appoint the eleventh man and the vice-chairman.[38]

Despite the possibility of a sharp division on the board, in practice disagreements and voting splits have apparently been as common among workers' representatives as between workers and the management group. Generally the tendency has been to achieve a broad consensus.[39]

Labor Directors in Coal and Steel

The codetermination law also provides for the appointment of a labor director to the managing board of a coal or steel company. The labor director is appointed in the same way as other directors by the supervisory board. (The top managing board, which has day-to-day executive responsibility for the firm, usually consists of three members.) However, the labor director cannot be appointed or removed against the votes of the majority of the workers' group on the supervisory board.[40]

The labor director has a joint responsibility with other directors for managing the firm under the general direction of the supervisory board. He also has special responsibility for "personnel questions, job evaluation, schooling and occupational training, social questions, old age pensions, sickness benefits, social housing, works libraries, works medical services, accident prevention," and a variety of cultural activities in the firm.[41]

Theoretically, a labor director can "always be outvoted by his fellow-managers on the executive board," but this rarely occurs. As Michael Fogarty comments, "Placed in a managerial position, and instructed by law and custom to behave as a manager, the labor director does in practice behave in this way and not as a union negotiator." On the other hand, Fogarty adds, the labor director "must not forget his obligation to keep communication open with the union, the works council and employee representatives on the supervisory board."[42]

It is difficult to measure the results of codetermination. The worst fears of some company officials—that it would lead to chaos, socialism, and the like—have certainly not been realized. Most managers now seem to feel it is "working well in their own" firm, although they remain suspicious of the principle as a whole.[43]

On the union side, some academic critics originally feared that co-determination (and in particular feared that the labor director's office) would undermine the militancy of German unions. These critics' views were summed up as follows: "It has been said that in steel and coal when the worker goes to see his boss he finds his union representative and when he goes to see his union representative he finds his boss."[44]

These fears have not been realized. German unions have actually grown in militance in the past half-dozen years—for reasons that have nothing to do with codetermination. The DGB does recognize, however, that codetermination, in its present German form, represents a clear break with old concepts of the class struggle. In an article published early in 1966,[45] a DGB executive board member writes: "If the German Trade unions demand co-determination for labour, then they at the same time recognize the rights of co-determination of the representatives of capital." On the other hand, the German labor movement is pressing for the extension of codetermination—full parity on all company boards—in all industry. Indeed, in the spring of 1968 the DGB launched a new, wide campaign in support of codetermination in all industry.[46]

The economic effects of codetermination in coal and steel also seem to elude precise measurement. Fogarty feels that the improved climate of industrial relations "played some part in enabling German steel firms to increase their productivity in the 50's." At the same time the improved climate seems to have made the coal and steel companies pacesetters in improving fringe benefits, with some resulting price pressures. The gain to productivity, then, seems to be offset by a possible inflation loss, with "no clear cut effect on over-all economic efficiency."[47]

There also appears to be broad agreement that the general structure of works councils, worker representation on supervisory boards throughout German industry, and the labor directors in coal and steel have helped to "humanize" labor relations in the country.

The pressure for workers' participation in management seems to be growing in many countries. It comes from unions in many instances, from governments who see it as a device to increase productivity and/or to divert unions from all-out concentration on consumption, and from some managers who are concerned with the problem of worker motivation. It grows in developed countries and it grows even more in less developed countries.

It is particularly difficult for anyone rooted in the American industrial-relations setting to appraise the value and prospects of worker-participation systems. This movement has had only the most limited support in modern American social history. The traditions of American capitalism and entrepreneurship run strongly, indeed belligerently, against the concept of joint management either as a right or as a necessity. The modern American labor movement, with a few exceptions and unlike almost every other Western trade-union movement, has been either hostile or indifferent to worker participation in management. For a brief period, in the 1940s, some groups in the CIO, particularly under the leadership of Philip Murray and the United Steelworkers Union (a CIO affiliate), advocated joint labor-management councils in industry.[48] But this movement did not embrace many unions or leaders and petered out in the early fifties.

Wartime in the United States, as in many other Western countries, is often a period when there is an increase in joint labor-management committees to improve production. A great many such committees were established during World War II, with federal government encouragement and assistance; but their functions were often not too well defined; in any event, these committees only rarely survived the war period.[49]

There continue to be, of course, a fair number of *individual* formal union-company efforts to collaborate in improving production. These efforts seem to be growing in number in recent years in the United States.[50]

The special problems created by automation and rapid technological change have given rise to important new union-management committees, notably in such U.S. companies as Armour Meat Packing and Kaiser Steel, and also in the West Coast longshore industry. These committees try to deal with technological change, as it affects labor and management, on a year-round basis. There are likely to be many more such union-management arrangements in the years to come as automation renders obsolete many old organization and job patterns and practices.

Perhaps the most lasting effects of the earlier CIO interest in labor-management cooperation, and particularly the steelworkers' interest in these forms of collaboration, derive from the work and plans of Joseph Scanlon, at one time research director of the Steelworkers Union. In the main, however, the so-called Scanlon plan has come to be a device that emphasizes the sharing among workers and management of gains from cost reduction. In cruder applications, some have turned it into simple profit sharing.[51]

Worker Participation Involves More Than Material Rewards

The ultimate validity of the movement for worker participation in management cannot rest simply, or even primarily, upon mere material rewards for the individual. The movement must provide for such material rewards, of course. In the Western world today, however, if the "idea" of worker participation is to be successful, it will be responsive to the fact that, with a minimum decent existence assured to most workers, the real problem is to probe for new, added motivation.

Worker participation, if it grows successfully, will also no doubt reflect the rising levels of education throughout the population and the widening desire for participation in many contemporary institutions in addition to the place of work.[52] These same trends have probably strengthened the movement in Europe.

Perhaps the greatest practical difficulty in making the various systems of worker participation in management more effective is worker indifference and/or ignorance. Studies have revealed that even where plans for these systems are well worked out and set up at the "top," there is often "a profound ignorance among the workers of the mechanism of these institutions, and even of their fundamental objectives." In the case of codetermination, the systems are seen "essentially as a means of improving material conditions"; in British joint consultation, they are seen as "dealing more fairly with individual complaints."[53]

This suggests that as long as material conditions are very unsatisfactory, or as long as adequate machinery is lacking to deal with individual employees' grievances, it will be difficult to move workers to participate significantly in the "higher" problems of an enterprise. In the absence of good grievance machinery, workers will often use, to meet grievance needs, the machinery designed to help contribute to better management and production.[54]

It is also quite possible that many workers find the rigors of an eight- or nine-hour day under modern industrial conditions quite taxing and have little desire or energy left over for additional, different types of activity related to their work.

Finally, one of the most difficult barriers to bridge is the one between the worker and his immediate superior. Plans for worker participation, however, are usually limited to providing middle- or high-level representation and consultation with management.[55]

The performance of workers' representatives on management councils, moreover, has tended to be disappointing in terms of their taking a real interest in the business and in managerial problems. This has been true both in developed and in underdeveloped countries. In Yugoslavia, for example, where the formal structure provides not for worker participation but full *worker management*,[56] similar disappoint-

188   WORKER CONTROL OF INDUSTRY

ments are encountered. According to case studies, the elected manual workers on the management council are generally silent when it comes to problems of production, design, output, and the like. They defer to white-collar employees, the engineer who may also be a council member, and to the plant manager who may also sit as an equal. The workers' delegates spring into action when individual grievances are at issue, or when questions of wages or the allocation of enterprise-built housing are at stake.[57]

To some extent special education courses for workers may overcome some of their backwardness; indeed, nearly every country that is experimenting with worker participation in management is providing some special training courses for the worker representatives.

In any event, it would appear that, in the immediate future, Western workers and their unions—with better pay, more education, and industrial experience—are likely to have a better chance to be effective in new managerial tasks than workers in the less developed nations. In developing countries, devices like worker participation can, perhaps, help in the fundamental tasks of acclimatizing and adapting new workers to the rigors of industrial life.

There may be an even greater difficulty than ignorance to overcome, however. Rolf Dahrendorf argues that the functions of workers and management are not the same, and it is futile to expect someone who has advanced into management not to think and function as a "manager." Moreover, the inevitable, hierarchic character of modern organization, such as the individual enterprise, Dahrendorf holds, creates an inevitable unequal distribution of power and a certain amount of conflict.[58]

One can concede that some continuing conflict is inevitable. On the other hand, areas of accommodation and integration are expanding. The operation of and interest in systems of worker participation in management is growing, and this participation will certainly continue to be an element of great importance in industrial relations abroad.

In the United States any serious union movement for worker participation in the management of private industry would, at the very least, probably await a new generation of union leaders. Some forms of greater participation in management in the United States may, however, grow in the public employment area where unionism is newer and expanding rapidly. The presence of a large number of white-collar and professional employees in the public sector unions may also enhance the possibilities of the unions' assuming wider functions in this area.

Finally, there seems widespread agreement that even if the economic effects remain unverified in Western countries, and though workers have not rallied very actively to management participation systems, the improvement that such systems has effected in industrial relations generally has usually been considerable.[59]

N O T E S

1. On the origins and early development of the movement for worker control see Daniel Bell, "One Road from Marx: On the Vision of Socialism, and the Fate of Workers' Control, in Socialist Thought," *World Politics,* July 1959; Frederic Meyers, "Workers' Control of Industry in Europe," *The Southwestern Social Science Quarterly,* September 1958; and Adolf Sturmthal, *Workers Councils* (Cambridge, Mass.: Harvard University Press, 1964), Chap. I. For a brief period at the end of World War I, the example of the Councils of Soldiers and Peasants in the first stages of the Russian Revolution also added to the prestige of works councils, among workers elsewhere in Europe, and especially in Germany. See C. W. Guillebaud, *The Works Council, A German Experiment in Industrial Germany* (Cambridge: University Press, 1928), pp. 5–6. Today Soviet Communist leaders are generally opposed to socialist programs, such as those advocated by Yugoslav Communist leaders, which stress the role of workers' councils.

2. For information on the movement in the United States, as one example, see Douglas McGregor, *Leadership and Motivation* (Cambridge: Massachusetts Institute of Technology Press, 1966), and *The Human Side of Enterprise* (New York: McGraw-Hill, 1960).

3. For good general accounts of the scope of the European workers' management movement, see Sturmthal, *op. cit.,* and H. A. Clegg, *A New Approach to Industrial Democracy* (Oxford, Eng.: Basil Blackwell, 1960). Milton Derber has traced the concept of industrial democracy in American labor history. As he indicates, despite the more limited and pragmatic thrust of American unions, they have often, nevertheless, sought a share in management decision-making in many specific areas that have been associated with the European workers' management movement. Generally, however, U. S. labor has not been interested in formal managerial power. See Derber's "The Idea of Industrial Democracy in America: 1898–1915 [and] 1915–1935," *Labor History,* Fall 1966 and Winter 1967.

4. *Information Bulletin of the Netherlands Federation of Trade Unions* (*NVV*), No. 87 (March 1966). A similar mixture of greater job control and a formal voice in actual plant management is contained in a new "Campaign for Industrial Democracy," which was launched by the Danish LO in February 1968. See *Danish Labour News,* Information Bulletin from the LO, February 1968, pp 3–5.

5. *ICFTU Economic and Social Bulletin,* September-October, 1966.

6. *Ibid.*

7. Worker or union participation in economic planning, manpower policy-making, and the like has been dealt with in Chapter IV. The relationships between different types of worker or union participation at various levels of the economy often cannot be separated. See, for example, a recent useful general review of the field in Kenneth F. Walker and L. Greyfie de Bellecombe, "Workers' Participation in Management, The Concept and its Implementation," *International Institute for Labour Studies Bulletin,* February 1967, pp. 67–100.

8. *Consultation and Cooperation Between Employers and Workers at the Level of the Enterprise,* Labour-Management Relations Series: No. 13 (Geneva: International Labour Organisation, 1962).

9. Article 10 of the law of February 22, 1945, contained in *Les comités d'entreprise* (Paris: Confédération Générale du Travail Force Ouvrière, 1966), p. 94. A similar provision is contained in the Netherlands law, while in Belgium only trade unions can present lists of candidates. *Session d'études syndicales sur les conseils d'en-*

treprise, rapport final, July 1956 (Paris: Organisation Européene de Cooperation Economique, 1956), p. 39. In the German case, discussed below, there is no formal union connection with the naming of candidates. British consultation is not based on the law, and union relationships to the committees vary. In Scandinavian countries, where the councils are founded by a basic agreement between the central union bodies and the central employers' association, this problem does not arise.

10. See the recent amendment to the French law in *International Labour Review,* April 1967. As a result of the great strikes in France during the spring of 1968, additional steps were to be taken to strengthen the unions' role in the process of worker participation in management.

11. On the eve of the sixth congress of the Confederation of Yugoslav Trade Unions, its official monthly journal (published in English) had four articles dealing with the subject of the role of the trade union in society and its relation to the self-management system. See *Yugoslav Trade Unions,* July 1968. The Yugoslav experience with workers' management is still difficult to appraise, but one useful description can be found in International Labour Office, *Workers' Management in Yugoslavia* (Geneva: International Labour Office, 1962). For another appraisal see Sturmthal, *op. cit.,* Chap. IV.

12. *Industrial Relations Handbook* (London: Ministry of Labour, Her Majesty's Stationery Office, 1961), pp. 15–16, 144–145.

13. Dorothea de Schweinitz, *Labor Management Consultation in the Factory* (Honolulu, University of Hawaii, 1966), p. 20.

14. *Ibid.,* p. 76.

15. J. A. Banks, *Industrial Participation, Theory and Practice, A Case Study* (Liverpool, Eng.: Liverpool University Press, 1963), esp. Chap. 3 and Conclusion; and National Institute of Industrial Psychology, *Joint Consulation in British Industry* (London: Staples Press, 1952), pp. 63–64.

16. A description of the rules in effect in eleven European countries may be found in *Consultation and Cooperation Between Employers and Workers at the Level of the Enterprise, op. cit.,* esp. pp. 17–23.

17. De Schweinitz, *op. cit.,* pp. 20–22.

18. Adapted from *ibid.,* pp. 62–63.

19. *Report, 95th Annual Trades Union Congress* (Brighton, Eng.: 1963), p. 279.

20. For a critique of the operation of joint consultation in Britain, see Clegg, *op. cit.,* pp. 37–41.

21. For the Commission's full views on union participation in management see: *Royal Commission on Trade Unions and Employers' Associations 1965–1968 Report* (London: Her Majesty's Stationery Office, 1968), pp. 257–260. The Labour Party, at about the same time as the TUC, called for extending worker and union participation in the management of industry. Although the party recognized the opportunity to do this was greatest in the nationalized industries, it also argued the case for a similar development in the private sector, including such new legislation as might be necessary to achieve this objective. See *Industrial Democracy, Working Party Report* (London: Labour Party, 1967).

22. On the steel industry worker representation plan see *Labour, TUC Information Broadsheet,* April 1968.

23. Dr. Alfons Klein, *Codetermination and the Law Governing Work Councils and Staff Representation in the Public Services,* Social Policy in Germany, A Survey in Monographs, No. 23 (Essen, West Germany: Federal Ministry of Labour and the Social Structure, 1963), pp. 6–7 (hereinafter cited as *Codetermination*). This is one of a series on social policy available both in German and in English. I have used the English edition.

24. For a useful summary of German labor at the time of the Weimar Republic,

see Nathan Reich, *Labour Relations in Republican Germany* (New York: Oxford University Press, 1938).

25. The case of Sweden is worth noting. As previously noted, works councils in Scandinavian countries usually rest on private agreements between unions and management. In Sweden, the councils are based on a special agreement between the Swedish Employers' Confederation, the Confederation of Swedish Trade Unions (LO), and the Central Organization of Salaried Employees (TCO). The objectives of this agreement are to maintain "continuous collaboration between employer and employees for the achievement of the best possible production; providing opportunities for employees to gain insight into the economic and technical conditions and financial results of the business; promoting employment security, and safety, health and satisfaction in the work; promoting vocational training within the firm; and generally promoting good production and working conditions within the firm." See Andren and Holms Boktryckeri, *Agreements Regarding Works Councils* (Stockholm: 1959). The basic agreement was written in 1946 and has been amended several times since. Councils are limited to firms of fifty or more workers (subject to extension to smaller establishments by mutual agreement), where one party or the other (i.e., local management or local union) requests that one be established. In most Continental countries the law makes compulsory the establishment of a works council, provided size and other general conditions are met.

26. In France there are also two separate electoral colleges. The first is for workers and white-collar salaried employees; the second, for which separate elections are held, takes in engineers, foremen, and some supervisors. In Belgium, the law sets up two groups, workers and salaried (or white-collar) employees. In France and the Netherlands the head of a firm is a member and chairman of the council. In Belgium he is also a member. *Sessions d'etudes syndicales sur les conceils d'entreprise, op. cit.,* pp. 36–37.

27. Klein, *Codetermination, op. cit.,* pp. 17–25. In those countries where the worker members of the council are selected from union lists, the possibility of secrecy is somewhat less and the penalties are rarely stipulated. See *Les comités d'entreprise, op. cit.,* p. 91.

28. *Ibid.,* p. 27.

29. Sturmthal, *op. cit.,* p. 78.

30. In most other Western European countries the councils' powers are largely advisory, except in the social field, where worker management of canteens, vacation colonies, etc., is on a joint basis or may even be almost completely in the hands of the workers' group.

31. Klein, *op. cit.,* pp. 33–36.

32. *Ibid.,* pp. 37–39.

33. De Schweinitz, *op. cit.,* pp. 31–32.

34. De Schweinitz, *op. cit.,* p. 33.

35. Sturmthal, *op. cit.,* p. 82; see also De Schweinitz, *op. cit.,* pp. 33–34.

36. *Basic Programme of the German Trade Union Federation—DGB,* Dusseldorf, 1963, p. 13. This has been reaffirmed since 1963.

37. On the ideological and political background to this struggle, see Paul Fisher, "Labor Co-determination in Germany," *Social Research,* December, 1951, and Herbert J. Spiro, *The Politics of German Codetermination* (Cambridge, Mass.: Harvard University Press, 1958).

38. Klein, *Codetermination, op. cit.,* pp. 49–50. As of 1963 there were 1,250 members of boards of supervision of coal and steel companies who were appointed under the law. Of these, 578 represented the employees; nearly all of them were trade unionists, and 28% of them were full-time union officials.

39. Michael Fogarty, "Codetermination and Company Structure in Germany," *British Journal of Industrial Relations*, March 1964, p. 104. Fogarty traces the special evolution of company law in Germany and the way in which the growing sense of the public responsibility of supervisory boards has facilitated the acceptance of codetermination. Our concentration here, of course, is on the industrial-relations aspects of codetermination.

40. Klein, *Codetermination, op. cit.,* p. 51.

41. Ludwig Rosenberg, *The Codetermination Rights of Workers in Germany* (Dusseldorf: Federal Republic of Germany, n.d.), p. 10.

42. Fogarty, *op. cit.,* pp. 104–105. Fogarty also finds that, if employee representatives in the various organs of codetermination "are forced to rate one organ against another, the highest vote seems to go equally to the supervisory board and the works council, with the labour director some way behind."

43. *Ibid.,* p. 96.

44. Quoted in Clark Kerr, "The Trade Union Movement and the Redistribution of Power in Postwar Germany," *The Quarterly Journal of Economics,* November 1954, p. 560.

45. "Co-Determination Instead of Class Warfare, DGB Proclaims Its Faith in Democracy," *DGB News Letter,* Dusseldorf, March 1966, p. 7.

46. See for example the article by Dr. Friedhelm Farthmann, "Industrial Democracy, the German Way," *Free Labour World* (ICFTU), May 1968.

47. Fogarty, *op. cit.,* p. 14. Another recent *general* survey of worker participation in management concludes, "In Germany, where it has gone further, opinion would appear to be virtually unanimous in the groups concerned that the system of co-determination exerts no influence whatever in the economic field." Walker and de Bellecombe, *op. cit.,* p. 93.

48. We have already mentioned the earlier exceptions: the Industrial Workers of the World and some small socialist groups in the American labor movement. A major reason why American labor has been less interested in worker participation in management plans has been the great strength of unions at the job level. As previously noted, these participation plans are sometimes a means for extending worker job control, often lacking under European union-management agreements. The CIO interest in joint industry councils reflected, in part, the influence of modern, liberal Catholic social thought on a few key (CIO) leaders. See the Industry Council Program presented by Philip Murray (who was president of both the CIO and the Steelworkers) to the 1941 CIO Convention, as well as some discussion of this issue, in Clinton S. Golden and Harold Ruttenberg (both, then, top officials of the Steelworkers), *The Dynamics of Industrial Democracy* (New York: Harper & Row, 1942), pp. 343–351. Mention should also be made of earlier labor-management collaboration plans in the railway and clothing industries.

49. Dorothea de Schweinitz, *Labor and Management in Common Enterprise* (Cambridge: Harvard University Press, 1949). During World War II, Walter Reuther, then vice-president of the CIO's United Automobile Workers, proposed a top-level labor-management-government board to plan and run the aircraft industry, in order to expedite the output of warplanes. See Walter P. Reuther, "500 Planes a Day," *Selected Papers* (New York: Pyramid Books, 1964), Chap. I.

50. See the recent survey of "cooperative provisions" in major union-management agreements in the United States in the *Monthly Labor Review,* March 1966 (major agreements cover 1,000 or more employees). This Labor Department study, however, "found a continued reluctance on the part of management and unions to enter formal cooperation agreements" to improve production. Even where clauses pledging cooperation were to be found, "in the overwhelming number of cases, no

formal machinery was established to implement these clauses." An interesting if small minority of agreements do make such provisions, and these will doubtless be the subject of study in the years ahead.

51. For Scanlon himself, and for his successors, the plan was to involve the participation by workers in production decisions right on the shop floor, and it was not to be limited merely to agreeing on a formula for cost savings or profit sharing. Fred Lesieur (ed.), *The Scanlon Plan* (New York: Wiley, 1958).

52. A student remarked to me in the course of a long discussion of the subject that "even in the P.T.A. [Parent-Teachers Associations] today, no one likes to take any decision before discussion, participation, and consensus are forthcoming. It's hard to believe it won't spread to the work place." I am indebted to my students for several long discussions on these matters, and particularly to Arie Shirom, who served as my research assistant.

53. Walker and de Bellecombe, *op. cit.,* p. 82 and p. 75.

54. Experience in less-developed countries strongly supports the view that if they do not have effective, regular grievance channels, workers are likely to be suspicious about efforts to institute plans for worker consultation in management. In other cases, in the absence of effective unions, workers turn such plans into regular grievance and negotiation machinery. See, for instance, Saad Ed Din Fawzi, *The Labour Movement in Sudan* (London: Oxford University Press, 1957), pp. 43–57; T. M. Yesufu, *Industrial Relations in Nigeria* (London: Oxford University Press, 1962), pp. 54–57; and Charles A. Myers, *Labor Problems in the Industrialization of India* (Cambridge, Mass.: Harvard University Press, 1958), pp. 126—128.

55. Walker and de Bellecombe, *op. cit.,* p. 75. The same authors (p. 95) do find that in those few cases "where participation has taken the form of reorganization of the work on a basis of autonomous, responsible groups" right on the work floor, productivity has definitely risen. This has apparently also been accompanied by a greater sense of interest and work satisfaction.

56. There are, of course, controls external to the firm that are exercised by the state, the local community, the local union, and Communist Party bodies.

57. Jiri Kolaji, *Workers' Councils, the Yugoslav Experience* (London: Tavistock, 1965), esp. Chaps. 2 and 3. A similar complaint comes from India where a government report on joint management councils notes, "In most cases workers' representatives seem to care more for the enlargement of the amenities and facilities, and in a few cases the redressal of grievances, than about larger problems such as increasing productivity, reducing absenteeism, effecting economies, and suggesting the methods for more efficient utilization of plant and equipment." *Reports on the Working of Joint Management Councils* (New Delhi: Government of India, Ministry of Labour and Employment, 1965), p. 4.

58. Rolf Dahrendorf, *Class and Class Conflict in Industrial Society* (Stanford, California: University Press, 1961).

59. Walker and de Bellecombe, *op. cit.,* pp. 96–98, cite the experience in France, Sweden, Germany, and Britain to this effect.

X

The Development of White-Collar Unionism[1]

WE have noted that in several Western European countries—Germany and Great Britain are good examples—trade-union membership, after advancing sharply in the immediate postwar period, has begun to stagnate in relationship to the increasing labor force. The same phenomenon has also been somewhat characteristic of U.S. union membership for over a decade. The primary cause has been the relative decline of blue-collar (manual) workers vis-à-vis white-collar (nonmanual) workers. For the most part the major trade-union federations in Western Europe and in the United States have, of course, been traditionally dominated by, and have catered to, manual workers.

Both in the United States and in parts of Western Europe the "problem" of organizing the rapidly growing white-collar force (or the opportunity to do so) has become one of the issues most generally discussed in union circles. Several missions of U.S. trade unionists have been sent to Western Europe in recent years to study white-collar work and to appraise the organizing methods of several apparently more successful European white-collar unions.[2]

White-Collar Unions: A Long History

Trade unionism among European white-collar employees began long before World War II and, indeed, in some countries before World War I. For the most part, however, unions of white-collar employees, as distinguished from more purely professional and mutual types of societies, were not numerically well established before World War II. Somewhat of an exception to this were the countries of Central Europe, notably Germany[3] and Austria. In these countries, continuity of feudal-guild concepts of organization and the granting of special legal status to white-collar employees resulted in the organization of a fairly large number of white-collar unions and union-like organizations. Certain white-collar occupations—for example, in retailing, insurance, and banking—followed a recognized guild apprentice structure, and this also encouraged organization.

In Sweden, the white-collar workers' federation traces the main lines of its origins to shortly after World War I—in the 1920s—but its membership was modest until well into the 1930s. In still other European countries white-collar unions of modest strength were also to be found before World War II.[4]

As compared with the degree of unionization of blue-collar workers, however, the greatest growth of white-collar unionism in Western Europe has come about since World War II. This recent increase in white-collar unionism can be traced to a number of forces—economic, social, and political—as well as to adaptation by unions of structural forms, policies, and activities to white-collar workers' needs and desires. A few of these forces parallel developments in the United States, but in some instances they are unique to Europe and to some of the individual countries that are being studied here. And in some cases it is difficult to establish a clear cause-and-effect relationship.

The Extent of White-Collar Unionism

Precise measurement of the degree of white-collar unionism in Western Europe is almost impossible, particularly if one is interested in making comparisons with American statistics.[5] As a general rule, it is probable that the higher the percentage of blue-collar unionism in a country, the higher the percentage of white-collar unionism.

Thus, white-collar unionism appears to be most advanced in Sweden, Denmark, and Austria. In Sweden, around 90 percent of the manuals are unionized, and approximately 70 percent of the nonmanuals are in unions. In Denmark, the comparable figures are 70 percent for manuals and around 60 percent for nonmanuals. Figures on unionization (in the private economy) in Austria show 75 percent unionization for manuals and around 60 percent for nonmanuals.

White-collar employees are usually organized to a greater degree in government than in private employment. In Sweden, for example, in private employment about 50 percent of the nonmanuals are unionized, as compared with approximately 75–80 percent in government.

Although unionization among nonmanuals has been growing in many other countries, it does not approach the degree of organization in Austria, Sweden, or Denmark. In Great Britain, although individual white-collar unions have been growing rapidly in recent years,[6] their membership still does not exceed around 25–30 percent of the total employed, as against about 50 percent for blue-collar unions. This takes in both public and private employment and, as might be expected, white-collar unionization is higher in the public sector.

In Germany, whereas more than 40 percent of the privately employed blue-collar workers are unionized, the white-collar figure is less than 25 percent. In the Netherlands, about 20 percent of the privately employed white-collar workers are unionized, compared with around 50 percent of the privately employed blue-collar workers.

While these figures show great variation in the degree of unionization among white-collar workers, in most of these countries notable progress has been made only in the past twenty years or so. For example, the Swedish Central Organization of Salaried Employees (TCO), as of 1966 numbered 577,000 members; when formally established in 1944, by a merger of previously organized bodies in the private and public sectors, it could claim but 175,000 members. Similarly, the Austrian Union of Nonmanual Workers in Private Industry (GAP), with a membership of about 256,000 in 1964 and today the second largest affiliate of the Austrian Federation of Trade Unions (ÖGB), had only 147,000 members in 1951. The GAP has been one of the fastest-growing unions in the ÖGB for many years.

Figures on trade-union membership in France are difficult to arrive at. As in so many trade-union matters, however, France tends to be an exception among most Western European countries in that white-collar unionization may be relatively higher than blue-collar. This is apparently due in part to the extensive unionization in the public sector. Michel Crozier writes, "The public service is, by far, the sector most 'unionized' in the French economy. The percentage of dues payers can perhaps be estimated at an average of 40% of the employees, against only 15% in the private sector."[7]

While comparisons between Europe and the United States are difficult, it can be estimated that in the United States close to 3 million nonmanual workers are in unions, or aproximately 11 percent of those normally eligible for unionism. In contrast (depending upon the assumed potential), around 50 percent of U.S. manual workers are unionized. One reason why nonmanual unionism is less advanced in the United States is that government employees have begun to organize in large numbers only in recent years. In the United States as in Western Europe, however, individual white-collar and government-employee unions are generally among the fastest growing. During a recent three-year period, for example, while the AFL-CIO increased by some 7 percent, several major government-employee unions grew at many times that rate. For much of the past decade, while many manual unions in private industry were declining or stationary, government unions were increasing. Nonmanual government-employee membership does not account for all of this increase, but this sector of unionism is also growing significantly.

Note Tables 6 through 9.

TABLE 6. *Trends in U.S. Public Employment and Government Union Membership (000)*

Year	All Public Employment	Federal	State & Local	Union Membership* as % of Public Employment
1947	5,474	1,892	3,582	N.A
1956	7,277	2,209	5,069	12.6
1964	9,596	2,348	7,249	15.1
1966	10,871	2,564	8,307	15.8

N.A. Not available.
SOURCE: U.S. Department of Labor.
* Union figures include small number of blue-collar union members of U.S.-based unions operating in Canada. Membership figures do not include the many independent "associations" functioning in public employment.

TABLE 7. *Trade-Union Membership,* * U.S.-Based Unions (000) 1956–1966.*

	1956	1966	% change 1956–1966
Nongovernment	17,189	17,892	+4
Government	915	1,717	+88

TABLE 8. *Trade Union Membership,* * Industrial Distribution, U.S.*

	Mfg.	Nonmfg. (Private)	
1956	8,839 (48.8%)	8,350 (46.1%)	915 (5.1%)
1964	8,342 (46.6%)	8,125 (45.3%)	1,453 (8.1%)
1966	8,769 (45.8%)	8,640 (45.2%)	1,717 (9.0%)

* SOURCE: See Table 6 footnote.

The Retail Clerks, one of the AFL-CIO's largest white-collar affiliates in private industry, grew from 291,000 to 472,000, around 62 percent, in this same 10-year period.

Independent White-Collar Associations

In addition to the traditional and generally known white-collar union organizations, one also finds, in several European countries, independent associations or unions that cater to civil service employees. Often these

TABLE 9. *Membership Changes, AFL-CIO and Other Unions (in 000)*

	1956–57	1966–67	% Change
AFL-CIO	12,883	13,781	7
American Federation of Government Employees	56	196	250
American Federation of State, County and Municipal Employees	147	297	102
American Federation of Teachers	48	125	160

SOURCE: *Report of the Executive Council of the AFL-CIO, Seventh Convention,* Bal Harbour, Florida, Dec. 7, 1967 (Washington, D.C.: American Federation of Labor and Congress of Industrial Organizations, 1967), pp. 35–38. The figures presented are annual averages for the 2-year biennial periods shown. In the case of these rapidly growing government unions, the figures tend to underestimate their strength considerably. The State, County and Municipal Employees, for example, were approaching the 400,000 member mark by the summer of 1968. The AFL-CIO figures for 1956–1957 do not include any members in unions that were expelled in 1957 and after.

bodies are a "cross" between a mutual society, a professional guild, a "company union," and a regular union, though some seem to have evolved into full-fledged unions. It is also interesting to observe that, according to one study done several years ago in the United States, some 392,000 employees in state and local service were to be found in similar types of independent associations.[8] A number of associations that formerly limited themselves to mutual insurance, fraternal and recreational activities, as well as to the general protection of the civil service system, have, in the past few years, taken advantage of new legislation in several states. They have accepted the principle of collective negotiation and have begun to sign collective agreements where possible. The growth and spread in the United States of collective-bargaining programs among independent professional groups such as nurses' and teachers' associations is part of the same trend.

The transition that such associations must make to reach the point where they fully accept the need for, and value of, bargaining is often difficult. Not all such associations make the shift successfully. Some may merge with more orthodox unions in the process while others that are in conflict with regular unions may lose out entirely.

Forces Underlying Growth: Labor-Force Trends

While labor-force statistics for recent years are not available for all Western European countries, data that are available clearly illustrate that the relatively greater growth of white-collar versus blue-collar employment, so familiar a trend in the United States, has also been taking place in Western Europe. In Austria, for example, between 1934 and 1960 salaried (i.e., white-collar) employees rose from approximately 23 to 36 percent of all employees. In Sweden, between 1940 and 1960 the white-collar percentage of the total labor force rose from 20 percent to 35 percent of employment (excluding the self-employed). In Germany, if one excludes the civil service, other white-collar employees increased from 20 percent of the labor force in 1950 to 26 percent in 1958. In Great Britain, from 1931 to 1961, white-collar employees increased from 23 to 36 percent. In most countries the increase in government activities and employment has accelerated the growth of white-collar employment. In Canada, between 1951 and 1961, the number of white-collar employees increased at a rate of 3.6 percent annually, while the corresponding increase for the entire labor force was only 2.1 percent.[9]

This increase in the European white-collar force has created more concentrated areas of white-collar employment and has facilitated the efforts of unions to organize white-collar workers. Some of the bonds of personal identification that the white-collar employee had with his employer began to weaken or break down among larger pools of employees. For example, the Clerical and Administrative Workers' Union of Great Britain, in appealing to office workers to unionize themselves, notes:

The clerical labor force of a single employer may now number several thousands, concentrated in one or two administrative offices in the center of cities or spread through the country. In these circumstances, there can be no question of personal contact between employer and clerk. A hierarchy of managers and departmental heads stands between the clerk and his ultimate employer, the board of directors, from whence come the policy decisions affecting his conditions. The personal and individual salary, with the personal and individual contact, has disappeared, and however employers may seek to disguise the fact by maintaining a system of merit increases, they cannot avoid establishing group standards of payment to correspond with the grouping of work.[10]

Despite oft-expressed union optimism, the mere increase in *numbers* of white-collar office employees may not, in some cases, make the new office workers necessarily receptive to unionism. The *new* workers are *often truly new*. More and more of them come from families with manual backgrounds. While their new job status and working conditions may not compare favorably with those of white-collar clerks of twenty or thirty years ago, they probably do compare favorably with those of yesterday and today in the manual work lives of their parents, older brothers, or sisters. This is likely to be the standard of comparison rather than any bygone superior status enjoyed by white-collar employees of another generation. It is this state of affairs that helps account for the very meager success of union organizing efforts among white-collar employees in U.S. industry—despite the great increase in the number of white-collar

THE DEVELOPMENT OF WHITE-COLLAR UNIONISM

workers employed. In the United States today, for example, white-collar employees in industry, even if they do not belong to unions, are probably by and large still more secure in their jobs than the average manual worker.

The growing importance of government employment, coupled with the well-established pattern of unionization among most government employees, including white-collar workers, accounts for some of the progress European unions have made among privately employed nonmanuals.

Blue-Collar Unionism Stimulates White-Collar Unionism

The great upsurge and strengthening of manual workers' unionism in the last few decades in a number of European countries has also contributed to the spread of white-collar unionism. Organization of white-collar workers becomes a necessity when a predominantly manual workers' union federation and the highest-ranking employers' association are decisively influencing top economic and social matters in a nation, including the setting of a national wage policy or the determination of training and retraining programs.[11]

In Sweden, for example, the spread of unionism among white-collar employees, including college graduates in professional fields, has undoubtedly been due in part to the high degree of organization and the great political and social effectiveness of the manual workers' union during the past thirty years.

The Swedish Confederation of Professional Associations (SACO), a union of college-trained professional workers, asks rhetorically, "Why did the people with academic qualifications organize in separate professional organizations with trade-union purposes?" It answers its own question, "It is, after all, quite a natural thing in itself that a social group should be compelled to organize in a society in which all other groups are organized. Otherwise it risks being discarded and forgotten."[12]

With the increase in union membership since World War II and the development in several countries of national wage-determination systems in which public policy plays a large role, the classical labor market has given way to a "collective bargaining" labor market, in which union and management institutions take over much of the original market's power. As a consequence, large groups, including those in white-collar occupations, are impelled to organize themselves in order to participate in the wage-setting process.

In Great Britain, efforts of the Conservative government to introduce some sort of a national wage policy and a pay pause in 1961–1962 led to a militant outburst by certain professional white-collar union groups— groups that are ordinarily less well organized and have a less militant tradition than manual workers. When the government sought to exercise the policy, it provoked demonstrations by the nurses and the teachers (an already well-organized group).

The phenomenon of militant white-collar employee reaction to what they believe has been a relative worsening of their position has not been confined to Britain. Serious strikes or threats of strikes have occurred among doctors, nurses, and teachers in Canada, Belgium, Sweden, and elsewhere in recent years. It need hardly be added that the same phenomenon has occurred among nurses and teachers in the United States. In France, government employee strikes or demonstrations have become common, and for similar reasons. These displays of white-collar militance are likely to recur in the future, as the relatively new unions begin to exert their potentially great power.

Employer-Association Bargaining as a Factor in White-Collar Unionism

In some Western European countries the centralization of employer associations and their role in area or industry-wide bargaining has added to the pressure on white-collar workers in private industry to join unions.[13]

In Austria, the central secretary of the Union of Nonmanual Workers in Private Industry states that the existence of "the powerful employers' organizations has an effect in the case of those middle class nonmanual workers who have a strong aversion to organization in a quite particular sense: it is not merely a question of recognizing the necessity of becoming trade-union organized—this is also supplemented with some such remarks as: 'Oh, well, if even the bosses need an organization, it can't be as bad as all that.' "[14]

The pattern of bargaining with employer associations, so characteristic of Western Europe, facilitates white-collar unionism. This differs of course with the situation in the United States, where each union must generally struggle to win bargaining rights, employer by employer. In the United States, moreover, white-collar employee units (especially in manufacturing) tend to be relatively small. As a result, organizing them is often a slow and costly process.

In Europe, again as compared with the situation in the United States, associations tend to bargain with manual workers. It is therefore more difficult for individual employers to take a "principled" or ideological stand against bargaining with white-collar employees. Furthermore, when a European white-collar union wins recognition with and through an employers' association, it automatically receives recognition at all of the firms affiliated with the association. By the same token, after an association has extended recognition, it acts as a counterforce against the efforts of any individual firms to wriggle out of bargaining with a white-collar union.

One stimulant of European white-collar unionism has been the relatively greater economic advance of manual workers through their unions—especially in the past fifteen years or so.

The British Clerical and Administrative Workers' Union says that another

. . . factor bearing on the changed position of the office worker is the improved status of the productive worker. The statement can be misunderstood. The improvements which the unions have brought about in the position of the manual worker do not in themselves adversely affect the clerical worker and recognition of the value of work performed by other workers is welcomed by him. Indeed, the trade union clerk has actively worked for and contributed to the raising of living standards generally.

The problem arises through the fact that the concentration on the value of direct production and the productive worker which has been a feature of the past 20 years has been accompanied by a denigration of the value of other forms of work, including office work. The bright boy has been encouraged to take up a craft or technical training. Office work has been regarded as the refuge of the second best.[15]

In Australia, nonmanual workers have been taking to unionism for similar reasons. Ross M. Martin noted that nonmanual workers ". . . believe they no longer hold the superior social and economic position they once enjoyed in relation to manual workers. . . . they [also] fear that promotional opportunities and even the security of nonmanual work may diminish in the future." Equally important, "Non-manual employees feel that employers no longer treat them with the respect they deserve. . . . their disgust has been heightened by the belief that . . . governments discriminate in favor of the manual unions."[16]

In Sweden, relative economic disadvantage appears to have been the main reason why college graduates established the Swedish Confederation of Professional Associations (SACO). SACO describes the unfavorable economic trends for professional employees that helped lead to their unionization:

1. The costs of studying increased and consequently the amount of the debts incurred while studying;
2. the ratio of higher appointments to lower paid posts worsened;
3. the cost of living increased;
4. the pressure of taxation on those income groups in which university graduates are to be found increased enormously, owing to the fact that the progressive scale of taxation was altered so that the amounts due on higher incomes increased more steeply;

5. towards the end of the thirties and at the beginning of the forties, university graduates in a number of branches found it impossible to obtain employment; (and)
6. the policy of equalizing incomes was put into effect with increasing stringency thus reducing the chances of obtaining compensation, through higher salaries in later life, for the years devoted to study and for the unpaid or badly paid probationary years.[17]

An important part of SACO's membership, higher-level civil servants and teachers, conducted a serious strike in 1966 in Sweden (where serious strikes have become rare). It was directed, in part, against the general wage agreement that the Swedish Federation of Trade Unions and the Employers' Association had negotiated earlier in the year. The government sought to negotiate somewhat similar terms with public employees, but SACO rejected them. The strike also stemmed, in part, from the government's failure to provide tax relief for upper-income employees, who argued that the combination of inflation and high marginal tax rates made the manual workers' settlement of little or no real value to professional employees. SACO and other Swedish government white-collar employee unions were successful in winning a substantially larger increase than the manual workers had negotiated, although only SACO was caught up in a strike.[18]

Wage movements as between white- and blue-collar workers in the United States seem to have followed a somewhat different course, at least in recent years. From 1950 to 1963, for example, while all male laborers enjoyed a 55 percent increase in median annual income, the increase for clerical and kindred employees was 71 percent and for professionals and technicals, 88 percent. These increases from 1950 to 1963 contrast with those from 1939 to 1950, when the annual median income of laborers rose 175 percent, as compared with an increase of 111 percent for clericals and 114 percent for professionals and technicals.[19]

During the 1939–50 period, many of the same forces favoring blue-collar workers in Europe were also operating in the United States: There was a very pressing demand for manufactured goods, the labor market for all skills (manual and nonmanual) was in tight supply; the low birth rates of the thirties led to only modest additions to the labor force; and so on. In addition, manual workers in many industries in the United States were in the first phases of successful unionism, and they exercised strong bargaining power. Since the mid-fifties, frequent periods of slackness in manufacturing and related industries—plus the growing need for clericals, technicals, and porfessionals—seems to have tilted the labor market more favorably toward nonmanuals, especially professionals.

It is not yet clear whether (or when) similar developments will overtake the European labor market, although there are a few significant signs.[20]

In the case of some groups of professional employees in Europe, an infringement of their professional rights spurred them to militancy and eventual unionization. It is interesting that, in the 1962 dispute between the New York City Board of Education and unionized teachers, the issues that aroused the teachers as much as anything else involved the assignment of such nonprofessional tasks as bus patrol and cafeteria watch.

The research of Professor S. M. Miller on professionalism and organization among nurses in the United States suggests that similar work issues also lie behind the unionization agitation in this profession.[21]

In the case of engineers in American industry, studies indicate that infringement of professional status is one of the forces behind the emergence of unionism among them since World War II.[22]

Increases in employment of professionals seem to be extremely important as a force which has created great unrest and movement toward unionism among these groups. A special report of the International Labor Organization comments on the great increase in the numbers of employed professionals:

The liberal, scientific and allied professions are among those which are experiencing the greatest upheavals, both qualitative and quantitative. The relative proportion of workers engaged in such occupations . . . as a whole tends to increase as the level of development rises.[23]

Between 1947 and 1966, for example, total employment in the United States rose only 28 percent; professionals and technicals increased 146 percent as compared with 65 percent for clericals; and there was only a 13 percent increase for semiskilled manual workers. The number of employed unskilled laborers actually declined in this same period.[24]

While there may not necessarily be direct relationships between the growth in numbers of professional employees and their resort to unionism, this seems to be true in many important professions. Increased numbers often lead to new forms of administrative and bureaucratic control of professional work as well as some decline in the individual organizational status of the professional. (These problems are, of course, largely confined to employed as opposed to self-employed professionals.)

Although professional unionism is a relatively new phenomenon, it does seem that unionized professionals are likely to be among the most militant of white-collar unionists. A keener sense of occupational identity seems to strengthen their group identity. In addition, their professional status probably gives them a greater freedom of job mobility—particularly in today's labor market—than is the case with many other white-collar occupations.

Clearly evident as another important element in professional restlessness has been a general reaction against the equalitarian policies in practice in most democratic countries during the twentieth century. The general increase in higher education, the spread of progressive income tax systems, the income transfer effects of social welfare programs, the impact of powerful manual worker unions—these and other forces seem to have reduced the special economic and social status of many professional groups. This reduction in status also leads many of them to turn to organization in different forms, including unionism as we have generally known it among other types of workers.[25]

Special Legal Status of European White-Collar Workers

In listing the elements that have facilitated the organization of white-collar workers, one should call attention to the special legal status they sometimes enjoy in European countries. In some Western European nations, there are, for example, special and usually more liberal social-security retirement laws and health laws governing white-collar as against blue-collar workers. The legally established vacation privileges of white-collar employees have often been superior to blue-collar privileges. This was especially true before World War II. In addition, protection against dismissal, under the law, is often stronger for white-collar employees.

The necessity to lobby for the preservation of this separate and generally superior status has probably encouraged unionization of some categories of white-collar workers—especially in the past decade, during which time the blue-collar unions have begun to close the gap by strong bargaining. For example, the desire to protect what usually has been a superior social-security retirement arrangement is obviously of considerable importance here.

As far as the superior vacation or social insurance benefits enjoyed by white-collar workers is concerned, during the past decades unionized blue-collar employees in several European countries have begun to press their governments to extend to them these same benefits (by changing the legislation). Where white- and blue-collars are members of the same labor federation, this can become a delicate political issue, as the white-collar unions and their members may object to such leveling.[26]

Generally, employers in Western Europe, as in the United States, have been more reluctant to negotiate and sign agreements with white-collar workers than with blue-collar workers. This traditional reluctance stems, in part, from the fact that most of today's white-collar functions were historically "once performed by the employer" and are still, in the employer's mind, managerial.[27] It might also be noted that in most European countries, employers, when confronted with the necessity to bargain with white-collar workers prefer to see them in separate unions —separate, that is, from the manual workers' unions.

Judging from the experiences of several countries, it appears that if unionization of privately employed white-collar workers is looked upon as a desirable public objective, special governmental intervention is often required to bring it about. The situation in Sweden offers one example. Although Swedish employers had long recognized the rights of manual workers to unionize and sign collective agreements, it took the passage of special legislation in 1936 to open the door fully to private white-collar union recognition in Sweden.

Recently several British experts and some British union leaders have recommended a special union recognition tribunal to expedite the development of white-collar unionism in that country. George Sayers Bain writes:

If the trade union movement is to continue to play an effective role in the British industrial relations system, it must reverse the present downward trend of the density of unionisation by expanding its membership among the poorly-organised areas of the labour force, particularly among the rapidly increasing number of white-collar employees in private industry. Second, a major obstruction to the expansion of union membership in these areas is employers' refusal to recognise unions and their pursuance of policies designed to discourage or prohibit their employees from joining them. Third, most white-collar unions, and even some manual unions, have obtained recognition from private employers largely as a result of government policies, and these unions are unlikely to obtain further major concessions of recognition without government assistance. These generalisations, in sum, lead to the conclusion that the continued growth and effectiveness of the British trade union movement largely depend upon government action to encourage union recognition.[28]

The TUC itself proposed to the Royal Commission that in disputes over recognition either union or management be empowered to bring about arbitration of such a dispute, if it so desired.[29] The Royal Commission Report in June 1968 did not specifically prescribe a new recognition tribunal, but it assigned this problem to a proposed new permanent Industrial Relations Commisison (which would have other functions as well). The Royal Commission expressed general agreement with a proposal by Allan Flanders that such a new Industrial Relations Commission should have the power to conduct secret elections to determine union representativity. The Commission, however, with the exception of only one of its twelve members, inclined to avoid prescribing any penalties for companies and unions that did not comply with such representative determinations as might be made. The pressure of public opinion would, apparently, be the principal enforcing device for the Industrial Relations Commission.[30]

During the twentieth century as the problems of union recognition for particular major sectors of the labor force have come to the fore in the United States, special government intervention to assist the unions to establish themselves has been required. This was true, for example, of the railroad workers in the 1920s (various railway labor acts were passed), the mass production workers of the 1930s (the National Labor Relations Act), and government employees in the 1960s (Federal Executive Order 10988 to expedite federal employee unionism as well as the recent spate of special legislation in a number of states to encourage unionism and regulate industrial relations among state and local government employees).

Whether or not special legislation may be enacted some day in the United States to encourage private white-collar unionism is impossible to forecast at present. In any case, it is not being suggested that the need for special legislation to expedite private white-collar unionism is universal even among Western European countries. Such legislation has not been necessary in countries like Switzerland, Austria, or France, which represent a wide spectrum of countries with varied union and industrial relations systems.

Unionization of Foremen and Supervisors

Another factor that explains the appeal of unionism to white-collar workers is the high degree of unionization, in Western Europe, of foremen (in charge of blue-collar employees) and supervisors (in charge of white-collar employees). In a society where social hierarchy and group status—whether of the feudal, guild, mercantile, or capitalist variety—have always been more deeply entrenched than in the United States, it is not surprising that even managerial employees have found it desirable (and not so difficult) to organize. Added to this, in the foremen's case, was of course the "risk of being ground between the millstones of two other very strong groups, namely the workers' union organizations on the one hand, and the employers on the other."[31] Moreover, long experience with unionism makes a manual worker more easily persuaded of its value after he has moved up to foreman.[32]

While foremen and supervisors are well organized within a few of the traditional European labor federations, the stronger unions covering these workers usually are either independent or part of a separate white-collar federation as such. In Denmark, for example, the union is independent. In Sweden, the foremen have formed an important, separate union in the TCO, and many supervisors in industry and government are members of other TCO affiliates.[33] In Austria, the GAP takes in both foremen and supervisors. In France, despite relatively weak union organization and membership among manuals, the unionization of supervisors and foremen is surprisingly strong.[34] Structurally, in France, these unions usually have engineers, supervisors, and foremen in one organization. One such union, the independent General Confederation of Supervisory Employees (Confédération Générale des Cadres [CGC]), includes in its ranks some management personnel in executive levels that are close to the very top.

European unionists stress that supervisors who join unions thereby set an example that frequently induces lower-level white-collar workers to sign up. This is cited as a factor in unionization among large groups of government white-collar employees in France and England (in England this is especially true of the National Association of Local Government Officers).

Moreover, the typical white-collar worker is likely to have aspirations for a higher position—more so than the manual worker. This is because the continuum between supervision and other levels of white-collar work, which is found in many office situations, is not found in most manual working situations, where no advancement is possible beyond the foreman level. In Sweden, the TCO recognizes that the large increase in white-collar employment has reduced the possibilities of individual advancement, but it notes, "Almost all salaried (white collar) employees regard opportunity for promotion as a practical reality—an essential difference between salaried employees and manual workers."[35] In Britain, one of the broad objectives of the Clerical and Administrative Workers Union is "to keep open avenues of promotion for those who make office work their career." Especially when the union is able to span almost all occupations in the office, including at least some of those in supervision, its general appeal is strengthened. Members can see the union as a control point in the promotion process, since it has the right to bargain on higher posts. Crozier points out that one of the real appeals of the public employee unions of France's Force Ouvrière is the influence of their "recommendations in the matter of promotions."[36]

Contrary to what might be expected by American students and practitioners in the labor-relations field, the problem of dual loyalty on the part of unionized supervisors seems to be taken right in stride in Western Europe. These supervisors carry out their supervisory functions, yet, when the occasion arises, they can bargain as employees about their wages and working conditions—and do so right across the table from very top management.[37]

Several European white-collar union leaders, on learning that unionization of supervisors is extremely difficult under U.S. labor laws and practice, have expressed the view that this would greatly hinder the unionization of white-collar workers in the United States. In this connection, the experience of U.S. unions in both private and public employment is relevant. Some of the organizing gains by the Retail Clerks

Association in California in the late 1930s seemed to be due in part to the fact that store managers could then be included in the union.[38] Similarly, a number of locals of the American Federation of State, County and Municipal Employees have found that signing up supervisors is frequently a key factor in organizing white-collar employees in state and local public employment.[39]

Executive Order 10988 (January 17, 1962) was designed to encourage unionism among federal employees. It is still too early to tell whether it borrowed too heavily from the National Labor Relations Act as amended by Taft-Hartley in the way in which it seems to limit the inclusion of so-called "supervisors" in bargaining units.

Structure of Nonmanual Unionism

The variety in the structure of nonmanual unionism in Western Europe is considerable. Moreover, the forms of unionism and the bargaining patterns often differ from those we regard as normal in the United States, but not much more than do some European manual union forms and practices differ from those in the United States. These differences, of course, reflect differences, among others, in the organization of the economy and in the traditions among employers. (In Europe, we have noted, employer associations play a more important role, and there are fewer large corporate industrial units.)

As in the United States, there is continuing debate in several European federations as to the "best" union structure within which to organize white-collar employees—whether it is better to combine them into industrial unions with manual workers in the same plants, whether to organize them in "craft" unions, or whether to combine them in some other way.[40]

AUSTRIA AND GERMANY. The forms of white-collar unionism are quite varied, even in those countries where most of the unionized white-collar employees have been organized within the central, traditional, and once almost completely manual-dominated labor federations. In Austria, for instance, the White Collar Workers Union in Private Industry and Commerce (GAP) is a separate affiliate of the Austrian Federation of Trade Unions and it covers white-collar workers throughout the private sector—in banking, insurance, manufacturing, forestry, and so on. The decision not to include white-collar workers within the industrial unions was made after difficult and protracted debates, which ended in 1951. On the other hand, within the German Federation of Trade Unions (DGB), after a similar debate, it was decided to organize the nonmanual employees into the sixteen basic industrial unions. Office and technical employees in the textile industry, for example, would be organized in the one textile union.[41]

The DGB has unionized approximately 1.3 million white-collar employees in private and public employment.[42] While many of them are in public employment, a few of the large industrial unions operating in the private sector have made considerable progress in unionizing the white-collar workers in their jurisdictions. The giant German Metalworkers Union has a nonmanual membership of around 200,000, and the Chemical, Paper and Ceramics Union has more than 60,000 nonmanual members. The DGB does have one predominantly white-collar affiliate in the banking, commerce, and insurance field, which has over 100,000 members.

In the past few years the DGB has been caught up in a major campaign to unionize officers (commissioned and noncommissioned) in the armed forces. At the center of this campaign, which has met with some success, is the DGB's large public-employees' union, which has approximately 1 million members, covering manual and nonmanual employees in all levels of government—federal, state, and local—but which does not include public postal and transport employees, who are in separate DGB unions. Some ordinary trade-union considerations are involved in this campaign, such as pensions, allowances, and the like. There is no intent, however, to interfere in any way with usual military considerations, such as transfers, battle assignments, and so on.

The decision to accept army officers into the DGB occasioned some soul-searching among leaders of the traditionally antimilitarist German trade-union movement. A major reason why it was made lay in the conviction that this was one way to insure fuller integration of the German armed forces into the democratic society. DGB leaders therefore believe that this broad sociopolitical goal can be accomplished even if only some of the officers become unionized.[43]

Similar considerations have led the public-employees' union to enroll jurists. Members of the bench have traditionally been recruited from the more conservative layers of German society. The labor movement believes that even if only a minority of German jurists is enrolled, this can have a democratic, leavening effect on the judiciary.

Outside the DGB there is an independent union devoted to organizing white-collar workers across the board, that is, in both private and public employment. This union is the Deutsche Angestellten Gewerkschaft (DAG), with a membership of over 470,000. The DAG was born largely out of the dissatisfaction of certain nonmanual worker groups with the DGB decision in favor of complete industrial unionism. These groups refused to give up their special white-collar classification.[44]

Aside from the DGB and DAG, there are several other organizations engaged in unionizing nonmanual employees in Germany. The most important is the Deutscher Beamtenbund, a union devoted to organizing only classified civil service employees. Its membership of around 700,000 is virtually all nonmanual. A smaller organization, the Christian-National Trade Union for White Collar Employees, also competes in the non-manual field.

SWEDEN. A separate federation—separate, that is, from the traditional manual workers' federation—has unionized the bulk of the white-collar employees in Sweden. The Swedish Central Organization of Salaried Employees (TCO), which has already been mentioned, is the center of white-collar unionization. Indeed, in Sweden even the professional employees—the so-called diploma or college-graduate types—have organized a separate central federation.

The Swedish Federation of Trade Unions (LO), the manual workers' federation, has some nonmanual membership in its Commercial Workers Union, including substantial numbers of lower-level nonmanuals in commerce.[45] LO also has organized a fair number of lower level nonmanuals in public employment, including many in communications. But LO seems never to have made a strong and concerted drive to organize nonmanuals generally. This eventually helped pave the way for TCO, as a separate nonmanual federation.

The TCO is a combination of unions of a predominantly vertical (industrial) character, along with a few horizontal (craft) unions. The largest TCO union is the Swedish Union of Clerical and Technical Employees in Industry, a vertical union that covers all types of office employees and, in some instances, managerial employees in private industry outside of commerce or trade. This union has a membership of 170,000 (1966), which is around 30 percent of the entire TCO. Until 1968 the second largest union in the TCO was a craft type, the Swedish Union of Foremen and Supervisors, which takes in those categories of workers in private industries and numbers over 54,000 members, but this union withdrew from TCO in a craft-industrial dispute at the beginning of 1968. The Union of Commercial Employees in Sweden, third largest TCO affiliate, has jurisdiction over nonmanual workers in most of the retail and wholesale trade. Other important occupational or craft unions in the TCO include the Swedish Nurses Association, the Swedish Union of Policemen, and the Union of Noncommissioned Officers in the Defense Forces. (The commissioned officers are well organized in a small, independent government-employees' federation.)

SACO, the Swedish federation of professional (or diploma) employees' unions, has to some extent been built on the foundation of the country's various professional societies and associations. If one conceived of the American Pharmaceutical Association, the American Medical Association, or the Society of Archivists explicitly taking over union and collective-bargaining functions along with their professional tasks, he could begin to have a picture of some of the important affiliates of SACO. In addition to promoting the professional interests and occupations of their members, Swedish professional associations have also committed themselves to "safeguard the social and economic interests of the members" (the words quoted are from the constitution of the Swedish Medical Association). Union organization extends so far in Sweden that the SACO includes a union that takes in clergymen (recall that the church is supported by the state in Sweden). The engineering and secondary school teachers' unions, unlike the doctors' or architects' unions, are separate from the professional association in these fields. In the dental field, union and professional activities are also carried on by separate organizations, although their relations are close and cordial.[46]

The great majority of unionized professionals, including doctors, jurists, and clergymen, are directly or indirectly employed by the state, and SACO's membership of over 90,000 is concentrated primarily in public employment. The four largest of its thirty-one affiliates, which account for over 50 percent of its membership, are the Swedish Medical Association, largely employed in relation to the Swedish system of socialized medicine; the Swedish Association of Graduate Engineers; the National Association of Swedish Teachers (these are employed in higher level secondary or *gymnasium* type schools; most Swedish teachers, in other types of schools are members of the TCO); and the Swedish Federation of Jurists (largely employed as administrators in the public employment).

THE NETHERLANDS.   In the Netherlands, there are three main central labor movements: the Netherlands Federation of Trade Unions (the socialist-oriented NVV), the Netherlands Catholic Workers' Movement (Catholic-oriented KAB), and the National Federation of Christian Workers (Protestant-oriented CNV). In these movements the forms of nonmanual unionism are even more varied. Thus in the NVV, the leading Dutch labor federation, by a clear-cut organizational decision at the end of World War II, nonmanual workers were slotted into their "appropriate" industrial unions—for example, the nonmanuals in metal plants were "assigned" to the metalworkers union. The NVV also established one central union, Mercurius, to cover all employees in commercial establishments as well as nonmanual workers who fall outside of the traditional industrial lines (e.g., banks, insurance companies, private hospitals). The principle of organizing nonmanuals into their appropriate "industrial" unions has also been largely followed by the CNV, but within the KAB, white-collar workers tend to be organized on craft lines.[47]

GREAT BRITAIN.   The traditionally greater variety and overlapping in the forms of organization in British manual-worker unions tend to hold for nonmanual unions. In describing the nonmanual affiliates of the British Trades Union Congress, the secretary of the TUC Nonmanual Workers Advisory Committee mentions three types of organization:

Horizontal: In which nonmanual employees irrespective of their industry are in the same union. Examples may be found in the Clerical and Administrative Workers' Union and the Association of Supervisory Staffs, Executives, and Technicians. The most successful union of this type is considered to be the Draughtsmen and Allied Technicians' Association.

Vertical: In which the clerical staffs may be in the same union as the manual workers whether skilled, semiskilled, or laborers, for example, National Union of Mineworkers and National Association of Theatrical and Kine Employees.

Occupational: In which nonmanual workers within an industry or service have separate unions—Transport Salaried Staffs Association, National Union of Bank Employees, Civil Service Clerical Association, etc. This type has by far the most nonmanual members in Britain.[48]

As an example of some of the overlapping, office employees in the nationalized coal industry are unionized in both the National Union of Mineworkers and the Clerical and Administrative Workers' Union, both affiliated with the TUC. The need for some consolidation of the numerous, relatively small white-collar unions into larger units has been under discussion for a number of years.[49] Early in 1968 the Association of Supervisory Staffs, Executives, and Technicians merged with the Association of Scientific Workers. Perhaps partially as a defensive measure to this merger, the Draughtsmen and Allied Technicians' Association reopened merger negotiations with the large and powerful Amalgamated Engineering Union (there had been some merger discussions between these two unions in the past). The Clerical and Administrative Workers' Union also seems to be in similar conversations with the giant General Transport and Workers' Union, which already has a special section for staff employees in industry. Sharp jurisdictional conflicts over which union should organize a particular group of white-collar employees are not uncommon in Great Britain.

One of the TUC's largest nonmanual worker concentrations is in the Union of Shop, Distributive and Allied Workers (USDAW), which takes in both manual and nonmanual employees in the retail and wholesale trade field. In an earlier period, much of USDAW's strength was based in the British co-op field. In Western Europe a number of commercial-employee unions affiliated with predominantly manual-worker federations owe their origin to traditional labor co-op ties. Unionization among the employees of cooperative stores and warehouses was (and is) almost an automatic procedure.

In addition to the TUC and its nonmanual affiliates, there are a few important independent white-collar unions in Great Britain. The largest of these is The National Union of Teachers, also an independent, which has a membership of over 215,000. Several other independent unions—or staff associations, as they are generally termed—are also operating in the national civil service. The National Association of Local Government Officers, with a membership of 338,000, affiliated with the TUC late in 1964, after a long history of independence.

DENMARK. In Denmark, unionized nonmanual employees are divided between the Danish Federation of Labor (LO), and a loosely organized, independent, white-collar federation, the Federation of Civil Servants and Salaried Employees (FTF). Within the LO, more than half of the white-collar membership is concentrated in the Danish Retail Clerks and Office Workers Union (HK), with a membership of over 100,000. The HK is the second largest union in the LO and its fastest-growing major affiliate. It takes in white-collar workers in some public employment. (Most of the privately employed white-collar workers are in trade. Most of the publicly employed white-collar workers are in civil service unions, some are in the LO, some in the FTF; a few are in independent unions.)

The FTF is only about fifteen years old. It has a membership of over 140,000, primarily in public employment. It includes a teachers' union of around 25,000, a nurses' union of 33,000, and several important higher level civil service workers' unions. The FTF has a thinly manned headquarters secretariat, is a very "loose" organization, and has not yet developed into a federation comparable to the TCO in Sweden, with which it has fraternal relations.

Some Danish white-collar workers are organized independently of both the FTF and the LO. A union of foremen and technicians, covering both public and private employment, numbers over 25,000. Most of these workers have moved up from a manual background. An early agreement by the LO with Danish employer associations not to take in foremen seems to account for the union's independent status.

White-Collar Unions and Politics

Compared with unionized manual workers, nonmanual unionists tend to be less "political" or less apt to support or relate to the traditional labor-socialist party.[50] (The interest of nonmanuals in *political issues* as such, may, however, equal or exceed that of the average manual worker.)

In Great Britain, where a union member may elect not to pay any union political levies, this practice of "contracting out" of such payments is more prevalent in nonmanual TUC affiliates. Moreover, a nonmanual union, even though part of the TUC, is a bit less likely to affiliate with the British Labour Party than is the average manual workers' union; the National Union of Bank Employees is a case in point. Also, the principal reason why members of the National Association of Local Government Officers (NALGO) for many years resisted its officers' efforts to affiliate with the British TUC was the feeling that affiliation "implied support for the Labour Party."[51]

There is a feeling of general "uneasiness" in some white-collar unions that are part of a manually dominated, political-party-oriented labor federation. The bank employees' union that was mentioned a moment ago is a good example. At the 1965 annual convention of the TUC this union introduced a resolution noting that "the party-political discussions frequently carried out within the TUC has created an obstacle to the increased membership of those non-manual unions affiliated to the TUC and has been a factor militating against an increase in the number of affiliated trade unions catering for non-manual employees." The bank union went on to propose that the convention instruct the TUC General Council to conduct "an investigation; whereby means could be created to effect a clear organizational differentiation between industrial and economic debate and activity of the TUC," on the one hand, "and the party-political debate and activity of those unions affiliated to the Labor Party on the other."

The TUC General Secretary responded that "I am a trade unionist from top to bottom, but all my life is in politics. . . . Almost everything we do at the TUC leads to a political conclusion." After further debate, in which more leftist white-collar unionists also criticized the bank union's proposal, it was rejected.[52]

Among white-collar unions affiliated with the Norwegian Federation of Trade Unions (LO), it has been observed that they "try to adjust themselves to the neutralist [political] tendencies of their actual and potential membership." An analysis of union journals published during the 1957 election campaign showed "that all working class unions . . . took a clear partisan stand [in favor of the Labor Party], whereas white collar unions affiliated [with the LO] tended to be weakly engaged, or not engaged at all." Few white-collar local unions tend to be "collectively affiliated" with the Labor Party, unlike the manual local unions.[53]

Both the Swedish TCO and the German DAG are neutral as far as ties with political parties are concerned, even though they take positions on specific political issues. Although members of both organizations clearly tend to be more conservative, politically, than manual unionists, many of their leaders come from or are personally sympathetic to the Socialist Party.

In Austria, most of the leaders of the nonmanual GAP may be personally committed and active socialists, but they attribute the more successful unionization of nonmanuals since World War II, in part, to the formal depoliticalization of the Austrian Federation of Trade Unions.[54] This formal political nonpartisanship made it easier to take in all groups of the work force, including the Catholics, who had been strong among the white-collar groups in the pre-World War II era.

Collective Bargaining, Wage Structures, and Strikes

COLLECTIVE BARGAINING. For the most part, white-collar collective-bargaining structures and patterns (only a few key factors are discussed here) tend to follow those practiced in the blue-collar field. Where a high degree of centralization in bargaining has developed—as, for example, in Sweden—there also tend to be centralized patterns in white-collar union bargaining. In Sweden, the bargaining structure in the manufacturing sector is, in fact, in some ways even more centralized for nonmanual than for manual employees. The two key white-collar unions, the Swedish Union of Clerical and Technical Employees in Industry (SIF) and the Swedish Foremen's Association (SAF), negotiate a central bargain for all white-collar employees in all manufacturing. By contrast, bargaining for manual workers is on an industry-wide basis, as in the case of metals, textiles, chemicals, and so on.

In other countries where industry-wide bargaining between national unions and associations has become the pattern (as, for example, in the British engineering industries), unions covering the clerks and draftsmen have also negotiated national agreements with the appropriate employers' associations. In Germany, in the private sector of the economy, the pattern of bargaining is largely set by the large industrial unions, many of which negotiate separately with industry-wide employers' associations for both the white-collar and blue-collar workers. Where plural unionism has been the prevailing practice, as in the Netherlands and France, it is common for more than one union to have representation rights in a given white-collar unit.

While it is difficult to generalize, key economic bargaining power in almost every Western European country continues to rest—with a few exceptions—with the manual unions and/or the manual federations (if there is a separate white-collar federation). Under these circumstances, the white-collar unions, as far as general economic movements are concerned, tend to be followers rather than leaders. Whether this is due primarily to the greater militance of the manual workers' unions, their longer experience, and their greater numerical strength is difficult to say. Also helping to account for the bargaining leadership of the manual unions is the strong demand for blue-collar workers in the postwar labor market, with its great emphasis upon the reconstruction and reequipment of European industry, and the later expansion of markets in consumer durable goods.

WAGE STRUCTURES. The stronger economic impact of the manual unions is in part accounted for by the special character of white-collar wage bargaining in the private sector. In nearly every country, one finds that white-collar wages are more individualized, or less standardized, than manual workers' wages.

Exemplifying the extreme in the individualized approach is the Swedish Union of Clerical and Technical Employees in Industry (SIF), which maintains:

. . . every employee should receive a salary equivalent to his proficiency, position, education, age, and years of service. No schedule of salary rates for employees exists in Swedish industry; instead, salaries are determined quite individually. This does not mean, however, that SIF is inactive when it comes to improving salary conditions for its members. Collective bargaining takes place each year in almost every company where the salaried employees are organized.[55]

Under this system, each year (or every two years, as the case may be) a bargain is made that specifically recognizes that additional individual increases (a significant percentage of the average) will thereafter be negotiated at each place of work. These negotiations and adjustments are based upon individual merit, length of service, special skills, and so forth. If the plant-level negotiations do not produce agreement, the matter may be taken up in central negotiations. To back up the local negotiations, the unions make comprehensive salary surveys and classification studies; furnishing one's own salary data is virtually a condition of membership in the SIF. The union is thus able to guide the individual in negotiations by telling him the prevailing levels for given jobs in given areas and giving him similar pertinent information. In some ways, this comprehensive effort concerning individual wages gives the union a greater hold on membership interest than can be achieved by the manual worker unions in negotiating general wage scales.[56]

In Britain, the draughtsmen's union also makes extensive wage surveys to assist its members in negotiating at the local level. It has installed an advanced electronic data-processing system to help it with its wage analyses.[57]

In the United States, where there is a relatively large concentration of engineering and technical personnel in private employment, one can already discern a special emphasis upon wage research, even though unionism has only barely begun among these employees. Individual merit systems, which result in individual as against uniform wage rates, makes the provision of wage-research data a major service function for engineering unionism.[58]

Returning to SIF's approach to wage-bargaining, one should note that this union represents an extreme even in Sweden, inasmuch as no general occupational scales are sought. In white-collar bargaining by other Swedish unions (for example, in commerce as well as in government), there are standardized salary schedules—though again not as standardized as for manual work.[59]

While most European white-collar unions do not go as far as the SIF in accepting an individual salary structure, many accept and consider factors that individualize the salary schedule considerably. Frequently, only job minimums are negotiated across the board, and beyond this a variety of "individual" factors affect the employee's wage. For example, under Dutch collective agreements, a white-collar employee's salary depends not only upon what branch of industry he works in and what class of job he holds, but also upon the employee's sex, age, and/or seniority, and merit rating. The degree of union participation or control in the merit-rating process varies widely. The use of individual merit ratings, age factors, and male/female distinction are fairly widespread in European white-collar salary schemes.

Regular longevity increases are quite common for banking employees. In Great Britain, for instance, there is provision for regular wage increases (to some extent related to job advancement) between ages seventeen and thirty-one. The National Union of Banking Employees has accepted this custom, though it seeks some changes in the progression pace, scale, and so on.

At present, as the economies of Western Europe become more dynamic, systems based on such rigid longevity requirements are causing concern because of the difficulties they create in recruiting younger personnel for some jobs. Several banking and insurance company executives expressed this concern to the author in recent years.

STRIKES. Whether for reasons of outlook or tradition, strikes and strike action tend to be considerably less practiced or accepted by unionized white-collar workers than by unionized blue-collar workers (and, as discussed earlier, less practiced and accepted by European than by American blue-collar workers). White-collar workers are less interested in strikes even in some cases where they are in the same union as blue-collar workers. The German Metalworkers Union is a good example. No one in that union expects white-collar clerical workers to strike, even when the blue-collar workers go out. Because of their predominantly manual background, foremen and technicians may be a little closer to the blue-collar workers in their acceptance of strike action.

In Austria, on the other hand, there appears to be no significant distinction between the manuals and nonmanuals as far as strike techniques and policies are concerned. In Great Britain the situation seems to vary with the union. For example, the Draughtsmen—which has a strong sense of craft pride and has a large number of members who have been apprenticed and upgraded from the manual ranks—appears to be as militant as any other union in the TUC. Unions like the bank employees' and the clerical workers' seem, however, to put less emphasis on strike action.

Where the nonmanuals are in a separate federation, as in Sweden, strike action becomes more complicated. The TCO refers to:

. . . the very difficult intermediary position occupied by salaried employees in the event of dispute. Theoretically, salaried employees in large industrial enterprises have the same right as manual workers to come out on strike. But the result of such a strike would be that the manual workers of the enterprise would immediately be plunged into unemployment and this, in many cases, rules out the possibility of strike action. Manual workers, on the other hand, need not have such inhibitions. The employers cannot lay off salaried employees in the event of a labor dispute; and it is stipulated in salaried employees' agreements that their wages cannot be reduced until a strike has been proceeding for at least 3 months—and even then not below 60 per cent of the normal amount, a further condition being that working hours are reduced accordingly. Under their agreements, salaried employees are, in principle, neutral in the event of a labor dispute, nor are they obliged to carry out work causing a strike.[60]

Considerable emphasis must be given to the fact that under no circumstances are nonmanual employees expected to perform the work of manuals who are on strike. It is true in Great Britain, too, that while the white-collar unions follow a policy of making no common cause with blue-collar strikes, they carefully avoid doing any of the work of blue-collar workers who are out on strike.

Industrial Relations in the Public Service[61]

In Western Europe, there is, of course, great variation from country to country concerning the rights of unionization and bargaining of public employees. At the outset it is necessary to distinguish between civil servants (usually nonmanuals whose job tenure is more or less permanent, unless they commit very grave offenses), and nonestablished, or noncivil service public employees. The latter might include workers in publicly owned gas or electrical plants, coal mines, local public transportation systems or railroads, nationalized factories, ports, and so on. As far as this noncivil service group is concerned, their bargaining and strike rights have evolved to the point where they approach or equal those of employees in the private sector of the economy. Usually they can negotiate collective agreements like those in private industry, may strike on occasion, and take other action similar to that of the privately employed. Where necessary, collective agreements may be subject to ratification by public legislation bodies.[62] Unfortunately for students of comparative industrial relations, workers in certain services in some countries—as, for example, the operating personnel on railroads—are civil servants, while in other services, they are not. Nevertheless the broad distinction between the two groups, as set forth above, will hold.

The status of the civil servant has undergone an enormous transformation in the past thirty or forty years. Civil servants were, for a long time, a highly privileged, special caste of workers, whose *personal conduct* was even subject to public scrutiny and regulation,[63] and for whom the ordinary rights of unionization and negotiation, let alone strikes, were nearly unthinkable. As for strikes, penal sanctions were generally provided.

This state of affairs has changed substantially in every Western country. The forces behind the change have been (1) the growth in private employees' job security, resulting from a full-employment policy and the strengthening of collective bargaining, thereby rendering the security of civil servants less exclusive, (2) the great increase in the number of civil servants, reducing their individual status, and (3) the period of more or less continuous full or high employment in the past fifteen or twenty years, which make it all but impossible to apply severe sanctions against civil servants who strike or unionize, since it is next to impossible to replace them in large numbers, (4), which is a corollary of (3), the ability of unionized noncivil service employees to obtain benefits and working conditions equal to and in some cases better even than those that were formerly enjoyed only by civil servants, (5) the growth of the principle of collective decision-making and collective representation in modern society to which we have alluded.

Gradually, but at an accelerating rate in the past twenty years or so, civil servants have gained important negotiating rights. This has often passed from the stage of mere consultation up through the stage that involves the right to negotiate an effective collective agreement. In some countries, even where full negotiating rights have been achieved, this has not included the right to strike. However, in Scandanavia and France, even this right is explicitly provided now for most civil servants, if proper notice and other stipulated procedures are followed.

Where this right to strike is extended, as for instance in Norway, some groups are often excluded, such as higher-level civil servants, those in military service, and policemen. In Sweden, a special agreement has been negotiated between the various unions and the government to handle disputes that may be injurious to the community. A similar agreement between the employers' association and the unions operates in the private economy.[64]

In Norway and Denmark, the government has general powers to intervene in a dispute that may be harmful to the nation and to help impose by special legislation a settlement through compulsory arbitration.[65]

None of this should convey the idea that strikes among civil servants are common. They occur rarely, and they are often just one-day manifestations aimed at calling public attention to grievances.

In Britain, there is no law forbidding strikes in the civil service, but striking is a disciplinary offense. On the other hand, there is a system of compulsory arbitration to resolve unsettled disputes in Britain. Moreover, the British government has wide powers to negotiate with its employees, relatively free of parliamentary constraint, and it does so. Membership in "staff associations," as the civil service unions are termed, is encouraged by the government. Arbitration is limited to general issues such as wages, hours, and working conditions affecting whole classes of employees. These matters are generally negotiated for the whole or large parts of the civil service, with unions sitting in for the employees', and a specially empowered representative from the Treasury sitting in for the government. Together they form the so-called Whitley Council.[66] Individual grievance cases which are taken up by the unions directly with the ministries are not subject to arbitration but can be appealed to the courts. Union and management representatives indicate that practically all individual cases are settled to the satisfaction of both parties within the ministries.

As for Germany, although its constitution establishes a general right to strike, this right is generally held not to extend to civil servants. Other classes of public employees, such as manual workers and white-collar employees who do not have civil service status, do have the right to strike. The constitution of Germany's public employees' union provides that policemen, firemen, and the military cannot take part in strikes.

Although wages and other basic benefits of civil servants are usually established by law, collective agreements concerning wages in general, basic wage schedules, and classifications have also come to play a major role in some countries. These agreements are usually subject to ratification by the appropriate legislative body (e.g., Parliament in the case of a national civil service agreement, the municipal government in a negotiation involving municipal employees), but eventually such ratification becomes a formality in cases in which responsible public officials and unions have completed their negotiations. In several countries agreements negotiated by state authorities and civil service unions no longer even require ratification.

Enhancing this evolution in Europe is the practice of party government. Since control of the legislature and control of the executive branch usually go hand in hand in Europe, and since party discipline is stricter

THE DEVELOPMENT OF WHITE-COLLAR UNIONISM

than in the United States, obtaining legislative approval for an agreement negotiated by the executive is virtually automatic. Obviously these same conditions are lacking in U.S. government and politics, and their absence is likely to result in important differences in the evolution of public-employee bargaining as compared with Europe.

Generally speaking, where unions of civil servants have won the right to negotiate agreements, including basic wage schedules, this has been accompanied by major structural changes within the union movement. Larger groupings of unions, cartels, or joint bargaining committees become necessary, if the unions are to have an impact upon basic civil service regulations affecting all employees. In some countries this need has led to the amalgamation of public-employee unions.

A similar development seems likely to take place in the United States as unions which represent only particular groups of employees (in a particular occupation or department) come up against civil service regulations which cover all employees in the service. This was virtually anticipated by the so-called Lindsay report that concerned problems and procedures in public-employee bargaining in New York City. This report recommended that New York City bargain on basic economic benefits affecting "Career and Salary Plan Employees, only with an employee organization or council or group of employee organizations representing more than 50% of all Career and Salary Plan Employees."[67]

The present highly defensive position of most civil service agencies (federal, state, or local) about bargaining over civil service regulations or wage classifications is likely to be breached when coalitions or amalgamations of unions come to confront them.

White-Collar Unionism Likely to Increase

Borrowing from the past experience of manual unions and improvising new forms and policies, European white-collar workers are taking to unionism in increasing numbers and in a variety of forms. Social, economic, and political forces in Western Europe—and the very successes of white-collar unions in the past decade—indicate that this latest wave of organization will continue to rise.

It is likely that the influx of white-collar employees will prove to be an important source for new leadership in the trade unions of Western Europe. Increasing demands throughout the labor movement for case presentation, technical analysis, and similar operations give the white-collar employee, with his greater literary and technical training, certain important advantages. There is already some indication that he is coming to the top in a growing number of union situations.

In the United States, the prospects for white-collar union growth are likely to be influenced by some of the same underlying forces, such as, for example, the increasing importance of collective representation in national social and economic decision-making.

The degree to which the need for general representation can act as a pressure toward unionization—and even as a pressure that drives independently organized groups toward affiliation with already established powerful labor federations—is well illustrated by recent British labor history. We have already noted that the affiliation of the National Association of Local Government Officers (NALGO) with the TUC late in 1964 was due, in part, to its desire to participate effectively in Britain's new industrial-planning machinery, the National Economic Development Council. This could be accomplished only as an affiliate of the TUC. Six months after NALGO's affiliation, the officers of the independent Society of Civil Servants, which two years earlier had rejected affiliation with the TUC (by membership referendum vote), began to take steps to affiliate. It did so because "the largest white collar union, NALGO, had decided on affiliation," and also because the need to influence the government's new wage-price policy made affiliation with the TUC desirable. As the union examined this new policy, it concluded that "the declaration of intent on prices and incomes meant *that negotiations must take place through the TUC.*"[68]

The British National Union of Teachers, which jealously guards its professional status and independence, in April 1965 instructed its executive council to "consider affiliation to the British Trades Union Congress despite the fact many NUT members still regard [TUC] as a cloth capped ogre." Even the decision to investigate the possibility of affiliation came with difficulty. But speakers at NUT's delegate convention noted that most civil service workers and a great many white-collar employees were already in TUC. Even more important, as one delegate put it:

The real basic issue is that nowadays the TUC is an instrument of government in this country. Irrespective of whatever party is in power, you will find that the TUC is consulted on all pronouncements of government and on all major legislation affecting working people in this country.

The same speaker went on to state that teachers were not serving on the new regional planning boards, "but surely education should be at the forefront of any planning reorganisation in this country at this time."[69]

Later in 1965, after a long debate, the NUT executive council rejected affiliation "at this time." Consideration of professional status and desire for unity with other non-TUC affiliated teacher associations finally tipped the balance in favor of nonaffiliation.[70] Pressures on the NUT are likely to continue as economic planning deepens in Great Britain.

Even if the need for national representation excludes the idea of affiliation with the central federation that is traditionally dominated by manual workers, it is apt to lead nonmanuals into increased militance and a greater desire for political power. Such has been the case with some clerical, professional, and semiprofessional groups in Norway. One Norwegian writer has described their reaction as a form of "middle-class protest."[71]

The same broad combination of forces that has stimulated the development of white-collar unionism in most of Western Europe is likely to produce similar results in the United States in the years ahead. The wider acceptance of unionism by society, the need to be represented in what is increasingly a group-oriented and group decision-making economy, the increasing number of white-collar workers with some consequent loss of "individualism," the encouragement now given to federal employees to unionize—these and related factors already seem to be having an important effect on the growth of teachers', nurses', and government employees' unions in the United States.[72] The deeper hold of individualism, as well as the generally superior economic status of American white-collar employees, seems, however, to slow the rate of white-collar union growth.

Aside from the matter of the development of white-collar worker representation, it is also important to note that if some effective unity is not realized ultimately between manual and nonmanual organizations in most Western countries (including the United States), the power of the labor *movement,* as such, could be eroded. As yet, however, one cannot see serious signs of such an erosion, and there are some forces operating to counter such a development.

NOTES

1. In this chapter we treat the white-collar worker group as a whole, for the most part. (In European parlance "employee" a better word than "worker," as the latter is usually limited to employees who do manual work.) We distinguish to some extent, between privately employed and publicly employed white-collar workers. We have also singled out professional and supervisory employees to some slight degree. Space precludes our going beyond this classification, but many sociologists make other useful subdivisions of the white-collar group. Rolf Dahrendorf, for example, distinguishes particularly between white-collar employees who are part of the power structure of management (whether private or public) and those whose power status, in relation to management, is not substantially different from manual employees. "Recent Changes in the Class Structure of European Societies," *Daedalus,* Winter 1964.

2. See the *Role of Office Workers, Technicians and Engineers in Social and Economic Development,* a report prepared by the Canadian and American Trade Union Study Group, May 4–June 3, 1962, under the auspices of the Organisation

for Economic Cooperation and Development, Division for Social Affairs (OECD) Paris, 69pp. (Mimeographed.) Just a few years before, the United Automobile Workers sent a three-man mission to Europe to make a similar study.

3. For a description of white-collar unionism in pre-Hitler Germany, see Richard Seidel, *The Trade Union Movement of Germany*, No. 7–8 (Amsterdam: International Federation of Trade Unions, 1928); see especially Bernhard Goring's "Non-Manual Workers' Trade Union Movement," pp. 133–154. Useful, brief histories of white-collar unions in Austria, France, Britain, Germany, and Sweden are included in the chapters on these countries in Adolf Sturmthal (ed.), *White Collar Trade Unions* (Urbana: Illinois University Press, 1966).

4. The same situation, i.e., the existence of a fair number of white-collar unions of rather limited strength, also obtained in the United States before World War II. For a brief history of white-collar unionism in the United States, see my chapter in Sturmthal (ed.), *op. cit.*, Chap. 8.

5. Generally, when Europeans estimate the degree of unionization, they determine the ratio of union members to the total employed or to the civilian labor force, with the possible exclusion of the self-employed. Thus they may include farm workers, foremen, supervisors, and managers, etc. Foremen and supervisors are highly organized, although generally in separate unions from rank-and-file workers.

6. From 1948 to 1964, for example, the National Union of Bank Employees increased its membership from 28,583 to 56,224; the Clerical and Administrative Workers Union, from 38,493 to 79,177; and the Draughtsmen and Allied Technicians' Association increased from 45,049 to 65,843 in 1960. Between 1948 and 1964 the manual-worker membership of the British Trades Union Congress (TUC), to which all of these unions are affiliated, increased only approximately 0.6%, while white-collar TUC membership increased approximately 33.6%, according to George S. Bain in "The Growth of White Collar Unionism in Great Britain," *British Journal of Industrial Relations*, November 1966, p. 319.

7. Michel Crozier, *Le Monde des Employés de Bureau* (Paris: Aux Editions de Seuil, 1965), p. 56.

8. Joseph Krislov, "The Independent Public Employee Association: Characteristics and Functions," *Industrial and Labor Relations Review*, July 1962, pp. 510–520. In a letter to the writer, dated February 26, 1968, the President of the Assembly of Government Employees, a loose association of some 26 independent state affiliates (state employees only), reported a membership of 429,692 as of Nov. 1, 1967.

9. These data are derived from a number of sources, and perfect accuracy is not possible because the occupational definitions on which they are based vary from country to country. For a general summary of some of these trends, see Otto Nordensiköld, "Trends in Nonmanual Employment and Their Social Effects," *International Nonmanual Workers Conference*, Nov. 3–4, 1961 (Brussels: International Confederation of Free Trade Unions, 1962), pp. 11–27. I have also used *Problems of Nonmanual Workers, Including Technicians, Supervisory Staff, etc.*, Report 7, International Labour Conference, Forty-Third Session, 1959, (Geneva: International Labour Office, 1959); *Non-manual Workers: Problems and Prospects*, Report of the Director General, Part I, International Labour Conference Fifty-First Session, 1967 (Geneva: International Labour Office, 1967); Sturmthal (ed.), *op. cit.;* and Bain, *op. cit.*, p. 306.

10. *Office Workers in the Mid-Twentieth Century*, (London: Twentieth Century Press, n.d. *ca.* 1960 or 1961), p. 4.

11. One is led to speculate about what long-term union organizational effects upon nonmanual workers may stem from such new U.S. institutions as the President's Advisory Committee on Labor-Management Policy, and other such bodies, all of which include representation from the AFL-CIO.

12. *Swedish Professional Associations as Trade Unions,* (Stockholm: Swedish Confederation of Professional Associations, 1959), p. 4.

13. In Western Europe the employer associations are not only comparatively strong, but employers have come to depend on their associations. These factors have led to a higher degree of unionization among manual workers as compared with the United States. This is particularly true in the case of firms with a relatively small number of employees, which are frequently so difficult to unionize in the United States. In certain industries like the (men's and women's) garment industry, printing, trucking, and construction, where employer-association-union bargaining is a common practice, the degree of organization among small employers is also high in the United States.

14. *International Nonmanual Workers' Conference, op. cit.,* p. 31.

15. *Office Workers in the Mid-Twentieth Century, op. cit.,* p. 5.

16. Ross M. Martin, "Australian Professional and White Collar Unions," *Industrial Relations,* October 1965, pp. 98–99.

17. *Swedish Professional Associations as Trade Unions, op. cit.,* p. 5. Similar pressures have been operating on Norwegian professional employees, who have often found themselves in opposition to the egalitarian-tending policies of the Norwegian Federation of Trade Unions (LO), as well as those of the Labor government which governed until 1965. The result has been to drive many professionals into a tighter, more militant organization. See Egil Fivelsdal, "White Collar Unions and the Norwegian Labor Movement," *Industrial Relations,* October 1965.

18. For a description of professional unionism in Sweden as well as an analysis of the strike of 1966, see the author's "Professional Unionism in Sweden," *Industrial Relations,* February 1969.

19. *Current Population Reports, Consumer Income,* Series P-60 (Washington, D.C.: Bureau of the Census, various numbers and years).

20. On trends in Britain, see "Has the Salariat Prospered?" *The Economist,* I and II (May 23 and 30, 1964). This article suggests that the salaried employee (roughly equivalent to the white-collar worker) fared very poorly in relationship to the wage earner (manual employee) from roughly 1938 to 1955. Since 1956 the salariat has kept pace with the wage earner, and in the upper echelons even has made relative gains at his expense. Elsewhere in Europe it would seem that the booming economy, which is keeping demand high throughout the labor market, has probably enabled the better-organized manual workers at least to maintain the advantages gained during and after World War II. On the longer-term trends of differentials between various occupational groups in Britain, see Guy Routh, *Occupation and Pay in Great Britain* (Cambridge: University Press, 1965). Routh's work seems to indicate that during the past 50 years or so most of the professional groups suffered some declines relative to manual workers.

21. S. M. Miller, "Professionalization, Organization, and Economic Advance in the Nursing Profession," *New York State Nurse,* March 1961, pp. 10–12, 15. For a recent survey of these and related aspects of professional unionism, see the symposium, "Professional and White Collar Unionism: An International Comparison," *Industrial Relations,* October 1965, especially the articles by Joseph Ben-David, Ken Prandy, Ross Martin, George Straus, and the writer.

22. Richard E. Walton, *The Impact of the Professional Engineering Union: A Study of Collective Bargaining Among Engineers and Scientists and Its Significance for Management* (Boston: Graduate School of Business Administration, Harvard University, 1961), pp. 21–22.

23. *Non-Manual Workers, op. cit.,* p. 14.

24. *Manpower Report of the President, April 1967* (Washington: U.S. Department of Labor, U.S. Government Printing Office, 1967), pp. 201, 211.

25. For studies by political scientists which analyze the reactions of two professional bodies as "political pressure groups" see Harry Eckstein, *Pressure Group Politics: The Case of the British Medical Association* (Stanford: Stanford University Press: 1960) and James M. Clark, *Teachers and Politics in France, A Pressure Group Study of the Fédération de l'Education Nationale* (Syracuse: Syracuse University Press, 1967).

26. Such, for example, has been the case in both Austria and Germany. See Sturmthal (ed.), *op. cit.*, pp. 85–88, and 158–160.

27. Fritz Croner, "Salaried Employees in Modern Society," *International Labour Review,* February 1954, p. 105.

28. George Sayers Bain, *Trade Union Growth and Recognition,* Research Papers 6, *Royal Commision on Trade Unions and Employers' Associations* (London: Her Majesty's Stationery Office, 1967), p. 99. Also see Allan Flanders, *Collective Bargaining: Prescription for Change* (London: Faber and Faber, 1967).

29. See *Trade Unionism, The Evidence of the Trades Union Congress to the Royal Commission on Trade Unions and Employers' Associations,* 2d ed. (London: Trades Union Congress, 1967), pp. 112–113.

30. *Royal Commission on Trade Unions and Employers' Associations* (London: Her Majesty's Stationery Office, 1968), esp. pp. 64–65. The commission did favor allowing either union or management, unilaterally, to obtain an arbitration ruling in cases of recognition disputes. Presumably, if enacted into law, this would enable unions to demand representation elections.

31. *SAF, The Swedish Foremen's Association,* (Stockholm: 1953), p. 8.

32. Similar forces were operating in the United States in the early 1940s to create a favorable climate for organizing foremen. However, the failure of the labor movement to take full advantage of this situation, followed by the Taft-Hartley Act (1947), which placed restrictions on the unionization of foremen, cut down what might otherwise have been a significant union development.

33. In 1966 a long-smoldering dispute erupted in the TCO as the foremen's union seemed to be claiming rights over all supervisors and foremen, many of whom were members of other TCO affiliates. The foremen's union disaffiliated from TCO on January 1, 1968, taking more than 50,000 members with them.

34. Virtually at the outset of the nationwide coal miners' strike in France in the early part of 1963, the foremen's and engineers' unions announced their general solidarity with the miners.

35. *TCO, Central Organization of Salaried Employees in Sweden* (Stockholm: 1953 ed.), pp. 13–14.

36. Crozier, *op. cit.*, p. 57.

37. Supervisory unionism is one of the most exotic of European labor practices in the eyes of many U.S. union and management men who visit abroad. They find it hard to understand the pattern of dual loyalty which enables supervisors to fulfill their responsibilities to management on the one hand, and on other occasions be part of a union "bargain" which covers their own wages, hours, and working conditions. Yet such dual loyalty is really not so far removed from that of millions of American workers who feel a real sense of allegiance to their companies, on the one hand, and a strong loyalty to their union, on the other. See Theodore V. Purcell, *The Worker Speaks His Mind on Company and Union* (Cambridge, Mass: Harvard University Press, 1953), *passim*.

38. The present national president of the Retail Clerks was once a retail store manager in Oakland, Calif.

39. Col. E. A. Garey, Wisconsin's State Director of Personnel, and his Senior Personnel Examiner, Arnold S. Zander (national president of the union for over thirty years), founded what was to become the American Federation of State, County

and Municipal Employes in 1932. Both Garey and Zander were in supervisory positions. See Leo Kramer, *Labor's Paradox, The American Federation of State, County and Municipal Employees, AFL-CIO,* (New York: Wiley, 1962).

40. The structural problem of organizing white-collar workers even plagues the communist-controlled Metalworkers Federation (FIOM) of Italy's CGIL, which comments, self-critically:

As is known there exists no organizational structures which would provide for the active presence of the trade union among the white collar workers. This shortcoming—by now a historical and structural reality of the industrial trade unions in our country—is disclosed both by the absence of specific autonomous bodies at the national or sectional levels and by the absence of organisms functioning with the trade union having some tasks or real connections with the workers concerned.

If there are only a few thousand white collar workers and technicians within the FIOM this is due purely to organisational reasons and not to trade union policy toward this category.

See *CGIL News Bulletin* (Rome), No. 15, October 1963, p. 21. This article goes on to discuss the need to assure technicians sufficient "real autonomy" within the industrial FIOM, or risk their forming a separate union (pp. 26–27).

41. A good brief description of the structure of the DGB today can be found in Franz Lepinski, *The German Trade Union Movement,* (3rd ed. 1964). Available from the DGB.

42. The DGB itself estimated its membership among white-collar employees, not including civil servants, at 861,160 at the end of 1966.

43. This statement is based on conversations with some officials of the public-employees' union. Only officers are being recruited, on the theory that the rank and file are not permanently oriented to a career in the armed forces. The union has already recruited members ranging from noncommissioned officers to top-level generals. The decision to accept army officers into the DGB triggered a storm in German political life. Eventually it led to the replacement of the minister of defense, under pressure from top military officers who opposed the move. This opposition seems now to have died down, as the campaign proceeds.

44. In pre-Hitler Germany there was a very strong, independent white-collar federation, and to some extent the DAG carries on this tradition. See the chapter on German white-collar unionism in Sturmthal (ed.), *op. cit.,* pp. 142–150.

45. Until recently there was jurisdictional friction between this union and the TCO commercial workers' union, but this now seems to have been worked out. TCO's relations with the Swedish Confederation of Professional Associations (SACO) have been more strained than its relations with LO. (Both TCO and LO are affiliated with the International Confederation of Free Trade Unions.) TCO tends to believe there is no real necessity for a third federation of professional employees. Some of these professional employees belong to the TCO, but the large majority are in SACO.

46. See the author's "Professional Unionism in Sweden," *op. cit.,* for a longer discussion of SACO.

47. The Catholic federation has recently taken action to begin some structural reorganization looking to more industrial forms of unionism that would embrace white-collar workers along with manuals (resistance from foremen's and technician's unions still persist, however, in the KAB). See "The Catholic Trade Union Movement of the Netherlands Takes on a New Appearance," *Labour* (Brussels: International Federation of Christian Trade Unions, June 1964), pp. 137–140.

48. W. A. Widden, "The Place of Nonmanual Workers in the Trade Union

Structure," *International Nonmanual Workers' Conference, op. cit.,* p. 39. A bitter conflict erupted, in 1968–1969, between craft and industrial unions in the TUC and an independent white-collar "staff association," as to which organization should represent the white-collar employees in the nationalized steel industry.

49. For a proposal to consolidate all unionized clerical-office and related employees into one national union, see *Trade Union Membership* (London: Political and Economic Planning, 1962), and *The Observer,* July 1, 1962.

50. According to Richard Rose, the British Labour Party polled approximately a two-thirds vote among manual workers in the 1959 election, but only about one-fifth among the nonmanual occupations. See Mark Abrams and Richard Rose, *Must Labour Lose?* (London: Penguin Books, 1960), p. 76. In the 1966 general election, 28% of all nonmanuals voted Labour, and this shift seemed to account for the party's decisive victory. Letter of Mark Abrams to the author, April 7, 1967.

51. D. Volker, "NALGO's Affiliation to the T.U.C.," *British Journal of Industrial Relations,* March 1966. This article presents an interesting study of the pressures upon an independent employees' association to affiliate with the main body of labor, in an era of national wage policies, industrial planning, etc., when representation on public bodies is primarily through the central federation of labor, in this case the TUC. Also on NALGO, see the valuable book by Alec Spoor, *White Collar Union, 60 Years of NALGO* (London: William Heinemann, 1967).

52. *The Guardian* (Daily), September 11, 1965.

53. Fivelsdal, *op. cit.,* p. 39.

54. In contrast to the situation before 1930, when each major political party and/or religious group had its "own" union federation, the Austrians created a unified trade-union center after World War II—a center that has no direct official ties with any political party. In the 1959 elections for representation in the Austrian Chambers of Labor, among the manual workers the socialists polled 74% of the vote, as against 49% among nonmanuals. The Catholic Party candidates received 34.5% of the nonmanuals' vote with communists, nationalists, and others polling small percentages. Sturmthal (ed.), *op. cit.,* p. 83.

55. *Some Facts About SIF, the Swedish Union of Clerical and Technical Employees in Industry* (Stockholm: n.d., *ca.* 1951), p. 10.

56. In addition to wage surveys, the SIF has helped to develop the job-classification system for clerical and technical employees that has now become standard throughout most of Swedish industry. See *The Classification System of the TCO, Summary Description,* (Stockholm, TCO, 1961).

57. *Draughtsmen and Allied Technicians Association, Its Structure and Work,* (London, 1962), pp. 16–17.

58. See, for example, *Survey of Salaries, March 1963* (Burbank, Calif.: Lockheed Section of the Engineers and Scientists Guild).

59. The acceptance of more individualized wage treatment in some European countries even among manual workers goes beyond U.S. practice. Skilled metalworkers in Denmark, for example, have minimums set by national negotiations, but once these are completed, individual workers proceed to negotiations on their own behalf. A very good description of white-collar union wage policy in Sweden is contained in *The Wage Policy of White Collar Worker Unions in Sweden* (Stockholm: TCO, The Central Organization of Salaried Employees in Sweden, 1964).

60. *TCO, Central Organization of Salaried Employees in Sweden, op. cit.,* p. 31. It should be noted that serious strikes are a rarity in Sweden.

61. No attempt is made here to provide detail on the great variety of practices and institutions that have grown up in Western countries around unionization and bargaining in the public service. A few generalizations are presented to give a sense of the evolution of this area of industrial relations. The literature is vast, as each

country has been the subject of scholarly work; but I have made use of the valuable publication of the Public Services International (an autonomous union body, associated with the International Confederation of Free Trade Unions), which groups public-service unions from many different countries: *Negotiating Rights of Public Services and the Right to Strike in the Public Service* (London, Public Services International, 1966). In addition to survey essays by Professor Folke Schmidt (Sweden) on "Negotiating Rights of Public Servants" and "The Right to Strike in the Public Service," by Professor Marc Somerhausen (Belgium), this volume contains reports by the PSI-affiliated unions from fifteen countries on the rights of negotiation of public employees. Visits to Britain, Sweden, and Germany in 1968 made possible by a grant of funds from the University of Wisconsin International Studies Program also provided much useful data on public employee bargaining in those three countries.

62. To some extent the same distinction can be drawn in U.S. federal employment between so-called classified civil servants and other types of public employees. There is a large body of federal employees who are not within the classified civil service. Until recently, at least, unionism had made more progress among these workers (government arsenals, shipyards, etc.), particularly among skilled craftsmen, than among classified civil servants.

63. For example, in Germany civil servants are technically subject even today to the public regulation that "games of chance may be played in good company [only] so long as one's economic independence is not thereby jeopardized." As summarized by Somerhausen, *op. cit.*, p. 29.

64. For a description of the basic features of the bargaining system for Swedish public employees, see *Collective Bargaining Rights of Swedish Civil Servants* (Stockholm: TCO, 1968).

65. A useful discussion of the different methods employed to deal with critical strikes, including those by public employees, may be found in "Provisions Regarding Public Interest Disputes in Selected Countries," *Labor Developments Abroad* (Washington, D.C.: U.S. Department of Labor, April, 1966), pp. 1–4.

66. An excellent short, official description of this process can be found in *Staff Relations in the Civil Service, H.M. Treasury*, 4th ed. (London: Her Majesty's Stationery Office, 1965).

67. *Lindsay Report* (so named here for identification purposes, but there is no title) (New York: 1966), pp. 7–8. (Mimeographed.) This report was prepared with the help of the American Arbitration Association, representatives of some New York City labor unions, and some public officials. Unlike many other reports on this subject in recent years, this one did not get overwhelmed with the single issue of the possibilities of strikes by public-employee unions. On the contrary, it was concerned primarily with expediting public-employee bargaining and offered many creative ideas to accomplish this objective. While the report was not fully implemented, New York City did set up procedures that enabled one union, the largest in the city, to bargain as a kind of "chosen instrument" on fringe benefits for most of the city employees in 1967.

68. *The Guardian* (Daily), May 21, 1965. The Society did not affiliate in 1965, but it and several other higher-level civil service groups were seriously considering affiliation with the TUC, again, in the spring of 1968.

69. *The Times* (Daily), London, April 23, 1965.

70. *The Guardian* (Daily), October 12, 1965. For an interesting case-history analysis of the forces sometimes counter to conventional unionism and professionalism among British teachers, see W. Roy, "Membership Participation in the National Union of Teachers," *British Journal of Industrial Relations*, July 1964, pp. 189–208. In the spring of 1968 the NUT again took up the matter of affiliation with TUC.

This latest move seems, in part, to have been motivated by the decision of one of its competitors, the National Association of Schoolmasters, to such affiliation with the TUC.

71. Fivelsdal, *op. cit.*, p. 86.

72. For a sketch of the trends, problems, and prospects of white-collar unionism in the United States, see the chapter by the author in Sturmthal (ed.), *op. cit.*, as well as his article, "Public Employee Bargaining in Europe: What Lessons for the United States?" *Industrial Relations Research Association, Proceedings of the Twenty-First Annual Winter Meeting, December 29–30, 1968* (Madison: Industrial Relations Research Association, 1969), pp. 48–58.

XI

Unions and Wage Bargaining, A Comparison of
Europe and United States

URING MOST OF ITS MODERN HISTORY the American union movement
has tended to mass its greatest power in the drive for higher wages. There
has been interest, of course, in other bargaining items, particularly, since
the early 1950s, in the so-called fringe benefits, including many devices
to provide greater economic security. But the traditional American emphasis upon the here and now, the still prevalent belief in high social
mobility, have kept the drive of the union movement strongest where its
power lay to begin with—in the collective-bargaining struggle for higher
wages.

Among European unions, on the other hand, the very structure of
the bargaining process, the economic environment, the nature of the
union "bond," and the character of the wage and benefit system—all have
led to a less concerted emphasis upon a goal of bargaining for maximum
wages.

Differences in Bargaining Structure Affect Union Wage Policies

Where bargaining is by nationwide agreement for each industry (or
covers all employers in the same industry in a large area), as is the case
in much of Europe, inevitably more consideration must be given to the
least efficient—the so-called marginal—producers. As such consideration
becomes a factor, the thrust for higher wages is greatly blunted.

Take the typical American union that operates in a national product
market (steel, automobiles, and rubber are leading examples of products
in the mass-production field). The union sets its sights on the top company or companies when it begins to bargain for a new contract. It obtains
the best possible settlement with this company or companies and then
seeks to "spread" it to other firms in the industry. (While our example

has been chosen for the mass-production industries, even among the unions that bargain in the smaller local markets—which involve the building trades, the printers, the truckdrivers, and many others—one can generally observe the same tendency to drive for the maximum possible bargain and to ignore the least efficient firms.)

The European union usually sits down with the association that represents all the firms in an industry—highly efficient, average, and least efficient—and together they bargain for and reach a more "average" settlement or, indeed, a settlement that will not jeopardize even the marginal producers. Where appropriate, these national bargaining agreements include special regional differentials or variations. It is not surprising that European unions, operating under these constraints, have not, historically, made the all-out effort in wage-bargaining that characterizes American wage-bargaining.

Needless to say, these two contrasting bargaining "models" are oversimplified. To give one instance of how reality can differ from the model: For years the United Automobile Workers has sought, unsuccessfully for the most part, to make "ability to pay" (the company's profit position) a major criterion in its bargaining with the General Motors Corporation, whose profit-making ability exceeds by far that of its major competitors. The UAW has never been able to achieve anything like a "maximum possible" bargain (indefinable anyway!) with General Motors. Indeed, if it did so and attempted to reach the same settlement with the other two major automobile producers, the settlement might threaten the very existence of these producers! On the other hand, this union—and we give it as a leading but by no means absolutely singular example of mass-production industry bargaining—has *not* shaped its basic bargaining policy to fit the needs of the numerous, smaller, sometimes marginal manufacturers in the automobile industry.[1]

In Europe, the interests or the economic position of the smaller, less efficient companies in a given industry often count for more than those of the larger firms under the system of national industry (or area-wide) bargaining. Often, of course, the larger firms have been content to "hide" behind the less efficient firms and willingly accept a modest settlement.

Several factors explain what appears to be the more restrained policies of European unionism. To begin with, the very nature of the "bond" of the labor movement is a restraining force. Where the area of concern, under a socialist or class philosophy, is *all* the workers, the power of the unions can hardly be concentrated on just the "lead sectors" of an industry. Traditional concepts of solidarity dictate that the needs and interests of the less well-paid employees of poorer firms must count for as much, if not more, than the best-paid employees of more affluent firms. If necessary, the union exerts its power in the larger, more affluent firms in order to squeeze out something from the industry as a whole; in this way it can bring at least some benefit to all the workers. This might be less than the maximum obtainable from the efficient firms, but more than the workers in the weak firms could achieve on their own. This solidarity has softened somewhat in recent years, but it still remains a significant force.

European unions have traditionally been more fearful than American unions of driving *any* firms out of business by aggressive wage policies. They are also more sensitive to the possible impact of their wage policies on costs—policies that might weaken their countries position vis-à-vis other countries. Prevalent in some countries, too, is a strong fear of the danger of inflation, which might result from an aggressive wage policy. German unions, for example, have never forgotten the terrible inflation of the early 1920s.

American notions of competition and "the devil take the hindmost" have had little counterpart in Europe among either unions or business-men. In many industries the European system of protective cartel organization helped cultivate an attitude that regarded the loss of any firm as a matter of common concern. This, of course, reinforced the willingness of both management and labor to bargain on an association-wide basis, which, in turn, raised the marginal producer to a key position.

Trade Needs Influence European Wage Bargaining

The great dependence of the typical Western European country upon world trade has undoubtedly been a restraining factor in union wage-bargaining. Imports of raw materials and other goods typically account for close to 20 percent of a European nation's total output, and must be paid for by exports of similar magnitude. It is therefore easy to see why European unions and workers, as well as managers and governments, have been more conscious than their American counterparts about weighing the impact of wage demands on the cost of exports (see Table 10).

An awareness of foreign trade and the possible impact of bargaining upon it has increased in some American industries and unions in recent years. The widespread publicity given to the balance-of-payments difficulties of the United States may also have made some unions more sensitive to the "foreign competition argument," and perhaps a little less aggressive in their wage drives.

This is true in spite of the fact that the U.S. trade position (as opposed to the balance of payments) has generally been strong, with some surpluses of exports over imports of merchandise and no serious signs of overall declines in competitive cost efficiency. In any event, ex-

TABLE 10. *Exports as Percentage of Gross National Product (1964)*

Country	Exports—Percentage of GNP
Austria	17.0
Belgium-Luxembourg	36.3
Denmark	23.3
France	10.2
Germany (West)	15.6
Great Britain	13.4
Ireland	27.2
Italy	12.0
Netherlands	34.4
Norway	20.7
Sweden	21.0
Switzerland	20.6
United States	4.1

SOURCE: *The OECD Observer*, Paris, February 1966, p. 24.

ports account for no more than 4 or 5 percent of the gross national product compared with the average of close to 20 percent for Western European countries. Under these circumstances it is doubtful that foreign trade will ever play the role in the United States that it does in Western Europe.

The Trend in Europe Toward Wage-Setting at the Local Level

While we have emphasized the nationwide, industry-wide character of European bargaining, it must be added that in the past ten years or so these patterns have broken down in many ways. A national bargaining agreement has come more and more to represent minimum wage standards for a given industry. In many key firms, in fact, especially in Germany, France, and England (Italy may also be cited), the actual wages for most jobs are far above the minimums prescribed in the collective agreement.

In the face of the European economic boom many employers have been forced to offer wages well above the minimums to help recruit as well as to hold work forces. This has created a difficult situation for French and German unions particularly, as some employers in these countries have seized the initiative in wage-setting, a practice that has been most notable in the large firms in the metal industries, where markets have expanded spectacularly since the early 1950s.[2]

In Britain, wage movements above the nationally bargained minimums in metalworking (in the so-called engineering and shipbuilding industries) have often been spearheaded by the militant action of the union shop stewards at local work sites.

The net effect of developments such as these in France, Germany, and Britain has been at least partial loss of control over wage determination by the national unions in these countries.

This loss of union control can be exaggerated, however. In the first place, only in a minority of dynamic industries or firms is there a significant spread between the nationally bargained rates and the actual rates paid. Second, some unions have taken direct steps to prevent their power from slipping away. They have become more active in local plant committees (France and Germany), or reached out to develop more effective relationships with local union stewards (Great Britain). In the case of France, some unions have been moving away from sole dependence upon nationally or regionally negotiated agreements and have come to advocate agreements negotiated at the firm; they do so in order to take advantage of the possibility of bargaining for higher wages at the firm level.

In Italy, the 1962 and 1963 agreements between the unions and the metal industries, and more generally with the federation of Italian employers, specifically recognized the right of unions to negotiate at the plant level on piece rates, production bonuses, and so on. The purpose here was to stop the employers from handling these problems unilaterally or in conjunction with the locally elected workers' plant committees (*Commissione Interne*, which are not directly under union control). The practice of union wage-bargaining at the plant level is becoming fairly widespread in the larger firms in Italian industry. The unions' tactic in many cases has been to sign special productivity-sharing agreements with management at this level.[3]

There was some softening of the economy in Germany in 1966 and 1967, and German metal unions reported that employers, in some instances, were withdrawing benefits they had voluntarily granted in earlier years—benefits that had not been incorporated into collective agreements. The metal unions protested these moves, and in some cases were able to reverse them in the labor courts.[4]

Returning to the situation in Britain, one British writer has argued that unless the unions supplement more effectively the system of national agreements with organized bargaining at the factory level, "They will slowly lose control of the actuality of wages in this country."[5] The necessity for unions and management to close the gap between the wage provided in the typical national agreement as against what is actually bargained for and operative at the plant level was a major conclusion of the Royal Commission on Trade Unions and Employers' Associations in its 1968 report.

All these changes and problems reflect the fact that European industry has become much more dynamic in the past decade and a half. The older, broad patterns of bargaining were better adapted to the pre-

World War II European capitalism, which was more stable and expanded more slowly.

To the extent that worker and class solidarity has declined in these past fifteen years, this too has opened the door to greater differentiation in wage levels on a firm-by-firm basis.

For France and Italy, one must also mention the role of a few key companies whose more liberal wage- and employee-benefit programs have been used as an industrial-relations instrument to loosen the hold on their workers of the communist unions. For example, the Renault Company, a French government-owned firm, for several years seemed to be moving in this direction; it signed separate agreements, which it initiated with the free (as opposed to the communist) unions—agreements that provided important breakthroughs for its workers.

Even as these trends toward "differentiated" bargaining are developing, however, national wage policy systems of control are also being introduced in a number of countries, and these lead back toward uniformity in wage movements.

Wage Differentials and Wage Structures

As might be expected, the variations in types of industries, the relative importance of argriculture, and the great differences in productivity make it difficult to compare the wage structures of Western European countries and to compare these in turn with wage structures in the United States. Certain general trends can be observed, however.

One finds, for example, a fairly steady long-term narrowing of occupational differentials in practically all the Western countries. Moreover, this narrowing process appears to be more rapid when the demand for labor is strong, particularly during wartime periods.[6]

In the United States it is estimated that the differentials between skilled and unskilled, which were as much as 100 percent in 1907, had generally been halved by 1947. Since the early 1950s the narrowing of differentials has been reduced and has perhaps even been reversed in a few industries. This resulted from the relative softness in the labor market in the late 1950s and early 1960s which weakened the position of unskilled workers in particular. Unemployment has tended to be more serious among blue-collar than among white-collar employees.

Despite any possible trend away from closing the gap between skilled and unskilled workers in recent years, these differentials nevertheless remain much higher in the United States than in Western Europe. One can think of a "typical" spread of 40 to 50 percent from top to bottom in a U.S. union-company wage scale, a European schedule would be much less spread out and might only show a 15 or 20 percent difference between the rates paid for unskilled on the bottom and skilled workers on top.

The long-term narrowing trend both in the United States and Europe also reflects factors other than supply and demand, and most significantly the general heightening in educational attainment throughout the population. More and more young workers now enter the labor force with a secondary-school diploma (or its equivalent in Europe). Thus, differences in skill within the work force have been lessening.

The reduction in differentials may also be a tribute to the superior bargaining strength of the better-organized manual workers in all Western countries during the twentieth century. For the United States this advantage of superior organization seems to have been most effective from 1940 to the early 1950s. Since then less favorable labor-market factors have been offsetting the superior bargaining strength of manual workers as compared with nonmanual employees.

The European pattern of narrower occupational wage differentials is also, in part, a result of the more egalitarian approach to bargaining. Precepts of socialism and a wider worker solidarity have led European unions to concentrate upon more equal wage settlements and wage structures. The earlier (and still wider) unionization of less skilled workers also helped make wage differentials narrower than in the United States, where unionism was for so many years largely concentrated among skilled workers.[7]

Just as some European employers and local union leaders have used the recent wave of prosperity and the tight labor market to obtain wage scales well above nationally negotiated minimums, so have employers and skilled workers used these factors to reverse the differential narrowing process. Payments above the negotiated scales for skilled workers have become increasingly common in many European countries.

"Wage drift" is the term that labor economists use to describe the general net result of all these devices or tendencies that lead to wage payments over and above those stipulated in collective agreements. To some extent there are always some forces creating a wage drift, even in less prosperous times; but this process has become more widespread and of greater moment during the sustained economic boom in post-World War II in Europe.[8]

Furthermore, under depressed economic conditions, unions and union members in some cases will wink at negotiated wage levels established in collective agreements and will work "below scale." This was not uncommon in the U.S. construction industry during the depression of the thirties.

When comparing union influence in the United States and Europe, not as much can be said about interindustry wage relationships as about occupational differentials. These relationships appear to be fairly stable, and indeed the ranking of industries, according to earnings of workers, seem to show interesting similarities from country to country.[9] The spread of unionism and/or the influence of union wage-setting patterns in more sectors of the economy would of course tend in the long run to minimize perceptible union impact upon particular industries.

Wage Levels and Trends: Some Comparisons

The rapid growth in world trade after World War II has heightened interest in comparing national wage levels and the movements upward (or downward) in wages and wage costs. Also, the intensified interest in economic development and rising living standards has resulted in improved data comparing hourly wage levels and living standards in the various countries.

Numerous agencies, both national and international, now periodically undertake surveys to shed light on relative wage levels, movements, and labor costs. Despite all this work, it is still difficult to make "true" comparisons. Problems of converting wages in different currencies into a common measurement, differences in industry mix (e.g., steel may be of major importance in one country and nonexistent or minor in another), differences in relative levels of taxation on wages and salaries, different levels of social security benefits, the amount of fringe benefits, differences in buying habits—all these and other factors make comparisons difficult and the results they yield limited; but the fascination to do so and the necessity to make such comparisons remain.

Table 11, which is derived from data from several sources concerning average hourly earnings plus supplementary benefits (social security, welfare plans, vacations, paid holidays, etc.), provides an interesting comparison of the United States with nine other countries.

Table 11 is generally consistent with other surveys, although there are modest variations. The European Economic Community, which has become an important source of comparative wage and labor cost data, surveyed wages and other labor costs in the community in 1962, and on the basis of labor-cost indices for fifteen industries ranked its five major member nations as follows: Germany, 100; France, 92; Belgium, 84; Netherlands, 83; Italy, 82.[10]

Not all supplementary benefits or charges are included in Table 11; these might change the rankings a bit and also reduce the relative superiority of the United States slightly. Perhaps of greatest importance, from a technical viewpoint, is that straight conversion of foreign earnings into U.S. currency, under prevailing exchange rates as in this study, tends to overstate the relative advantage of U.S. workers compared with the real purchasing power of workers in other countries. Also, it is diffi-

TABLE 11. *Average Hourly Earnings and Supplementary Benefits, All Manufacturing Industries*

Country	Date	Average Hourly Earnings (U.S. Currency)	Supplementary Benefits as % of Earnings*	Total Hourly Expenditures, Earnings Plus Benefits
Belgium	Oct. '63	$ .73	31	.95
Canada	Aug. '64	1.87	16	2.10
France	Mar. '64	.70	51	1.06
Germany				
(West)	Jan. '64	.91	35	1.23
Great Britain	Apr. '64	1.09 (men)	14	1.24
		.62 (women)	14	.71
Italy	Mar. '64	.56	74	.97
Netherlands	Oct. '63	.65	30	.85
Sweden	May '64	1.37	15	1.58
Switzerland†	Oct. '63	1.04	15	1.20
U.S.A.	Aug. '64	2.52	18	2.97

* Supplementary benefits include employer payments to government-established social security plans and to nonstatutory welfare plans, workmen's compensation plans, family allowances, paid annual holidays and vacation and other nonregular premiums, expenditures for workers' houses and similar charges. These expenditures are charges to employers in addition to wages as such. Many of the charges in Europe—e.g., family allowances or payments for workers' housing—have no real counterpart in the United States.
† Skilled and semiskilled men.

cult to give a full estimate of the value of public services, which are more developed in some European countries than in the United States.

Gunnar Myrdal, discussing economic growth and wealth in the United States and elsewhere, notes:

. . . comparisons over currency boundaries, however, have inherent difficulties to which national accountancy experts have still devoted too little interest. In addition to the ordinarily recognized ones related to the inadequacy of exchange rates for measuring differences in purchasing power, there are values not counted—such as economies in the collective organization of health facilities and other essential consumption items and, in general, values from a better organized society. Comparatively speaking, metropolitan areas in the United States are less well planned, and relatively more tools and activities are permitted to cause disutilities that are not subtracted in the accounting. The lower productivity and incomes of people in the segregated slums for Negroes and other submerged groups in the United States are reflected in the figures, but hardly in the grave disadvantages and costs this misery causes society.[11]

As previously suggested, European labor movements, compared with American unions, have historically concentrated more of their effort on nonwage items, ranging from social security, including family allowances and national health insurance, to housing subsidies, longer vacations, and the like. As a result, the direct wage counts for less in estimating the total income of a European worker.

It is frequently difficult to estimate the precise differences between countries as far as the comparative values of these nonwage items are concerned. On the one hand, they are *income only when paid out to and received* by workers; on the other hand, they are all actual *charges paid by* employers, to workers in some cases, and in other instances to the government in the form of taxes, levies, and so on, some of which may never actually reach the workers!

One British economist has roughly estimated the cost of these supplements in 1961 to European and U.S. manufacturing firms as ranging from 23.64 percent (in the United States) to 56.93 percent (in Italy).

TABLE 12. *Supplementary Labor Costs, European and U.S. Manufacturing Industries, 1961*

Country	% Payroll
Belgium	32.92
France	50.22
Germany (West)	35.09
Great Britain	13.90 (1960)
Italy	56.93
Netherlands	33.09
Sweden	13.60 (1958)
U.S.A.	23.64

SOURCE: Adapted from G. L. Reid, "Supplementary Labour Costs in Europe and Britain," in G. L. Reid and D. J. Robertson (eds.), *Fringe Benefits, Labour Costs and Social Security* (London: G. Allen, 1965), Chap. 4. This source shows relatively lower percentages for Sweden and Britain, but this may reflect different methods of financing certain benefits. Thus, in Britain a large share of social security costs are financed out of general revenue, to which employers do contribute in the form of income taxation. Reid also suggests that the figures for the U.S., based on U.S. Chamber of Commerce surveys, probably have a "considerable upward bias" when compared to more recent U.S. government studies.

The bulk of these supplementary costs are usually in the form of obligatory social security payments. These, for example, accounted for better than 60 percent of the total supplementary labor costs in France and Italy in 1959.[12]

Because social security is financed in varying ways by different countries, Table 12 presents only one view of the problem. For these eight countries, for example, one finds ratios between social security expenditures (regardless of source of income) and gross national product that in some respects give a fairer estimate of country "effort" or degree of worker protection in the social security area (see Table 13). Going

TABLE 13. *Percentage of Social Security Benefits to Gross National Product, 1963*

Belgium	13.8
Canada	9.8
France	14.6
Germany (West)	15.3
Great Britain	11.2
Italy	12.8
Netherlands	12.7
Norway	10.6
Sweden	13.5
Switzerland	7.4
U.S.A.	6.2

SOURCE: International Labor Organisation, *The Cost of Social Security* (Geneva: I.L.O., 1967).

into further refinements with this set of data, however, lies beyond the scope of this book.

Again, a note of caution must be struck. One cannot tell from these gross statistics, useful as they may be, how much a worker himself may be contributing (and this varies considerably between countries) to these social security outlays. Recall, too, that a number of areas "normally" covered under social security in Europe are covered to an important extent in the United States by employer payments into private insurance and other funds.

If the wage and benefit drive in collective bargaining by many European unions does not seem as sharp as the drive in the United States, Tables 12 and 13 help account for it. When employer expenditures for social security payments (in ratio to wages) are considerably larger than in the United States, and nonbargainable items make up 30 percent or 40 percent of a worker's income (family allowances, health insurance, housing allowances, etc.), less is at stake in direct wage negotiations between unions and employers. Furthermore, "sting" is added to United States bargaining because some of these important items that are exclusively in the public legislative sector in Europe are part of collective bargaining in the United States.

Metalworkers: International Wage Comparisons

As we have observed, gross average figures for manufacturing can conceal important differences in relative wages. It is useful to take just a few industries, where comparisons can be more meaningful, and compare wages and other labor costs on a country-by-country basis. Table 14 shows for ten selected countries 1965 annual hourly earnings and em-

TABLE 14. *Annual Hourly Earnings and Wage Costs, 1965
Steel and Automobile Industries*

	Steel Industry		Automobile Industry	
	Hrly. Earnings	Hrly. Employer Wage Costs	Hrly. Earnings	Hrly. Employer Wage Costs
Belgium	$1.14	$1.68	$1.08	$1.59
Denmark	1.55	1.79	1.70	1.92
France	0.80	1.45	0.96	1.74
Germany (West)	1.10	1.56	1.08	1.61
Great Britain	1.31	1.44	1.45	1.56
Italy	0.80	1.37	0.89	1.50
Netherlands	1.13	1.82	0.94	1.32
Norway	1.37	1.73	1.29	1.63
Sweden	1.65	2.01	1.67	2.03
U.S.A.	3.48	4.47	3.34	4.36

SOURCE: *Annual Survey of Wages and Working Conditions, Production and Employment in the Principal Branches of the Metal Industry, 1965* (Geneva: International Metalworkers Federation, 1967), pp. 2–3.
Hourly earnings include "average direct wages (time or piece work wages) including cost of living allowances, any allowances for overtime, night or Sunday work, bonuses for special responsibility, for heavy or dirty or dangerous work, production bonuses, etc. . . . to obtain wage costs, the following factors were added to the value of (hourly earnings) . . . legal or contractual social insurance, contributions to insurance institutions, paid vacations, public holidays and other days with leave of absence on pay, average cost per hour of family allowances paid by the employer or contributions to family allowance equalisation funds, together with any other payments by the employer not coming under any of the classifications listed." Definitions of hourly earnings, hourly wage costs, etc., are to be found in the same study, p. 72. The original data are in Swiss francs, which have been converted on the basis of official exchange rates into U.S. dollars and cents, with the dollar taken at 4.37282 Swiss francs.

ployer hourly wage costs for the basic steel and automobile manufacturing industries.

We are also indebted to the International Metalworkers Federation (IMF) for comparative data on weekly hour schedules and the number of paid days of vacation and holidays in the metal industries late in 1967. Since the metal industries in the United States do not have the same uniformities as the metal industries in most of Europe (bargaining and agreements in the United States being more on a firm rather than an industry basis, as is the case in Europe), the IMF has used the automobile and steel industries' major company union-management contracts.

Europeans generally enjoy longer paid vacations than Americans and perhaps more paid holidays. But when these benefits are measured against the shorter U.S. work week (Europeans have a longer regular work week, and employers schedule more overtime in most of Europe),

TABLE 15. *Length of Work Week, Paid Vacations, and Paid Holidays in Metals Industries, 1966–1967*

	Hours of Work Week Stipulated in Collective Agreement	Days of Paid Vacation After		Number of Paid Holidays
		1 Yr. Service	5 Yrs. Service	
Belgium	44	18	18	10
Denmark	44	18	18	9
France	—	24	24	6–8
Germany (West)	40	18–22	22	9–10
Great Britain	40	12	12	6–8
Italy	44–47*	12	14	15–17
Netherlands	45	15	15	6
Norway	45*	24	24	8–10
Sweden	44*	24	24	10
Switzerland	44	12–24	12–24	8
U.S.A.	40	auto 10–12½	15–20	11
		steel 5	10*	8*

SOURCE: International Metalworkers Federation, Geneva, 1967, same as in Table 14, with supplementary material on 1966 and 1967 also furnished by the IMF. The paid holidays in most European countries are laid down by statute. Needless to say, each new round of negotiations in a particular country brings some changes, and the data in this table are approximately as of the latter half of 1967. A very useful historical survey of the changes in worktime in major industrial nations can be found in Archibald A. Evans, "Work and Leisure, 1919–1969," *International Labor Review* (January 1969).

* U.S. automobile agreements also provided 4 weeks (20 days) after 15 years; steel agreements provided 2 weeks (10 days) after 3 years; 3 weeks after 10 years, and 4 weeks after 20 years or more, as well as 13 weeks every 5 years for senior employees. Paid holidays and vacations were further liberalized in the U.S. steel industry as a result of negotiations in the summer of 1968. In Italy new contracts provided for progressive reduction of the work week in practically all metal industries in 1968 and 1969. In Norway working hours were reduced to 42½ in July 1968, and in Sweden working hours were reduced to 42½ by January 1, 1969. Denmark reduced its work week to 42½ hours in June of 1968. Switzerland has longer vacations for very long service and older employees. In several European countries there is a legal requirement that the employer pay extra vacation pay (i.e., in addition to the regular pay for the vacation period).

the amount of work actually scheduled and performed over the year is probably less in the United States (taking the metal industry as a basis for comparison).[13] On the other hand, the work week has been cut rather sharply in Western Europe during the past five or six years, and one can probably anticipate further reductions in the direction of a basic 40-hour week, the objective of most European union movements. The higher average levels of educational attainment (years spent in school) in the United States probably result in shorter work lives for American workers when compared to most European countries.

Recent Wage Trends: European Gains

Current differences aside, it is also of interest to compare actual trends in wage movements. All of the data suggest that while the differences between U.S. and European wages remain high, the increases have been relatively greater in Europe in the past ten or twelve years.

Table 16 shows the general increase in wages in maufacturing in five European countries, expressing European wages as a percentage of total U.S. wages from 1950 to 1964.

TABLE 16. *Hourly Earnings in Manufacturing in 5 European Countries as % U.S. Earnings*

	1950	1953	1962	1963	1964*
France	16.1%	20.4%	20.8%	21.8%	22.7%
Germany (West)	21.2	21.8	33.8	35.2	36.9
Great Britain	27.1	28.0	34.6	35.1	36.8
Italy	15.9	15.5	18.1	21.7	23.6
Sweden	42.5	42.1	54.1	57.0	—
U.S.A.	100.0	100.0	100.0	100.0	100.0

* Estimated. Swedish figures not available for 1964.

SOURCE: *First National City Bank, Monthly Letter, New York,* April 1962, and letters from same to the author, May 5 and 21 and November 23, 1965, and November 29, 1966. The bank's chief source has been the National Institute of Economic and Social Research's *Economic Review.* Figures for France tend to be understated because of the effects of devaluation in that country. (Note: Figures represent direct wages paid and do not include fringes, subsidies, etc.)

Since 1953 European wage levels have advanced steadily and European manufacturing workers have made substantial gains relative to workers in the United States. According to the survey by the First National City Bank, Swedish average hourly earnings, which were 42.1 percent of the U.S. level in 1953, were 57.0 percent by 1963; Germany showed the greatest relative gain—from 21.2 percent in 1950 to 36.8 percent in 1964. Indeed, so rapid have been wage increases in Germany that they came up to the level of Great Britain by 1963. If one takes into account increases since then, as well as the higher level of employer-supported labor benefits in Germany (as compared with Britain), German hourly wages now stand high in Western Europe, exceeded only by those paid in several smaller countries. All countries in the survey made some gains relative to levels in the United States during most of the 1950s and early 1960s.

The absolute differences between European and American earnings remain very large, of course. In fact, these absolute differentials have not yet begun to close despite the relatively larger percentage gains made by European workers.

Between 1961 and 1963, for example, according to surveys by the International Metalworkers, direct hourly earnings of German automobile workers increased approximately 18 percent, while steelworkers made a 12 percent advance. In the United States the increase for automobile workers was 8 percent and for steelworkers, 4 percent.

In absolute terms, however, according to the IMF surveys, U.S. automobile workers advanced their wages 1.00½ Swiss francs per hour between 1961 and 1963 (from 12.55 to 13.55½ Swiss francs), while German automobile workers moved up to .58 Swiss francs (from 3.28 to 3.86). U.S. steelworkers showed a .54 Swiss-franc-per-hour increase (from 14.05 to 14.59), as compared with German steelworkers .47 increase (from 3.68½ to 4.15¼) in the same years.

The absolute gaps continued to widen slightly during these years, even though the relative gap (European wages as a percentage of American wages) was closing substantially.

The example of automobiles and steel puts the American situation in a more favorable light, since the impact of unionism on wages is stronger in the United States than in most other industries (although U.S. steel wages were unusually stable in those particular years, inasmuch as the union concentrated most heavily upon certain fringes). On the other hand, German workers' wage increases were among the largest in Western Europe during these same years.

In any event, if European workers continue to make substantially larger percentage gains than American workers in the years ahead, they will begin to close not only the relative gap but the absolute gap as well.

Unit Labor Cost Trends

The tables on wages and supplementary benefits shed light on trends in comparative earnings and in living standards. For comparative purposes it is also important to relate these trends to changes in productivity. By combining earnings and productivity data, it is possible to construct unit-labor-cost indices; these indicate what is happening to the competitive position of the industries of one country as compared with that of other countries.

Until now in this chapter we have been reviewing trends in employee wages and costs of supplementary benefits. While these reveal

TABLE 17. *Indexes of Unit Labor Cost in Manufacturing for Selected Countries, 1950–64*

	1950	1951	1952	1953	1954	1955	1956	1957	1958	1959	1960	1961	1962	1963	1964
Canada	77	84	90	92	94	91	93	100	101	101	104	103	102	103	103
France	50	67	76	80	82	87	92	100	113	115	115	123	132	141	142
Germany (West)	87	97	95	93	92	92	99	100	103	102	105	111	119	123	123
Great Britain	69	74	83	84	85	88	96	100	105	104	105	113	117	116	116
Netherlands	72	78	81	78	81	85	92	100	103	98	100	108	111	119	126
Sweden	60	69	83	87	91	95	99	100	102	101	102	106	113	116	116
U.S.A.	76	82	86	90	92	90	97	100	102	102	106	105	104	105	105

SOURCE: John Chandler and Patrick C. Jackman, "Cost Trend in Nine Industrial Nations," *Monthly Labor Review,* September 1965, p. 1065.

what an employer is paying for a given unit of work time (in the examples the unit is one hour), they do not indicate actual unit labor costs for given amounts of production. These are the more decisive costs in determining price policies, an employer's ability to compete against other employers, and the ability of employers of one nation to compete against those of other nations in foreign markets.

Let us assume, for example, that an employer has a total payroll cost (wages and supplementary employee benefit costs: in short, a total labor expenditure) of $1 per hour at the beginning of a five-year period. Let us assume, further, that this total hourly labor expenditure increased 100 percent, to $2 per hour over five years. Assume, also, that in the first year the output per worker in his plant had been 10 widgets per hour. At $1 per hour, therefore, each widget had a unit labor cost of 10¢ (10 widgets divided into $1). Assume that five years later productivity of each worker per man hour has risen to 20 widgets. Although the employer's costs for each hour of labor has risen to $2, his unit labor cost per widget would still be 10¢ (20 widgets divided into $2). Under these conditions, the employer's competitive position, as far as unit labor costs are concerned, would be unchanged, and he could maintain a stable price. On the other hand, if productivity had not improved, with output still at 10 widgets per man hour and with labor costs now $2 per hour, the unit labor cost would be 20¢ (per widget). To put it another way, *an index of unit labor costs* would have increased from 100 to 200.

Measured in terms of unit labor costs, the United States has had a relatively favorable time of it in recent years. Table 17 shows indices of unit labor costs in manufacturing for selected countries between 1950 and 1964. (Of the major Western European nations, only Italy has been excluded, and because precisely comparable data is lacking; but data that is nearly comparable indicates that in recent years Italy's experience is close to that of other Western European countries.)

As the authors of a study of these trends conclude: "From 1950 to 1957 unit labor cost in the United States rose about the same as the average of the other countries." Since 1957 "the trends . . . resulted in a great improvement in the cost position of the United States relative to its trading partners."[14] During the years from 1957 to 1964 unit labor costs in the United States rose only .6 percent per year, an average that was bettered only by Canada. Table 18 shows the average annual trends in total expenditure on labor costs and unit labor cost trends broken down into the periods of 1950–1957 and 1957–1964.

As can readily be seen, the pace of increases in wages and related benefits (total labor expenditure) has been somewhat slower in the United States and Canada, and this helps to account for their superior position in unit labor costs in recent years. On the other hand, Great Britain, with a level of labor expenditures not too much in excess of the United

TABLE 18. *Percentage Increases in Manufacturing Total Labor Expenditure and Unit Labor Costs Annual Averages*

| | 1950–1957 | | 1957–1964 | |
	Labor Expenditure	Unit Labor Cost	Labor Expenditure	Unit Labor Cost
Canada	7.4%	2.9%	4.4%	.3%
France	14.2	8.5	11.1	4.9
Germany (West)	13.1	1.2	12.0	3.5
Great Britain	8.6	5.0	5.9	2.3
Netherlands	10.5	4.0	10.0	3.4
Sweden	10.4	7.3	8.8	2.5
U.S.A.	6.7	3.5	4.3	.6

SOURCE: Chandler and Jackman, *op. cit.*, p. 1066.

States and Canada in the 1957–1964 period, shows a much larger rise in unit labor costs, reflecting of course smaller increases in productivity.

Chandler and Jackman also note that from 1957 to 1964 the total rate of increase in manufacturing production was substantially slower in the United States and Canada than in Western Europe, save for Great Britain.[15]

Unemployment Rate Higher in the United States Than in Western Europe

Some of the advantages enjoyed by the United States in unit labor costs during recent years may be because its rate of unemployment has been higher than that of Western Europe. In fact, rates of unemployment, not only for the United States but for Canada as well, have been considerably higher than those of Western Europe, as Table 19 suggests.

Clearly, production and labor-market conditions have usually been less "tight" in the United States (and Canada) than in Western Europe during recent years. This has doubtless contributed to a less pressing demand for labor, a less advantageous bargaining position for unions, and lesser pressures on unit labor costs. The net result has been more stable prices in the United States.

On the other hand, the continuing favorable trade position of the United States in 1965 and 1966, when unemployment was falling, suggests that the relationship of loose labor markets and lower unit labor costs may not be too exact.

Whatever the precise reasons may be, one can conclude, however,

TABLE 19. *Rate of Unemployment, Selected Countries, 1959–1966*

	1959	1960	1961	1962	1963	1964	1965	1966
Canada	6.0%	7.0%	7.2%	5.9%	5.5%	4.7%	3.9%	3.6%
France	2.8	2.6	2.0	2.0	2.4	1.9	2.3	2.4
Germany (West)	1.6	.7	.4	.4	.4	.4	.3	.4
Great Britain	3.1	2.4	2.3	2.8	3.4	2.4	2.1	2.3
Italy	5.7	4.3	3.7	3.2	2.7	3.0	4.0	4.3
Sweden	N.A.	N.A.	1.5	1.5	1.7	1.6	1.2	1.6
U.S.A.	5.5	5.6	6.7	5.6	5.7	5.2	4.6	3.9

SOURCE: Arthur F. Neef and Rosa A. Holland, "Comparative Unemployment Rates, 1964–1965" *Monthly Labor Review*, April 1967. Data from different countries have been adjusted to U.S. definitions of employment and unemployment so that the figures are comparable.

that favorable trends in unit labor costs, regardless of the relative absolute amount of increases in other benefits, helped to provide favorable trade opportunities for U.S. industry as a whole. American unions continued to bargain for increases in wages and fringe benefits, but these added up to less pressure, relatively, on U.S. prices, than on prices in Western Europe.[16] As the U.S. economic boom continued in 1966 and 1967, unit labor costs rose a bit faster.

Even at that point, however, U. S. unit labor cost trends were not unfavorable as compared to most other industrial nations; but the U. S. trade position did begin to show some deterioration by the late sixties, indicating that factors other than unit labor costs were also crucial in determining the trade positions of different countries.

N O T E S

1. In recent years some smaller firms facing economic dificulties have broken away from national bargaining patterns in steel, automobile, and other industries.

2. See Arthur Ross, "Prosperity and Labor Relations in Europe: The Case of West Germany," *Quarterly Journal of Economics*, August 1962, and "Prosperity and Labor Relations in Western Europe, France and Italy," *Industrial and Labor Relations Review*, October 1962.

3. See *Italian Labor Documents*, No. 15 (International Service of the Department of Research of the Confederazione Italiana Sindicati Lavoratori [CISL], 1963).

4. *I.M.F. News*, May 1967.

5. D. J. Robertson, *Factory Wages and Structure and National Agreements* (Cambridge: Cambridge University Press, 1960). In proposing that Britain move to a "two tier" bargaining approach, i.e., a combination of bargaining at the national industry level (to set minimums for the industry) and factory or firm wage bargaining (to reflect local profit, productivity, and other conditions), Norman Ross recognizes the far-reaching implications of this for trade-union and employer-association reorganization. See his *Workshop Bargaining: A New Approach*, Fabian Tract 366

(London: Fabian Society, March 1966), *passim*. Allan Flanders proposes a three-tier bargaining system. The first tier would set a national wage policy, and within that framework industry negotiations would proceed at the second tier. The third tier of bargaining would be at the enterprise level. *Industrial Relations: What is Wrong With the System?* (London: Faber and Faber, 1965), esp. Chap 6.

6. *Wages and Labour Mobility* (Paris: Organisation for Economic Cooperation and Development, 1965), esp. Chap. II, "Changes in Wage Structures."

7. See Adolf Sturmthal (ed.), *Contemporary Collective Bargaining in Seven Countries* (Ithaca, N.Y.: Institute of International Industrial and Labor Relations, Cornell University, 1957), pp. 334–343. Also see Lloyd G. Reynolds and Cynthia H. Taft, *The Evolution of Wage Structure* (New Haven, Conn.: Yale University Press, 1956).

8. For a good general treatment of wage drift, see Brent Hansen and Gosta Rehn, "On Wage Drift: A Problem of Money-Wage Dynamics," *Twenty-Five Economic Essays in Honour of Erik Lindahl* (Stockholm: 1957). Also see William Fellner, *et al.*, "A Note on Wage Drift," *The Problem of Rising Prices* (Paris: Organisation for European Economic Cooperation, 1961), pp. 67–68. Also see S. Eskilsson, "Wage Drift and Inflation," in Anthony D. Smith, ed., *The Labour Market and Inflation* (London: Macmillan, 1968).

9. *Wages and Labour Mobility, op. cit.,* pp. 22–27.

10. See *Labour in the European Community* (Washington, D.C.: April 1965), p. 3. This is a summary of a larger study, *Enquête sur les salaires dans les industries de la communauté économique Européene, 1962* (Brussels: European Economic Community, 1964). The number of institutions and sources for comparative intercountry wage and labor cost data are numerous. In addition to those cited in this chapter: the International Labour Organisation, which makes an inquiry each October (usually published six to nine months later); the Associazione Industriale Lombarda, Milan, which compares labor costs in Europe, published every few years (*Comparison of European Wages and Labour Costs,* Milan, 1966); the Swedish Employers' Confederation (*Direct and Total Wage Costs for Workers, International Survey 1957–1964,* Stockholm, 1965). Recently the European Free Trade Association has published material on wage costs in eighteen industries in eleven European countries and the U.S. (A summary of this survey was published in the *T&GW Record,* June 1967. This is the journal of the British Transport and General Workers' Union.) Of almost encyclopedic character on wage and income trends in postwar Europe is the United Nations' *Incomes in Postwar Europe: A Study of Policies, Growth and Distribution* (Geneva: United Nations, 1967). This is Part 2 of an economic survey of Europe made in 1965. A valuable historical survey (for the period 1860–1960) of wage and hour trends in five industrial nations (France, Germany, Sweden, Great Britain and the United States) appeared just as our volume was completed: E. H. Phelps Brown and Margaret H. Browne, *A Century of Pay* (New York: St. Martin's Press, 1968).

11. Gunnar Myrdal, "Economic Growth and Economic Policy in the United States," *Supplement to Svenska Handelsbanken's Economic Review,* No. 3 (1965), p. 3.

12. Reid and Robertson, *op. cit.* (see Table 12 source note), p. 100.

13. In a number of countries the benefits noted in Table 15 are provided primarily by statute. It should also be pointed out that collective bargaining is relatively more "effective" in the automobile and steel industries in the U.S. than in most other sectors, and to this extent benefits for the "average" U.S. worker may be relatively less advantageous.

14. Chandler and Jackman, *op. cit.* (see Table 17 source note), pp. 1064–1065.

15. *Ibid.,* p. 1066.

16. Continuing favorable trade balances in merchandise exports over imports reflected the relatively stable unit labor costs in the United States during the years surveyed above. This should not be confused with U.S. balance-of-payment difficulties, which were not being caused by unfavorable trade trends, but also reflected capital movements out of the country, military and economic expenditures abroad, and other factors. The tables and data in this section have admittedly been of a general character. If one could compare unit labor costs in specific export industries, country by country, it might be easier to judge union bargaining impact upon foreign competition. As yet we do not have sufficient, comparable data in this much detail, but the data seem to be convincing as regards the trends of labor costs in the United States as opposed to most other nations. One recent study by the U.S. Bureau of Labor Statistics, *An International Comparison of Unit Labor Cost in the Iron and Steel Industry 1964: United States, France, Germany, United Kingdom*, Bulletin 1580 (Washington: U.S. Department of Labor, 1968), does provide detailed data on this one industry.

XII

Development of National Wage Policy Systems

THE most noteworthy development in wage setting within Western industrial-relations systems since World War II has been the increase in national wage policies or controls (or incomes policy, as it is commonly termed in Europe). Efforts to impose, or achieve by consensus, some uniformity in wage movements have been made in a number of European countries, including Sweden, Norway, Denmark, Austria, and the Netherlands. More recently, similar steps have been taken in Great Britain and in the United States, and the issue has been under intensive consideration in France.[1]

National wage policies, as a significant influence in Western industrial-relations systems, dates from the time of World War II. Before this, government intervention to establish minimum-wage levels and union-management-negotiated national wage levels in particular industries were quite common in Western countries. Policies and institutions designed to give general coherence or uniform direction to wage movements were generally unknown, however.

Under some compulsory arbitration systems (notably in Australia[2]) and under legislation in some countries whereby the terms of labor-management agreements could be extended to entire industries, including nonunionized firms (see Chapter VII), there was some movement toward a more nationally directed wage system. But these limited experiments were (or are) not really comparable to policies designed to gear all wage movements to a general formula, as is the case under a national wage or incomes policy. The formula is also called "guideposts" or "guiding-light system." (The name varies from country to country.)

The tremendous industrial mobilization triggered by World War II, coupled with highly effective mass trade-union movements (for the first time in the history of a few of the Western countries) brought about national wage-control programs.

The United States is a good example. During World War I a

254

National War Labor Board was established to help control industrial relations. Its prime concern, however, was to quash industrial disputes and prevent strikes. In World War II the government again established a National War Labor Board. As before, this board sought to prevent strikes that could disrupt the war effort. A major part of its time and effort came to be devoted, however, to controlling wage movements; this was done in order to support economic stabilization. The difference between the scope and activities of the two boards can be explained by the fact that in World War II (1) industrial mobilization was greater and (2) a mass trade-union movement was putting pressure upon costs and prices by pursuing wage increases.

Increasing Use of Wage-Controls in Peacetime

Special economic conditions and pressures led a number of Western European nations after World War II to establish national wage policies and/or control systems. Most of the countries were confronted with large reconstruction tasks that necessitated a great diversion of resources into plant and equipment. This diversion, in turn, led to a shortage of consumer goods and created inflationary pressures. At the same time all these nations were struggling to regain their world trade markets. These objectives were being pursued at the same time that a determination throughout the Western world to prevent the recurrence of depressions, like the one in the thirties, and to underwrite full employment was also evolving. The net effect of these developments was to lower the threshold to price increases. The need to curtail inflation, whatever its source, led to wage- (and price-) control programs of varying types. Occasionally, as for example in the case of Sweden, a labor ideology of solidarity and a desire to use collective bargaining to move lower wage levels upward, at the relative expense of better paid groups, has also promoted acceptance of a national wage-bargaining approach, even in "ordinary" times.

With the completion of reconstruction and the return to "normalcy," it might have been anticipated that national wage policies or control systems would disappear from Western democracies, which have usually prided themselves on the voluntaristic character of their industrial-relations systems. Such has not been the case. Nearly every country in Western Europe in the past decade has either experimented with or seriously considered some form of a national wage or income policy. In recent years the United States also took a few steps in this direction, with the formulation of national wage and price guideposts, beginning in 1962 with the *Economic Report of the President* and his Council of Economic Advisers. (The United States abandoned the guideposts early in 1969.)

The methods employed to effect wage control or guidance have varied considerably. Some countries (Sweden and Denmark are good examples) have relied primarily upon high-level negotiations between the leading labor federation (the equivalent of the AFL-CIO) and the large employer associations.

High government authorities (of central planning bureaus and the ministries of social affairs and finance) usually keep in close touch with the negotiations. They provide the negotiators with the economic prospects for the year ahead, the trends in productivity, the country's trade needs, and so on. Their purpose is to help the parties reach a more "rational" settlement in keeping with the nation's economic possibilities and needs.

Norway has also tried to pursue a national wage policy that depends primarily on agreement between central union federations and employer associations, although in the years immediately following World War II a high degree of direct government control was accepted. More recently, central negotiations that involve all unions and employers have received less acceptance in Norway than in Denmark and Sweden. Negotiations in Norway usually proceed on an industry-wide basis; however, government still exercises considerable influence directly if negotiations stall and strikes threaten. It also exercises its influence indirectly via pressures on both labor and management.[3]

Under some arrangements, and Denmark is a case, in point, if voluntary negotiations fail to produce a settlement, government "mediators" intervene and propose new terms for the negotiating parties. Also, and again Denmark affords an example, if the parties do not accept the settlement, the government may impose it upon them by legislative enactment, which produces what is in effect compulsory arbitration. In recent years this type of government-imposed settlement has also occurred on several occasions in Norway. Sweden, on the other hand, has continued on a more voluntaristic basis; the negotiating parties have managed to bargain through to a national agreement each time (usually covering a one- or two-year period), and there has been no resort to compulsory government arbitration.

Generally speaking, these negotiations result in one overall settlement involving wages and related benefits (a uniform wage increase, a cut in weekly hours, etc.), but there may be special adjustments. These adjustments are (1) for women workers, who are still quite underpaid in relationship to men (as yet there is only modest acceptance in Europe of the principle of equal pay for equal work), (2) for workers in lower paid industries or occupations, (3) for workers (in the form of special increments) who have not had the advantages generally accruing to pieceworkers in an expanding economy, and (4) for other groups. From time to time, national wage bargaining also adjusts working hours, modifies vacation benefits, and touches upon other important fringe areas. The national settlement is applied uniformly to all workers in all industries covered in the negotiations.

Negotiations involving white-collar workers are usually conducted after, and separately from, the blue-collar federation settlement. Special variations may occur, but the general framework is set by the first top-level bargain that is struck by the major labor federation and the employers' association.

In situations like those in Sweden and Denmark, the government does not set forth a national wage policy of its own. It seeks to influence the parties, but the settlement is a national one in the sense that it covers the great majority of unionized wage earners in one broad bargain.

Since some conceive of national "policy making" as a government function only, it can be argued that mere centralized national negotiation of wages, in and of itself, is not a wage-policy system. This, indeed, was the argument of a high-level team of experts from five nations who reported on this and related matters to an intergovernmental agency several years ago.[4]

This argument seems difficult to accept, however. Certainly the Scandinavian efforts in this field have been directed to the same objective as those pursued by more formal wage-control systems, as in the Netherlands and Austria. Moreover, should wage- or income-policy systems prove to be necessary in the long run, the predominantly voluntaristic types may prove to be as effective (or no less ineffective!) than the more formal ones. Tolerance by labor and management of controls even in the face of emergency economic conditions, such as inflation or a balance of payments deficit, seems to vary inversely with the period of time these controls have been in operation, particularly where the government is an active participant in the process.

Direct Government Involvement in Control Systems

Confronted with a serious inflationary threat in the mid-fifties, the Austrian labor movement took the initiative in calling for establishment of a joint price-wage control board. The government cooperated, and in 1957 a joint council was set up for the regulation of wages and prices. In addition to representatives of both the union and the employers' associations, the council includes the federal chancellor, the minister of trade, the minister of social administration, and the minister of the interior.

Procedure requires that no wage demand is to be made of an employer and no price increase is to be put into effect before the matter is submitted to the joint council. Special standing subcommittees of the council are set up to pass upon proposed new wage claims or price increases. Employer groups and unions are represented on each of these subcommittees.

Generally speaking, under this arrangement the joint council tries to keep wage increases in proportion to the increase in productivity in the particular industry in which the union is making its demand. It then is in a position to press the industry to absorb all or a large part of the cost of any wage increase without raising prices.

Enforcement of the council's decisions ultimately depends upon the ability of the Austrian trade union federation and the employers' associations to keep their members "in line." The council has no power of legal sanction, and the system is basically voluntary. The minister of the interior may, however, subject to price control those industries or firms that increase prices without prior approval of the council. The minister is authorized to do so by legislation that gives the government power to regulate prices.[5]

Common to all national wage policies or systems has been the effort to link wage increases with productivity by one device or another. Most efforts, at least at the outset, are designed to limit wage increases in relationship to the increase in the level of national productivity. This level is usually determined on the basis of either a very recent trend or the prospect for the year ahead.[6]

Where very formal control systems have been used, in time a general guideline based on national productivity trends seems to break down or shift to a more differentiated basis. It then becomes permissible to negotiate wage variations related closely to the varying productivity (and perhaps profit) levels of different industries. Wages are then geared to productivity trends within given industries. Such, for example, has been the case in the Netherlands.[7]

The problem of the productivity of individual firms and industries can also be troublesome under a national wage policy. In an effort to encourage increases in output, the British Labour government has established an exception to the national wage formula and has permitted larger wage increases where it can be demonstrated that new labor-management agreements were directly related to plans to increase productivity. Whether such agreements truly provide for relaxation of old work restrictions, greater worker effort, and so on, can be next to impossible to determine, in practice. Moreover, they can occasion much bitterness where labor and management, on the one side, and government, on the other, disagree as to whether a new agreement will truly increase productivity.

The British National Board for Prices and Incomes issued a special set of regulations and standards, late in 1966, to determine whether a new pay and productivity agreement could be properly qualified for approval. Soon, however, it was in head-on conflict with the Electrical Trades Union and the Electrical Contracting Industry over an agreement adopted by these parties to increase productivity by providing substantial pay increases in certain jobs, these increases to come out of the savings effected by eliminating certain other jobs. The board judged the savings insufficient and in some respects too vague to warrant its approval of the agreement.[8]

The experience of the Netherlands illustrates still another general problem in the effort of some European countries to control wages; namely the effect of changes in wage policies of different countries on each other. Thus, the liberalization in the wage control system that was forced upon the employers and the unions after several years of operation seems to have been, in part, caused by the Netherlands' economic partners in Western Europe pursuing less controlled wage policies, and there was some danger of a serious exodus of skilled workers from the Netherlands to these other countries, notably to Germany.[9]

Aside from productivity and the interrelatedness of wage policies, the other major factor usually influencing wage policy under a national control system is the cost of living. Theoretically there should be no substantial changes in the cost of living under a perfectly effective wage-policy system geared to productivity increases. Practically, however, weaknesses in the wage-policy system that involved its administration— as well as outside forces beyond administrative control—have led to price increases in all countries that have experimented with national wage policies. Generally, this problem is anticipated by accepting the necessity of adjusting wages in line with price changes over the course of time, and also of adjusting them in line with increased productivity.

Adjustment of wages to price increases, usually pegged to the national cost-of-living index, becomes a virtual necessity if the operation of the income policy is geared to collective agreements that run beyond one year. In Norway, for example, the chief economist of the Ministry of Finance notes:

> The wage earners, on their side, have made it a condition for accepting such long contract periods that they should be given a certain guarantee of the purchasing power of their earnings. The guarantee has been in the form of the price escalator clause.[10]

If wages are renegotiated on a yearly basis (every two years in some cases), any cost-of-living increase can be taken into account at that time, along with changes in productivity. In other cases long-term wage agreements may provide for semi-annual reviews of changes in the cost of living; these reviews then lead to any necessary adjustments.

Those who shaped American wage policy, particularly the Council of Economic Advisers, were very reluctant to admit the cost of living into wage-increase formulas. As long as the cost of living was rising no more than 1 or 1½ percent a year, this was not a critical problem. The 1966 consumer price rise in excess of 3 percent annually made this position difficult to hold.

While the council was still not willing to accede to these pressures and change its wage guideposts, which were limited to a national productivity formula, the Secretary of Labor recognized the changed circumstances. He accepted "completely" the idea that consumer price increases must be taken into account, at least partly, in any guidepost formula.[11]

Effectiveness of Wage Policy Systems

It is still difficult to appraise the economic effectiveness of the various national wage policies or control systems that have been tried by Western countries in the past decade.[12] Generally, upward price movements throughout the world make it difficult to differentiate between the economic records of countries that have tried and countries that have not tried peacetime wage-control policies. If, however, it can be assumed that one principal objective of any wage or income policy is to restrain upward price movements, the available data are not too encouraging to the advocates of wage controls.

For a time one country or another seems to do relatively well in controlling prices, but then comes a period of inflation. For example, a group of international experts, in a report for the OEEC in 1961, heaped great praise upon the very formal incomes system of the Netherlands; but print was hardly dry on their report when the system virtually came apart. Between 1962 and 1965 the Netherlands witnessed a worse price explosion than most of its Western competitors.[13]

From the data in Table 20 a case could be made that prices would be better off without formal wage policies. Certainly the United States, Italy, and Germany, which operated without wage policies during most of these fifteen years, have superior records. On the other hand, France, which also lacked a wage policy, had the poorest official price record. One can argue that there were, of course, special circumstances; the case cannot be made, to say the least, that countries like the Netherlands or Sweden, which have experimented with formal or informal wage policies, pay pauses, and the like have done any better.[14]

Admittedly, comparisons among countries may not be the most accurate standard of judgment in weighing the value of wage controls or incomes policies. Ideally, one should judge what might have happened in a given country with or without such controls, but this is virtually im-

TABLE 20. *Index of Wholesale Prices, Selected Countries*
1950–1965 (1957 = 100)

	1950	1962	1965
France	72.4	125.7	136.5
Germany (West)	81.8	102.6	107.4
Great Britain	77.1	107.6	118.4
Italy	101.3	99.3	111.3
Netherlands	81.3	96.2	108.5
Sweden	70.9	104.6	119.2
U.S.A.	87.7	101.6	103.5

SOURCE: *Unit Labor Cost in Manufacturing, Trends in Nine Countries,* Bulletin 1518 (Washington, D.C.: Bureau of Labor Statistics, U.S. Department of Labor, 1966). In the case of France, particularly, the problem of "competitiveness" is hard to prove from these figures, since that country went through a severe official currency devaluation in these years. Needless to say, other price indices are equally reliable in evaluating comparative price performance, but they too yield no conclusive results. The use of unit labor cost indices, perhaps the most important indicator for policy makers, makes the U.S. performance even more impressive.

possible. A better argument might hold that, in terms of a country's goals, even a temporary holdback of price-wage movements for a given period of time, as the Netherlands' control system seemed to accomplish in the more immediate post-World War II period and in the 1950s, was worth the effort.

Some economists have made efforts to demonstrate correlations between wage-price movements and levels of unemployment prevailing in a given country. The classical argument in this situation is that the lower the level of unemployment the more rapid the wage-price movements. Again the data do not demonstrate that such close relations always prevail nor how long the time lag may be before a given level of unemployment affects wage and price levels.[15]

Although it remains difficult to judge the economic effectiveness of national wage policies, it is useful to describe some of the basic factors which can be seen either as necessary *institutional* prerequisites or results of the operation of such systems—particularly as they affect the labor movements and industrial relations systems.

Factors Influencing Union Acceptance of National Wage Policies

To secure union acceptance or support for a national wage policy in peacetime, the labor movement must be confident of the society's ability to maintain a strong, full-employment economy. Lacking such confidence (or, more properly, if a given economy has not maintained a strong full-employment pattern over a period of years), it becomes difficult to engage the trade-union movement even in a discussion of national wage policy.

On the other hand, when full employment has been sustained for a very long period in peacetime, and inflationary pressures persist, a national labor movement may even reach the conclusion that a national wage policy is an absolutely indispensable part of a planned, sustained full-employment economy. Sweden's LO, as one example, reached this conclusion, and took the lead in formulating the case for a planned central wage policy.[16] In this instance uncoordinated or excessive union wage pressures came to be regarded as potentially dangerous obstacles or bottlenecks in maintaining full employment and a high rate of economic growth.

Where such confidence exists in the employment situation, the union movement may accept a national wage policy as part of a total plan to insure the improvement of living standards and real wages. This seems to be the way in which the 1964 British Trades Union Congress expressed its willingness to cooperate in a planning effort with (what it hoped would be) a new Labour government on the eve of the 1964 election. One British trade-union leader described this as "a planned growth of incomes."[17] When the Labour government did take over, George Brown, the first Labour government minister directly responsible for developing the incomes policy, described it's goal as "the fullest growth of wages." He insisted:

This [policy] does not mean another sterile wage freeze and it does not mean the end of free collective bargaining. The essence of the challenge is how to plan for the fullest growth of the economy and the fullest growth of wages and salaries with the *fairest* possible distribution of the growth of wages that can be managed.[18]

The switch of the British Trades Union Congress from opposition to a wage or income policy to a position of cautious support—in keeping with the switch from a Conservative to a Labour government—illustrates another typical precondition for the successful development of such a policy. In virtually every European nation in which a national wage policy was first established in peacetime, the government in power either was socialist-led or was a coalition that included a socialist party. Often, too, in such a government the ministry of labor, key to the formulation and execution of a wage policy, was under the leadership of a socialist.[19]

The experience of the United States also supports this general conclusion about the need for a prolabor government as an important force in gaining any acceptance for a national wage policy.

Conservative journalist Arthur Krock of *The New York Times* called attention to the fact that the effort to introduce a "non-inflationary" wage policy could better be attempted under a Democratic administration like that of John F. Kennedy than under either President Dwight D. Eisenhower or Richard M. Nixon. Shortly after President Kennedy had set forth the first national wage guideline philosophy, Krock wrote:

Although the Eisenhower administration compromised with labor in taking small, cautious steps toward restoring the social-economic balance in the national community, and candidate Nixon's intervention in the steel strike of 1959 ended in results which were praised by the union leaders, Kennedy entered the 1960 campaign with better union credentials. Important among these was the strongly pro-labor Los Angeles platform. Hence it is much more probable that a Kennedy than a Nixon administration can influence the unions against a continuance of the inflationary cycle represented by wage and other contract demands exceeding the productivity increase formula.

In the same column, written just after the conclusion of the 1962 steel contract negotiations, Mr. Krock went on to praise the influence of President Kennedy and his Secretary of Labor, Arthur J. Goldberg, in persuading the steel union and steel management to accept "a contract which would provide no solid ground for a rise in steel prices."[20]

Another factor in facilitating organized labor's support of wage policies is its involvement in the development of such plans. John Dunlop has argued that one reason why the U.S. government's wage guideposts proved relatively unsuccessful in recent years stems from the failure to involve labor and management in formulation and administration of the policies:

Business and labor leaders have little respect for the current guideposts, in part because they had no role in drafting them. In our society interest groups must have a role—not a controlling role—in the formulation of wage-price policy if they are to conform to it.[21]

Enlisting participation by labor in the administration of a wage-control program may have other positive values for government. When the union movement accepts the program, a part of the pressure from below, which may develop against the controls, is diverted from government and aimed at the top union hierarchy, which shares in the responsibility for the control system.

Another condition of union acceptance of a national wage policy is related to labor's confidence in the intent and ability of the government to carry through a program of "equal sacrifice" for all economic groups. The effort of the Conservative government to put into operation an incomes policy in Great Britain in the early 1960s is again a good case in point. This policy was roundly criticized by the British unions on the ground that only wages were being controlled. It seemed almost an afterthought that moves were made to control other forms of income. The new

Labour government (1965) announced its intention to couple an incomes policy with some new taxes on capital gains and possibly with some forms of price and income control—all of which, among other things, were intended to assure the unions that other groups were being called upon to contribute to the solution of Britain's economic difficulties.

This problem of relative equity and the containment of incomes other than wages has produced strange twists in bargaining relationships in some countries. The Danish Federation of Trade Unions and the chief employers' organization in that country adopted a new procedure for negotiation in 1964; they agreed "to aim at seeing that this income policy embraces all recipients of income in the society." It was also agreed that this would involve joint pressure upon the government whose "legislative powers are able to secure this objective." The union had felt that after the 1961 agreement "those who draw incomes outside of the trade union movement properly speaking succeeded in securing far greater income advances than did the workers. . . . The trade union movement wishes there to be no recurrence of this."[22] A new European literature is now being developed, under pressure from the unions, on the subject of control of nonwage incomes and prices in relation to wage controls.[23]

A similar example of labor's demand for "equal sacrifice" took place in the United States in 1966. While continuing to express hostility to the so-called guideposts, President George Meany of the AFL-CIO indicated labor's willingness to cooperate in a national emergency "over-all stabilization" program:

If the President concludes there is such a national emergency as to require extraordinary over-all stabilization measures, he will have the complete wholehearted support of the labor movement. This would mean every economic factor—all costs, prices, profits, wages, being equally restrained. All America would be sharing equally the costs and the sacrifices of a national problem.[24]

Most major economic groups in a democratic society must experience a fairly high degree of national consensus—a sense of commonly perceived danger to the economy—before serious consideration will be given to the types of control, or even self-discipline, that go into the operation of a national wage policy. All European democratic countries that in peacetime have accepted a national wage policy as a replacement for traditional wage bargaining have been confronted with an existing or possible balance-of-payments crisis. In this situation anti-inflation wage policies become easier to pursue. This sort of crisis generally helps to develop a much wider sense of national consensus in all sectors of the society.

While there was continuous concern and debate about inflation and the influence of union pressures on prices in the United States during the 1950s, it is significant that the first formal effort to establish national wage guidelines did not occur until a great many people had become aware of the balance-of-payments crisis early in the 1960s. As long as a creeping inflation is "only" a source of "domestic" debate and concern, it is not likely to trigger "extreme" counterpolicies or interference with traditional union and collective-bargaining institutions. When critical, balance-of-payments considerations are thrown onto the scales, traditional resistance may give way.[25]

Union and Industrial-Relations Structures and National Wage Policies

It seems clear that it is easier to formulate and implement a national wage policy in a country where bargaining has developed along predominantly national, industrial lines. It was relatively easy for the Swedes, for example, to move from a system where most of the basic wage bargaining was through national industry-wide negotiations to a single top-level bargaining system (for manual workers) that sets out a general framework for all wage increases. Contrast this, for example, with the bargaining structure in the United States, where the *prevailing labor-management contract patterns* are set by plant, by company, or by occupation for a very *limited* geographical area.

Again, carrying out a national wage policy is more orderly where the predominant union structure is industrial in character. Denmark, for instance, offers a striking contrast to Sweden. In Denmark, where the union structure is highly craft-dominated, labor encounters greater difficulties. Jockeying between a variety of craft unions, plus the usual complications in labor-management negotiations, often makes it extremely difficult to strike a single national wage bargain in Denmark.

In 1965 the negotiations in Britain's engineering industry provide another apt example of the added difficulties that a predominantly craft-union structure can impose on national wage-policy negotiations. Enormous work by thirty-seven unions and the employers' association resulted in a long-term agreement, in December, 1965. It was generally felt that this agreement would be compatible with the kind of national wage-policy formula the new labor government was seeking. After the top-level negotiations were concluded, however, one of the unions, the Electrical Trades Union, raised serious objections to the agreement on the ground that it gave insufficient consideration to its skilled craft members.[26]

Even where national wage bargaining has been accepted by the entire labor movement, it is likely to produce somewhat different results among different industries and occupations. Under conditions of full employment, employers and workers, operating in tight labor markets, can often find the means to evade the national formulas to some extent. They do so by loosening incentive standards, upgrading workers to higher classifications, paying so-called black wages or under-the-counter payments in excess of regular classification rates, and so on. These processes lead to the wage drift described earlier, or "the difference between the actual earnings recorded in a sector during a period (e.g., a year) and the earnings which were expected to follow directly from the terms agreed under the contract for the period."[27]

In other words, if in a given industry a 10-cent increase is negotiated for a one-year contract, but at the end of the year average hourly earnings have risen 13 cents in the same industry, the wage drift is 3 cents (the difference between the negotiated 10 cents and the actual 13-cent increase).

To control this drift and to prevent evasions of the national wage policy formula, some union movements have become increasingly receptive to the introduction of more formal wage-classification and job-evaluation systems, especially where they have operated under national wage policies for a long time. This has been true in the Netherlands and in Sweden.[28]

Where a craft union structure predominates, the stresses and strains in wage movements under a national wage policy may occur between different groups of occupations. Thus, in Denmark wage drift is much more prevalent among skilled metalworkers (who have their own craft union) and often causes bitterness in the important general workers union, which caters to less skilled industrial workers.

As between industries, it appears that national wage-policy administration may be less successful (in the sense that evasions are greater and wage drift is higher) in industries where there are large numbers of employers or when the industry is working exclusively for sheltered domestic markets, as, for example, in the building industry. The "control" of building workers' wages has been a vexing problem for national wage policy advocates in the United States and Sweden. Most recently in Sweden and Norway there has been sympathetic consideration of the view that there must be concentration primarily on the wage-cost-price relationships in export industries, with less attention to so-called domestic-market industries.[29]

In addition, in many large European metal companies, where profits have been higher than in most other manufacturing sectors, employers have also tended to pass along various wage and related benefits over and beyond the national formula.

National Wage Policies and Their Effects on Union Structure

A national wage policy almost by definition indicates that the role and power of the top (federation) level of the labor movement has increased in relationship to lower levels of the movement. Formulation of demands, negotiations with the government as well as with top management, control over strikes—are among the powers that seem to gravitate toward the federation executives in a number of countries where national wage-policy systems have been in operation for some time. This has certainly been the case—and to an important extent—in Scandinavia, the Netherlands, and Austria.[30]

Moreover, unions or union leaders who can exercise political power also tend to come to the fore when national wage-policy decisions are to be made.[31] For example, in Denmark several years ago the leader of the metalworkers union, who was also a key socialist member of the parliament, played a central role in negotiations among unions, management, the various political parties, and the government. These negotiations went on during the period of crisis when the new national wage agreement, as well as accompanying tax, rent, and food price subsidies had to be worked out.

In Britain in 1965, top union leaders who were under pressure from the Labour government and its new incomes policy, decided to take on the almost bizarre task of screening in advance of negotiations proposed new wage increases to preserve a maximum of voluntarism in the bargaining process. The TUC agreed to recommend reductions in the proposals if they were "out of line."[32]

Although there have been several changes in the laws and regulations concerning incomes policy in Great Britain since 1965, the TUC has continued to "vet" (as it is termed in Britain) or pass upon claims of its affiliates before these are formally presented to management. On March 27, 1968, for example, the TUC Incomes Policy Committee considered 14 claims for increases, by 14 unions covering 796,788 workers. The committee found that one claim, covering 1,098 workers appeared "to be incompatible with the requirements of incomes policy." In the case of two claims covering 66,440 workers, the unions were asked to meet with a panel of the committee for further discussion. Some eleven claims, covering 729,250 workers were judged to present no objections and the unions were advised to proceed "with negotiations for a settlement of the claim as it stands."[33]

The Labour government has passed from what was, more or less, a freeze in the period between July 1966 to July 1967, and has sought a new guideline in wage policy. In April 1968 it set forth a new "ceiling of 3½ percent on wage, salary and dividend increases." In February 1968, just before the government formalized its guideline, the TUC had convoked what has come to be an annual conference of union executives. At this conference, the TUC presented its own economic review, which judged that with appropriate expansionist economic policies ". . . the economy should be allowed to grow at the rate of more than 6 percent." On this assumption and the linked assumption that productivity would rise by more than 5 percent, an increase in weekly pay of 5 percent seemed "compatible with stable labor costs across the economy as a whole," for the 1968–1969 period. (The TUC recommended that 1½ of the 5 percent should "be allowed for increases arising from local bargaining.")[34]

The TUC has continued to pass upon the wage claims which its affiliates continue to submit to it, presumably applying its own standards or norms. As unions have chafed under restraints, however, some of them, including several of the largest, began to pull out of the vetting system by the summer of 1968. They would continue, of course, to be subject to the government's policy which, among other things, includes government's power to delay negotiated settlements for as long as twelve months.

Informed observers estimate that the very setting up of the TUC screening process had the psychological effect of making many unions operate in a more "responsible" fashion, i.e., they formulated their demands with national income policy standards in mind. There is still the problem that under such a system, even after the demands have been formulated and vetted, they must be negotiated with employers.

In any event, the entire vetting experience to date has involved an enormous expansion of the role of the TUC, the central union body. The annual meetings of union executives and the economic reviews which are presented at them seem destined to continue. As a consequence of the annual review and the meeting, the TUC's influence on the wage policies of its affiliates is likely to be greater than in the past.

In the Netherlands, under the wage-price-control system, union and management leadership have also participated in the screening of proposed increases during much of the post-World War II period.

Generally speaking, where there is a tradition of worker solidarity and an acceptance of the principle of a powerful central labor federation, it is easier to operate an incomes policy. In Sweden, the LO found the central wage-bargaining system attractive because of its desire to provide larger increases for lower-paid workers who might otherwise have suffered a disadvantage in bargaining because of their particular industry or occupation.

The rather long "tolerance" of some forms of wage policy in the Netherlands, Austria, and Sweden seems clearly the result, in part, of similar factors. On the other hand, the less successful recent British efforts at voluntary income controls can be partially explained by the fact that the TUC and its affiliates are a less "solidaristic" movement. A

TUC mission to Sweden a few years back, in comparing the two labor movements, concluded, "The real differences lie in the sense of collective purpose that pervades the Swedish movement: in this sense there is no British trade union movement but only a collection of trade unions."[35]

The statement was almost prophetic. Put to the test under a labor government in 1965 and 1966, the British labor movement, and British society, simply proved unequal to the task of trying to operate a voluntary, central, uniform wage policy. Average wage increases went much beyond levels that were acceptable to the government and compatible with the country's balance-of-payments position and general productivity ability. The failure of the voluntary system prompted the government to freeze wages. During peacetime such an act is an extreme development for any market-oriented democracy.[36]

Does this British experience have any particular lessons for the United States?[37] Purely from a trade-union viewpoint, the AFL-CIO probably resembles the TUC more than any other movement in the world, even to the crucial characteristic that affiliated unions jealously guard their bargaining power from any intrusion by the central federation. Again, it is probably true that the TUC and the AFL-CIO are more alike, as compared with most other Western European labor centers, in that their members have less of that "sense of collective purpose" characteristic of movements in Sweden and in some other countries. (Lest this be taken *too* literally, it is worth recalling that the great wage drift, over the negotiated national wage formula, that persists in Sweden and other countries belies any absolute solidarity. In part the drift reflects the ability of more highly skilled workers to take advantage of their superior market position.)

If, then, the United States had to operate a strict wage-control policy in peacetime, it could probably not depend on voluntarism any more than the British. It should be added that economic circumstances in the United States are considerably different from those in Britain, and a need for strict wage controls seems less likely.

Effects of Wage Policy on Lower Levels of Labor Movement

As already indicated, long-term operation of a national wage policy may tend to reduce participation in critical wage negotiations by all but the very top officials of the labor movement. The integrated relationship with management and government that such a policy produces may render the top union leadership vulnerable to charges of bureaucratization. Where opposition Communist Party forces exist, they may seek to exploit some of the discontent that can arise from the limitations and restraints on normal collective bargaining that are produced by a national wage policy.[38]

It is also important to keep in mind that even where the central labor federation and most of its affiliated unions have accepted a national wage policy or even cooperated in constructing the control system, it is not uncommon to find certain unions, by no means necessarily under communist control, voicing opposition to the policy. For example, in Great Britain at present an important minority of unions has been opposing the newly emerging incomes policy, which has generally had the support of the Trades Union Congress asa whole.[39]

Aside from its effects on workers' sense of income equity, a system of national wage-policy bargaining can also lead to the neglect of many purely local bargaining grievances. Walter Galenson, writing of Denmark, says that there "has been a constant source of complaint by both parties, but particularly by the workers, who charge that minor demands which nonetheless are important to them are often shelved in the central bargaining sessions, to the detriment of sound industrial relations." Once a settlement is reached on major economic issues, there is heavy pressure on officials at the local level to avoid strikes and settle all other terms quickly.[40]

Further Economic Consequences of National Wage Policies

One student says that this "pursuit" of an incomes policy, in a number of Western countries during the 1960s, is marked by "fervent expectations" and a "curious unrealism." It is as though an incomes policy were a "magic road" or a "short-cut to an ideal economic world of steady prices and uninterrupted growth."[41]

The proponents of incomes policy chose to ignore the fact that they were asking wage earners and other groups to accept the existing division of wealth as basically fair and unalterable. They went on to argue that any effort to get more than one's fair share was self-defeating. As Andrew Shonfield says, ardent proponents of incomes policy assume a kind of "new Social Contract" in which different interest groups have accepted their relative positions. But among other things, this inevitably means that an incomes policy must take into account such problems as the taxation of capital and capital gains and the distribution of wealth.[42]

As a result, it is difficult to see how unions can keep out of many other areas of economic policy once a national wage policy remains in operation for some time. First of all, certainly, unions may insist upon some form of price control to go along with wage or income control, and they may possibly insist upon union participation in the agency that is set up to control prices. In both the Netherlands and Austria, for example, the institutions that have been developed to handle wage and price controls provide for union representation.

The process may go well beyond even this level, as in Denmark. National wage negotiations there have tended to become a crisis period during which "deals" are made on tax policy, food subsidies, and rent control as well as on wages. At the time of the 1962 settlement, the General Workers Union, representing the lower-income unskilled and semiskilled workers, took the lead in fighting for a raise in the income-tax exemptions for low-wage workers. At this time the socialist-led government was insisting on enacting a major sales tax to absorb the excess purchasing power it feared the wage settlement would create. The General Workers sought to offset the effects of the new sales tax on low-income families by getting the government to raise the amount of income to be completely exempt from income taxation—something which would be of prime benefit to the low-income workers and families.

During 1964, in Austria, the Federation of Trade Unions joined the employers' organizations on the Joint Price and Wages Council (the agency that administers the national wage and price policies) in recommending that the government take steps to reduce tariffs (in order to encourage import competition) and to use the balance-of-payments surpluses that had been built up in recent years (in order to reduce price pressures in domestic markets). From its beginning the federation had apparently looked upon the price-wage council as a device to help bring about union participation in the formulation of overall national economic policy.[43]

Wage Policies Encourage Employee Organization

It should now be readily appreciated that the institution of a national wage policy, in one form or another, is likely to spread union participation into many aspects of policy-making in a democratic society. As suggested earlier, a national wage policy may also have the effect of compelling any remaining unorganized large groups in the society—such as white-collar workers, farmers, or professionals—to organize in order to participate in these same processes and to protect their own interests.

Even where union participation does not involve a role in economic planning, but is limited to the function of making national wage policy, other employee groups are under pressure to organize. No national wage policy is absolutely uniform in its application. There are always variations, exceptions, special applications, and the like. Without organization, a given white-collar group, for instance, may be unable to argue its case before the control body (that is, of course, if the national wage policy involves a control body).

In the United States, foremen and nurses began their most serious efforts to engage in union types of activities during World War II when the National War Labor Board was controlling wages under a general wage formula (which, however, had provisions for exceptions). In order to carry a case before the board for treatment as an exception, it was necessary to create an organization of one form or another.

Wherever a national wage policy is put into operation, it is also likely to pose special problems for public employees. These problems differ from those of privately employed workers. Given the cracks and loopholes that are inevitable in the private economic sector of a democratic society, unions and employers can generally find some means of modifying broad national wage formulas. Moreover, in the private sector some groups of white-collar employees work on an individual salary basis, and this, too, permits private employers fairly wide latitude in evading wage formulas if they want to offset tight labor-market pressures by granting more than formula wage increases. The government, however, often sets the stiffest and least yielding wage formula for its own employees. Here there is likely to be very little wage drift. Some of the rising militance of public employees in many countries in recent years is attributable to their reactions against national wage policies.

As more and more groups organize for bargaining in a society, and as public desire for full employment becomes firmly institutionalized, traditional atomistic, supply-and-demand concepts of the labor market seem less workable. The results of formal, national systems of wage-policy control do not demonstrate, at least not yet, their superiority over traditional market forces. The future, however, is likely to see even more experimentation with such policies. Reconciling these policies—and the control systems that they may entail—with some of the historic freedoms of unions and management will be one of the challenging industrial-relations issues in the years ahead.

NOTES

1. References cited elsewhere in this chapter concern the experience of countries that have already made extensive use of national wage policy "systems." For the United States, see especially *Economic Report of the President,* together with *The Annual Report of the Council of Economic Advisers* (Washington, D.C.: Government Printing Office, January 1962), pp. 16–17, 167–190. Subsequent reports of the President and the Council of Economic Advisers spell out further details of the so-called wage-price guideposts, but see especially the 1964 *Report,* pp. 112–120.

Although the Conservative government began to move toward the establishment of a system of "guiding lights" for wage control in the early 1960s, only under the new Labour government (1965) have detailed plans to control incomes (including wages) been instituted. In France, planning and fiscal government officials in recent years have also stressed the desire for an "incomes policy," but as yet no formal system has been fully developed, or accepted by labor and management. The importance of minimum wage setting by government in France—as well as the relatively extensive state ownership of transport, industrial, and mining properties—gives the government considerable power over the labor market at all times. The policy concepts of the French government are summarized by Jan Dessau in "Recent Discussion on Incomes Policy in France," *British Journal of Industrial Relations,* November 1964, pp. 356–359; and by Neil W. Chamberlain, *Incomes Policy in France, Industrial Relations Research Association, Proceedings of The Nineteenth Annual Winter Meeting* (Madison, Wisconsin: Industrial Relations Research Association, December 28–29, 1966), pp. 116–124.

2. As one Australian scholar remarks, wage policy resulted not "from any deliberate legislative design." Rather, it developed from the fact that industrial relations, generally, have long operated under a system of state-imposed compulsory arbitration. As federal authorities (and state authorities) assumed responsibility for settlement of disputes, almost inevitably they had to fashion some sort of a wage policy as well. J. E. Isaac and G. W. Ford (eds.), *Australian Labour Economics Readings* (Melbourne: Sun Books, 1967), p. 3 (from the excellent introduction by the editors). Part I of this volume includes a number of illuminating readings on Australia's relatively long experience with national wage setting.

3. Mark W. Leiserson, *A Brief Interpretative Survey of Wage-Price Problems in Europe,* Study Paper No. 11 (Joint Economic Committee, 86th Congress, 1st Session, Washington, D.C.: U.S. Government Printing Office, 1959), pp. 43–45. This short study contains useful capsule descriptions of the policies and mechanisms of national wage controls in Sweden, the Netherlands, and Great Britain, as well as in Norway —all as of the late 1950s. For two recent, very good analyses of the Swedish incomes-policy system and some of the problems it has been encountering see: Jean Mouly, "Wages Policy in Sweden," *International Labour Review,* March 1967; and Steven D. Anderman, "Central Wage Negotiation in Sweden: Recent Problems and Developments," *British Journal of Industrial Relations,* November 1967.

4. William Fellner *et al., The Problem of Rising Prices* (Paris: Organisation for European Economic Cooperation, 1961), p. 58.

5. Anton Proksch, "The Austrian Joint Wage and Price Council," *International Labour Review,* March 1961, pp. 229–247; and *Labor Developments Abroad* (Washington, D. C.: U.S. Department of Labor, July 1963), pp. 1–2.

6. The U.S. Council of Economic Advisers based its wage guideposts upon a moving average of annual productivity increases during the past five years. See *Economic Report of the President* (1964), *op. cit.,* p. 115. In 1966, when this average threatened to lift the guideposts considerably, the council departed from it and kept to the figure set forth in its earlier reports.

7. Murray Edelman and R. W. Fleming, *The Politics of Wage Price Decisions,* (Urbana: University of Illinois Press, 1965), Chap. 5; and Ellen M. Bussey, "Recent Wage Control Policy in the Netherlands," *Monthly Labor Review,* May 1964, pp. 517–521.

8. The board's standards appear in *Ministry of Labour Gazette,* December 1966. For the reaction of the Electrical Trades Union, generally a supporter of the incomes policy, see "Who Needs Enemies?" in its journal, *Electron,* January 1967. For good descriptions of many aspects of so-called productivity bargaining in the context of the British incomes policy, see Lloyd Ulman, "Under Severe Restraint: British

Incomes Policy," *Industrial Relations,* May 1967, and Robert B. McKersie *The Significance of Productivity Bargaining,* paper presented to First World Congress *International Industrial Relations Association* (Geneva: September 4–8, 1967). (Mimeographed.)

9. For a good short summary of the Netherlands' experience, see David C. Smith, *Income Policies, Some Foreign Experiences and Their Relevance for Canada,* prepared for the Economic Council of Canada (Ottawa: Queen's Printer, 1966), Chap. 6. This volume is a valuable analysis of many of the issues posed by the institution of wage or income policies.

10. Hermod Skanland, "Incomes Policy: Norwegian Experience," *British Journal of Industrial Relations,* November 1964, p. 311.

11. *The New York Times,* September 13, 1966. Accepting the 3.2 productivity guidepost and recognizing the 3.5 cost-of-living increase in 1965–1966, the Secretary of Labor felt a 5% annual wage rise might not be "out of line." *The New York Times,* November 18, 1966. After 1966 the Secretary of Labor seemed to have withdrawn from this discussion. In its 1968 report the Council of Economic Advisers continued to oppose formal acceptance of the cost of living in its wage formula but seemed to recognize that as a practical matter negotiated wage settlements in 1968 would reflect price changes to some degree. The Nixon administration dropped the policy altogether in 1969.

12. The literature on this subject is becoming voluminous. In addition to studies already cited in this chapter, see B. C. Roberts, *National Wages Policy in War and Peace* (London: Allen, 1958); H. A. Turner and H. Zoeteweij, *Prices, Wages and Incomes Policies in Industrialised Market Economics* (Geneva: International Labour Office, 1966); and *British Journal of Industrial Relations,* Vol. II, No. 3 (November 1964). This issue is almost entirely devoted to the experience of various countries with "incomes policy." An evaluation of the United States' experience is John Sheaham's *The Wage-Price Guideposts* (Washington, D.C.: The Brookings Institution, 1967), and a critique of the guideposts' assumptions and application is Edward F. Denison, *Guideposts for Wages and Prices, Criteria and Consistency* (Ann Arbor: University of Michigan Press, 1968).

13. See Fellner *et al., op. cit.,* pp. 60–61, 388–390.

14. Information for Canada, Switzerland, Belgium, Denmark, and Norway does little to help determine whether countries with or without wage or income policies fared better. Taking the Consumer Price Index as a measure, eleven European countries, the U.S. and Canada ranked as follows in total price changes from 1953 to 1963:

Switzerland	108.6	−NC	Netherlands	129.4	−C
United States	114.0	−NC	Great Britain	130.2	−NC
Canada	115.2	−NC	Norway	134.1	−C
Belgium	115.2	−NC	Sweden	137.0	−C
Germany (West)	120.6	−NC	Denmark	140.7	−C
Italy	128.4	−NC	France	150.6	−NC

SOURCE: *O.E.C.D. Statistical Bulletin* (Paris: Organisation for Economic Cooperation and Development. I have used various issues of this monthly publication to construct this table.) C stands for controls or a wage policy during this period; NC stands for no controls or wage policy. Whether a wage policy or control system existed in part or in whole during these 10 years has been interpreted in the text. Thus, the Swedish national "single" or "frame" bargaining system, which does not involve government directly, is classified as an effort to effect a wage policy or control. The more formal Netherlands system is also placed in this classification. Technically, the U.S. wage guideposts were issued in 1962, but it was not until 1965 that the government began to press for them in a more systematic manner.

15. The best-known article in support of the unemployment-level wage move-

ment relationships is A. W. Phillips, "The Relations between Unemployment and the Rate of Change of Money Wage Rates in the United Kingdom, 1862–1957," *Economica,* November 1958. While economists have come to doubt any simple relationship in this area, a Swedish economist has recently argued that throughout Europe, allowing for a stipulated time lag, a close correlation can be demonstrated between levels of unemployment and wage movements—with subsequent efforts on labor costs. He suggests that since the problem is so often one of the effects of wage movements on the prices of goods that enter into foreign trade, it is more appropriate to judge the data for all of Western Europe together. See Karl-Olof Faxen, "The Swedish Cost Problem and the Range of Action for a Swedish Incomes Policy," *Skandinaviska Banken Quarterly Review,* March 1967.

16. See, for example, *Trade Unions and Full Employment* (Stockholm: LO, 1953), and T. L. Johnston (ed.), *Economic Expansion and Structural Change, A Trade Union Manifesto* (London: G. Allen, 1963).

17. *Report of the 90th Annual Trade Union Congress* (Blackpool: Trades Union Congress, September 7–10, 1964), p. 446–452.

18. "The Need for an Incomes Policy," *Socialist International Information,* December 19, 1964, p. 308.

19. Much of the erosion of the Netherlands' postwar wage policy began when its principal architect, socialist leader M. Suurhoff, along with the rest of the Socialist Party, left the government coalition.

20. *The New York Times,* March 30, 1962. The action by steel companies to raise prices and the intervention of President Kennedy to set aside these increases occurred after this column was written.

21. George P. Shultz and Robert Z. Albier, eds., *Guidelines, Informal Controls and the Market Place* (Chicago: University of Chicago Press, 1966), p. 90.

22. *Economic and Social Bulletin* (Brussels: International Confederation of Free Trade Unions, November–December 1964), p. 16. In setting its national wage-bargaining time schedules for 1966, the Norwegian Federation of Trade Unions also sought to prevent industrial workers from being disadvantaged vis-à-vis others. It fixed bargaining dates so that "the settlements both for agriculture and fisheries should be ready, so that their contents are known before the reply of the LO is given" to the employers. *Trade Union News Bulletin From Norway,* Oslo, January 1966, p. 6.

23. *Non-Wage Incomes and Prices Policy* (Paris: Organisation for Economic Cooperation and Developement, 1966).

24. George Meany, quoted by AFL-CIO Research Director Nathaniel Goldfinger in *News From the AFL-CIO,* February 14, 1966.

25. Among other reasons why the implementation of a national income policy will probably continue to encounter great obstacles in France (and Italy) is the existence of a plural union structure out of which no broad national consensus is likely to emerge between the free union federations and the major communist-led federation. Plural unionism as such, however, need not necessarily prevent such consensus, as the experience of the Netherlands with major socialist, Catholic, and Protestant federations demonstrates.

26. *The Daily Guardian* (Manchester), December 14, 1965. In Sweden or Austria, where union structure tends to be more purely industrial in character, only one or at most a few unions would be involved in negotiations with the "engineering" industry.

27. T. L. Johnston, *Collective Bargaining in Sweden* (Cambridge, Mass.: Harvard University Press, 1962), p. 246.

28. In the United States, the United Steelworkers' acceptance and promotion, along with major steel companies, of a national job-evaluation plan stemmed in part from its desire to insure a more uniform wage structure throughout the steel in-

dustry. It is also significant that the job-evaluation plan covering this industry was first directed by the National War Labor Board when it was "administering" wages by formula during World War II.

29. Walter Galenson writes of Norway's so-called sheltered industries, including construction that under the national wage policy their "high level of wages is due at least in part to the monopoly position enjoyed by these industries," which do not have to compete in foreign markets. See *Labor in Norway* (Cambridge, Mass.: Harvard University Press, 1949), p. 234. Swedish employers have protested against the exceptionally high wage structure that has developed in the building industry even in the face of centralized, uniform wage negotiations and settlements. See *LO, Information to Foreign Countries* No. 6, Stockholm, June-July 1965, p. 22. (Mimeographed.) Settlements higher than the guideposts during 1965 and 1966 in the U.S. construction industry led the government to bring heavy pressure against several building trades unions. *The New York Times,* March 22 and 31, 1966. On the keynote of the wage bargaining margin in export industries, so far as price stability in Sweden is concerned, see Erik Lundberg, "The Margin for Wage Increases," *Skandinavisica Banken Quarterly Review,* I (1969), 1–5.

30. A national wage policy has also resulted in increased power for employers' associations, as compared with the power of individual employers, in Western European countries.

31. For some years now, key labor leadership in U.S. railway negotiations, which often end up in high government offices, seems to go to men who have special skills in dealing with government agencies.

32. *The Guardian* (Daily). See the issue of September 9, 1965 for the action of the TUC, and the issue of October 19, 1965 for the hesitant following of the same path by the Confederation of British Industry. The CBI seemed even more reluctant than the TUC to accept this task, especially with respect to prices. See *The Guardian,* November 12, 1965. In practice, the CBI has not carried out price screening in the way in which the TUC has taken on the wage task.

33. *Industrial News* issued for the use of the press by the Trades Union Congress, "TUC Incomes Policy Bulletin No. 10, March 1968." On other occasions the TUC vetting committee has found that a much higher percentage of unions' claims were incompatible with the incomes policy.

34. For the government's position see *Productivity, Prices and Incomes Policy in 1968 and 1969* (London: Her Majesty's Stationery Office, 1968). The TUC position is to be found in Trades Union Congress, *Economic Review and Report of a Conference of Executive Committees of Affiliated Organisations 1968* (London: Trades Union Congress, 1968).

35. *Sweden, Its Unions and Industrial Relations* (London: Trades Union Congress, 1963), p. 23.

36. Even the official freeze did not seem to gain full compliance in Britain. At least two white-collar unions reported in their journals, without company names, wage-increase agreements they had negotiated after the freeze, and presumably in violation of it. See *DATA Journal*—organ of the Draughtsmen and Allied Technicians' Association—for October 1966: "Despite the Government's freeze DATA has, nevertheless, been able to reach settlements in recent weeks with a number of firms. Publicity is not being given to these settlements because of the obvious difficulties which might be created. At its last meeting the executive committee of DATA decided to advise members to continue to pursue claims in the normal manner." Somewhat similar items were to be found in ASSET, the journal of the Association of Supervisory Staffs, Executives and Technicians.

37. For an interesting comparison of British and U.S. wage policies, see D. J. Robertson, *Guideposts and Norms: Contrasts in U.S. and U.K. Wage Policy,* Reprint

No. 294 (Berkeley: Institute of Industrial Relations, University of California, 1967). A sharp *American* critique of British industrial relations policies and parctices is Lloyd Ulman's chapter in Richard E. Caves (ed.), *Britain's Economic Prospects* (Washington, D.C.: The Brookings Institution, 1968). David Smith's chapter in the same volume traces the operation of Britain's "Income Policy" in economic policy terms.

38. See, for example, Olaf Davison, "who profits by the 'Block Solution'?" *World Trade Union Movement,* May 1964, pp. 23–25. (This is a journal of the communist-controlled World Federation of Trade Unions). The article attacks the Danish labor movement and the socialist party for their participation in national wage policy negotiations, which also include agreements on taxes, prices, etc.

39. For a short but effective critique by Britain's largest union, see Harry Nicholas, Acting General Secretary, Transport and General Workers' Union, *Our View on Incomes Policy* (London: Transport and General Workers Union, n.d., *ca.,* 1965). By late 1966 and 1967, nearly all important TUC leaders had become increasingly critical of the government's wage policy. In March 1967, top TUC leaders won support of the great majority of its affiliates, including the largest unions, for a more voluntaristic incomes policy. This new proposal still did not represent a full break with the Labour government. See *Incomes Policy,* speech by George Woodcock, TUC General Secretary, March 2, 1967, Trades Union Congress; and TUC *Industrial News,* March 8, 1967.

40. Walter Galenson, *The Danish System of Industrial Relations* (Cambridge, Mass.: Harvard University Press, 1952), p. 120.

41. Andrew Shonfield, *Modern Capitalism, The Changing Balance of Public and Private Power* (New York: Oxford University Press, 1965), p. 217.

42. *Ibid.,* p. 219.

43. See the *Economic and Social Bulletin* (Brussels: International Confederation of Free Trade Unions, July-August 1964), pp. 26–29, for details of this joint state-mont; and also see Turner and Zoeteweij, *op. cit.,* p. 103.

XIII

Conflict and Integration in Western
Trade-Union Development

RADE UNIONS in modern Western history have in many respects developed in two seemingly contradictory ways. One of these processes is the apparently endless struggle for employees' rights at the work-site level, whether we are talking about a factory, office, construction location, mine, or railroad. Whether an enterprise is privately owned or publicly controlled, the very nature of the worker's position, somewhere at the bottom of a chain of command, makes him react to pressures of management as well as to job stresses and strains. Unionism is, of course, a vehicle for the expression of this reaction. Presumably these reactions and this function of unionism will continue indefinitely, as long as work in modern industrial organization has some hierarchical character.

The second developmental process takes place on a social and economic plane. In this case, unionism evolves as a force which integrates workers into society. This contrasts, in some respects, with the phenomenon of worker reaction that we have just described. In retrospect, on this social and economic plane, unionism has enabled large masses of workers to participate in the broad political and economic decision-making processes of a modern state. When it functions in this way, unionism relates workers more effectively to other forces in a society.

Although this latter aspect of unionism appears as an integrating force today, it actually had its modern beginnings during the last half of the nineteenth century with the workers' movements (unions and labor parties) for basic citizenship rights, including social, political and legal equality. So broad were the workers' needs and demands at that time that the programs of labor called for nothing less than a revolution in society—a revolution typically (though not always) framed in the Marxism of the day. This struggle left a permanent political mark upon the labor movements of Western Europe. It helps to account for the continued use of the socialist (or social democratic) label by most of Western European labor today.[1]

During the closing decades of the nineteenth century and the early years of the twentieth century, European workers won their citizenship rights—they won voting rights for themselves, educational opportunity for their children, and a large measure of social and legal equality. These great advances, achieved step by step, produced no dramatic revolution; instead, the very fact that they were gradual led to the insinuation of the labor movement into key institutional processes of the society. This is what is meant by the process of integration in union development.

Obviously the two processes of labor development do not have totally different characteristics. By serving as a "reactor" and constructive channel for workers' grievances and stresses at the job level, unionism, although based on conflict, in some ways also helps to maintain the worker as an integral part of the social order; but in this function there lies a certain *continuing* sense of hostility and conflict toward management. But it should also be observed that as unions participate in the broader decision-making processes in their societies, they often take positions in opposition to those of other groups. The very form of this integrative process—union representation on public boards, planning commissions, and the like—does not however, breed the same kind of hostility conflict that the enterprise or job relationship does. The integration process operates among equals, that is, organizations with equal standing and recognition in the decision-making processes. This contrasts with the enterprise, where the worker reacts from an inferior, hierarchical power position vis-à-vis management. Thus the two developmental processes we have been discussing produce their own particular types of hostility and conflict.

The foregoing is not intended as a new full-blown theory of trade unionism! Too great a flux in modern industrial life including automation and a more rapid rate of economic growth, the rise of unions in developing countries, aspects of labor development in such communist-style countries as Yugoslavia—all these forces make the times inauspicious for a new "universal" theory.

It should be noted, nevertheless, that some of the apparent disagreements between older theories of the labor movement seem to dissolve in the context of the two basic union processes we are describing. Thus, Selig Perlman's theory of unionism based on and keyed to job consciousness, job protection, and a philosophy of scarcity "fits" in part the first process of unionism, that is, its role in the representation of the worker at the work site. J. B. S. Hardman's concept of unions as economic and political power centers in modern society is consistent with the second process, as would also be Frank Tannenbaum's theory of the union as re-creating some of the social bonds characteristic of pre-market domi-nated economies.[2]

If communist labor theorists would admit the reality of conflict at the work-site level, and the need to express it openly, even unions in Soviet-bloc countries might fit these two categories to a degree! Such a superficial comparison with Soviet-style unions, however, really sug-gests that unions and industrial-relations systems are only subsystems of larger social and economic orders, and comparisons of institutions as between "orders" must be made with great caution. Critical differences exist in the social origins and natures of these orders. To illustrate the point with one such difference: The struggle for *individual* rights and freedom, so characteristic of the development of Western countries, has been lacking for the most part in non-Western countries. It has no real counterpart, for example, in Japanese history, and it will certainly not take the form of a primarily middle-class bourgeois struggle in many of the newer societies of Asia and Africa. Moreover, in the absence of this tradition, unions in the new societies will have philosophies and aspira-tions somewhat different from those of the West. It is easy to forget to what extent the struggles and goals of Western labor were shaped by the desires of workers to obtain some of the same status and freedom enjoyed by the bourgeoisie.

Unions as Channels for Conflict at the Job or Enterprise Level

To turn briefly to the first of these enduring functions or processes—namely, unions as channels for conflict at the local level—even if one hypothesizes a completely democratic and/or socialized economy, with worker representation in management, some hierarchy of powers or authority seems to be inherent in the very nature of modern economic organization. Functionally there are still managers and the managed. Under these circumstances, job problems will always be viewed differently by workers and management. Under these circumstances, too, groups in conflict seem inevitable in modern industrial organization. This conflict, of course, need not take, and in most of the world does not take, the form of Marxian class warfare, with all its revolutionary implications;[3] but conflict it is, and there is no reason to believe it will disappear. This remains true even as time and experience soften the rougher aspects of conflict, as areas of labor-management cooperation are enlarged, and as improved social machinery is developed to resolve *most* industrial con-flict without resort to open social ruptures in the form of strikes.[4]

The channels within which this conflict typically finds expression in modern Western industrial society tend to be conservative in character.

The rise of trade unions and the spread of collective agreements as the vehicles that channelize most of the conflict almost inevitably make the process conservative in tone.

Once recognized at the work site, the union has a great stake in preserving its role and functions. It exists to channelize worker discontent, but if it approaches this task without sufficient caution, it endangers its role in the enterprise and possibly the enterprise itself. This danger arises on the one hand from the fact that management nearly everywhere (with the possible exception of publicly managed enterprises) is usually tolerant toward unions only because they possess power and only rarely because it genuinely wants to embrace them as necessary social institutions. On the other hand, the union must also satisfy some of the practical day-to-day needs of its members if it is to survive and prosper. Experience demonstrates that obtaining satisfaction for workers derived *solely* from agitation is not likely to provide an enduring basis for union membership in modern industrial life.

It has already been noted that the very act of winning written collective agreements helps blunt any revolutionary thrust of the union movement. The written agreement involves acceptance of at least temporary periods of collaboration and compromise. Protest by radical forces in the labor movement against written agreements as manifestations of class collaboration recur in Western labor history.

The spread of written collective agreements (and the eventual acceptance even of some enterprise as contrasted with mere industry-wide agreements by communist unions in France and Italy as noted in Chapter VII) suggests, however, that they are necessary to check an employer's arbitrary, managerial power. Codes of law can substitute to a certain degree, as can a very powerful, militant union (functioning without an agreement); but neither is apt to be as fully effective as a well-administered collective agreement in protecting the day-to-day needs of workers on the job.[5]

The necessity of defending and advocating workers' interests has lain behind the accumulation of strike funds, union treasury reserves, and a more permanent form of union organization. This has brought with it an almost inherent caution or conservatism. Progress, almost necessarily, becomes a day-by-day, step-by-step affair at the industrial level.

But in spite of the gradualism, the institutionalization of conflict by means of collective agreements, the rise of unions with *their own* institutional needs, and the widening areas of cooperation between labor and management, the nature of the industrial process and the industrial hierarchy suggest that conflict itself will persist in modern economic life. It is difficult to conceive of modern economic organization without large numbers of workers in positions where they will to some extent feel "put upon" by the organization and its management. To the degree that areas and techniques of accommodation grow in industrial relations, use of the formal strike may continue to decline, although new problems such as automation or national wage policies will produce strains from time to time. The spread of unionism to new white-collar employees, both private and public, may further reduce strikes, since these groups usually come to collective bargaining without the same history of conflict and struggle that characterizes blue-collar employees. Nonetheless, the need to regulate or handle conflict at the work level has its own basis for continuity in union development.

Unions as Major Decision-Making Bodies

As already noted, the process of industrial conflict and the unions' role in dealing with it also tends to produce countertendencies: the collective agreement, the maturer relationship with management, and more cautious action by labor. In a larger sense, these tendencies are part of the second basic process of union development which leads to the integration of workers into the broad decision-making processes of modern economic life. Western labor movements, which in Europe embrace labor parties and cooperatives as well as trade unions, have constantly gone beyond the work site to influence legislation, public administration, and policy-making. As the various labor movements succeeded in changing the social order, in order to make it more responsive to workers' needs and aspirations, they also were caught up in its processes.

The achievement of basic citizenship rights, the construction of effective social security systems, the attainment of workers' housing cooperatives, cooperative travel and recreation associations, and the like—these successes helped to give the labor movements a sense of institutional equality in the society. By World War I most workers and labor movements had become sharply aware that they had more to lose than their chains.

In the 1920s and especially during the post-World War II period, this process of advanced social control blossomed. Labor movements have participated increasingly in industrial planning, labor-market and manpower operations, wage and price control boards, and other planning efforts. In many instances these functions are not merely advisory but involve the actual making of decisions. (See Chapter IV. Although our analysis has concentrated upon the role of socialist-oriented unions, it should be added that the Christian union movements have come to the same role in their respective countries.)

These enlarged responsibilities and functions take many forms. Recently one large American union, the United Automobile Workers, announced that its own newly established nonprofit social research institute had accepted a grant of over $67,000 from the U.S. Department of Health, Education, and Welfare to study the uses of certain benefits paid to survivors of deceased workers in the automobile industry. The study itself is no cause for surprise, but the establishment of a nonprofit institute by a union is, however, new, and the union's acceptance of a direct government research grant breaks new ground.[6]

The wider responsibilities of the union at the national level of society help integrate workers into the social order, but at the same time they may create tension within the labor hierarchy. Critical decisions made at the top seem increasingly remote from leaders and workers in the shop. Strikes are often frowned upon by top-level labor echelons, whose concern is more and more with the larger issues of economic growth, full employment, social welfare, inflation, and balance of payments.

In Great Britain, strikes in recent years have been overwhelmingly "unofficial"—in other words, they have been called without the support of official union leaders and outside the regular machinery that is set up by the unions and managements for handling disputes. To a lesser but significant extent, the same development can be observed in a few other European countries. In the United States, union-management relationships in key industries like automobiles and steel have matured considerably at the national level; but the usual biennial or triennial signing of a new agreement, setting forth national wages and working-condition benefits, is often met with protests and work stoppages by many individual local unions who find that their specific shop problems are neglected or are sacrificed to "larger" considerations.

The gap between the larger goals pursued by top labor leaders and the shop-level goals pursued by local union leaders may in part be the result of a communications problem.[7] It is more probable, however, that it is primarily a deeper manifestation of the two contradictory processes of union development. It is therefore not likely to disappear in the course of time. To the extent that the top-level planning efforts meet with continued success in the form of high levels of employment and rising living standards, the strains and frictions should, however, generally be bearable on all sides.[8]

The unrest of the union rank and file may also reflect some uncertainty about the nature of the new planning process, its relationship to traditional organs of decision-making in a democracy (such as parliaments), and doubts as to whether unions can function on an equal basis with representatives of industry in this area of activity. This, of course, is part and parcel of the broader social question of reconciling new forms of social power and control—the planning mechanism—with older, governmental institutions.[9]

A survey of Western labor evolution suggests that it is likely to develop further in the direction of national integration. The pace and precise character of labor integration will of course vary from country to country. But even as progress in participation and integration continues, conflict at the work level is also likely to persist.

Even at this level, however, the union role may be increasingly complicated by the actions of some large employers who seem to shun the traditional lines of conflict and try to assume some new initiative themselves in humanizing work relations.[10]

The changes in union policy and structure to meet these new challenges will not be accomplished without organizational friction in most countries. Traditional programs, policies, slogans, and tactics do not yield easily. A steady stream of articles inside and outside the union press testifies to the search for new paths. "What are we here for?" asked the General Secretary of the Trades Union Congress during its 1962 Congress as he reexamined the purposes of the British union movement.[11]

There are no simple or direct answers to George Woodcock's question. The institutions and processes involved are dynamic and pragmatic in character, and answers seem to come from the process itself. One can, however, draw some encouragement from the successful, evolutionary transformation of Western labor movements that has already occurred in the past seven or eight decades (with France and Italy as exceptions to some extent). Despite periods of difficulty and bogging down occasionally, they continue to evolve as important institutions of complex, changing societies.

NOTES

1. The reader wil recall that labor's early struggle for the rights of citizenship was not as protracted or as difficult in the United States, but it was characteristic of much of U.S. union effort in the 1820s and 1830s. In any event, as earlier noted, this struggle was completed, for white male adults, several decades before the modern American labor movement took form.

2. Selig Perlman, *Theory of the Labor Movement* (New York: Augustus M. Kelley, 1949; first printing, 1928). J. B. S. Hardman, "Labor in Mid Passage," *Harvard Business Review*, January-February 1953, pp. 39–48; Frank Tannenbaum, *A Philosophy of Labor* (New York: Knopf, 1951). For an early and somewhat different statement of the "integrative" aspects of Western trade-union development, see W. Milne-Bailey, *Trade Unions and the State* (London: G. Allen, 1934). Also see Sidney and Beatrice Webb, Part III, "Trade Union Theory," *Industrial Democracy* (London: Longmans, Green, 1902), especially Chap. IV, "Trade Unionism and Democracy."

3. Rolf Dahrendorf, criticizing the Marxian theory of class and class conflict, redefines class in his theory: "The term 'class' signifies conflict groups that are generated by the differential distribution of authority in imperatively coordinated associations" such as business enterprises and other organizations. Dahrendorf notes that despite

the great rise in the standard of living of Western workers, the public is "baffled" by "the continued reality of strikes." He argues that this bafflement simply fails to recognize that "conflicts are ultimately generated by relations of authority, i.e., by differentiation of dominating and subjected groups." See *Class and Class Conflict in Industrial Society* (Stanford, Calif.: Stanford University Press, 1961), pp. 204, 253–254. There is a tendency among some "later day" Marxists, who have stressed the theme of alienation of the worker in modern industrial society, to follow Dahrendorf (and others) in accepting the inevitability of "conflict" even under "socialism." See, for example, a summary of the views of the Polish sociologist Adam Schaff, in Z. A. Jordan's "Socialism, Alienation and Political Power," *Survey*, July 1966.

4. This general formulation of the nature of job or enterprise conflict in modern industrial society admittedly applies primarily to *industrial* workers and managers. There is evidence, nevertheless, that even in the case of white-collar and professional employees, where they are employed in large numbers, hierarchical and conflict strains often develop. The issues in conflict, especially in the case of professional employees, may be somewhat different in character from those that arise in purely *industrial* situations. Again, it should be noted that the intensity of union-management job conflict varies from country to country and seems to take its most intense form in England and the United States.

5. Needless to say, this judgment reflects the writer's American biases. Codes of law, labor courts, and the like, as indicated in Chapter VIII, play a much more substantive role in Western European labor relations than in the United States.

6. *IMF News in Brief* (Geneva: International Metalworkers, No. 23, September 1965). Also see *News from UAW, UAW Forms Research Institute* (Detroit: United Automobile Workers, August 3, 1965). A number of American unions have also accepted grants, under federal manpower legislation, to upgrade the skills of their members or to train less skilled workers.

7. Contrasting the relative unity between rank and file and top leadership in the Swedish labor movement with the rather serious breaches between these levels in the British Trades Union Congress, one leading British labor journalist writes, ". . . one of the first factors in his success that Mr. Arne Geijer, President of LO in Sweden, mentioned to me was the existence in every trade union branch of two, three or more men and women who 'really understand and accept' what their leaders in Stockholm are trying to do for their benefit when they agree to restraint in wages. The Swedish unions give large numbers of their members courses (often residential ones) in economics and the way in which their labor market system works." This same journalist contrasted this with the British workers' education effort, and spoke of its "limited kind of training in the basic functions of a shop steward . . . in most courses." See John Cole, "The Price of Obstinacy," *Encounter*, July 1963, p. 62.

8. The nonunion critic of the union movement today, especially in the United States and Great Britain, is usually short-tempered with the second of these processes: the narrower, more self-centered conflict at the work-site level. This process produces the occasionally discomforting strike, higher wages that are often translated into higher consumer prices, etc. These critics forget that this level of labor activity lies at the very foundations of the movement. The more "socially" preferred activities, labor's support for planning, social welfare, the expansion of educational opportunities, and the like—these would hardly be possible without the existence or support of the base of the union pyramid.

9. Andrew Shonfield has raised some searching questions about the problem of bringing the planning process inside government machinery and under democratic control. He notes, for example, that in France union leaders are "without authority" in important industry-planning commissions, and that the businessmen are inclined to cut them out of discussions when these are alleged to involve "business secrets."

Modern Capitalism, The Changing Balance of Public and Private Power (London: Oxford University Press, 1965), p. 232.

10. Jean-Daniel Reynaud makes much of this tendency and the possibility that the union role within the enterprise may be reduced in his "The Future of Industrial Relations in Western European Approaches and Perspectives," *International Institute for Labor Studies, Bulletin,* February, 1968. Reynaud is correct in his judgment of the more enlightened views of many modern employers, but he may be overly influenced by the relatively weak position of French unionism at the enterprise level as he judges the potential problems of all European unions. As was suggested in Chapter VIII above, the more dynamic character of European enterprise today is actually provoking new activities and structural reorganization by many unions, at the plant level.

11. For a discussion of this issue in Britain, see PEP, *Trade Unions in a Changing Society* (London: Political and Economic Planning, 1963). Also see the interesting interview of George Woodcock in "British Unions on the Move," *Free Labor World,* February 1963. While it is outside the scope of this volume, similar soul-searching and self-critical reflection go on in the "middle-class world," which tries to reconcile traditional concepts of individualism and liberalism with the enlarged role of the state in social welfare and planning today.

PART TWO *Unions and Industrial Relations in the New Nations*

XIV

Trade-Union Development in the New Nations:

A Comparative View

T

Types of Unionism in the West

O UNDERSTAND the special qualities of unionism in the development of the new nations, it is helpful to review union evolution in the Western World.

Without exception, the first unions in the West were formed in the eighteenth and nineteenth centuries as a reaction to, or as part of, the process of capitalist development. The spread of the market economy, with the resulting alienation of the worker from control over the sale of his products, stands out as one clear, common characteristic of the development of unions in the West. Market growth was a prime force, first in isolating the worker in the new productive process and then in motivating him, in many instances, to organize collectively to regain some control over his economic destiny. Sidney and Beatrice Webb have given a classic summation of this development:

This fundamental condition of Trade Unionism we discover in the economic revolution through which certain industries were passing. . . . the great bulk of the workers ceased to be independent producers, themselves controlling the processes, and owning the materials and the product of their labour, and had passed into the condition of life-long wage earners, possessing neither the instruments of production nor the commodity in its finished state.[1]

Though similar in origin, unions in the West are broadly and basically of two different types: the American type and the Continental European type. British unions fall somewhere in between, and unions in Latin countries also diverge somewhat from the general Continental pattern.[2]

From their modern beginnings, most Continental unions were part of a complex that embraced a labor-socialist party as well as a union movement. Class barriers—social, economic, and political—were real in nineteenth-century Europe, and labor movements took on revolutionary, class qualities in their struggle against them. Workers in the United States had long since gained basic citizenship rights, and they went forward in the framework of the American Federation of Labor to concentrate on "business" or, more exclusively, economic unionism. American unions, with rare exceptions, established no continuing attachment to any political party or class programs.

Although there are two different principal patterns of unionism in the West, they have certain critical characteristics in common. First and foremost, for purposes of comparison with other societies, all have been shaped by their struggle with private, capitalist employers. The state assumed some role in the economic development of Western nations, but the prime task in this development everywhere fell to the private, capitalist sector.

The development of unions in the West was also deeply affected by the fact that political modernization—out of which emerged the modern, rationally administered national state—was largely accomplished before the appearance of modern unionism, which dates from the last decades of the nineteenth century. Of importance, too, was the fact that political and economic modernization proceeded along *separate* tracks, each with its own sets of leaders and groups.

To an important extent, unionism had to develop its own "private" counterthrust to meet *private*, independent capitalist management, which played the central role in Western economic development. Labor's struggles for economic and political rights, while often interrelated (especially in Europe, as we have already noted), were also separable operationally, because of the private character of capitalism, as opposed to the public struggle for political rights.

This state of affairs imparted many distinct characteristics to unionism in the West. It made it easier for unions to develop their own clear-cut institutions separate from the labor political parties. And it encouraged development by the unions of independent systems of financial support. (Today European labor parties are often dependent upon the unions for financial support; there is no union dependence for financial support on labor or socialist parties.) It led the unions to develop their own leaders who were not financially dependent upon political parties.

To an important extent Western labor movements remained outside society, politically and economically, for a number of decades while they carried on their struggles. Only in recent decades has this position changed; today union movements are integrated into society. This process of integration is still fairly new and, as yet, it is difficult to grasp its full implications for Western labor movements.[3]

Forces Shaping Unionism in Developing Nations

Space precludes consideration of all the major forces that are shaping unionism in the developing nations. Concentration here is on political and economic forces, although a fuller treatment would demand that religious, communal, tribal, and caste influences be treated, as well as special climatic and population factors.

The term "developing nations," or, in this context, the non-Western World, refers to so many countries that we must be very cautious before making any generalizations. For every general proposition about union development in the less developed countries, there are at least a few and often a score of exceptions. Far less than in the Western world can one find any great uniformity in class, cultural, or political background and history. Moreover, since less developed nations, as compared with Western nations, can vary all the way from a gross national product of $50 or $60 per capita up to $500 or $600 per capita, we are here concentrating primarily on the lower and middle parts of this range. In terms of geography, our concentration will be mainly upon Asia and Africa. Latin America, where the per capita product is higher, and where political development is advanced by comparison with most of the non-West, will be treated more briefly.

Political Unionism in Developing Areas

What are the characteristics or forces that distinguish or shape the development of unionism in the newly developing societies, particularly when this process is compared with what we know about Western development? To begin with, there is the striking fact that in most of these nations political modernization and economic modernization are proceeding side by side. Colonialism has barely come to an end, and the new societies are faced with the twofold task of structuring new forms of political government while they strive for accelerated economic development. This places a strain on all groups in the society, and trade unions are no exception.

In many of the developing areas, in the time before independence was achieved, the unions were part of the nationalist struggle for freedom against the colonial powers. A working alliance, formal or informal, between unions and nationalist parties was a logical development in many cases. As we suggested earlier, when workers lack citizenship rights, labor movements are inevitably highly politicized. When such rights are lacking for the great majority of the society, as was the case in the colonial areas, the political sweep can be even more irresistible.[4]

The nature of the anticolonial struggle in many of these countries amplified the political tone of union activity. In Africa, where there was hardly any significant *native* manager-owner middle class, and where industry was foreign-owned and managed by another *race*, trade-union activity, even when conceived with exclusively economic goals in view, almost inevitably had social and political overtones. Audrey Wipper, writing of union development in French West Africa, comments, ". . . the pattern of labor conflict highlighted the hostility between the Europeans and Africans. The institutional complex was so geared as to focus protest onto that twin-headed ogre, the 'capitalism-colonialism' issue, the abolition of which was seen as the panacea of all ills."[5]

So heavy was the impact of politics in many of the developing societies during the period when trade unions were being formed, that it frequently was the local or national political leader who took the initiative to form the first unions. Many of the new unions were shaped by a mixture of motives that included concern for the workers' economic plight and the desire to build a political base.

Much has been made of the domination of unionism in the developing nations by "outsiders." To many Western trade unionists, this has been a source of concern, an uneasy feeling that the union leaders in the new countries were merely using the unions for their own purely political ends. A distinguished participant in Indian trade-union development shows the other side of the coin, however:

The workers were not, however, in a position to take upon themselves the task of organisation. They were illiterate, ignorant and backward. . . . They were not a homogeneous mass, having come to the factory from different parts of the country. There was a wide social gulf between them and the employers and managers and other officers. . . . They were afraid of the employers and their officers and of the police and the government. In this situation, they needed some outside assistance to get over their initial feelings of fear and nervousness and to learn the rudiments of agitation and organisation. Some eminent public men, political leaders and social workers came forward during those early years of the movement to render that much needed and invaluable assistance.[6]

The inability of manual workers to communicate with management even in the latter's language, whether English, French, or Dutch, often made for dependence upon "outside," educated leaders. In parts of Asia, notably India and Ceylon, where caste played such a major role in the relationships between groups, the workers almost invariably turned to higher caste, more educated leaders to present their cases to management or government.

Jobs for skilled manual workers, such as craftsmen or railway engineers in many of the most important enterprises (mines or railways) were usually not open to African blacks, but were reserved for Europeans or Indians. As a consequence, skilled craftsmen—who everywhere in the

West were the early, natural leaders of the union movement—were often not available to help Africans unionize. In a number of early union efforts, this also made for some dependence on outside white-collar workers.

In major Asian countries, modern industrial organization was often introduced abruptly, more or less superimposed on the rest of the economy, and the old-style craftsman or artisan was not drawn into the industrial process. As a result, industrial workers (such as those in India) did not come from the ranks of artisans or craftworkers who tended to remain in the villages. Harold Butler writes that as a consequence, there were "few well-knit bodies of skilled craftsmen such as formed the backbone of trade union development in Western countries."[7]

Scalapino, similarly noting the tendency of craft and handicraft workers in Japan to remain outside the modern economy, and preserve their small-employer, guild-like attitudes, observes that this served to "restrict working-class consciousness and union activities among a portion of the labor aristocracy who, in many cases in the West, were pioneers in craft unionism." He adds that most "handicraft and building trades workers" found the "transition into modernism exceedingly difficult," and generally "they refused to identify themselves with any portion of modern industrial labor, and stoutly rejected participation in the labor movement."[8]

In most less-developed societies, ignorance and illiteracy, as well as tribal, caste, regional, or religious differences among workers, made it less possible for them to take effective, day-to-day, industrial action. It was often easier to call the workers into the street for a short, political type of demonstration at which they vented their numerous grievances than it was to hold them together in a tight, disciplined strike for "bread and butter" bargaining. Incidentally, this continues to be the case with many of the unions, even after national independence has been gained.

The very weakness of the unions also continues to lead them to rely upon government and the exercise of political power. In many instances, a government arbitration award might bring more benefits than would any direct action against the employer.

But whatever the reasons, the political coloration of unionism in the new countries was deep and continues to be deep. It affects the very forms of unionism. In Africa and Asia the primitive economic base has made it difficult for industrial or craft unions of the Western type to emerge. There are usually not enough printers, machinists, or textile-mill workers with which to form a base for individual national unions in their trades or industries. Also, political factors tend to press unions structurally into geographic rather than industrial forms. Political leaders came to understand that a local, regional, or broad national locus of union power was likely to be more adaptable for political purposes than the power of industrial or craft unions, which might have formed the base for a more purely economic effort. A report on British Guiana in 1949 noted:

In British Guiana, as in the rest of the West Indies, politics are the all absorbing concern of the people and trade unionism there has reversed the natural pattern by developing the political before the industrial aspects of organisation. There have thus been examples of "personalities" founding organisations with one eye to political gain . . . more than to the real benefit of the worker.[9]

After independence comes, such leaders as serve the union movement may also be attracted by better paid or more prestigious positions in government. The following complaint of the Nyasaland Trade Union Federation has been echoed in many countries:

Perhaps the biggest problem of all facing the Nyasaland trade-unions today is that of leadership. We are under no illusion that the present trade-union leadership is the best the country has to offer. But here we come up against the phenomenon that so many educated people are being canalised into the political movement at the expense of the labour movement. It is unfortunately true that to many Nyasas an easy way into the legislative council is more important than the interest of the workers.[10]

One of the more effective, highly charismatic leaders of a general workers' union in the Bombay area of India entered politics and scored a spectacular upset election victory in the 1967 parliamentary elections. His political prestige seemed to soar in succeeding months, but he subsequently seems to have lost control of parts of his union. This particular union clearly seems to be suffering from the leader's need to divide his time between political and union activities.

As literacy and industrial experience advance in less-developed countries, the availability of potential union leaders who come directly from the ranks of the industrially employed will undoubtedly increase. At the same time there is likely to be a growth of unions more in keeping with the industrial needs of workers, including stronger national unions as opposed to unions that concentrate on political objectives.

Party and State Pressures on Unionism
Following Independence

Even after independence is achieved, political ties between union and party may persist; in any case party and/or governmental pressures on unions to conform to overall political goals and programs are great. Confronted with such great divisive forces as tribalism, communalism, regionalism, and the vestiges of colonialism—as well as the desire for rapid economic development—the concept of any fundamental separation between unions and government, or between unions and parties, seems impossible to many political leaders in the new countries. This is especially so in Africa, where the new political regimes lack deep roots and seek support anywhere they can find it. To African party leaders who have helped to build the unions or have collaborated closely with them in the struggle for liberation, the idea that each shall now go his own way is unacceptable.

Julius Nyerere, political leader of Tanzania, argues:

The Trade Union Movement was, and is, part and parcel of the whole Nationalist Movement. In the early days (before independence) when a Trade Union went on strike, for instance, and its members were in dire need of funds to keep them going, we saw no doctrine which would be abrogated by our giving financial support from the political wing to the industrial wing of the same Nationalist Movement. It would clearly have been ridiculous to preach . . . [a] doctrine of "independence" of the T.F.L. [Tanganyika Federation of Labour] from political control and so deny them the assistance they needed from T.A.N.U. [nationalist political alliance].[11]

By the same token, Nyerere argues, the union continues to be part of the nationalist movement after independence. "Trade Unions and the Political organisations are prongs, or 'legs' of the same Nationalists' Movement. . . . In Africa there are no traditional, contending classes, and governments are socialist, the government represents the workers, and the workers can no more be independent of it, than can it be independent of the workers."

While this doctrine of the necessity for organic activity between trade unions and the governing party is fairly widespread in Africa, there have been important exceptions in countries like Nigeria or the Congo.

Where private enterprise has a significant role in the economy (Malaya is a good example) and/or where political power has been more diffused by reason of regional or tribal differentiation (Nigeria), there has been less pressure on the unions to renounce their independence and enter into full collaboration (or subordination) to the party or government apparatus. Also, where political institutions seem to be more firmly planted, as in India and even in Ceylon, greater union independence and union pluralism are more probable. These are only variations in degree, however (though degree can, admittedly, be crucial here), and the pressures for control of the unions and/or industrial relations are great virtually everywhere in the less developed world.

Generally, as long as its own legitimacy remains uncertain, a new government finds it hard to accept the "independence" of any other force in the country. Trade unions can be particularly suspect since they are concentrated in the modern sector of the society—among people who can readily be mobilized, even though their numbers are small. The key role of numerically small trade unions in serious uprisings in several African governments in the past half dozen years (including Dahomey and Congo-Brazaaville) is a tribute to their potential power in the new societies.

The methods of controlling unions in situations like these vary, but the attempt to limit their independence is almost universal. African unions are sometimes incorporated into the broad government-party coalition that is ruling the nation (Tunis and Algeria are good examples).

When a nation has won independence, and the government is strong, the methods of controlling unions are more varied. In Ghana and Tanganyika the unions were "reorganized," reduced in number, and placed under direct state control; their top leaders became subject to government approval or appointment. Finances for the unions generally come from a government-imposed checkoff of workers' dues. Kenya has taken steps in the same direction, though the process of control has not been quite as total.[12]

Government concern with the potential political strength of unions in some countries has led to the specific legal prohibition of union "political" activities. Formally, at least, this has been a pattern quite common in Latin America—though the unions themselves often do not observe it. The device has also been employed in other areas; in Egypt, for example, legislation prohibits unions from "dealing with political questions." In Malaya, where direct political activity by the unions is regarded with some suspicion by the government, the law regulating unions nonetheless specifically permits political funds for the support of candidates and parties, for political literature, and for like political activities. Contributions to such funds are strictly voluntary, however, and are made only by members "who specifically agree to contribute"—who are said to "contract in" for political contributions.[13]

Perhaps detailed union registration laws constitute the most general method of government control over unionism in many of the new societies. While such laws are not uncommon in the West, they are more comprehensive in the new countries and give control authorities wide powers of intervention in union life. Especially in ex-British colonies, union registration laws are an inheritance from the pre-independence period. As such they were often disliked by the unions that were struggling against colonialism. If anything, however, the tendency during postindependence has been to strengthen the government's hands under these laws. (Legally required registration of unions is also widespread in Latin America.)

The involvement of unions in politics is not, however, merely a result of state or party pressure upon them. Confronted with a situation in which the whole of a society is being constructed, the unions can hardly keep away from politics. Political modernization and economic modernization are simultaneous and interrelated processes in Asia and Africa, and to a lesser but still significant extent in parts of Latin America.

Relations of Unions and Parties in the New Nations

As we have observed, unions in the West today are independent of government and have relatively free relationships with political parties. Development along these lines tends to be the exception rather than the rule in much of the developing world. It can be argued that the political commitment of non-Western unionism is paralleling pre-World War I European union development, as far as the struggle for workers' citizenship rights is concerned. But the relationship of this early European labor movement to political and governmental forces was more voluntaristic in nature. Moreover, as workers' basic legal and social rights are established in the new societies, there is not likely to be any rapid depoliticalization of the labor movements or easing of government controls over them. Economic forces also produce a different, more state-related form of unionism from that which developed in the West.

This matter of trade-union independence and the nature of the trade-union "function" in the new societies of Asia and Africa—and, to some extent, in the countries of Latin America—is one of the most debated issues in international trade-union forums. Earlier in this chapter Julius Nyerere was quoted on the necessity for unity between the ruling party and the unions. His view is commonly held in many of the new countries.

On the other hand, the long-time General Secretary of the International Confederation of Free Trade Unions (ICFTU), Omar Becu, was very much concerned with this tendency of governments in the new societies to infringe upon trade-union freedom. He therefore wrote a thoughtful, major article on the subject, in which he addressed himself both to the unions, who he feared might confuse their functions and thereby jeopardize their independence, and to the political authorities. He noted that the International Labour Organization in several of its basic conventions has sought to set forth the necessity for unions to preserve their independence. Even in cases where unions "decide to establish relations with a political party or to undertake constitutional political action, as a means towards the advancement of their economic and social objectives," this should not "compromise the continuance of the trade-union movement or its social and economic functions irrespective of political changes in the country."

Agreeing with the general proposition, Becu added, ". . . trade-unions have a primary responsibility toward their members in the service of whom they have a continuous and fundamental task to perform. They have the specific obligation to prove their effectiveness in the field with which they are most directly concerned, that of collective bargaining—free and voluntary cooperation with other progressive forces is necessary for the common weal, but no political party, however close its affinities with the trade union movement may be, is in a position to carry out the everyday activities of the trade-unions."[14]

R. J. Magongo, General Secretary of the Tanganyika Federation of Labor, some years before its absorption by the government, also opposed Nyerere's view of the union movement. While accepting the necessity for cooperation between unions and government, Magongo argued: "If trade unions are to do their job properly and efficiently, their freedom has to be maintained. By this I mean that trade unions should be free from domination by any political party." Unless such freedom can be maintained, the very function of the unions is jeopardized if "they are no longer free. . . . they cannot fulfill their obligations to their members nor indeed to the nation as a whole, for they do not act on their own policies but by direction of the political party in power."[15]

Unions and the Government in Kenya

The debate continues in Asia and Africa. The difficulties and dilemmas of trade-union development in the new countries are exemplified by what has happened in Kenya. Tom Mboya, a high-ranking cabinet minister and former General Secretary of the Kenya Federation of Labour (KFL) has argued for a middle-of-the-road position on the question of union independence and responsibility. Mboya calls upon the labor movement to realize that today there is no place for yesterday's obstructiveness (slowdowns and even industrial-sabotage), which was "sometimes found to be proper means in the battle to free our countries from imperialism." Unions must rethink their relationships and functions and adopt new attitudes on work and cooperation in the now free and independent states.

Mboya calls upon union leaders to reeducate "their followers to change their attitudes towards the government." Difficult as it may be, union members must be persuaded, "that the businessman who yesterday was the arch-supporter of the colonialist regime today becomes the colleague of their nationalist government." The unions must also "persuade the workers that if we are to progress, they must put greater effort into their work."[16]

Virtually as soon as it became an independent nation, Kenya established its industrial-relations system on the foundation of a voluntary, negotiated Charter of Industrial Relations (1962), to which government, the Kenya Employers' Federation, and the Kenya Federation of Labour were all signatories. This charter spelled out and sought to facilitate the process of union recognition, the conclusion of agreements between unions and managements, and the peaceful, though voluntary, settlement of disputes. The unions also agreed to discourage bad work practices among employees.[17]

Because of reluctance by management in a number of cases to extend full recognition to the unions and because of a series of difficult strikes and severe conflicts between competing union groups, the Kenyan government took new action. Today the matter of industrial relations is much more closely controlled, and the government has the right to impose compulsory arbitration in disputes.[18] Unions are closely supervised under a registration law that has been made more strict. The unions in Kenya have been reorganized by government action; only a single new federation is permitted, which operates under close government surveillance and replaces the groups who in the past were in competition.[19]

Under these new statutes, the unions can benefit from a form of compulsory checkoff, but since this is imposed and controlled by the government, union independence is in some ways lessened.[20]

Although in recent years government control over unions and industrial relations has been considerably extended in Kenya, it is still a far cry from the pattern in Tanganyika and in some other African states where the unions are virtually incorporated into the ruling party and/or the state.

The Singapore National Trade Union Congress has made a particularly eloquent and subtle statement of this problem of union freedom in the difficult political circumstances confronting the new countries of Asia and Africa. The SNTUC recognizes the difficulty of maintaining a separation between unions and political parties, especially because so many of the basic problems of union members (better health, education for their children, more rapid economic development, etc.) call for political action.

The SNTUC also appreciates the highly divisive, centrifugal forces at work in the new societies, and the need for all modern forces to overcome the "inertia of tradition." It observes, by way of summary, that the two movements, the political movement and the union movement, "each in full freedom should reach an agreement to which both can give full hearted loyalty."

The SNTUC realizes the difficulties of reaching such an accord under political conditions prevailing in most of the new states of Asia, "where there is no established national tradition to keep differences within national bounds, where personal tribal or communal, and ideological interests diverge, where elite ability is scarce, where the organised democratic dialogue of public debate is considered as a waste of abilities and as hostile to action." If agreement is not possible, asks the SNTUC, "can agreement be reached by compromise, and consultation between [the] separate organisations, the primacy of the political moment being accepted." Or, in the absence of agreement or compromise, "must the trade Union movement become a disciplined subordinate of [the] political movement."[21]

Union and Party in Algeria

Practically speaking, one often finds even the most politically committed union movement drifting toward some independence of action in the new countries. Algeria is a good example. Here the movement was begun by the underground nationalist forces in the struggle against France in 1954.

When Algeria became independent, the union movement was included in the ruling party's total governing complex. In spite of this close relationship and control, on two occasions the government has felt compelled to intervene directly and almost brutally, in order to change the unions' top leadership, which it found to be too independent and demanding.

The union (Union Générale des Travailleurs Algériens), despite its unwavering devotion to the cause of the party program and to socialism, feels itself shut out of party councils on critical decision-making. Moreover, many of its members accuse the UGTA of not being militant enough, while the political leaders charge it with posing too many problems and with agitating even to the point of being in opposition.

The U.G.T.A., mass organization of the Party led and inspired by the militants and composed of producers is most devoted and concerned for the cause of Socialism, and can in no manner be accused or suspected of deviationism. . . . However, it has not had its fair position either in the councils of the party or in the affairs of economic life.

And,

. . . paradoxically, our Organisation finds itself charged by the workers for its lack of aggressiveness in pressing their legitimate demands.

While, at the same time, the political leaders of the country

. . . accuse it of raising difficulties, provoking agitation, even of being an opposition.

As a result the "union movement finds itself between the hammer and the anvil."[22]

In Tunisia, where ties between the ruling Neo-Destur Party and the union movement have been somewhat looser, on several ocassions the government has nevertheless seen fit to change the leadership of the union movement.

Indian National Trade Union Congress and the Congress Party

Even in countries where there is more than one party, the ideological ties between unions and government (where the labor-oriented party is in power) can be troublesome. The Indian National Trade Union Congress, identified with the ruling Congress Party of India since the union was founded in 1947, is a good case in point. In July 1966 the INTUC devoted a special seminar ("the first of its kind in the history of our Organization") to these party-union relationships. The results were highly publicized in the union press.

The seminar issued a declaration to the effect that INTUC was independent politically and that no special labor party should be organized. It did note, however, that both itself and the Congress Party "have been inspired and influenced by Mahatma Gandhi and Pandit Jawaharlal Nehru and cherish identical aims and ideology within their respective spheres, which are virtually complimentary." The INTUC, not surprisingly, has worked closely with the Congress.

INTUC complains that some party leaders are not satisfied with the support the union renders and "are demanding servile allegiance of it." For its part, INTUC fears that it is being used by the party, without being given a real role in decision-making. INTUC calls for reestablishment by the party of the policy "of inviting the INTUC President to the meetings of the Congress Working Committee and . . . [to set up] a Labor Liaison Cell in the AICC." It also calls upon the party "to take INTUC into confidence and consult it when electing candidates for Constituencies in which the Labour vote is a factor worth reckoning." This hardly sounds like union independence of parties. There is also a bitter undertone in the statement charging that some Congress Party officials favor other labor leaders who may be claiming a connection with the INTUC without its approval.[23]

As far as collective bargaining is concerned, the INTUC seems to have been assisted from time to time by the ruling Congress Party government in such matters as official recognition, decisions on wage boards, and the like. On the other hand, there are other union federations in India (as well as rival, opposition political parties), and these have been able to take a more independent and militant line in many situations where INTUC has behaved "responsibly"—in other words, with an eye on its partner, the ruling party. As a result, INTUC's appeal to workers in a number of industrial situations has deteriorated in recent years. For this reason, too, the INTUC has become restive in its relationship with the Congress Party.

Unions and the Ruling Party in Mexico: A Case of Assimilation

In a few of the developing countries this vexing issue of party-union relationships seems to have reached a steadier and an apparently workable and mutually satisfactory relationship. Such is the case in a few Latin American countries, where development, both economic and political, is more "advanced" than in most of Asia and Africa. This offers an insight into one possible line of union evolution.

A prime example is Mexico. Here the unions have come to constitute one large and reliable section of the ruling revolutionary party. The unions are assigned their quota of candidates on the party's ticket for legislative offices and a share of the party's patronage. Also, they have some voice in the party's programs and councils.[24]

Where such an equilibrium is reached and the union movement begins to fit into the institutions of a newly developing nation, as in Mexico and in a few other Latin American countries, the movement can become the target of new charges. In some of these instances it is alleged that the unions, in return for modest gains for their own members, neglect the interests of the great mass of people, including the peasantry, most of whom are still terribly poor.[25]

Unions: Part of the Establishment in Some Latin American Countries

Victor Alba, long a student of labor in Latin America, believes that the assimilation of the unions into the ruling power structure in a number of countries eliminates them as a potential source of further social revolution.[26] He comments on the unionized worker's preoccupation with "immediate aims" because "Exploitation is so blatant that any theoretical explanation is useless," and concern with "the future" is too remote. Alba, though a dedicated democrat, sounds almost like Lenin in his criticism of the union's mere "economism" in Latin America, at a time when, in Alba's view, social reform and revolution, including sweeping land reform, continue to be the need of the day.[27]

A somewhat similar analysis of the role of Latin American unions has been made by an American scholar, Henry Landsberger. He finds that, in spite of the radical, seemingly revolutionary statements of many labor leaders, "Labor's goals are economic, not ideological," and not revolu-

302

tionary or very radical. He adds that "its means for reaching these goals are via politics" because the societies have been so structured that decisions flow more readily through the political apparatus than via industry itself. Moreover, many sectors of labor seem to have more political than economic power, partly because of Latin America's stagnant development and partly because of its more rapid political development."[28]

The problem of union-party-government relationships recurs constantly in the less developed countries. While we have described one general, very widespread pattern of relationships and problems, this one pattern does not hold, of course, for all countries.

To mention a few other possibilities: In several Latin American nations, the heritage of feudalism and capitalism seems to have cast a few important labor movements into a position of deep class hostility to the social and economic order—a position somewhat resembling that of European labor in the nineteenth century. The labor movements in these countries, at least in this stage, do not fit well into the Alba-Landsberger pattern just described. In Japan, just now passing from a less to a more fully developed state, the union movement and the industrial-relations system seem at this stage of history to be a unique blend of both traditional and revolutionary forces.[29]

Persistence of Unionism in the New Nations

It is interesting to see that despite the difficulties they create, almost nowhere in the new countries of Asia and Africa is there a move to suppress unions entirely. The influence of the International Labour Organisation and its standards of protection for unions and the right to bargain, which have long enjoyed great prestige in the less-developed nations, help account for the wary attitude of governments toward unions. The pressure of international trade-union organizations, such as the International Confederation of Free Trade Unions, is an additional supportive factor for many union movements in new countries. Finally, a general identification of unionism with modernism has developed in the present era.

While the potential importance of unionism for modernization is still insufficiently understood, one does find growing appreciation of this aspect of labor development. Unionism contributes to modernization, for example, through integration of ethnic groups. In discussing such integration, the distinguished Indian sociologist, N. K. Bose, has noted that despite the increase of urban groups in India, very few are actually bringing about "integration of the [many] ethnic groups." In his study of Calcutta, only two organizations were contributing to such integration, one was the Rotary Club. The other, however, is the union movement. Of the latter, he writes, it is "in the labor unions where workmen from different cultural backgrounds do unite to promote their collective interests."[30]

NOTES

1. Sidney and Beatrice Webb, *The History of Trade Unionism* 1st ed. (London: Longmans, Green, 1894). For a similar, "market" explanation of the emergence of American unionism, see John R. Commons and Associates, *History of Labor in the United States* (New York: Macmillan, 1918), Chap. I–III.

2. See Chaps. I, II, III, VI.

3. See Chap. XIII.

4. On the "inevitability" of political unionism under these conditions, see Bruce Millen, *The Political Role of Labor in Developing Countries* (Washington, D.C.: Brookings Institution, 1963).

5. "A Comparative Study of Nascent Unionism in French West Africa and the Philippines," *Economic Development and Cultural Change,* October 1964, p. 40. Elliot Berg and Jeffery Butler believe that the political involvement of unions and politics in parts of middle Africa has been exaggerated. "Trade Unions and Politics in Middle Africa," in James Coleman and Carl Rosberg (eds.), *Political Parties and National Integration in Tropical Africa* (Berkeley: University of California Press, 1964). While the preindependence period may be a subject of debate, as far as union involvement in politics in particular African countries is concerned, there is little doubt that politics and state action drastically influence the unions in the post-independence period nearly everywhere.

6. V. B. Karnik, *Indian Trade Unions, A Survey* (Bombay: Labor Education Service, 1966), p. 28.

7. Butler quoted in *Ibid.,* p. 21.

8. See the chapter by Robert A. Scalapino on Japan, in Walter Galenson, (ed.) *Labor and Economic Development* (New York: Wiley, 1959), p. 95.

9. Quoted in Walter Bowen, *Colonial Trade-Unions* (London: Fabian Colonial Bureau, 1954), p. 7.

10. *Free Labour World,* April 1961.

11. Julius Nyerere, "The African Trade Unions," speech, Dar Es Salaam, December 1960. As the newest of the developing areas, Africa has been the subject of a series of useful studies on unions and politics. See Jean Meynaud, *Trade Unionism in Africa* (London: Methuen, 1967); Ioan Davies, *African Trade Unions* (London: Penguin Books, 1966); and George Lynd, *The Politics of African Trade Unionism* (New York: Praeger, 1968).

12. We write here of the unions in "Nkrumah's" Ghana. See Douglas Rimmer, "The New Industrial Relations in Ghana," *Industrial and Labor Relations Review,* January 1961. Since the overthrow of Nkrumah's Ghana, the reorganized trade-union movement in that country seems to have become more independent, apparently with the assent of the new government. On the other hand, the new union movement seemingly has accepted some of the structural reforms that the Nkrumah government pressed on unions. In Tanganyika, the 1964 trade-union law required that the reorganized National Union of Tanganyika Workers become part of "The Tanganyika African National Union (the ruling political party) and do everything in its power

to promote the policies" of TANU. Also see *The Policy on Trade Union Organization in Kenya* (Nairobi: Republic of Kenya, Government Printer of Kenya, 1965); and *The Trades Disputes Act, 1965* (Nairobi: Republic of Kenya, Government Printer of Kenya, 1965).

13. On Latin America, see Roberto Vernengo, "Freedom of Association and Industrial Relations in Latin America," *International Labour Review,* May 1956, and "Labor Legislation and Collective Bargaining in the Americas," *International Labour Review,* October 1961. For Egypt, see *Labour Survey of North Africa* (Geneva: International Labour Office, 1960), pp. 154–155. And on Malaya, see *The Trade Union Situation in the Federation of Malaya* (Geneva: International Labour Office, 1962), p. 68.

14. Omar Becu, "Free Trade Unions in the Developing Countries," *Free Labor World,* July 1961.

15. *Spearhead,* January 1962. This issue of the journal, published at Dar Es Salaam but now defunct, carried an interesting exchange of views in a seminar on "Trade Unions in Under-Developed Countries."

16. Tom Mboya, "Trade Unions and Development," *Venture,* January 1964.

17. *ICFTU Social and Economic Bulletin,* January–February, 1963. The ICFTU, to which the KFL was then affiliated, hailed ". . . the exemplary value . . . and the importance" of this charter and reproduced it in full. A similar charter was signed in Uganda by government, unions, and management in 1964. The text of this charter appears in *ICFTU Economic and Social Bulletin,* September–October 1964. These are, I believe, the only cases of their kind in the new countries.

18. *The Trade Disputes Act of 1965* (Nairobi: Republic of Kenya, Government Printer of Kenya, 1965).

19. The top officer of the new federation is chosen by the government from a group of three nominated by the federation's governing council (which consists of a representative from each affiliate).

20. *The Policy on Trade Union Organization in Kenya, op. cit.* Part of the check-off goes into a government development investment fund.

21. Singapore National Trade Union Congress, *The Problems of Workers in Developing Countries,* Working Papers Presented by the Central Committee of the Singapore National Trades Union Congress to the International Labour Seminar, October 18, 1965 (Singapore, 1965) p. 7. This was a seminar convened by the SNTUC to discuss the general problem of labor and the role of the trade union in development. Self-consciously, but consistently steering its careful path, the SNTUC accepted the government's special Employment Act of 1968, which imposed new restrictions on unions and workers, including a maximum of forty-eight hours of overtime work for any individual worker per month. This overtime limit was designed to help share the work in a labor market in which unemployment was already high and where it was expected to be even more of a problem when Great Britain withdrew its military forces and closed its shipyard operation in the early 1970s. Although some workers would lose as much as 40 percent of their earnings because of the cut in overtime, the SNTUC viewed the act "in the context of . . . a newly independent nation fighting for its economic survival. This means that short-term demands will have to be subordinated to long term ends." *Asian Labour* (January 1969), p. 22. In drafting this legislation the government accepted a number of changes proposed by the SNTUC.

22. Statement by the Executive Committee of the Union Générale des Travailleurs Algériens (UGTA), then under pressure from the party and government. *Syndicalisme,* July 23, 1966. (*Syndicalisme* is the organ of the CFDT in France. CFDT has had close fraternal relations with the UGTA for many years.) There is an

almost desperate quality about the statement as the UGTA defends its loyalty to the party, declaring it "is with the Party; is behind the Party, is of the Party; is in the Party."

23. "INTUC Top-Level Seminar's Consensus," *The Indian Worker,* October 24, 1966. Harold Crouch's *Trade Unions and Politics in India* (Bombay: Manaktalas, 1966) is an outstanding treatment of the complex relations between the various parties and union federations in India.

24. On the overall structure and operations, including the unions' role, of Mexico's ruling Partido Revolucionario Institucional (PRI), see Robert E. Scott, *Mexican Government in Transition* (Urbana: University of Illinois Press, 1964). For a more detailed view of just the union-PRI relationships, see Frederic Meyers, "Party Government and the Labour Movement in Mexico: Two Case Studies," in Arthur M. Ross (ed.), *Industrial Relations and Economic Development,* (London: Macmillan, 1966), Chap. 7.

25. The condition of the masses remains at such a low level in Mexico, despite some general economic growth, that it leads some observers to question whether the unions have benefited even their members. Oscar Lewis's pioneering field study of the Mexican poor is a case in point. His central figure, Sanchez, remarks, ". . . there has been progress and some have benefited, thanks to the government that have concerned themselves with workers." By and large, it is the unionized workers who have particularly benefited. But Sanchez does not see it that way; however, his comments are principally about the poor, who are not really represented in the PRI. He adds, "In the thirty years I've been in Mexico City, the life of the poor people has changed very little, very little." On unions, he complains about the structure of representation, which gives them a role in the party and government. "I do not see that the unions help the worker much. I see the Sindicato as a cave, a trap, to exploit the mass of workers. The leaders become rich with the workers' money and I ask myself why the government allows such a thing. Isn't it possible to arrange things in favor of the workers without having leaders? If the government could eliminate the unions and make special departments to work out matters between the workers and the bosses, all that money they collect every month from the workers' dues could be used to build schools, hospitals and other things for the workers' children, instead of buying cars and homes for the leaders." Oscar Lewis, *The Children of Sanchez, Autobiography of a Mexican Family* (New York: Vintage Books, 1961), pp. 495–496.

26. Victor Alba suggested this as a possible hypothesis in an early work, *Le Mouvement Ouvrier en Amérique Latine,* (Paris: Les Éditions Ouvrières, 1953). Alba has returned to this theme in numerous, scattered writings in recent years. He now seems to place his hopes for leadership more in the so-called middle layers of the population. For later statements of Alba, in English, which are quoted here in part in the text, see *Dissent,* Autumn 1962, and A. O. Hirschman (ed.), *Latin American Issues* (New York: Twentieth Century Fund, 1961), Chap. 2. After this volume had gone to the printer, Alba published a new major volume in English: *Politics and the Labor Movement in Latin America* (Stanford, Calif.: Stanford University Press, 1968).

27. See pp. 111–112, in this text, on Lenin's criticism of trade union "economism."

28. "The Labor Elite in Latin America: Is it Revolutionary?" in Seymour M. Lipset and A. Solari (eds.), *Elites in Latin America* (New York: Oxford University Press, 1967). For an interesting description of the way in which industrial relations can be shaped into a process of "political bargaining," in a very broad and fundamental way, see James L. Payne, *Labor and Politics in Peru* (New Haven, Conn.: Yale University Press, 1965).

29. The literature on postwar Japanese labor development is large and growing

rapidly. One of the most useful works is *The Changing Patterns of Industrial Relations,* Proceedings of the International Conference on Industrial Relations (Tokyo: Japan Institute of Labour, 1965). On the blend and conflict of traditional versus modern factors in Japanese labor, see especially the essays of Professors H. Kawada, K. Odaka, K. Okochi, and I. Nakayama. This volume also contains many other interesting, descriptive essays on Japanese unionism and industrial relations, as well as several chapters on comparative studies. Also, on the unions' blend of modern and traditional forces, see Solomon Levine, "Japanese Trade-Unionism as a Model in Economic Development," in E. M. Kassalow (ed.), *National Labor Movements in the Postwar World* (Evanston, Ill.: Northwestern University Press, 1963), Chap. 8. A useful historical analysis of the forces shaping Japanese labor development is the chapter by Robert A. Scalapino in Galenson, *op. cit.*

30. N. K. Bose, "Calcutta: A Premature Metropolis," *Scientific American,* September 1965, p. 102. An as yet unpublished study by one of my students, M. Van den Bogaert, of port and dock unions in Bombay and Calcutta adds evidence to the integrative role of the unions among these workers.

XV

Industrial Relations in the New Countries:

Economic Setting and Problems

NO FORCE was more crucial in shaping unionism in the West than its relationship to the capitalist system of free enterprise, which is at the core of the European and American economies. While no single generalization will hold about the central developing force in the economies of the new countries, in almost none of the Asian and African countries can it be said that the capitalist system of free enterprise has the same position or weight that it carried in Western Europe and the United States.

Whether it is because of the sheer problem of trying to overcome backwardness in the face of an already well-developed Western world—whether it is because of the striking industrial (if not agricultural) gains of that large and late-developing nation, the Soviet Union—or whether it is because of a colonial heritage in which the government was often the chief employer and economic policy maker, the prime development mechanism of the great majority of nations that have gained independence after World War II is central government planning.

Almost from the start of the "independence era," most unions in the new countries have faced the reality that critical decisions about wage policy, employment, and many other working conditions must, in part at least, be bargained through with government. The government is often the largest employer; it has many ideas as to what is an appropriate wage and employment policy. This state of affairs means that even if the unions should be inclined to lean toward more purely economic-industrial action, they find they must be "in politics" to obtain economic decisions favorable to their members.

Unions, Investment, Consumption, and Development

Not only is central planning the rule of the day in most new countries, but for most planners development is synonymous with capital accumulation at all costs. The union, with its built-in drive for the economic advancement of its members, runs up against the planner's model of all-out sacrifice of immediate consumption in favor of capital accumulation for development. As a result, when a country has become independent, the unions often find themselves in a hostile economic environment.

In a paper prepared even before he assumed his government responsibilities, Asoka Mehta, who served as chief government planner in India for a number of years, foresaw a stark fate for unions in newly independent countries. For Mehta, consumption-oriented unions were well and good for the developed Western world, but in the "underdeveloped countries . . . the chief problem is economic growth, and, therefore the major question for unions is subordination of immediate wage gains and similar considerations to the development of the country." Unions should promote "labor productivity through propaganda," and also "educate their members to give up extra spendthrift habits of the labor class," thereby adding to capital accumulation. Mehta concludes, "The economic implications of such trade union behavior are twofold: (1) to restrict consumption and (2) to bring about an increase in the desired levels of production."[1]

It is curious how this grim, bleak picture of development pervades so many countries. Whether attributable to Marxist theory or capitalist history, there is almost everywhere a feeling of resignation, a feeling that development must be a grinding process, as in nineteenth century England or twentieth century Soviet Russia. The work in recent years by some distinguished scholars, the United Nations, and the International Labour Organisation indicates that a strategic investment in human resources—including decent social and economic conditions for workers, as well as expenditures for housing, health, education, and the like—are crucial to truly effective development. Countries should no more expect to have to duplicate nineteenth century English working conditions than they should expect to duplicate the "dark, satanic mills" of that country. The mills have long since been scrapped or assigned to museums. Also, it is no more appropriate to view the labor force in similar outmoded terms.[2]

Urban Versus Rural Income and the Union Role

African political leaders often formulate the same sort of "sacrifice" role for unions, but in slightly different terms. In the name of African socialism, for example, Leopold Senghor rejects union demands for "a raise in salary." His "most important objection stems from a comparison between the respective standards of living of city dwellers—government employees, workers and laborers—and of the peasants who constitute more than 90% of the population. It could not serve the public interest to increase the disproportion between the living standards of the classes now in process of formation."[3]

That urban wage earners, particularly unionized groups, must not be allowed to extend their already advantageous position relative to the rural population is a recurring theme among leaders in the developing countries in Africa. The militant position taken by the Nigerian Federal Minister of Finance in 1963 and 1964 against wage increases ("increases in salaries and wages would only benefit that small section of one vast population."[4]) helped precipitate a great general strike. In the longer run this conflict also contributed to the unrest that led to the 1965–1966 military coup.

It is at least debatable whether this policy of stabilizing or reducing the income gap between urban or modern economic sector workers and those in rural areas and traditional activities is consonant with effective development policy. The Dutch development economist L. J. Zimmerman reports that in the course of industrialization it appears to be characteristic for agricultural or primary sector income (generally defined to include farming, forestry, hunting, and fishing, but usually predominantly farming) to deteriorate first and then to remain stable at a ratio below half of that in the other sector of the economy. Substantial upward movement of agricultural income in relationship to other income seems to occur in very advanced stages of industrialization, after the agricultural population falls off sharply. At this point the welfare state takes over with farm subsidy programs. Other evidence, gathered by Simon Kuznets, also supports the finding that in successfully developing countries to date (notably Western countries and Japan) per capita income in agriculture tends to lag behind income in manufacturing.[5]

Government Wage Policy

Because even weak labor movements can be a potential political danger, governments in the new countries usually do not find it practical to impose a wage freeze. Some compromise is usually reached between the demands of the unions and the planners' desire for a freeze.

It is easy to exaggerate the unions' power and potential for inflation. All the socially divisive factors cited earlier severely limit worker and union solidarity and the unions' bargaining power. In most countries, too, overpopulation and substantial unemployment (and underemployment) militates against any runaway union-urban wage push.[6]

In India, for example, the reluctance of trade unions to make a clean break with government intervention and forms of compulsory arbitration is explained by their feelings of weakness in the face of population pressures, workers' ignorance, and related factors. A few well-structured unions have been ready to junk the system of government controls in effect since 1947 but most top leaders and the major federations apparently have been afraid to go it alone.

Confronted with a proposal during the 1950s to switch away from compulsory adjudication of disputes, all four Indian federations took a stand in opposition. Even the communist-controlled All Indian Trade Union Congress "urged freedom for workers to strike or to take a case to a tribunal." While there is concern with the excessive delays in clearing cases in the government legal machinery, the response of an official of the socialist-oriented Hind Mazdoor Sabha is typical: ". . . I have urged abolition of the Appellate Tribunal because of added expense and delays, but I feel that Industrial Tribunals are necessary to get justice for workers who are too weak." Some management groups seemed more favorably disposed to dismantling some of the government control machinery.[7] By 1968, however, when the subject was one of many being investigated by a National Labor Commission, union positions had changed somewhat. A number of important leaders and federations were clearly opposed to the continuation of the tribunals, and were willing to run the risks of a more voluntary bargaining system. The INTUC, however, still seems to favor the compulsory arbitration-tribunal system. Related to the discussion about strengthening the voluntaristic aspects of collective bargaining in India, have been suggestions—backed by some of the unions—to eliminate plural union representation at the work place. It is proposed to substitute something like the United States system under which one majority union has exclusive bargaining rights for all the employees in a given work place.[8]

The very delays complained about as regards wage and grievance settlement may be a deliberate policy of the Indian government. India does not try to freeze wages or directly to refuse the claims of unions. It does contain them by means of fairly elaborate machinery, draws cases out for months and years, but almost invariably makes awards that do represent some advance for workers or that at least help them to keep abreast of the rising living costs—costs generated by the inflation that seems to accompany development.

While the degree of government control over or influence on wages varies in the new countries, it is fairly extensive in most of Africa and Asia. The implications for union behavior in wage-setting are important. Even wage decisions that remain at the industrial level rather than at the national, governmental level may be made through government-sponsored wage boards or commissions, often tripartite in character (with union, management, and government representation). Such wage boards are employed extensively in India and Ceylon.

In Africa, the great surplus population in cities, workers' ignorance of the labor market, and the motivating force of social concern lead many governments, and some governments elsewhere in the developing world, to establish general minimum wages to protect labor. Unlike minimum wages that affect only a relatively small minority of workers in a developed country like the United States, government-established minimums in Africa may set the effective, real wages for many or most workers in particular regions or industries.[9]

Wage differentials in the new nations of Asia and Africa often strike Western observers as unusually large. Whereas the ratios between skilled and unskilled workers in the European countries today may be no more than 1.5 to 1, and even lower, in the new countries the ratios may be 3, 4, and 5 to 1, as the following table shows.

It is by no means certain (research data is lacking here) that at a comparable stage (say, in the first half of the nineteenth century) European wage differentials were not as great as those in some less-developed nations today. But given their commitment to planned, rapid economic development, the new countries are often not prepared to accept a "free" wage policy and the effects of time and development to reduce differentials. Deliberate policies are frequently adopted by the government to try to reduce differentials.

This question of differentials has also been complicated, especially in Africa, by the fact that certain skilled and professional jobs have traditionally been held by white Europeans brought in during the colonial period. These Europeans have been receiving a special, large differential, larger than what their superior skills alone might command. As they are replaced by natives, the question arises as to whether the latter should receive the same pay, thereby perpetuating enormous differentials within the wage structure. This can prove a difficult question for unions, especially since the transition from white to native employees may involve a long period of time during which some Europeans and natives work side by side doing the same job at vastly different rates of pay.

It places a great strain on the unions to accept lower pay for their members because the original differential had social and geographical elements in it (as an example, Europeans were not residing in their home countries and were receiving extra compensation for this). These social and geographical elements should not be included in a new, modern wage structure. If large differentials are preserved and passed on to the native replacements, they may create pressure to push up wages in many other jobs, produce inflation, and possibly dissipate capital needed for development.[10]

TABLE 21. *Wages of Different Occupations Expressed as Percentage of Wages of Unskilled Laborers in Manufacturing or Construction Industries, Selected Cities*

Carpenters		Garage Mechanics		Painters	
Place	*Percentage*	*Place*	*Percentage*	*Place*	*Percentage*
Manchester, Eng.	122	Germany	104	Manchester	122
Helsinki, Finland	126	Netherlands	105	Netherlands	125
Netherlands	126	Manchester	106	Cyprus	129
Cyprus	129	Spain	108	Manila	132
Manila, Luzon	132	Bangkok	111	Spain	134
Spain	134	Melbourne	117	Melbourne	135
Melbourne, Aus.	137	Cyprus	123	Helsinki	136
Germany (F.R.)	145	Helsinki	127	Germany (F.R.)	142
Stockholm, Sweden	146	Madagascar	167	Stockholm	142
Douala, Cameroun	156	Manila	208	Madagascar	148
Conakry, Guinea	183	Accra	210	Dakar	155
Madagascar	185	Douala	217	Douala	156
Lagos, Nigeria (E. Region)	189	Malaya	219	Conakry	158
Abidjan, Ivory Coast	206	Brazzaville	222	Abidjan	160
Accra, Africa	210	Dakar	239	Lagos (E. Region)	189
Brazzaville, Congo	219	Bangui	251	Accra	196
Bangui, Central African Rep.	220	Conakry	322	Bangui	216
Dakar, Senegal	227	Abidjan	490	Brazzaville	219
Malaya	305	Nairobi	707	Bangkok	244
Bangkok, Siam	311			Nairobi	250
Nairobi, Kenya	536			Malaya	270

SOURCE: International Labour Office, Report to the Government of Ghana, *op. cit.*, pp. 64, 66, 67. The figures are based upon a 1960–1961 ILO survey. For some cities, average rates have been used. In other instances minimum rates for the jobs are given, and in still others average earnings or prevailing rates are shown.

With unions as fragile as most of them are in the new countries, with widespread illiteracy among workers, with the state using a heavy hand nearly everywhere it can reach, it is perhaps surprising that there is any bargaining at all. All the more so when we consider that union pluralism is also a factor.

In the ex-British colonies particularly, legislation made it almost too easy to organize unions. Commonly, under legislation inspired by the colonial office, as few as seven persons could form a union, asked to be registered, and begin to function. Given this opportunity, and given the great diversity in political outlook, plural unionism became quite common in many British colonial areas, and it has continued in the new era of independence. Ceylon and India are good examples.[11]

Thus, one finds many unions—indeed, often too many unions to make for effective bargaining. The laws have also encouraged the development of a large number of so-called house unions, that is, unions confined to one firm or enterprise. House unions are in operation in many parts of ex-British Africa and Asia.

B. C. Roberts and L. G. de Bellecombe find, despite these obstacles to bargaining, a surprisingly good number of written agreements and functioning bargaining relationships at the enterprise level in ex-British Africa. Strikes are fairly well controlled; the government can intervene when strikes threaten essential services.[12]

Roberts and de Bellecombe find a different pattern in the ex-French colonies in Africa. Here far greater centralization of control prevails, and, somewhat in the French tradition, the central government plays a major role in determining the nature and content of collective agreements. The unions, too, operate along more centralized lines, and there is little bargaining at the level of the individual firm or shop.[13] Labour Courts usually are employed to resolve disputes at the local level, and strikes are well controlled or prevented entirely.

One must not appraise at face value forms of organization and bargaining that seem to be similar to those of the West. Closer examination reveals that they are somewhat different. Some of the bargaining and agreements in a less-developed area like Africa are apt to be superficial, and often manipulated by employers.

A field study of a plantation union in the Cameroons of Nigeria indicated that members looked upon unions quite differently from the way union members in the West do. To some it was a kind of intermediary, "just like parents to whom the workers could come and tell things . . . they guided the workers and told them not to make trouble." Others believed "that the unions' main activity was to encourage the men to work hard, or that it was an organization to discipline the workers."[14]

The strongest unions in Africa, not surprisingly, are in the mines, the railroads, the plantations, the docks, and, in many instances, in public employment. These large concentrations of employees, under modern management, often provide a broader membership base for union development.

As the unions and the industrial-relations systems have evolved since independence, some of the differences between French and British Africa which Roberts and de Bellecombe found as a result of original colonial influence (such as the lesser role of government in the British areas) are disappearing. The tendency of the state to exert control over the entire system and not only to control but even to take over the unions in some cases, has been described in the previous chapter.

In Asia, there are more examples of sophisticated union development and collective bargaining. A greater degree of industrialization, somewhat more political stability, a large private sector—out of these and other forces have developed a number of well-established unions and effective bargaining. Government influence is not absent, however. In India, for example, strikes are highly restricted; and, as previously noted, a government system of compulsory adjudication of disputes plays a strong role in industrial relations.

In Malaya, on the other hand, one finds a fairly free system of bargaining; there are some very strong unions, including the well-known National Union of Plantation Workers.

Already an enormous variety in collective-bargaining practice exists in Africa and Asia, and, given the variation in conditions and traditions from country to country, this variety is likely to grow in the years ahead as industrialization progresses.

Union forms mirror these changes. We have earlier referred (in the previous chapter) to the tendency for unionism that is geographically based, as contrasted with industrial or craft forms of unionism, to be most conspicuous and powerful in its earliest stages of development. As communications improve, as industry becomes more developed, and as markets grow, however, industrial unionism does emerge. Such beginnings can be found in India, for example—in banking, textiles, railways, iron and steel, docks, and a few other industries.

Class and Class Conflict

In many of the new countries, extensive government control over industrial management and wage policy tends to render irrelevant traditional Marxian and other Western socialist notions of class and class conflict. Nearly every new society proclaims itself socialist, and class divisions and forms of conflict are rejected. Such claims are heard most frequently and almost everywhere in Africa, as "there are no classes in our society" or "no classes exist in Africa, let alone antagonistic classes." The Kenyan white paper on African socialism declares:

The sharp class divisions that once existed in Europe have no place in African socialism and no parallel in African society. No class problem arose in the traditional African society and none exists today among Africans. The class problem in Africa, therefore, is largely one of prevention.[15]

In rejecting Marxist forms of socialism, Africans have struggled to replace it with their own doctrine. Although widely discussed, African socialism remains only vaguely defined. One element common to most socialist programs in Africa is great emphasis upon work and the obligation of all persons to work for the development of society.[16]

To the degree that decision-making power over wage policy, investment, marketing, and the like is largely in government hands, class and class conflict in the new African societies may not take a European-Marxist form. This is not the same as saying that conflict does not and will not exist. Actually there have been some severe strikes, even in "socialist" Africa. These strikes, not surprisingly, are often directed against the government, and on two grounds. First, if the government has considerable power over wage, tax, and employment policy, worker pressure may come to be directed at this policy. Second, while traditional entrepreneur-worker forms of conflict may not be predominant in some of the new societies, there is deep resentment among less well-paid workers and civil servants against the high-living styles of many of the ministers and top government leaders. Strikes among civil servants and other groups have in part been triggered by these "newer" forms of conflict and resentment.[17] Conflict actually grows out of the different positions groups occupy in authority systems. Such differences in position can derive from bureaucratic as well as purely economic or production relationships as were more basic in the West. There is no reason to believe that group conflict and hostility based on differences in status and power will cease, *even* in "socialist" societies.

Moreover, while Marxism, and Marxist style, are not common in the programs of many labor movements in the new countries, it is found in some. Where, as in India and Japan, for example, there is a major, indigenous bourgeoisie class and a longer history of industrialism, the labor movement has largely clustered around leaders and unions professing the most "advanced" Marxist-Leninist ideas of class conflict and demands for a workers' socialist society.

At first glance it may seem curious that while Marxism as the program of labor movements has nearly disappeared in developed Western societies, it thrives in industrializing India and Japan (as well as in parts of Latin America). During our discussion of the earlier developmental stages of European unionism, however, we have already suggested that to an important extent Marxism may be a formulation of workers' reactions to the shattering impact of industrialism and modernization—it may reflect the alienation of the "traditional" workers in the early urban industrial setting. As Adam B. Ulam observes, "In an industrializing society the appeal of Marxism rests on the fact that its intermediate aim, the overthrow of capitalism, coincides with the proletariat's instinctive reaction against industrialism." As industrialization proceeds, and the sense of shock wears off, says Ulam, Marxism tends to be replaced by "laborism" (really reformist socialism, as we know it).[18]

Ulam's work helps explain the popularity of Marxism in some societies of Latin America and Asia that are still in the early stages of industrialization. But he underestimates more purely class forces. The relatively weak appeal and influence of traditional Marxism in Black Africa, as already suggested, seems to be at least partially due to the absence of a major indigenous bourgeoisie, property-owning class. Because the state assumes the major role in the drive for development in most of Africa, Marxism will probably not become a prevailing language of protest among workers, even in the earlier stages of industrialization.

Unionism and Economic Planning

Faced with the reality of central planning by government, many unions in the new countries have been compelled to seek a role in the planning process itself. This contrasts, of course, with the relatively late entry by unions in the West into the area of manpower, incomes, and industrial planning.

Unions in the new countries frequently find that government is anxious to divert them not only from their own ambitions but from a "combative" and "consumptionist" posture and to direct them toward a more "positive," responsible role in development. The Kenyan government report on African socialism begins its list of tasks for trade unions as follows:

Government will assist trade unions to become involved in economic activities such as cooperatives, housing schemes, training schemes, workers' discipline and productivity, and in general, to accept their social responsibilities.[19]

Some unions in the new countries have their own lists of tasks for themselves, which are included in their constitutions. One of their goals is to participate in overcoming underdevelopment.

Relatively weak and numerically small union (and employer) organizations are accorded representation on economic and social bodies of all types, ranging from general planning councils to social security administration agencies. In a number of African countries this is, in part, a carry-over of French institutions and influence. It can be found, however, in a few ex-British colonies as well. In Algeria the basic governmental charter, in setting forth the framework for planning, states:

No plan is possible without conscious participation and active collaboration by the workers. . . . This participation must be enlisted not only during the execution of the plan, but more importantly, during the preparation of the plan.[20]

In Tunisia, to help effectuate the role of the union movement in the "plan," the government provides for union representation in the top level *Conseil National du Plan* and in various industrial, regional, and local committees. Similar representation is accorded to unions in many other African countries.

In India the government, in enunciating the first of its five-year plans, declared, "Trade unions should be associated [with planning] at various levels—at the level of the undertaking, at the level of the industry, and at the regional and national levels." This association is accomplished primarily through union membership in *advisory* bodies, which the planning authorities consult directly or indirectly.[21]

It is still too early to fully evaluate the effectiveness of union participation in these planning functions. Lack of sufficiently trained leaders, the need to build a firmer membership base—these and other factors have tended to minimize most of the efforts to date. The ILO, commenting on the African situation a few years back, said that "so far it has not been possible in most cases to associate the employers' and workers' organizations to any real extent with the work of the planning agencies." The ILO's comments still hold true for most of the developing countries. But the effort and desire among the various parties continue.[22]

Coming now to Latin America, most of the unions there, as compared with those in Africa and Asia, have been less conspicuous in attaining any significant, formal role either in government economic planning machinery or in the management of enterprise. Perhaps the more deeply implanted traditional class structure and class barriers, plus greater reliance in Latin America upon more conventional, capitalist economic forms, account for the differences. In a sense, one can speak of new societies only in Asia and Africa, even though most of Latin America is still classified as less developed or underdeveloped.[23]

Related to the effort to involve workers and unions more deeply in the tasks of economic development is widespread legislation calling for the establishment of joint labor-management consultation at the plant or enterprise level. The purpose of such joint consultation is to raise productivity; experience with it is as yet limited, but some early efforts proved abortive as workers viewed them, with suspicion, as a poor substitute for effective trade-union channels of protest.[24] Lack of effective union channels to express grievances about wages and working conditions seems to reduce drastically the possibility of labor-management cooperation toward greater productivity.

Some progress in the establishment of joint consultation has been made in India, but even that government reports that workers are rather disinterested in matters concerning productivity and come to life only when their own grievances are involved. (See Chapter IX, footnote 57).

Unions and Cooperatives

Union efforts in the cooperative field are still new in most of the developing countries, but several have shown considerable promise. Interesting examples are the port and dock unions in Bombay and Calcutta, and the Textile Labor Association in Ahmedabad, India. The port unions have sponsored successful grocery and credit union cooperatives that have served their membership well. The textile union at Ahmedabad has run successful clinics, credit unions, and other coop ventures. Several Latin American unions have sponsored workers' coop housing projects.[25]

Where the rigors of development and centralized planning make it difficult for unions to achieve direct wage increases, benefits passed on through union-run cooperatives may be one of the best services that can be offered to members. Helping members and their families with housing, keeping them out of the hands of money lenders when they must borrow, and assisting them in the everyday purchase of lower priced groceries and bread can truly minister to their most basic needs. In turn, these activities strengthen the allegiance of members to the unions.

The general shortage of capital and the lack of entrepreneurial skills in some of the new societies may present an opportunity for union cooperatives to make a contribution to *industrial* development. The Israeli labor federation, Histadrut, is an outstanding example of a coop-oriented union movement that has made a central contribution to a country's economic and social development. Cooperatives sponsored by Histadrut own and operate most of the country's health and medical program; they run the largest construction firms in the country; and so on.[26]

It is not likely that many of the labor movements in the new countries can duplicate the Histadrut program in full. The background of Histadrut's leaders and many of its members (well adjusted and already introduced to modern urban living) gave it many advantages not found in other less-developed nations.

The International Confederation of Free Trade Unions, particularly its Asian branch, has given warm support to union-supported coop activities. The ICFTU in Asia has tried to strengthen worker savings associations in order to help accumulate coop capital, and it specifically calls for (1) the establishment of savings cooperatives "to be located in the area of the factory establishment, where the workers are employed"; (2) "thrift boxes" to be provided "to members for saving small amounts which can be deposited in savings accounts every day." The ICFTU has also supported the voluntary checkoff from workers' wages of savings each pay day, to be turned over to cooperative savings banks.[27]

With so much emphasis upon "new" functions, one must not over-look the presence in the developing countries of a small but important number of conventionally successful *individual* trade unions. Whether on the docks of Bombay or Calcutta, in the mercantile houses of Ceylon, in the banks of Singapore and Malaya, or at the oil fields of Venezuela, one finds some union collective-bargaining activity not dissimilar to that in the more developed Western countries. The leaders and members of these unions display a competence and devotion that compares favorably with that displayed anywhere else in the world.

On the whole, however, the evolution of unionism in the new countries still remains very much an open matter. Clearly, along with traditional representational bargaining functions, unions will be called upon to join the enormous effort required of present-day, less-developed societies. All groups in these societies who are dedicated to modernization and development find that to "break through the barriers of stagnation. . . . in the service of economic development" and to bear with the pressures of rising expectations and exploding populations calls for "a much more powerful ideology [than] was required to grease the intellectual and emotional wheels of industrialization in the West."[28] The unions' role in this great drama has also just begun.

N O T E S

1. Asoka Mehta, "The Mediating Role of the Trade Union in Underdeveloped Countries," *Economic Development and Cultural Change,* October 1957, pp. 16–23.

2. See Theodore W. Schultz (ed.), "Investment in Human Beings," *The Journal of Political Economy,* Supplement, October 1962, and his *Transforming Traditional Agriculture* (New Haven, Conn.: Yale University Press, 1964). Also see the United Nations, *Report on the World Situation* (New York: United Nations, 1961); and Walter Galenson and Graham Pyatt, *The Quality of Labor and Economic Development in Certain Countries* (Geneva: International Labour Office, 1964). These studies all suggest a significant relationship between substantial strategic investment in human resources and a more rapid rate of economic growth.

3. Leopold S. Senghor, *African Socialism* (New York: American Society of African Culture, 1959), p. 38. Frantz Fanon's *The Wretched Earth* (New York: Grove Press, 1968; original French edition, 1963), which has become something of

a left-wing, revolutionary bible in the new countries, charges that with the advent of independence, the trade unions have become part of the new, exploitative ruling classes (along with some party leaders)—all at the expense of the back-country peasants (see pp. 121–123).

4. *Budget Speech 1963, Chief the Honourable Festus Sam Okozie-Ebboh, C.M.G.M.P.* (Lagos: Federal Ministry of Information, Printing Division, 1963), pp. 17–18.

5. L. J. Zimmerman, *Poor Lands, Rich Lands: The Widening Gap* (New York: Random House, 1965), pp. 48–54. Kuznet's data on the ratio of per-person income in manufacturing to per-person income in agriculture in the early and later development periods of eleven important nations is well assembled by Everett E. Hagen, "An Economic Justification of Protectionism," *Quarterly Journal of Economics,* November 1958, esp. Table I, p. 501. Elliot Berg argues the case for a slowdown or halt of urban wages in Africa, citing evidence that urban workers are conspicuously better off than the rural population. See Arthur M. Ross (ed.), *Industrial Relations and Economic Development* (London: Macmillan, 1966), Chap. 9. Regardless of the near neo-classical logic of most planners in Asia and Africa, it does appear that they are bucking a trend that apparently has deep roots in the development process, i.e., a trend favoring the urbanite.

6. See Paul Fisher, "Unions in the Less Developed Countries: A Reappraisal of their Economic Role," in E. M. Kassalow (ed.), *National Labor Movements in the Postwar World* (Evanston, Ill.: Northwestern University Press, 1963), Chap. 4.

7. Charles Myers, *Labor Problems in the Industrialization of India* (Cambridge, Mass.: Harvard University Press, 1958), pp. 147–149.

8. An interesting analysis of these and other basic aspects of the Indian unions and industrial relations system is to be found in Van Dusen Kennedy, *Unions, Employers and Government, Essays on Indian Labour Questions* (Bombay: Manaktalas, 1966). The author is an American scholar with long experience in India.

9. For an interesting statement of the wage problems confronting one developing African country, see *Report to the Government of Ghana on Questions of Wage Policy,* ILO/TAP/GHANA/R-G (Geneva: International Labour Office, 1962). On Asia, see *Problems of Wage Policy in Asian Countries* (Geneva: International Labour Office, 1956). A general analysis of wage issues in these areas appears in H. A. Turner, *Wage Trends, Wage Policies, and Collective Bargaining: The Problems for Underdeveloped Countries,* (Cambridge, England: Cambridge Press, 1965). A very useful collection of papers on *Wage Policy Issues in Economic Development* was presented to a Symposium conducted by the International Labour Office at Egelund, Denmark in October, 1967. The paper by Elliot Berg, "Wage Structure in Less-Developed Countries," is especially useful. These papers will be published as a volume later. The book of Shreekant A. Palekar, while mainly concerned with India, deals with many of the important general issues of wage policy in less-developed countries. See his *Problems of Wage Policy for Economic Development, with Special Reference to India* (Bombay: Asia Publishing House, 1962). For a shorter statement of these problems and policies, see my "Wage Policy and Manpower Policy in Developing Nations," *Manpower in Economic and Social Growth, Proceedings of the Sixth International Manpower Seminar,* July 1–August 13, 1966 (Washington, D.C.: U.S. Department of Labor, 1967).

10. For two differing viewpoints, see Robert E. Baldwin, "Wage Policy in a Rural Economy—The Case of Northern Rhodesia," *Race,* November 1962, and "Do the Jobs Really Deserve the Rates," *Free Labour World,* April 1960. Also see Koje Taira, "Wage Differentials in Developing Countries," *International Labour Review,* March 1966.

11. On Ceylon, see *Labor Law in Practice in Ceylon,* Report No. 227, (Wash-

ington, D.C.: Bureau of Labor Statistics, U.S. Dept. of Labor, 1962). This is one of many such BLS reports prepared on various less developed countries. These reports are often very formal, but provide a good introduction into the legal framework of unionism and industrial relations in a given country. The literature on India is voluminous. The work of Charles Myers, *op. cit.*, is still one of the best, and a new edition is promised for 1969.

12. B. C. Roberts and L. G. de Bellecombe, *Collective Bargaining in African Countries*, (London: Macmillan; New York: St. Martins' Press, 1967), esp. pp. 22–30.

13. *Ibid.*, pp. 27–30.

14. W. A. Warmington, *A West African Trade Union, A Case Study of the Cameroons Development Corporation Workers' Union and its Relations with the Employers* (London: Oxford University Press, 1960), esp. Chap. V, "The Union and its Members." This inquiry was made in 1954, and doubtless workers have become somewhat more knowledgeable since then. Unions in the less-developed countries still fill very old and traditional roles in the eyes of their members. I am indebted to my student, M. Van den Bogaert, whose unpublished study of port workers in Bombay and Calcutta, where there are several strong, well-established unions, reveals that there also is a ritualistic side of these organizations in great urban centers. Mass demonstration called by the unions may, for example, serve as a replacement for older, religious, or tribal parades.

15. *African Socialism and its Application to Planning in Kenya* (Nairobi: Republic of Kenya, 1965), p. 12. The first two quotations are from the speeches and writings of Leopold Senghor, President of Senegal, and of Sékou Touré, political leader of Guinea. While it is easier to find African examples, one can find similar arguments by Asian leaders. For other statements about African countries rejecting the idea that there can be classes and for a general discussion of this issue, see William H. Friedland and Carl Roseberg, Jr. (eds.), *African Socialism* (Stanford, Calif.: Stanford University Press, 1964), esp. Chap. I.

16. See the publications cited in the preceding footnote and also Senghor, *op. cit.*, and the various platforms and pronouncements of most of the ruling African parties. A useful summary review is Manfred Halpern, "African Socialism: Some Unanswered Questions," *Africa Report*, November 1965.

17. For an excellent analysis of the key role of the public employee in social conflict in new states, see Robert N. Kearney, "Militant Public Trade Unionism in a New State: The Case of Ceylon," *The Journal of Asian Studies*, May 1966, pp. 397–412.

18. Adam B. Ulam, *The Unfinished Revolution, An Essay on the Sources of Influence of Marxism on Communism* (New York: Random House, 1964), p. 66.

19. *African Socialism and its Application to Planning in Kenya, op. cit.*, p. 56. Other functions related to industrial relations and wage-setting are stipulated, but all are obviously to be under the critical surveillance of government.

20. As quoted in Anisse Salah-Bey, "Trade Unions and Social Development in the Maghreb," *International Labour Review*, October 1966, p. 385.

21. N. Engineer, "Trade Unions and Plan Formulation in India," *International Labour Review*, September 1963.

22. *Industrial Relations in Certain African Countries*, Labour Management Relations Series: No. 22, proceedings of a seminar in Abidjan, October 1963 (Geneva: International Labour Organisation, 1964), pp. 145–146. One important example of successful union participation in planning is the trade-union federation, Histadrut, which has been a major force for development in Israel. The Western background of many of Histadrut's early leaders may help account for its somewhat exceptional role and success.

23. For a critical analysis of the role, or lack of it, of trade unions in planning

in Latin America, see *Report of the Director General, Social Development in the Americas,* Eighth Conference of the American States Members of the ILO (Geneva: International Labour Office, 1966), p. 95. The *International Labour Review,* monthly organ of the ILO, in 1966 and 1967 published a series of articles on union participation in planning in a number of less-developed countries. See the issues for April, October, and December 1966 and June, July, August, and December 1967.

24. Saad Ed Din Fawzi, *The Labour Movement in the Sudan* (London: Oxford University Press, 1957), pp. 43–57. For a lengthier discussion of the problems of workers' participation in the management of enterprise, see Chap. IX of this volume.

25. Numerous union coop examples in the less-developed nations can be found in a study which this author helped prepare for the United Nations Industrial Development Organization: *Trade Union Contributions to Industrial Development: Varieties of Economic and Social Experience* (New York: United Nations, 1967), pp. 144–171. (Mimeographed.) This study also includes other examples of union participation in non-collective bargaining activities which contribute to industrial development.

26. A good treatment of the Israeli labor movement is Irwin Sobel's chapter in Walter Galenson (ed.), *Labor in Developing Countries* (Berkeley: University of California Press, 1962).

27. *Report of the Experts' Conference on Cooperatives and Trade Unions* (International Cooperative Alliance and the Asian College of International Confederation of Free Trade Unions. (Mimeographed.) The conference was held in New Delhi, India, January 11–18, 1965.

28. Alexander Gerschenkron, *Economic Backwardness in Historical Perspective,* (New York: Praeger, 1962), pp. 24–26.

INDEX

Blue-collar (manual) workers, 85, 95
Bose, N. K., 303–4
British Guiana, 294
British trade unions, 6, 63, 99, 167, 171–172
  as conservative, 21, 55
  in dock and tramway strike, 51–52
  membership in, 87–90
  mergers of, 165, 166
  in plant bargaining, 161–65, 236–37
  policy consultation by, 60–61
  in political reform, 21–22
  religion affecting, 14–16
  shop stewards in, 161–64, 236, 237
  in social-insurance system, 67–68
  social reform by, 40
  white-collar, 196–97, 207, 213–15, 220
  See also Trades Union Congress (TUC)
Brown, George, 262
Bruin, J. J. de, 84
Bullock, Alan, 51, 52
Business unionism, 6, 22, 24–25
Butler, Harold, 293

Canada, 241, 248–50
  strikes in, 157, 202
Capitalism 7–9, 13, 133, 290
  in developing nations, 303, 308–9
  human needs under, 78–79
  overthrow of, 14, 20, 112, 317
  workers' fate under, 20
Central Organization of Salaried Employees (TCO), 77, 192, 216, 229
  membership in, 89, 197, 212–13
  on strikes, 220
  on white-collar workers, 208, 209, 212–13
Ceylon, 292, 295, 311, 314
Chandler, John, viii, 248, 250
Churchill, Sir Winston, 67
Class consciousness, 7–14, 85–87, 111, 289
  in collective bargaining, 152, 281
  in labor parties, 94
  in Latin America, 318
  in union membership, 141
  in written agreements, 131–32
  See also specific country
Class struggle (warfare), 67, 120, 144, 280, 284–85
  in codetermination, 186
  in developing nations, 315–17
  in New Zealand, 54
Clerical and Administrative Workers Union (British), 200, 203, 209

Closed shop, 142, 144–45
Codetermination, 180, 182, 184–86, 188, 193
Cole, G. D. H., 16
Collective action, 9, 13, 20, 72
Collective bargaining, 30, 66, 67, 71–72, 120, 139–45, 201, 243, 281, 298
  in developing nations, 301, 311, 314–315, 320
  grievance procedures in, 151–56, 167, 169, 188, 194, 222, 270, 293, 311, 319
  under national wage policy, 268, 270
  in public service, 220–23
  with white-collar workers, 206–7, 217–18, 282
  in worker control of industry, 175–76
  written agreements in, 131–32, 206, 281
  See also specific country
Collinet, Michel, 110
Communism, 69, 102, 269
Communist International, 112
Confédération Française Democratique du Travail (CFDT), 101–2, 117–124, 128, 135
Confédération Française des Travailleurs Chrétiens (CFTC), 101–2, 117–24, 128, 135
Confédération Générale des Cadres (CGC), 101–2, 209
Confédération Générale du Travail (CGT), 101–2, 105, 110, 113, 118–24, 131
Confederation of Christian Trade Unions (CSC), 88
Confederazione Generale Italiana Lavoro (CGIL), 121, 129, 131, 159, 229
Congress of Industrial Organizations (CIO), 63, 165–66
  on joint-management councils, 187, 193
  on social security system, 133, 148
  See also American Federation of Labor-Congress of Industrial Organizations (AFL-CIO)
Conway, Jim, 146
Crozier, Michel, 197, 209

Dahrendorf, Rolf, 189
Danish Federation of Labor (LO), 60, 166, 173, 215, 264
Danish trade unions, 90, 166, 171, 173, 196, 208, 215, 267
Deferre, Gaston, 121

German Salaried Workers' Union (DAG), 88, 211, 216
German Trade Union Federation (DGB), 53–54, 88, 96, 140–41, 147, 168, 210–11, 229
  on codetermination, 184, 186
German trade unions, 37–39, 90, 168
  industrial decision-making by, 69–70
  on May Day Demonstrations, 43–44, 48
  membership in, 87, 90
  militancy in, 186
  in plant bargaining, 160
  in political activities, 41–45, 53–54, 117
  unemployment insurance in, 67
  white-collar, 195, 197, 210–11, 217
Germany, 5
  codetermination in, 180, 182, 184–186, 193
  education in, 10
  employer associations in, 137
  in the Great Depression, 44–45
  grievance procedures in, 154
  guilds in, 13
  middle-class in, 86
  nationalization of industry in, 53, 184
  party-union relationships in, 63, 95–96
  political parties in, 37–39, 42-45, 107
  production committees in, 183
  public service in, 222, 231
  strikes in, 157, 222
  suffrage in, 9, 17, 30, 37, 42
  voting trends in, 91
  wages in, 236–37, 241, 244, 246, 247, 260, 261
  works councils in, 153, 154, 160, 180–183, 185, 186
Ghana, 296, 304
Goldberg, Arthur J., 263
Gompers, Samuel
  on labor parties, 22
  on local labor unions, 47
  on prohibition, 27
  on unemployment insurance, 68, 80
  on worker's passbook, 11, 68
  on written agreements, 131–32
Great Britain, see United Kingdom
Grievance procedures, 151–56, 167, 169, 188, 194, 270
  in developing nations, 293, 311, 319
  in public service, 222
Grutli Association, 36–37
Guilds, 12–13

Hamilton, Richard F., 86, 113

Hardie, Keir, 15
Hardman, J. B. S., 279
Hartz, Louis, 7–8, 12
Hatters secretariat, 35
Heilbroner, Robert, 8
Hilferding, Rudolf, 44–45
Histadrut, 319, 322
Hobsbawm, E. J., 14–15
Hobson, J. A., 51
Housing, 17, 50, 94, 182, 189, 282
  in developing nations, 309
Hunt, Richard N., 45, 49

Income, see Wages
India, 194, 292–95, 301, 303–4, 310–11, 314–16, 318, 319
Indian National Trade Union Congress (INTUC), 301–2, 311
Industrial relations systems, vi, 5–6, 130–46, 175
  in developing nations, 299, 308–19
  employer associations in, 137–38
  government's role in, 130, 132, 134–136, 147
  in public service, 220–23
  See also specific country; topic
Industrial Workers of the World (IWW), 132, 174, 193
Industry
  nationalization of, see Nationalization of industry
  worker control of, 174–89
International Confederation of Free Trade Unions, 303, 319–20
International Federation of Trade Unions, 35
International Labour Organization (ILO), 297, 303, 309, 318
International Metalworkers Federation, 244–45
Investment programs, 133
Italian Communist Party, 102, 129
Italian trade unions, 6, 8
  leftism in, 121–22
  membership in, 89, 90
  in plant bargaining, 160–61, 237
  plural unionism in, 119
Italy, 100–1, 104, 108, 121
  religion in, 106
  strikes in, 156–59
  violence in, 10
  voting trends in, 93
  wages in, 241, 244, 246, 260, 261
  worker's passbook in, 11

Jackman, Patrick C., 248, 250
Japan, 280, 293, 303, 310, 316

United States *(continued)*
    collective bargaining in, 6, 23, 24,
        63, 130, 132–37, 140, 142–43, 152,
        175, 199, 243
    education in, 10
    Federal Executive Order 10988, 208,
        210
    government decision-making in, 71–
        72, 79
    industrial relations in, 130, 132, 136
    legislation vs. collective bargaining
        in, 130, 132–35, 151
    manual worker in, 86
    National Labor Relations Act, 141,
        208, 210
    National War Labor Board, 255, 272,
        276
    public service in, 223, 231
    resistance to unionism in, 13
    suffrage in, 9
    strikes in, 126, 136, 156, 157, 159,
        255, 283
    trade unions in, *see* American trade
        unions; *and specific unions*
    unemployment in, 250–51
    unemployment insurance in, 68, 133
    unit labor costs in, 249, 261
    violence in, 24, 169
    wages in, 204, 218, 233–35, 238,
        240–41, 244, 246, 247, 254–55,
        259–66, 269, 274, 283
    worker-participation systems in, 187,
        189, 193
United Steelworkers Union (U.S.), 187,
    275–76

Vacations, 242, 244–45, 257
    legislation regulating, 132
    for white-collar workers, 206
    works councils on, 182
Van de Vall, Mark, 83–84
Voting trends, 58, 90–93
    See also specific country
Voting rights, 9, 66, 111, 279
    See also specific country

Wages, 11, 67, 94, 189, 233–51
    black (under-the-counter), 266
    in collective bargaining, 130–31,
        137–38, 233–34
    in developing nations, 308–13, 316,
        319
    electronic data-processing on, 218
    exports affecting, 235–36, 251, 253
    guaranteed annual, 133
    hourly, 240–41, 244

Wages *(continued)*
    longevity increases in, 219
    minimum, 312
    national policies on, 60, 168, 201,
        224, 238, 254–72, 282
    policy making on, 71, 76, 282
    in public service, 221–23
    research on, 218–19, 240
    set at local level, 236–38, 251, 265,
        268
    set at national level, 233–37, 265
    during strikes, 220
    unemployment affecting, 238, 250–51,
        261, 274–75
    wage differentials in, 238–39, 312
    wage drift in, 239, 266, 269, 272
    wage restraint in, 52, 53, 65, 285
    in white-collar unions, 218–19
    works councils on, 182
    See also specific country
Webb, Sidney and Beatrice, 30, 56–57,
    289
Welfare state, 83–84, 310
White-collar employment, 89–90, 95,
    200, 203
White-collar unions, 87–88, 97, 117,
    195–225, 285
    in Europe, 13, 195–96, 201–3
    for foremen and supervisors, 208–10,
        219
    history of, 105–00
    legal status of, 206
    militancy in, 201–2, 205, 220, 225,
        272
    on political issues, 215–17, 271, 272
    professional rights in, 205–6
    recognition of, 202–3, 207
    strikes by, 202, 204, 219–20, 282
    structure of, 210–15
    See also specific countries
Wilson, Harold, 16, 52–53, 94
Wipper, Audrey, 292
Wisconsin, University of, *vii*
Woodcock, George, 284
Work week, 244–45
Workers, as middle-class, 83, 85–86
Worker's passbook, 11, 68
Working class alienation, 100–1, 104,
    108, 110, 122, 285, 289, 317
Works councils, 75–76, 153, 154, 160,
    175–76, 180–83, 185, 186, 190–92
Woytinsky, W. S., 44–45, 49

Yugoslavia, 176, 188–89, 279

Zimmerman, L. J., 310